W9-ADD-876

Gramley Library
Salem College
Winston-Salem, NC 27108

Heirs of Fame

By Studiousnesse, *in* Vertue's *waies*
Men gaine an universall-praise.

ILLVSTR. XII.   Book.3

The *Square* whereon the *Globe* is placed, here,
Muſt *Vertue* be ; That *Globe* upon the *Square*,
Muſt meane the *World* ; The *Figure*, in the *Round*,
(Which in appearance doth her *Trumpet* ſound)
Was made for *Fame* ; The *Booke* ſhe beares, may ſhow,
What *Breath* it is, which makes her *Trumpet* blow :
The *Wreath*, incloſing all, was to intend
A glorious *Praiſe*, that never ſhall have end :
And, theſe, in one ſumm'd up, doe ſeeme to ſay ;
That, (if men *ſtudy* in a *vertuous-way*)
The *Trumpet* of a never-ceaſing *Fame*,
Shall through the *world* proclaime their praiſefull *Name.*

Emblem from George Wither,
A Collection of Emblemes, Ancient & Modern (London, 1624).

Heirs of Fame

Milton and Writers
of the English Renaissance

Edited by
Margo Swiss and David A. Kent

Lewisburg
Bucknell University Press
London: Associated University Presses

Gramley Library
Salem College
Winston-Salem, NC 27108

© 1995 by Associated University Presses

All rights reserved. Authorization to photocopy items for internal or personal use, or the internal or personal use of specific clients, is granted by the copyright owner, provided that a base fee of $10.00, plus eight cents per page, per copy is paid directly to the Copyright Clearance Center, 222 Rosewood Drive, Danvers, Massachusetts, 01923. [0-8387-5276-4/95 $10.00 + 8¢ pp, pc.]

Associated University Presses
440 Forsgate Drive
Cranbury, NJ 08512

Associated University Presses
25 Sicilian Avenue
London WC1A 2QH, England

Associated University Presses
P.O. Box 338, Port Credit
Mississauga, Ontario
Canada L5G 4L8

The paper used in this publication meets the requirements of the American National Standard for Permanence of Paper for Printed Library Materials Z39.48–1984.

Library of Congress Cataloging-in-Publication Data

Heirs of fame: Milton and writers of the English Renaissance / edited by Margo Swiss and David A. Kent.
    p   cm.
    Includes bibliographical references (p.) and index
    ISBN 0-8387-5276-4
    1 Milton, John, 1608-1674—Knowledge—Literature.   2. English literature—Early modern, 1500-1700—History and criticism.
3. Milton, John, 1608-1674—Contemporaries.   4. Influence (Literary, artistic, etc.)   5. Renaissance—England.   I. Swiss, Margo, 1946- .
II. Kent, David A., 1948-
PR3592.L5H45   1995
821'.4—dc20
                                                                94-213
                                                                CIP

PRINTED IN THE UNITED STATES OF AMERICA

For Margaret and Jonathan

Contents

Heirs of Fame

Introduction

MARGO SWISS and DAVID A. KENT

On Shakespeare, 1630

What needs my *Shakespeare* for his honor'd Bones
The labor of an age in piled Stones,
Or that his hallow'd relics should be hid
Under a Star-ypointing *Pyramid*?
Dear son of memory, great heir of Fame,
What need'st thou such weak witness of thy name?
Thou in our wonder and astonishment
Hast built thyself a livelong Monument.
For whilst to th'shame of slow-endeavoring art,
Thy easy numbers flow, and that each heart
Hath from the leaves of thy unvalu'd Book
Those Delphic lines with deep impression took,
Then thou our fancy of itself bereaving,
Dost make us Marble with too much conceiving;
And so Sepulcher'd in such pomp dost lie,
That Kings for such a Tomb would wish to die.

By its diction—"honor'd Bones," "hallow'd relics," "Dear son," "great heir of Fame,"—its tone of awe and "astonishment," and its movement from searching interrogatives to the accumulating power of assertion, Milton's "Epitaph" for Shakespeare evidently fulfils its generic functions of tribute and consolation. Just as the poem extravagantly praises "fancy's child" (*L'All*, 133), its sentiments about "Fame" and its implied valuation of literary tradition can be applied to Milton himself and, by extension, to the other Renaissance authors considered in this volume. If we listen to the author, Milton's attitude is unambiguous: the efficacy of "monumental" works such as Shakespeare's is confirmed by the aesthetic response that they have received and will continue to invite. A significant corollary to this

3

idea is that the "Fame" of "great" writers endures through the readers of their works. In a recent consideration of the "Epitaph," particularly the historical development of its genre and the reception of its text, John Shawcross has described the "Epitaph" as "an excellent original encomium that brings together many commonplaces in honor of a great poet."[1]

Furthermore, Milton's homage to Shakespeare adumbrates his own aspirations to fame through legitimate heirship in the tradition for which Shakespeare serves as exemplar. In the "Epitaph," his first poem to appear in print (with the exception of the Commencement piece), Milton inscribes himself within the literary tradition by invoking important predecessors. His epithet "ypointing," for example, is an archaism that looks back to Spenser, who himself had used it in imitation of Chaucer. The concluding couplet of the "Epitaph" has a distinctively Shakespearean ring and may allude to the scorned state of kings in sonnet 29. In addition, Milton recalls Shakespeare's sonnet 55 ("Not marble nor the gilded monuments / Of princes shall outlive this pow'rful rhyme") and, through that reference, the classical precedents of Horace on monuments (*Odes* 3.30) and Ovid on fame (*Metamorphoses* 15.871–79).[2] The conscious discipline with which Milton claims his place in literary tradition and with which he subsequently pursued his vocation as poet-priest, as political advocate, and finally as prophetical agent of God, eventually led to literary works that have become a source of both fame (as he would have hoped) and notoriety (as he might have expected).

Many contemporary readers now devalue the kind of wonder and awe that evidently engaged Milton in the works of Shakespeare. Some of the premises that characterize this skepticism include the indeterminacy of texts and the contingency of meaning, the fictions of author and originality, and the fallacies of intention and evaluation. Other readers, however, are beginning to reassert more conventional ideas about literature, the literary artist, and the function of criticism. For example, George Steiner has characterized the aesthetic experience itself as bringing "with it a radical calling towards change."[3] This change is not some political or social transformation. Rather, the change is personal, and it is one that we fear: the submission of ego to the power of art. This point is eloquently stated in *Real Presences*: "We flinch from the immediate pressures of mystery in poetic, in aesthetic acts of creation . . . the secondary is our narcotic. Like sleepwalkers, we are guarded by the numbing drone of the journalistic, of the theoretical, from the often harsh, imperious radiance of sheer presence" (49). Northrop Frye has connected creative presence in literature with a kind of "magic" that as an accidental effect of the poetic . . . nevertheless seems to open up a dimension beyond the craftsmanship of the creative process. In actual magic there is an *invoking* of an objective presence, or what seems to be one. Ascendant ideologies are nervous about unauthorized presences. . . . In certain moments of creation there may even be a feeling of actual communication with a personal but not subjective presence. A writer who has once had such feelings or experiences can hardly pretend to himself that he has not had them, whatever the clamoring of ideologies and doctrine around him may say.[4]

Presences in literature, as both Steiner and Frye describe them here, are what this volume explicitly affirms. The "Epitaph" reveals Milton engaged with the presence of Shakespeare, and the essays in this collection consider Milton in relation to other powerful literary presences.

There has been considerable debate about the implications of Milton's overtly laudatory "Epitaph." Paul Stevens has traced a critical "preoccupation with subversion" by various critics, summarizing readings by Paul de Man, John Guillory, and Jonathan Goldberg.[5] Stevens uses these subversive readings of Milton's "Epitaph" as a "convenient paradigm" of the dogmatic exclusiveness by which other "equally interesting possibilities" (377) have been ignored. In examining works by both Milton (*Comus*, "Il Penseroso," and *Paradise Lost*) and Shakespeare (*The Tempest*, his sonnets, and *The Winter's Tale*), as well as relevant texts from Aristotle, Donne, and Spenser, Stevens contextualizes the "Epitaph." He persuasively describes Milton's regard for Shakespeare's work as that of "wonder and astonishment," wherein the stasis so arduously seized upon by subversive readings is not death but instead figures the "ecstasy" of imaginative "rapture" that, in turn, heralds "prophecy" (385, 384). This reading of the "Epitaph," in contrast to "subversive" readings, demonstrates the benefits of "an intentionalist account of the poem" (382).[6]

In contextualizing the "Epitaph," Stevens engages in a method long recognized as appropriate to the signifying power of literary works as these exist within a tradition of texts. As Robert Alter has written, "Since antecedent texts can neither be ignored nor repeated verbatim . . . this process of infinite combination and permutation of texts, of simultaneous activation of 'texts,' is ineluctable in the making of literature."[7] The self-conscious consideration of one author by another, which Milton's poem "On Shakespeare" exemplifies, should not be described as a conspiracy for power and authority. It is simply the manner in which serious authors affirm a lineage and contribute to a tradition of literature which they value. As a result, "there is," explains Alter, "a backward-looking aspect of literature." This retrospective dimension to literature "cuts across political systems; writers, whatever their tacit and explicit ideological commitments, are often extraordinarily preoccupied with literature as an internally coherent, self-propelling set of models and norms" (27). Authors are "forced to enter into a dialogue or debate with their predecessors" (114). As Alter insists, "one reason for the cohesiveness of literary tradition over the stretch of almost three thousand years is its powerful impulse of self-recapitulation. Writers repeatedly work under the influence of a founding model, whether happily or not: they repeatedly return to origins, seeking to emulate, extend, transpose, or outdo some founder" (27). Authors recognize their debts to the past; its creations, contingent upon precedents within the tradition, are distinct from the commentary they elicit. This distinction depends upon what Steiner describes as "a priority in time." He elaborates this point: "the bringing into being of the work of art is prior to all other modes of its subsequent existence. It has precedence; it has right of way" (150). The present collection assumes this priority of literature over commentary, the formative interest writers take in one another, and the existence of a tradition to which Milton is central. The essays brought together here counterpoint Milton with other important Renaissance authors. In all of these studies the authors are very much alive as individuals, as is their intentionality. The contributors would doubtless approve Lawrence Lipking's endorsement of authorial identity: "authors comprise an elite . . . who *originate* a work and therefore own it, by copyright law or simply by fixing their names. Many are called writers, but few are chosen authors."[8]

Much recent criticism of Milton has been directed to his "contextualization"[9] in the seventeenth century; this volume, we believe, contributes to that undertaking. David Lowenstein and James Grantham Turner's volume of essays on Milton's prose, *Politics, poetics, and hermeneutics in Milton's prose*, for example, "propose[s] a complex relationship between text and context" that the editors describe as dialectical and "mutually constructive."[10] Similarly, in their introduction to *"The muses common-weale": Poetry and Politics in the Seventeenth Century*, Claude J. Summers and Ted-Larry Pebworth refer to "what is perhaps the most vital enterprise in current Renaissance literary scholarship, the re-contextualizing and re-historicizing of Renaissance literature." The essays in their collection focus especially "on the complex and subtle interplay of artistic technique and social context," with particular attention to the "turbulent" political setting.[11] The political dimensions of Renaissance literature have been emphasized in recent years, especially since David Norbrook's influential book, *Poetry and Politics in the English Renaissance*, which grew out of his observation that "some of the greatest English Renaissance poets were politicians, and all of them tried to influence public affairs through their writings."[12] Political considerations are important in several essays in the present collection. Many contributors emphasize other contextualizing influences, including Christian exegetical traditions, scriptural pretexts, patristic writings, moral imperatives and ideas; many of the authors considered (including Milton himself) were, after all, educated in theology, and several were ordained clergy.[13] Other contributors draw on biographical, social, and academic contexts.

As an epigraph to this collection, Milton's "On Shakespeare" reveals intertextual connections with his predecessors and demonstrates the legacy by which one author may fall "heir" to another. Such inheritances may not always be amicably received, but inheritances they are nonetheless. They act as foci of engagement between or among literary artists, generating new conceptions and visions, literary culture, and, eventually, critical and scholarly incentives. Moreover, the aesthetic and ideological concerns of literature are themselves the result of the author's interactive exchanges on several fronts: with the work of other authors (influential pretexts); with contemporary political, religious, and social forces (cultural contexts); and with the private task of writing (its intentionality or function). "All serious art, music, and literature is a *critical* act," as Steiner has written; "in a more particular sense, works of literature . . . embody expository reflection on, a value judgement of, the inheritance and context to which they pertain" (11).[14] Contextualizing is equally central to critical activity from Frye's perspective: "the central activity of criticism, which is the understanding of literature, is essentially one of establishing a context for the works of literature being studied. This means relating them to other things: to their context in the writer's life, in the writer's time, in the history of literature, and above all in the total structure of literature itself."[15] The presence of literary heirs, reacting to pretexts, contexts, and their own conceptions of intention, makes authors authentic critics of their tradition. Authors thus write with the authority of both creative artist and contextualizing critic.

The unifying strategy for this volume is the juxtaposition of Milton with other Renaissance writers.[16] As Annabel Patterson has said, the "coupling" of writers has been one of the major "processes of canonformation." She comments on this process:

> When we couple writers we usually imply a criterion of fit or at least explicable mating . . . we presumably give greater authority to relation-

ships that imply causality, even, or especially, if causality is defined as the influence of the one writer on the other. Most of such relationships are unidirectional, from the earlier to the later dead, and a plausible coupling requires either the successor's own testimony that the influence-relation existed, or other evidence that the influence-relation was strong enough to be formative; or, preferably, both.[17]

Patterson also indicates that criticism has usually emphasized the vertical relation of author to predecessor (over the horizontal relations between authors who are contemporary) and has figured literary influence "in terms of early modern English laws of inheritance" in which "primogeniture" (the father-son relation) is stressed (Patterson, 775). Given this long-established tendency, it will therefore not be surprising that no women authors are among the heirs discussed in the present collection of essays. As Barbara Kiefer Lewalski has observed,

> because we have only begun the recovery and analysis of elusive women's texts, many of them unpublished, uncertain of attribution, and in obscure archives, we still know very little about how early modern women read and wrote themselves and their world. And the few texts we have were virtually unknown before the present decade.[18]

These current efforts to retrieve the literary achievements of women during the Renaissance will undoubtedly establish new lines of inheritance in the near future and simultaneously modify the metaphors and conceptions governing relationships between writers in the English literary tradition.

In the meantime, the essays in this volume "couple" Renaissance writers with Milton both vertically and horizontally, sometimes following conventional patterns, at other times deviating from them. Milton is thus juxtaposed with predecessors such as Sidney, Spenser, Shakespeare, and Hooker, but his relationships with those whose lives overlapped with his, such as Jonson, Donne, Crashaw, Marvell, Hobbes, Bunyan, and Dryden are also examined. Coupling is not, however, strictly an academic maneuver or heuristic device imposed on literary figures to create a convenient network. Writers associate themselves by their receptive or antithetical response to other writers. Intersections occur; affiliations are formed and affirmed; others are denied, though even in denial or conflict there may be influence. Literature is always partly written within literature. In untangling the complex relations between texts and writers we increase our understanding of both. Juxtapositioning therefore illuminates individual achievements and throws authorial identities into greater relief.

The essays here that bring antithetical writers into relationship include those on Hooker, Jonson, Crashaw, Hobbes, and Dryden. P. G. Stanwood contrasts the ecclesiological beliefs of theologian and apologist Richard Hooker with the "puritan" Milton. Although they shared the tradition of natural law and right reason, their profound differences in matters such as episcopacy and perfectibility highlight the doctrinal polarities that divided England and helped to provoke civil war. John Creaser's essay on Ben Jonson and Milton, while acknowledging Milton's early poetic debt to Jonson and certain "affinities of temperament" they shared, also stresses fundamental differences. In examining their respective works, Creaser discriminates with exacting attention between forms of utterance and aspects of their sensibilities, between Jonson's art of "being" and Milton's art of "becoming." Milton and Crashaw are similarly antithetical personalities and literary figures. Through reference to historical documents and biographical details and by examining their parallel but radically opposite experiences at Cambridge and in Italy, Paul Parrish identifies differences in their religion, politics, and art. Charles Cantalupo and Steven Zwicker approach their topics from unconventional points of view. Instead of following the accepted view of Milton and Hobbes as "counter" spirits, Cantalupo presents *Leviathan* as a philosophical epic with generic similarities to *Paradise Lost*. Zwicker overturns the received accounts of the relationship between Milton and Dryden. The "anxiety of influence" usually ascribed to Dryden is instead imputed to Milton, and *Paradise Regained* is treated as Milton's response to the challenge of Dryden's heroic drama and the new literary culture it represented. These essays explore the work of other important writers without necessarily positing influence but, in doing so, help us to contextualize more effectively the literary works both of these writers and of Milton.

Several essays discuss the more expected alignments of Milton with other writers. Thomas P. Roche's study reaffirms the moral perspective linking Spenser and Milton. A verbal borrowing leads Roche into a penetrating analysis of how Spenser (and Sidney) portrayed evil and how Milton resolved its representation and genealogy. M. J. Doherty's essay on Sidney and Milton is an ambitious exploration of their relationship. The phoenix image is the enabling figure that permits Doherty to identify various strands of connection, including aesthetic technique, moral concepts, and the theme of vocational election. Stella Revard examines the central role of the marriage in Shakespeare's *The Tempest, Cymbeline,* and *The Winter's Tale* and suggests how these late romances affected Milton's handling of Adam and Eve in *Paradise Lost*. Diana Treviño Benet charts Andrew Marvell's changing attitudes toward Milton's claims to prophecy through two works, "Upon Appleton House" and "On Mr. Milton's *Paradise Lost*." Twenty years separate these two works, and their distinctive reactions to the older poet help measure Marvell's revised understanding of Milton's stature. Dennis Danielson is another contributor who employs a pattern of imagery as a way of assessing a relationship, in this case the shared imagery of nakedness and clothing in a comparison of John Bunyan with Milton. His account of their "spiritual integrity" defines the Puritan sensibility these writers share, shows how their values affect character and narrative action, and leads to a definition of their respective missions as Christian writers.

Two other essays contextualize Milton by turning to more fugitive sources in Christian tradition. Maren-Sofie Røstvig is well known for her interest in numerological structures in literary works. In her essay she analyzes Milton's *Poems* (1645) for evidence of "contexture." Drawing on a host of earlier texts, including the Psalms, Augustine, and Cassiodorus, as well as Spenser, Giles Fletcher, and Herbert, Røstvig presents evidence of hitherto unsuspected formal design and arrangement in Milton's poetry. Margo Swiss also invokes an established tradition revealed in theological and patristic writings—that of *Lachrymae Christi*. This approach allows her to use a sermon by John Donne ("Jesus wept") as a gloss on *Lycidas* and to argue how the three New Testament accounts of Christ's weeping form a three-part substructure in the three movements of Milton's elegy.

To read Milton in relation to other Renaissance writers involves a variety of competing concerns in different essays. Religion and politics are closely intertwined in the period, although different nuances operate when we are speaking of a conformist like Hooker, or a Roman Catholic like Dryden, a materialist like Hobbes, or a nonconformist like Bunyan. Biographical details may be important if Milton knew the other writer personally, as was the case with Marvell and Dryden; biography can also be used in other ways, as the essays on Jonson and Crashaw show, since forms of expression and details of personality are often interdependent. Denominational lines are often transcended in the cases of Christian traditions and aesthetic imitation or adoption, as the essays on Shakespeare, Spenser, and Donne suggest. Of course, critics have become reluctant to use the word *influence* when describing literary relations between writers. However, the introduction by Jay Clayton and Eric Rothstein to a recent book on the subject—*Influence and Intertextuality in Literary History*—licenses our use of influence, for the term may include the notions of context, of allusion, and of tradition, none of which is influence in a narrow sense but all of which are needed if the narrow sense is to be useful even for the purpose of charting originality. An expanded sense of influence allows one to shift one's attention from the transmission of motifs between authors to the transmutation of historically given material. This shift does not do away with author-centered criticism so much as broaden it to take into account the multifarious relations that can exist among authors.[19]

It is within this wider understanding of influence and contextualization that the present collection will find its place. Shakespeare, Milton, and the other Renaissance writers discussed in these essays have earned their legacy of remembrance. They are among the heirs of fame.

This volume of essays was conceived in sunny Italy during the memorable Third Milton Symposium at Vallombrosa and Florence in June 1988. Having proposed the project, we were very grateful for the responsiveness of several prospective contributors. We thank also Jack and Lorraine Roberts; their subsequent tour of Rome allowed some of us to make further plans. Additional thanks go to Barbara Lewalski and John Shawcross for their encouragement, and to Robert Adolph for his support over many years. For the benefit of their reflections on our introduction, we thank Pat Kennedy, Paul Stanwood, Michael Darling, and D. R. Ewen. Lastly, we thank Susan Rainey and the staff at the former Academic Technology Support Group, York University, Toronto, who diligently helped prepare this manuscript.

Unless otherwise indicated, all quotations from Milton's poetry are from Merritt Y. Hughes, ed. *Complete Poems and Major Prose of John Milton* (New York: Odyssey Press-Bobbs-Merrill, 1973). References to Milton's prose are from Don Wolfe et al., ed. *Complete Prose Works of John Milton*, 8 vols. (New Haven: Yale University Press, 1953–83) and are preceded by the abbreviation *CPW* and volume and page number. Standard abbreviations of Milton's writings are listed in Hughes, xv–xvi. "Milton, Dryden, and the Politcs of Literary Controversy" was first published in *Literature, Culture and Society in the Stuart Restoration,* ed. Gerald MacLean. Copyright 1994 Cambridge University Press. Reprinted with permission of Cambridge University Press.

Notes

1. John Shawcross, *John Milton and Influence: Presence in Literature, History and Culture* (Pittsburgh: Duquesne University Press, 1991), 14.

Gramley Library
Salem College
Winston-Salem, NC 27108

2. See *A Variorum Commentary on The Poems of John Milton*, vol. 2, part 1, eds. A. S. P. Woodhouse and Douglas Bush (New York: Columbia University Press, 1972), 209–12, where some of these echoes and parallels between the "Epitaph" and precedent texts are noted.

3. George Steiner, *Real Presences* (Chicago: University of Chicago Press, 1989), 143.

4. Northrop Frye, *Words with Power: Being a Second Study of the Bible and Literature* (New York: Harcourt Brace Jovanovich, 1990), 76.

5. Paul Stevens, "Subversion and Wonder in Milton's Epitaph 'On Shakespeare'," *English Literary Renaissance* 19 (Autumn 1989): 376.

6. Jerome J. McGann, *The Textual Condition* (Princeton: Princeton University Press, 1991), 9, 135, 64. Additional support for this approach can be found in some of the bibliographical facts surrounding the poem. These details support the empiricist arguments that McGann has made about the social nature of authorship and importance of considering the "textual condition" of a poem and the "impossibility" of "separating textual/editorial work from critical/interpretive work." To illustrate briefly, the "Epitaph," as we learn from the *Variorum Commentary* (203), was printed anonymously in the Second Folio of Shakespeare (1632) among other commendatory verses. Without concerning ourselves with the poem's textual history, we can quickly cite one detail that lends additional support to Stevens's position. That is the title under which the poem originally appeared: "An Epitaph on the admirable Dramaticke Poet, W. Shakespeare." The epithet "admirable" contains within its Latin root the verb to wonder or marvel at, and points to the "rhetoric of wonder" Stevens (382) wishes to describe.

7. Robert Alter, *The Pleasures of Reading in an Ideological Age* (New York: Simon and Schuster, 1989), 114.

8. Lawrence Lipking, "Life, Death, and Other Theories" in *Historical Studies and Literary Criticism*, ed. Jerome J. McGann (Madison: University of Wisconsin Press, 1985), 181.

9. Joseph Wittreich, Jr., *Interpreting 'Samson Agonistes'* (Princeton: Princeton University Press, 1986), 51.

10. David Lowenstein and James Grantham Turner, eds., *Politics, poetics, and hermeneutics in Milton's prose* (Cambridge: Cambridge University Press, 1990), 3.

11. Claude J. Summers and Ted-Larry Pebworth, eds., *"The muses commonweale": Poetry and Politics in the Seventeenth Century* (Columbia: University of Missouri Press, 1988), 2.

12. David Norbrook, *Poetry and Politics in the English Renaissance* (London: Routledge and Kegan Paul, 1984), 1.

13. "In the early seventeenth century, theology still afforded the most acceptable explanation of the facts of experience." Arthur Barker, *Milton and the Puritan Dilemma 1641–1660* (Toronto: University of Toronto Press, 1942), xxiv.

14. Christopher Ricks makes a related point: "The crucial constituting of what is tendentiously called the canon is effected not by academics and critics but by creative writers." See "What is at stake in the 'battle of the books'?" *The New Criterion* 8.1 (September 1989): 44.

15. Northrop Frye, "Criticism, Visible and Invisible" in *The Stubborn Structure: Essays on Criticism and Society* (London: Methuen, 1970), 88.

16. Among the studies of Milton and other major Renaissance authors, the following may be cited as examples: A. Kent Hieatt, *Chaucer, Spenser, Milton: Mythopoeic Continuities and Transformations* (Montreal: McGill–Queen's University Press, 1975); Maureen Quilligan, *Milton's Spenser: The Politics of Reading* (Ithaca: Cornell

University Press, 1983); Paul Stevens, *Imagination and the Presence of Shakespeare in Paradise Lost* (Madison: University of Wisconsin Press, 1985).

17. Annabel Patterson, "Couples, Canons, and the Uncouth: Spenser-and-Milton in Educational Theory," *Critical Inquiry* 16 (Summer 1990): 773. In fact, Patterson's article criticizes this conventional method. She advocates that the "coupling" of Spenser and Milton should be reconceived along radical and reformist lines.

18. "Writing Women and Reading the Renaissance," *Renaissance Quarterly* 44 (Winter 1991): 792. *See also* Barbara Kiefer Lewalski, *Writing Women in Jacobean England* (Cambridge: Harvard University Press, 1993).

19. Jay Clayton and Eric Rothstein, eds., *Influence and Intertextuality in Literary History* (Madison: University of Wisconsin Press, 1991), 6.

Spenser, Milton, and the Representation of Evil

THOMAS P. ROCHE, JR.

Although no one to my knowledge has ever doubted the influence of Spenser on Milton, neither has any one ever convinced me about where that influence appears or why. The index to the Columbia edition of Milton's works lists over 120 allusions to Spenser, but the majority of these citations turn out to be parallel passages in which both poets are describing natural events such as sunrise or sunset or moral conditions such as chastity or fighting dragons. They rarely give the assurance of direct verbal echoes that Milton had that line or that passage from Spenser in mind and intended the reader to recognize his use of his predecessor. The enterprise of annotating influences as exemplified in the editions of Merritt Hughes and Cary-Fowler proclaims a world of criticism that has quietly slipped away or fallen into the interstices of intertextuality. The whole question of influence, earlier seen as a happy borrowing from, or an ingenious improvement on, an earlier poet, has now become an anxiety, Oedipal and ugly. Verbal felicities, previously known as rhetorical colors, have now become wrenching psychological confrontations between poetic fathers and sons or daughters, all within the text, which sits quietly on the page. We have moved from the text as a construct to the text as a pretext to reveal the author's anxieties about the world he is creating and the world in which he lives. Mr. Tillyard's hierarchical world picture becomes the stultifying deity to be overcome by the satanic forces of the author, hounded by the presence of his precursor, and to be recreated in every act of reading the poem, with every man his own prophet.

Although I can agree with some of these Romantic or psychoanalytical readings, at least in part, I do not see Milton's relation to Spenser in this way. If we but attend to those citations of Spenser in Milton's prose, we will see that they all share one characteristic in common—a moral reading of Spenser. Milton chooses to mention the shepherd Palinode from the "Maye" eclogue in *Animadversions* (*CPW*, 1:722), Guyon in the often cited passage from *Areopagitica* (*CPW*, 2:516), Talus in *Eikonoklastes* (*CPW*, 3:390), the quotation from the Chronicle of Britain (*FQ*, 2.10.24) in the *History of Britain* (*CPW*, 5, pt. 1:17), and finally the references in the *Commonplace Book* to *A view of the present state of Ireland* (*CPW*, 1:465, 496).[1] All of these passages are Spenser at his most "sage and serious" moments, and these moments are the ones Milton chooses to punctuate and illuminate with his own most sage and serious admonitions because he dared "be known to think [Spenser] a better teacher than *Scotus* or *Aquinas*."

I will not discuss any of these passages, but I should point out that by choosing Guyon and Talus as the only characters from Spenser's poem to be named explicitly Milton takes up two of the most harried characters in twentieth-century criticism of Spenser: Guyon branded with the uncaring privileges of class and Talus receiving the full burden of oppressive power politics. Milton's references to them, on the other hand, show them as exemplars of a system of virtues that he read out of Spenser in ways that we seem now unable to fathom. Milton's choice of these two characters suggests his approval of Spenserian "rigor," for reasons very close to his not wanting the Lady in *Comus* to succumb to the blandishments of Comus and possibly why he, more than his modern readers, probably supported Elder Brother in his defense of chastity.

No matter what influence Chaucer had on Spenser, or Spenser on Milton, they were all influenced by philosophical assumptions common to them all, and it is these common philosophical assumptions that link them intellectually and that then further link them when they pick up verbal echoes of the previous poets to inscribe in their own poems. Chaucer's "thought" does not influence Spenser, Spenser's "thought" does not influence Milton, as if there were a separate empire of "poetic thought." Each later poet imitates structural configurations, verbal patterns, or significances that emerge from the common Christian tradition that binds all three together. And it will not do to claim that Chaucer is fourteenth-century Catholic, Spenser sixteenth-century Protestant, and Milton seventeenth-century Puritan, or any gradation of temporal or nominal distinctions among Christian sects popular today. We can attribute "sectarian politics" to the poets, if we must, but it is almost impossible to discriminate poetically among those sects because the large and clear images and symbols these poets use are meant to draw in and unify the large configurations of thought and emotion that enunciate Christian thought. Of course, Chaucer is "Catholic" because the Church of England to which he belonged was still attached to the See of Rome. Of course, Spenser is "Protestant" because his Church of England is no longer attached to the See of Rome. Of course, Milton is "Puritan" because he sees a different organization of the church from either Chaucer or Spenser. But all three are Christian poets and saw the difference in the Christianity of their predecessors, and in their language, and in the poetic task before them, and therefore the question of influence implies both tradition and innovation, but above all continuity of symbols. It will not do to see any of these poets primarily as "precursors" unless we understand how they read those earlier poets, whom they might have read merely as poets who simply lived earlier than they, within a living tradition.

Thus when Patrick Cullen rightly proclaims the trinity of the world, the flesh, and the devil as a major link between Spenser and Milton, and A. Kent Hieatt elegantly elaborates Edwin Greenlaw's early study of the passions in *Faerie Queene II* as an influence on Milton, we must also remember that these paradigms had a larger and more fulfilling life in the world outside poetry.[2] We might say that poetry was pre-empting philosophy, but we might more properly say that poetry was creating itself out of the forms of thought that characterize the period.

I think there is another, and more conscious, form of influence manifesting itself as imitation that sees into the heart of the earlier creation, such as Milton's depiction of Eve as perceived by Adam immediately after her return from her Satanic experience.[3]

> On th' other side, *Adam,* soon as he heard
> The fatal Trespass done by *Eve,* amaz'd,
> Astonied stood and Blank, while horror chill
> Ran through his veins, and all his joints relax'd;
> From his slack hand the Garland wreath'd for Eve
> Down dropp'd, and all the faded Roses shed:
> Speechless he stood and pale, till thus at length
> First to himself he inward silence broke.
>
> (*PL,* 9.888–95)

This is the only time that Milton uses the word *astonied,* and commentators have rung all the changes of meaning that can be expected, from Medusa-like petrifaction to astonishment, but I would like to suggest that Milton knew that he was using a word from Spenser, a word that is so like the Spenserian language that Ben Jonson despised that we do not remember that it is a word that Spenser uses on only four occasions in *The Faerie Queene,* the most important of which is the response of the Olympian gods and goddesses to the eruption of Mutabilitie in their midst:

> Whilst she thus spake, the Gods that gaue good eare
> > To her bold words, and marked well her grace,
> > Being of stature tall as any there
> > Of all the Gods, and beautiful of face
> > As any of the Goddesses in place,
> > Stood all *astonied*, like a sort of Steeres;
> > Mongst whom, some beast of strange & forraine race,
> > Vnwares is chaunc't, far straying from his peeres
> So did their ghastly gaze bewray their hidden feares.
> > > > > *(FQ,* 7.6.28; italics mine)[4]

At least two things stand out in Spenser's description of the gods' *astoniement:* she is as beautiful as they but a threat to them in ways that they do not want to admit. Spenser insists on the equality of their beauty, but he also insists on an Orwellian syllogism: All animals are equal, but some are more equal than others. The gods are "like a sort of Steeres," and Mutabilitie like "some beast of strange & forraine race, . . . far straying from his peeres." Spenser's shift to a bestial analogy in the latter part of the stanza points to a radical disjunction between his described observers (the gods) and their unstated opinions of the intruder, but his analogy maintains the parity between the enthroned gods and the interloper, even if his narrative and his xenophobic gods do not.[5]

I am suggesting, of course, that Milton makes Adam see Eve as Spenser's Mutabilitie and wants his reader to make the identification of the two through his use of the word *astonied.* Adam is precisely in the situation of the gods observing Mutabilitie: his relation to this beautiful creature has been called into question by her separatist activity in the garden, his very existence is threatened, but he cannot deny her beauty nor its claim upon him. This is not another parallel passage; it is an insight on the part of the later poet to clarify his own depiction of Adam and Eve. The threat and winsomeness of Spenser's Mutabilitie was not lost on Milton; he understood the allegorical fullness of Spenser's character as few later readers have, and he used it for his own poetic purpose through his appropriation of that single word *astonied.*

Milton presents Adam with the problem facing the Olympian gods. They bring Mutabilitie to a trial to convince both Mutabilitie and us, the readers, of the rightness of their claim; Adam argues merely with himself and is confronted by Eve's beauty:

Against his better knowledge, not deceiv'd,
But fondly overcome with Female charm.
Earth trembl'd from her entrails, as again
In pangs, and Nature gave a second groan,
Sky low'r'd and muttering Thunder, some sad drops
Wept at completing of the mortal Sin Original.
                                    (*PL*, 9.998–1004; italics mine)

The world of mutability enters Milton's poem through the beauty of
Eve and the doting of Adam, and the whole world is turned into a
grieving mother in labor. For both Spenser and Milton the world as we
know it has been born. "Never again would bird song be the same."

1

One of the most popular bromides about Milton is that the allegory of
Sin and Death in book 2, lines 629ff., is the only real allegory in *Paradise Lost*, but few will agree on why it is allegorical except for the
personification of Sin and Death and how and why it differs from
Spenserian allegory. I would like to take a different approach to that
episode of the poem, not because of the personification of Sin and
Death (I do not believe that allegory has very much to do with personification before the eighteenth century), but because it is the closest
that Milton gets to a philosophical genealogy of evil in his poem. My
discussion will lead me into disagreement with most of the recent
commentators on this episode,[6] but I hope that my diversion will be
thought worthy. Although I have known ever since I first read *Paradise Lost* that Satan's confrontation with Sin and Death brings him
(and us) as close to a genealogy of evil as he can get, I had not thought
much about the problem of genealogies of evil until I recently presented a lecture on this subject in Spenser and Sidney.[7] I have always been
troubled about Duessa's descent to Night to resuscitate Sansjoy in the
fifth canto of book 1 of *The Faerie Queene*. It is clearly a diabolical
imitation of Aeneas's descent to the underworld in book 6 of the
Aeneid, and it is Spenser's major attempt to treat the pre-Olympian
gods except for his depiction of Mutabilitie. It is therefore something
of a surprise to find how very few of Spenser's critics have given it
any attention in view of its enormous importance to the allegorical
structure of the book.

For our purposes allegory begins with that serpent in the garden of
Genesis, by which we have always understood Satan, the initiator of
evil in heaven and on earth:

And the great dragon, that olde serpent, called the deuil and Satan, was cast out, which deceiueth all the worlde; he was euen cast into the earth, & his Angels were cast out with him. (*Rev.* 12.9: Genevan version)

This passage from the Book of Revelation has much to do with our apprehension of evil, even though for most of us we have imbibed it first in a literary way from our reading of Milton, so much so that we as readers of English literature do not question the absence of Satan in other works. For example, Satan never appears in the *Arcadia*, which is no surprise, and only once in *The Faerie Queene*, which is a surprise, and there he appears as a mute, inglorious chauffeur to Lucifera in the House of Pride:

> And after all, vpon the wagon beame
>   Rode Sathan, with a smarting whip in hand,
>   With which he forward lasht the laesie teme,
>   So oft as Slowth still in the mire did stand.
>   Huge routs of people did about them band,
>   Showting for ioy, and still before their way
>   A foggie mist had couered all the land;
>   And vnderneath their feet, all scattered lay
> Dead sculs & bones of men, whose life had gone astray.
>   (*FQ*, 1.4.36)

This stanza is the culmination of the preceding twenty stanzas, in which we see in stanza 17 Lucifera climb into her coach, and then the reader is jumped ahead to the front of the six ill-assorted sins and beasts that carry her, three stanzas allotted to each sin, and then the single stanza devoted to Satan, who is seated directly in front of Lucifera. We have come full circle in this meaningless entourage. We have gone nowhere, and Satanic force is subordinated to the poetic fiction of the seven deadly sins. The reader moves through twenty stanzas, but there is no progress, and we end where we began with Lucifera, Pride, the primal sin, and it is only at this point that Spenser opens up his narrative again to tell us that Duessa was all the time "next vnto the chaire / Of proud Lucifera, as one of the traine," but we read her only now that the iconic static progress has been read. The power of Satan has been transferred to Lucifera, his poetic daughter, and she relinquishes her power to Duessa and to the arrival of Sansjoy, to whom I will return soon.

Spenser's abdication of dealing with Satan as the primal force of evil is in direct contrast with Tasso his predecessor in the epic form and with Milton his successor, both of whom give full scope to their depictions of Satan as an active force in their poems. The reader may need to be reminded of that powerful depiction of Satan at the beginning of the fourth book of *Gerusalemme liberata*. It is the same book in which Armida, the main enchantress of the poem, appears, and critics have usually taken Tasso's comment that "All episodes derive from this book" to mean that all the evils of the poem derive from the arrival of the enchantress.[8] I think that Tasso meant us to see that his depiction of Satan, who wants to undo Godfrey's efforts to win Jerusalem and unleashes all the powers of hell to do so, is the motive force behind Armida's appearance and activity in the poem. As a Jesuit graduate student pointed out to me long ago, Tasso, educated by the Jesuits, bases his depiction of Satan on the first of St. Ignatius Loyola's *Spiritual Exercises*, in which the retreatant is meant to visualize and focus on Satan as the main force of evil in this world.

Spenser's fiction of evil is different in that he begins and ends with images of evil at one remove from the primal names of the Christian depiction of evil because he elected to make the villain of book 1 a dragon, which any Christian reader of the period would know as an image of Satan. Within that metaphoric pattern it was even daring of Spenser to give Satan his unavailing seat on the beam of Lucifera's coach for the simple reason that he had already given the role of hypocrisy, deceit, and duplicity to Archimago, who separates Red Crosse from Una with his diabolically conceived "porn" show (*FQ*, 1.2.3–8).

Recent criticism has made such a fetish of the duplicity of words that I want to remind us that Archimago works mainly through images and that the separation he effects between Red Crosse and Una is because of the duplicity of things. Red Crosse cannot distinguish between Archimago's simulacra and Una; just a little later he cannot see that Fradubio's story refers to the very woman with whom he is now riding. All these errors are a matter of human perception. It would be wrong to spend most of our critical energies blaming Red Crosse for being morally wrong at this point in the narrative when it is more a matter of perception, surely one of the points Spenser wants to make and which he reinforces through Red Crosse's speechless observation of Lucifera's House of Pride and his aborted victory over Sansjoy, rescued by Duessa and that Virgilian cloud:

> Therewith his heauie hand he high gan reare,
> Him to haue slaine; when lo a darkesome clowd
> Vpon him fell: he no where doth appeare,
> But vanisht is. The Elfe him cals alowd
> But answer none receiues: the darkness him doth shrowd.
>
> (*FQ*, 1.5.13)

At this point, after this cloud of unknowing descends to shield San-sjoy, in imitation of Virgil's obscuring the body of Turnus from the eager view of Aeneas in book 11, occurs one of the strangest episodes in *The Faerie Queene*, the descent of Duessa to the realms of Night to cure the wounded Sansjoy. It is clearly Spenser's rendition of Aeneas's descent into the underworld, but it is equally clearly the closest that Spenser gets to a genealogy of evil in the whole poem. It is in the poem to explain the absence of Satan from Spenser's depiction of evil, and once again it is presented in terms of perception, with Duessa representing as much light as can penetrate the realm of Night. It is the downward sweep corresponding to the upward sweep of Mutabilitie into the heavens at the end of the poem. The episode is tripartite: the approach of Duessa to Night (stanzas 19–27); their descent into the classical hell with all its pendent sufferers (stanzas 28–36); and the myth of Aesculapius's damnation for the effrontery of redoing Hippolytus, for which reason he is being sought out to do the same for Sansjoy (stanzas 37–44).

It is the first of these parts that interests me here, the encounter between Duessa and Night. The second part—the descent to hell—merely domesticates Virgil's exposition in the *Aeneid*, and the Aesculapian recovery of Sansjoy leads to the usual Spenserian impasse, in which either nothing happens or Spenser chooses not to tell us about its outcome; in either case the narrative leaves Sansjoy in the intensive care unit of hell, and we never hear of him again.

The meeting of Duessa with Night is the first major confrontation of evil forces in the poem, and if I am not mistaken it was much in Milton's mind when he wrote the confrontation of Satan with Sin and Death. Both episodes deal with the confrontation of two forces of evil. Both episodes deal with the consequences of sin in which the progenitor does not recognize its offspring, and both episodes terminate in a recognition and alliance both horrendous and ultimately unavailing. Thus Satan has to be told by his daughter-wife who she is and what they did and then have pointed out to him the consequences of their actions in their offspring Death. Milton's male-female confrontation allows him to play on the subtle sexual encounter and on the problem of paternity.

Spenser, on the other hand, has two females confront each other, the suppliant daughter identifying herself to the ancient mother figure. There is no question of sexuality or paternity in Spenser, only the unrelenting matriarchal line discovering itself and revealing itself to us. There are no active males; only the wounded Sansjoy, the already dead Sansfoy, and the damned in the classical hell. "Phoebus cheareful face durst neuer vew" the "visage deadly sad" of Night (*FQ*,

1.5.20). No active males. Even Aesculapius will not achieve the triumph of plastic surgery for Sansjoy that he achieved for Hippolytus.
Duessa and Night take over a parodic replay of male heroic action. In
Virgil Aeneas goes to the underworld to find his father and the wisdom necessary to found Rome; in Spenser Duessa goes to the underworld to intercede with her great mother, and Spenser does this trick
with the most subtle use of light and dark imagery.

Duessa, having wept all day for the wounded Sansjoy, at the
approach of night "to the easterne coast of heuen makes speedy way,"
and there encounters the monolithic figure of Night, but before I
approach my allegorical reading of Duessa and Night, I had better
attend to the continuous allegory of the Sansboys, because it
entwines the separated adventures of Red Crosse and Una. In a
nation where church and state are one, as was the case for England in
the sixteenth century, there was a fear that faithlessness (Sansfoy)
would automatically lead to lawlessness (Sansloy); atheism would
lead to the breakdown of the law and hence the state. Spenser carries
this axiom one step further in creating Sansjoy, who is the logical
outcome of faithlessness and lawlessness, despair, civil mutiny with
no reward, action with no possibility of reconciliation, and that is
what Sansjoy represents in the poem, and that is also the reason that
Duessa espouses him.

Duessa's appearance at the moment when Night is to begin her
journey encompassing the earth is a reminiscence of Red Crosse's
encounter with Error in canto 1:

> But forth vnto the darksome hole he went,
> And looked in: his glistring armor made
> A litle glooming light, much like a shade,
> By which he saw the vgly monster plaine.
>
> (*FQ,* 1.1.14)

That is, the armor of righteousness, which he is wearing, is the only
source of light, the only means her thousand little monstrosities know
to hide within her mouth (*FQ,* 1.1.15). Here in canto 5 Duessa's
depraved glitter, her Roman pomp, is enough light to frighten Night,

> Where she all day did hide her hated hew. . . .

> Who when she saw *Duessa* sunny bright,
>   Adorned with gold and jewels shining cleare,
>   She greatly grew amazed at the sight,
>   And th'unacquainted light began to feare:
>   For never did such brightnesse there appeare,

> And would have backe retyred to her caue,
> Untill the witches speech she began to heare,
> Saying, yet o thou dreaded Dame, I craue
> Abide, till I have told the message, which I have.
>
> (*FQ*, 1.5.21)

The message is nothing more than complaint about Night's neglect of her fallen heroes, "old *Aveugles* sonnes," who just happen to be the lovers of Duessa, but this complaint about fallen nephews (Latin: *nipotes*) strikes a small chord in the heart of Night:

> Her feeling speeches some compassion moued
> In hart, and chaunge in that great mothers face:
> Yet pittie in her hart was neuer proued
> Till then: for euermore she hated, neuer loued.
>
> (*FQ*, 1.5.24)

Her response to Duessa's charge is the usual diabolical response about the tyranny of Jove, his favoritism to his own sons of day, and the admission that none can "breake the chayne of strong necessitee / Which fast is tyde to *Ioues* eternall seat." Even her feeble threat against all the sons of day to pay the price of blood spilt does not bring the hate-filled heart of Night over to Duessa's cause until Night asks her final question: "But what art thou, that telst of Nephews kilt?" (*FQ*, 1.5.26). This is an ultimate question, in fact, the ultimate matrilinear question. Not "who are you" but "who are you to speak of dead men?" It is a question that has not been commented on in Spenserian criticism. In view of the recent feminist interest in Spenser's poem, I think we ought to pay some attention to this crucial episode and to reconsider why Spenser is using these two female figures to present his genealogy of evil. The answer Duessa gives to Night persuades me that Spenser is not being antifeminist:

> I that do seeme not I, *Duessa* am,
> (Quoth she) how euer now in garments gilt,
> And gorgeous gold arrayd I to thee came;
> *Duessa* I, the daughter of Deceipt and Shame.
>
> Then bowing downe her aged backe, she kist
> The wicked witch, saying: In that faire face
> The false resemblance of Deceipt, I wist
> Did closely lurke, yet so true-seeming grace
> It carried, that I scarse in darkesome place
> Could it discerne, though I the mother bee
> Of falshood, and root of *Duessaes* race.

O welcome child, whom I haue longed to see,
And now haue seen vnwares. Lo now I go with thee.
(*FQ*, 1.5.26–27)

It is a sisterly reunion. By shifting his genealogy of evil from God-Satan to Night-Duessa Spenser is certainly "gendering" his depiction of evil in this episode, but I think it is unimportant in view of his constant upgrading of "gendering" in his depiction of Belphoebe, Britomart, and most of the "female" figures in the poem. To take such a modernist, or postmodernist, stance about such an unremittingly unmodern poet is to introduce issues into the reading of his poem, for which we will have to take harder knocks than we have given our predecessors.

Spenser turned the epic inside-out by naming the allegorical import of each book with the name of a virtue, and we have not caught up with his devious tactics in four hundred years. We are still perplexed about the problem of continuity between books. In each book except book 4 we are presented with a figure of evil that must be defeated by the knight of that book of such variety that any previous or subsequent writer would have dropped his pen. There is a dragon, a nymphomaniac, a pornographer, a mafioso warlord, and a giant pit bull, but as these modern instances suggest, my modern terminology for the evils depicted in *The Faerie Queene* shows only how far we have traveled from the world Spenser depicted.

2

Before turning to Milton's "reading" of this episode, I want to amplify my matrilinear explication of Duessa's descent to Night by bringing in another matrilinear genealogy of evil from Sidney's *Arcadia*. I am, of course, referring to the abortive efforts of Cecropia to get either Philoclea or Pamela to accept her son Amphialus as husband. The episodes occur in book 3, chapters 5–10, and they are the only occasion in the *Arcadia* in which Sidney reaches beyond his usual technique of relying on act-morality to assert a virtue-morality. The potential grandmother figure, Cecropia, is the instigator, and her object is to supplant her brother-in-law, Basilius, by marrying her son to one of his daughters, thus assuring the ascendancy of her line. Cecropia is not so awesomely dark and fearsome as Night; she is as close as anything named Cecropia can be to a human characterization. Sidney's characters always have an insight into their errors; they can see other actions that might have been possible. With Spenser's characters there is never any thought about past actions; there is never any possible action but the one Spenser tells. Within the gambit of allegory Spenser plumbs the depths of the allegorical sense, and Sidney wrings the heart out of the tropological sense. The evil depicted by Sidney comes from the evil actions of characters almost human, always dramatic. Sidney's narrative dramatizes what "to make of a diminished thing," our fallen condition. Spenser goes for the roots of that condition. In that sense the encounter of Duessa and Night is comparable with the confrontation of Cecropia and Pamela.

Neither set of figures is justly served by comparison to characters in novels, just as we would be misreading *Tom Jones* by placing too much emphasis on the fact that Tom is searching out Sophia (wisdom) when we all know that he is really after Sophia Western. In a similar way we may obliterate some of the more obnoxious characteristics of little Pearl in Hawthorne's *The Scarlet Letter* by remembering the Pearl of Great Price, but we as readers will destroy the fiction if we press too hard on the buttons of the names in these novels to achieve an allegorical reading. Just as surely we will destroy that fiction by neglecting the ancient tropes of Wisdom and Salvation as subliminal parts of the characters. It requires a delicate calibration of our literary responses to account for what we now consider tugs in opposite directions, but those tugs are absolutely necessary if we are not entirely to rule out the possibility of literary archaeology.

Victor Skretkowicz cites in his note to the Cecropia-Pamela section a reference to Mark Rose's treatment of the episode, in which Rose argues heroically for a pagan Arcadia, a Stoic Pamela, and a libertine Cecropia, citing Milton's objections to the inclusion of Pamela's prayer in Gaudens's defense of King Charles I in *Eikon Basilike* of 1649.[9] Milton had a very special rhetorical task to accomplish—the justification of regicide—and was not loath to use rhetorical tricks in pushing a political advantage. In the first place he calls Pamela's outburst a "prayer," for as such it is included in Gaudens's tract, but Milton knew full well that that was not its generic function in Sidney's *Arcadia*. It is a sermon set as a response to an attempted seduction of one woman by another, and once more the confrontation is brought about, as in Spenser, by the inadequacy of the male, Amphialus. In Sidney the confrontation does not lead to recognition as in Spenser but to condemnation: good facing evil. Pamela's sermon is deliberately neither Christian nor pagan; it is meant (in my opinion) to be a nexus between classical and Christian attitudes toward evil to convince the reader of the utter depravity of Cecropia, and in this objective I feel that Sidney was most successful, for he measures the success of Pamela's sermon by its effect on Cecropia's perception:

Thus she [Pamela] said; thus, she ended, with so fair a majesty of uncon-
quered virtue that captivity might seem to have authority over tyranny, so
foully was the filthiness of impiety discovered by the shining of her
unstained goodness—so far, as either Cecropia saw indeed, or else the
guilty amazement of a self-accusing conscience made her eyes untrue
judges of their natural object: that there was a light more than human
which gave a lustre to her perfection. But Cecropia, like a bat which,
though it have eyes to discern that there is a sun, yet hath so evil eyes that
it cannot delight in the sun, found a truth but could not love it; but, as
great persons are wont to make the wrong they have done to be a cause to
do the more wrong, her knowledge rose to no higher point but to envy a
worthier, and her will was no otherwise bent but the more to hate, the more
she found her enemy provided against her. (p. 363)

In a manner similar to Spenser's truncation of Satan in the House of
Pride, and his genealogy of evil as the confrontation of Duessa and
Night, Sidney traces his genealogy of evil only so far as Pamela's ser-
mon to Cecropia.

Neither Spenser nor Sidney can be considered less than Christian
believers, yet neither one pushed his orthodoxy to delineate a genealogy of evil originating with a male Satan figure. Both in their major
works chose to present us with two female figures in discourse to
expound their deepest probings of the problem of evil.

I think that Milton also saw this matrilinear proposal in Spenser
and Sidney, but he was faced with a political problem of a king killed,
sacrificed, defeated, whose defenders had included Sidney's fictional
plea in their hagiographical defense of the dead king as the prayer that
he spoke on the night before he was killed. The untruth of the alleged
prayer would have been enough to send Milton to his writing desk, but
I feel certain that the feminist format of the Sidneyan debate also contributed some reverberations of Milton's outrage. I cannot say that
Milton remembered his diatribe when he wrote the allegory of Sin and
·Death, but I think that there are enough parallels between Spenser's
descent to hell and Milton's description of Satan's ascent from hell to
suggest a genuine influence of the earlier poet on the later.

3

Duessa goes down; Satan flies, swims, floats up, and at the limits of
his newly imposed liminality he meets the first fruits of his error, his
wife and son, who have no names at this point in the epic since they
have not become the things they will be. The allegory is a study in
ontology.[10] What are Sin and Death without the fodder of human

flesh? At this point in history they have neither sting nor victory (1 Cor. 15:55).

Their genealogy has been traced to James 1.15: "Then when lust hath conceived, it bringeth forth sin; and sin, when it is finished, bringeth forth death." This Genevan version led John M. Steadman to want a fuller identification with Satan to establish "Lust" as Milton's source, and he suggested St. Basil's "Sixth Homily on the Hexameron."[11] That Milton concurred with the James reading is confirmed by the facts we learn from the episode: that Satan became enamoured of his newly begotten daughter, that from this union was born Death and that Death then proceeded to beget new sins from the body of his mother. The parody that Milton wrote must be examined with some care to see how the allegory is worked out narratively.

Once more the narrative is controlled by the nature of "human" perception. Satan first "arrives" in the vicinity of the gates of hell and observes two shapes, who are not named:

> The one seem'd Woman to the waist, and fair,
> But ended foul in many a scaly fold
> Voluminous and vast, a Serpent arm'd
> With mortal sting: about her middle round
> A cry of Hell Hounds never ceasing bark'd
> With wide *Cerberean* mouths full loud, and rung
> A hideous Peal: yet, when they list, would creep,
> If aught disturb'd thir noise, into her womb,
> And kennel there, yet there still bark'd and howl'd
> Within unseen.
>
> (*PL,* 2.650–59)

Milton has cleaned up the perplexing ambiguities of Spenser's description of Error in 1.1.14:

> His glistring armor made
> A litle glooming light, much like a shade,
> By which he saw the vgly monster plaine,
> Halfe like a serpent horribly displaide
> *But th'other halfe did womans shape retaine,*
> Most lothsom, filthie, foule, and full of vile disdaine.
>
> (Italics mine)

This is surely one of the most troublesome alexandrines that Spenser ever wrote, and no amount of justification about delayed modifiers will finally rescue him from the charge of antifeminism. Nonetheless, it should be remembered that, except for the feminine pronouns in the rest of the episode, the female aspect of Error is mentioned this once and then dropped from the poem. She is a dragon for the rest of the episode.

Milton makes the female part of Sin "fair" but transfers the entry-point for their spawn from the mouth of Error (stanzas 25–26) to the loins of Sin, giving a Lear-like repellency to his description and changing Spenser's insistence on the verbal power of his Error to the incestuous sexual fecundity of Sin. In fact, Milton changes the whole valence of this episode. He insists on questions of paternity and male dominance in his genealogy by describing the second shape, again unnamed, whose shapelessness and namelessness again reproduce the ineffectuality of the males in *Faerie Queene* 1.5—with these differences, that the unnamed Death is articulate, knowledgeable about the situation of his opponent, and aggressive in the mode of all later military aggression: he does carry "a dreadful dart" (2.672) to shake. Satan is not fighting Death, nor his son, but a shapeless, crowned opponent:

> So frown'd the mighty Combatants, that Hell
> Grew darker at thir frown, so matcht they stood;
> For never but once more was either like
> To meet so great a foe: and now great deeds
> Had been achiev'd, whereof all Hell had rung,
> Had not the Snaky Sorceress that sat
> Fast by Hell Gate, and kept the fatal Key,
> Ris'n, and with hideous outcry rush'd between.
>
> (*PL*, 2.719–26)

Milton shuffles the reader back and forth between the literal events and their full allegorical meaning. We are pushed forward to the final victory of Christ over Satan, Sin, and Death, "For never but once more was either like / To meet so great a foe"—again that victor unnamed, but then Milton trounces the possibility of heroic combat as in an *Iliad* or an *Aeneid* or a *Gerusalemme liberata* by slipping back to the time of the narrative: "and now great deeds / Had been achiev'd, whereof all Hell had rung."[12] No victory could be achieved by either of these combatants, and the potential stalemate is forestalled only through the timely intervention of Sin. It is a typical epic convention to forestall the confrontation between mighty opposites, either through goddess-induced clouds that obscure one of the opponents (*Iliad, Aeneid*) or inability of one of the combatants to meet the other (*Orlando furioso, Gerusalemme liberata*), but Milton introduces in the shuffling of his time scheme the possibility of a victory of

either Satan or Death, "whereof all Hell had rung," that would preclude the Fall as we know it.

The "portress of Hell Gate" intervenes, and it is only at this point
that we learn facts, names, and relationships. Satan is "Father";
unnamed shape is "only Son." Satan's response to this revelation of
relationships and the intervention in what would have been an epic
fight in any other epic are muted. He does not respond to the prophecy of his eventual defeat (*PL*, 2.731–34). What disturbs him is the
"strange . . . outcry" and the "words so strange / Thou interposest,"
which have interrupted his action, the intention of which he will not
reveal:

> till first I know of thee,
> What thing thou art, thus double-form'd, and why
> In this infernal Vale first met thou call'st
> Me Father, and that Phantasm call'st my Son?
> I know thee not, nor ever saw till now
> Sight more detestable than him and thee.
>
> (*PL,* 2.740–45)

The dramatic economy of this speech is remarkable in that it moves
rapidly from the polite abstraction of "thy outcry" and "thy words so
strange," to a threat of renewing his forestalled action, to a description of what he sees and his revulsion at the sight. Satan is now caught
in a situation that happens only to epic knights who suddenly have
revealed to them the evil mis-shape of the ladies with whom they have
colluded, for example, Red Crosse knight with Duessa (*FQ,*
1.8.46–50), but for Satan this is not to be a sight but a testimony,
given by his only-begotten daughter for his benefit and that of his
only-begotten son.

Sin reveals Satan's act of transgression for him and for us, and for
the first time *names* herself and her son (*PL,* 2.747–49):

> Hast thou forgot me then, and do I seem
> Now in thine eye so foul, once deem'd so fair
> In Heav'n

Sin continues without waiting for an answer because, of course, Satan
has forgotten what has happened to him. In one sense Sin is in the
same situation as Duessa in her descent to Night in that both must
inform their progenitor of what has happened. The fact that both
Duessa and Satan are the interlopers into new territory should not
becloud the fact that both Duessa and Sin are in rhetorical command
of the action. If Sin is not telling the true origin of evil, Satan does

not refute or contradict her, and thus we must accept her story of her birth as the nearest approach Milton can make to his genealogy of evil perhaps because Milton's God has empowered her with the key to hell, which is a genuinely allegorical statement.

The story she tells drives the ambiguity of all those female knights that emerge in the sixteenth-century epic romances of Boiardo, Ariosto, Tasso, and Spenser, back to a primal disorder, figured as an armed woman begotten by a single male parent: "A Goddess arm'd / Out of thy head I sprung" (*PL*, 2.757–58). The implications of this armed woman go much beyond the parody of Athene springing full-grown from the head of Zeus. Milton, virtually at the end of the long line of heroically armed warrior women from Boiardo through Spenser, cannot make his Eve into an armed woman because there is no armor for her to wear.

What armor there is to wear is worn by Sin in her birth from Satan's head, but it is only her memory of that event that informs Satan of his past. His vision of her at this moment in the poem owes more to that earlier Spenserian description of Error, to which I have already alluded, and it is here that I must disagree most strongly with Maureen Quilligan's description of this scene in which she "reads" Satan = God the Father; Sin = Holy Spirit; Death = Son.[13] Her analogical equations are not gendered correctly. Satan is certainly the father of this infernal trinity, but Sin must be "equated" with the Son, and Death with the Holy Spirit, as the narrative directs us to believe. Sin is the effective agent in this passage. Sin must do her work of telling Satan who he is, of opening the gates, of letting the Fortunate Fall occur so that the action of book 3 can occur before the action of book 9. Death in this episode, after his rodomontade with Satan, so fortunately interrupted by Sin, is nothing more than a greedy cypher, a negation of the work of the Holy Spirit.

More important, I would like to suggest that God's Son should become in Milton's parodic allegory Satan's daughter because of what Milton learned from Spenser's genealogy of evil both in *The Faerie Queene* and in the "procession" of paternity in Spenser's *An Hymne of Heauenly Loue*:

> It [God the Father] lov'd it selfe, because it selfe was faire;
> (For faire is lov'd;) and of it selfe begot
> Like to it selfe his eldest sonne and heire,
> Eternall, pure, and voide of sinfull blot,
> The firstling of his joy, in whom no jot
> Of loves dislike, or pride was to be found,
> Whom he therefore with equall honour crownd.

With him he reignd, before all time prescribed,
In endlesse glorie and immortall might,
Together with that third from them derived,
Most wise, most holy, most almightie Sprite.

(lines 29–39)

Spenser's insistence on the "faire"-ness of the Son in this passage may have been the verbal clue to urge Milton to make his own Sin "fair" (*PL*, 2.650) and female. It surely goes along with the beauty that Spenser grants to his Mutabilitie. What Milton has done in his allegory of Sin and Death is to intellectualize and translate Spenser's Mutabilitie back into the specifically Christian terms that Mutabilitie represents obliquely in Spenser's poem.

Ne shee the lawes of Nature only brake,
But eke of Iustice and of Policie:
And wrong of right, and bad of good did make,
And death for life exchanged foolishlie:
Since which, all liuing wights haue learn'd to die,
O pittious worke of MVTABILITIE!
By which, we all are subiect to that curse,
And death in stead of life haue sucked from our Nurse.

(*FQ*, 7.6.6)

Milton returns the matrilinear line of Spenser and Sidney to an exploration of paternity and sexuality, in which the father must learn of the daughter what his son means.

4

I began this essay with a reading of one word, *astonied*, which I suggested Milton had carefully borrowed from Spenser to indicate a connection between the return of Eve to Adam in book 9 and the reception of Mutabilitie by the Olympian gods. I did not press that initial reading to show a relationship between Spenser's Mutabilitie and Milton's Sin and Death because I did not want to obtrude the issues of allegorical reading so early in an essay intended to show how Spenser influenced Milton. Readers scatter at the mention of allegory and can rarely be brought back to the issues at stake. In the case of Spenser and Milton, Mutabilitie and Sin and Death are ultimate philosophical issues. To treat any of the three as purely literary artifacts, or personifications, is to deny a reality that faced Spenser and Milton, and also faces us (with the possible exception of Sin, which seems to have disappeared in the twentieth century). Spenser's presentation of evil seems to shrink from the almost omnipotent dragon of book 1 to the rabid canine of book 6, but his final presentation of evil in *The Faerie Queene* is the figure of Mutabilitie, fair as the gods and erroneous in her claims. She speaks to Jove with Satanic force, which he recognizes as the relic of the forces he overthrew in his defeat of the Giants ("and them destroied quite / Yet not so quite." *FQ*, 7.6.20). At the end of the "Mutabilitie Cantos" she is simply denied her claim by Nature (*FQ*, 7.7.58–59).[14] Evil, which began in Spenser as Error, simply ceases to exert influence and vanishes like Nature at the end of the "Mutabilitie Cantos," and if we consider the insignificance of evil in the *Fowre Hymnes* in comparison to the rapturous praise of light and love and beauty, we begin to believe that evil is little more than error exposed.

Milton was deeply influenced by this Spenser, but those Spenserian fictions were not enough for him, and he fought his way back to origins of evil that could only be approximated by returning to the richly obscure narrative of the early chapters of Genesis. Milton's Satan has titanic force and goes to a resounding defeat, which at least since the time of Blake has led some critics to see him as the hero of the poem, but it should be remembered that the history of his evil is revealed to him by his daughter, Sin, a gendering that I have tried to suggest Milton derives from the matrilinear genealogy of evil in Spenser and Sidney. The experience of reading Milton out of Spenser in this way clarifies some lines of influence, but it also poses some problems. There can be no question that Duessa and Night in Spenser and Cecropia in Sidney are as close to a genealogy of evil as these writers come.[15] Duessa, Night, Cecropia, Sin—are all female figures. They are bound up with the attempt to represent evil. I think that Milton attempted to "overgo" Spenser's finesse of the male in his representation of evil by introducing his abundantly energetic Satan into a world where he is instructed about the nature of paternity by his daughter-wife, thus completing the sexual paradigm eschewed by both Spenser and Sidney, in the most profound depiction of evil in English literature.

Notes

1. For a different view of these facts, see Annabel Patterson, "Couples, Canons, and the Uncouth: Spenser-and-Milton in Educational Theory," *Critical Inquiry* 16 (Summer 1990): 773–93.

2. Patrick Cullen, *Infernal Triad: The Flesh, the World and the Devil in Spenser and Milton* (Princeton: Princeton University Press, 1974); A. Kent Hieatt, *Chaucer, Spenser, Milton: Mythopoeic Continuities and Transformation* (Montreal: McGill-Queens University Press, 1975), 169–245.

3. In a fascinating paper on this subject, delivered at the 1990 Medieval Conference at Kalamazoo, Michigan, Professor Julia Walker concentrated on the verb *astonied*. I pointed out to her that this was a Spenserian word, and I hope that she will forgive my descant on her observations, which take another route than mine here.

4. All quotations from *The Faerie Queene* are from my edition (Penguin, 1989). The minor poems are taken from *The Yale Edition of the Shorter Poems of Edmund Spenser*, ed. William A. Oram, et al. (New Haven: Yale University Press, 1989). The other occurrences of *astonied* are *Visions of Bellay*, 9.1; *Shepheardes Calender*, "Julye," 227; *Muiopotmos*, 339; *Faerie Queene*, 1.2.15.8; 1.2.16.5; 1.6.9.8.

5. The obverse of this situation occurs in *FQ*, 1.6.9 where the word is used to describe the reaction of the fauns and satyrs to the appearance of Una, astonishment at a beauty beyond their comprehension.

6. Kathleen Williams, "Milton, Greatest Spenserian" in *Milton and the Line of Vision*, ed. Joseph Anthony Wittreich, Jr. (Madison: University of Wisconsin Press, 1975), 25–55; Maureen Quilligan, *Milton's Spenser: The Politics of Reading* (Ithaca: Cornell University Press, 1983); John Guillory, *Poetic Authority: Spenser, Milton, and Literary History* (New York: Columbia University Press, 1983).

7. The material for the Spenser and Sidney sections of this paper was originally delivered as the third Kathleen Williams Lecture at the International Medieval Conference at Kalamazoo, Michigan, 1990.

8. The line is quoted by Charles Nelson in his introduction to the Vintage edition of Edward Fairfax's English translation of Tasso but unfortunately with no reference to its source in Tasso's numerous letters. The closest I have come to finding the reference has been a letter written to Scipio Gonzaga: "La contenzione in se stessa e l'arti d'Armida sono *ex arte*, come quelle che procedono da un fonte, cioe dal consiglio infernale, e tendono a un fine medesimo e principalissimo, ch'e il disturbo de l'impresa." (Torquato Tasso, *Opere*, ed. Ettore Mazzali [Naples: Casa Editrice Fulvio Rossi, 1969, 1970], 2:867).

9. Mark Rose, *Heroic Love: Studies in Sidney and Spenser* (Cambridge: Harvard University Press, 1968), 56–62. All quotations are from *The Countess of Pembrokes Arcadia*, ed. Victor Skretkowicz (Oxford: Oxford University Press, 1987). On the subject of Gaudens's inclusion of Pamela's "prayer" one should still consult the careful and perverse discussion by William Empson in *Milton's God*, "Appendix" (London: Chatto and Windus, revised edition, 1981), 288–318.

10. See Stephen M. Fallon, "Milton's Sin and Death: The Ontology of Allegory in *Paradise Lost*," *ELR* 17 (1987): 329–50.

11. John M. Steadman, "Milton and St. Basil: The Genesis of Sin and Death," *MLN* 73 (1958): 83ff.; "Grosseteste on the Genealogy of Sin and Death," *Notes and Queries* 204 (1959): 367ff.

12. It seems to me incredible that the most brilliant Satanist of the twentieth century, William Empson, should make no mention of Sin and Death in his attempt to demolish the positions of C. S. Lewis and E. M. W. Tillyard, even in his revised edition of *Milton's God*.

13. Quilligan, *Spenser's Milton*, 88.

14. See Sherman Hawkins, "Mutabiltie and the Cycle of the Months" in *Form and Convention in the Poetry of Edmund Spenser*, ed. William Nelson (New York: Columbia University Press, 1961).

15. As one last parting shot at influence I wonder if Spenser's depiction of Echidna (*FQ*, 6.610ff.) does not owe something to Sidney's Cecropia.

Beyond Androgyny:
Sidney, Milton, and the Phoenix

M. J. DOHERTY

con la fenice la prova

(Petrarch, *Rime* 135)

God also made the phoenix.
(Tasso, *La Sette Giornate Del Mondo Creato*)

"A poet no industry can make, if his own genius be not carried into it," Sir Philip Sidney wrote in *The Defence of Poesie*. *Orator fit, poeta nascitur.*[1] John Milton the poet begins where Sidney dies but lives in glory—in a "copious Legend" (*SA*, 1737). Yet the Miltonic fulfill-ment of poetic promises Sidney did not live to flesh out has eluded our critical perception, perhaps because of the difference between flesh and spirit or letter and spirit we ourselves have tried to mark in the measure of words. Milton took demonstrated literary strategies from Sidney's poetics; but he also received from the image of the whole man the subtle and forceful will to transmit to an entire civi-lization an emblem of the Spirit engraved in his own poetic character. When we acknowledge in literary history that Milton is the locus classicus of our idea of the passionate English Protestant poet in the freedom of whose self-centering and self-renunciation the individual talent has risen repeatedly from the ashes of time, I think we are pay-ing our oblique respects to Sidney.

Sidney was the "Phenix" of his age, and in the diverse appearance and disappearance of this word in Milton's writings we gain some his-torical access to the passion of Milton's Sidney, which is a spiritual event caught in the body of language, a meeting of minds. The phoenix—unique, solitary, androgynous, regenerative, paradoxical, poetic, and sacred—is the constellating figure—variously a simile, metonymy, or paradox—in which Milton searches out the significance

of his desire for poetic fame and immortality and the spiritual implications of gender, generation, and regeneration. "This *Phenix* sweet
Sidney was the flower of curtesie," John Philip wrote in 1587. But for
Milton Sidney was also the seventeenth-century icon of a terrible,
holy Love in which death and rebirth were intertwined with his own
poetic and political identity and the erotic interlaced with the heroic.[2]
Sidney's death asked Milton to turn to a divinity beyond androgyny, to
make the flight of the phoenix no longer mythic but historical and
incarnate while transcending feminine and masculine spirits.

The "Patterne" Silence Makes

The quadricentenary in 1986 of Sidney's death has produced a literary
history illuminating the bond between Sidney and Milton. Elegized in
the names of his poetic characters, the "valorous" Astrophil and
"sage" Philisides, Sidney *dead* collected virtues—"curteus, valiant,
and liberall"—mythic identities—"Adonis," "Mars," "Mercury,"
"their Hannibal," "our Scipio, Cicero, and Petrarch"—and numberless
dedications.[3] During the years Milton was growing up, ambitious
writers appealed to Sidney's name as to a talisman for success.
Repeated publication of Sidney's writings during the seventeenth century exceeded editions of Shakespeare and Spenser.[4] These facts must
make us wonder at the critical submergence of Sidney, instigated by
Dryden and a change of taste in the Restoration and established by the
judgments of Hazlitt, which separated Sidney from any position of literary power by defining narrow categories of "imitation" and "originality."[5] The metamorphosis of Sidney's Pamela into Richardson's
makes one ask why she prays once more in *Eikon Basilike* and what
Milton makes of Sidney's *Arcadia* in its supposed association with the
King about to die (*Eikon*, *CPW*, 3:362–67).[6] With Lamb's connection
of Sidney's and Milton's "plainness" and "boldness" of spirit despite
political differences, Sidney's reputation began to resurrect.[7]
J. A. Symonds considered him the lesson bequeathed from Elizabethan to Victorian England that a virtuous Anglo-Saxon race would
continue to rise to "the grandest birth of future time," but the late
nineteenth-century identification of homoeroticism in the Sidney legend may actually have contributed to another critical silence.[8] Forty
years passed before Kenneth Myrick acknowledged the conjunction of
religion, politics, and writing in the temperaments of Sidney and Milton, marking the arrival of the passionate Sidney: "Sidney reminds us
sometimes," Myrick wrote, "of Milton's firm and ardent nature. Like
Milton the pamphleteer, he sometimes gives way to passion."[9]

Despite explicit allusions, echoes of *The Defence*, and Arcadian parallels, twentieth-century criticism discloses hardly any study of Milton's relation to Sidney for almost another forty years.[10] There are many passing remarks, but Dryden's assertion that Milton was the "Poetical Son of Spencer" and Spenser Milton's *"Original"* encouraged scholars to pursue this influence instead, and even the Spenser-Milton connection develops slowly according to Maureen Quilligan.[11] Where Sidney does reappear thoughtfully linked to Milton, Spenser is the mediator in what, for instance, A. S. P. Woodhouse called a shared "cultural inheritance" and Joseph A. Wittreich, Jr., the "visionary," prophetic tradition distinct from the "line of wit" expressed by Donne, Dryden, and Pope.[12] Prefacing his remarks about Sidney and Milton with several cautions on how the linkage of the two poets may seem "unwarranted" and "downright perverse" because of Milton's few "overt references" to Sidney, S. K. Heninger, Jr., nevertheless mediated the two poets with Spenser and du Bartas, arguing cogently from the effects of specific poems to shared causes in poetic theory: Sidney and Milton saw the poet as a "maker" who produced literary artifacts working like little worlds in their own right.[13] To date, the brief but intensely reflective essay on Sidney by Andrew D. Weiner in the *Milton Encyclopedia* is the only literary analysis that penetrates the aura of "the Milton industry" to explicate Milton's interested knowledge of *The Defence* and the *Arcadia*. Weiner concentrates the question of Milton's Sidney on Protestant poetics, bringing to light fundamental similarities and differences between the two poets.[14]

After a fashion, such literary history supports the idea that the Elizabethan aristocrat's play with his "unelected vocation" as a poet made a great moral demand on Milton by providing him with an anamorphic mirror in which to find the vision of his elected one (*Def.*, 75). The young Milton painstakingly discerns his "call" to seek the divine Beauty and to proclaim religious truth, and we must shed both modern Freudian notions of influence and eighteenth-century critical categories of originality and imitation if we are to grasp Milton's claim, which he made more in performance than in verbal testimony, to be not so much Sidney's "son" as his legitimate spiritual heir. We may be sure that Milton, the seventeenth-century exponent of the genetic argument that only a good man can compose a good oration or poem, would never have merely copied anyone (*Apology, CPW*, 1:874). Milton himself gives us the right term to apply when he argues that the poet himself must be a "true Poem," that is, "a composition and pattern of the best and honourablest things" (*Apology, CPW*, 1:890).[15]

Evolving from a sixteenth-century pronunciation of the word "patron," derived from *pater*, "pattern" gradually came to signify "exemplar" and "archetype," shifting senses by the end of the seventeenth century away from Spenser's "perfect paterne of a Poete" in Cuddie and toward "an original proposed for imitation" (Dryden's Spenser as Milton's "*Original*").[16] Far from patrilineal or patronal, Sidney played the part of such a Christian exemplar for Milton—an alter ego whose death reveals the vanity of human flesh, achievement, and history while the spiritual rebirth of his reputation actually demonstrates the transcendence of mortality.[17] Milton views the famous Sidney not as a father or social superior but as a brother—a messenger of the desirability of becoming one of the new kind of corporeal "angels" promised in the Incarnate Word as the "first frutes of them that slept" and the "first borne to manie brethren."[18]

An English development of the figure of the phoenix along "angelic" lines fed the contention between flesh and spirit, however, that promotes Milton's projection of an elegiac theme into his portrayal of angels and heroes. Although Sidney had provided ample play of erotic variations and couplings in the *Arcadia* and a sustained interrogation of desire in *Astrophil and Stella*, his own apotheosis as a phoenix occurs because of sudden death through his obedience to the Queen's mandate to go to the Netherlands, and not directly because of the triumph of his literary exposition of the erotic. This obedience to a death-summons, combined with the heroic journey Sidney did *not* take with Drake to the New World, is one Milton seems to internalize as the identifying feature of the Protestant poet who imitates no one but the only-begotten Son of God.[19] The angels of *Paradise Lost* rise or fall like heroes, consequently, as masculine, feminine, or androgynously gendered creatures who either flourish in the light of divine glory or degenerate in the multiple fallen forms of pagan gods and goddesses (*PL*, 1:423–31). Similarly, although only one angel in that poem, Raphael, is named as "A *Phoenix*, gaz'd by all" (*PL*, 5.272), others fulfill its role truly or falsely as Milton develops the metonymic attributes of the phoenix such as rarity, uniqueness, colored feathers, and fire in their portrayal. The Sidneian phoenix historically clarifies our knowledge of Milton's appropriation of the Elizabethan poet's legacy, but it is, nevertheless, an image fraught with ambivalences Milton had to sort out and did sort out in his prose and poetry.

Divine Bird, Unique on Earth

Almost half a century ago Kathleen Ellen Hartwell traced the philological links between classical myths of the phoenix and Milton's early use of the divine bird in *Epitaphium Damonis* to the allegory of

Christ in Lactantius's *De Ave Phoenice*. Her suggestion that "one idea of God that may have reached Milton by way of Lactantius is that of His sexlessness" deserves reexamination in the light of contemporary gender studies of Milton's poetry.[20] Divine "sexlessness" does not signify a denial of the erotic or an opposition of the erotic to true religion but, in the image of the sacred Phoenix, a gender-transcendent Love beyond even androgyny and known by human beings and angels alike as a transforming, regenerative fire. Both angelic and human characterizations of the erotic are, in this respect, mere representations of the completely self-contained and self-donating *eros* of God, which cannot be directly imagined. Lactantius's emphasis on divine sexlessness arose in the context of his pedagogical effort to disabuse Christian converts of the false religion in which they had been brought up on the amorous adventures of gods and goddesses.[21] As a fierce apologist for the emergence of the one true religion from the ashes of classical culture, Lactantius underwrites the sense in which Sidney and Milton also argue a phoenix-like regeneration of the poet as a Christian hero made in the image of the sacred Phoenix. Thus Sidney could go so far as to propose that the false deities of myth were better than the atheism brought in by philosophy. Now that the "light of Christ" has come and "Christianity hath taken away all hurtful belief" and "wrong opinions of the Deity," he implies, one is free to poeticize (*Def.*, 108). So, too, quoting Lactantius in *Of Reformation*, Milton proposes the difference between Christian revelation and myth as the difference between the believer's truth and the ancient's illusion. Lactantius warns us, he says, "against the vaine trust in Antiquity" and advises us to seek the "Truth . . . inbred to all" and "wisedome the gift of God," since those that follow the ancients "are led by others like bruit beasts" (*CPW*, 1:561–62).

In Philippe du Plessis Mornay's *The Trewnesse of the Christian religion*, part of which Sidney was said to have translated, the bond Lactantius may have created between Sidney and Milton on the subject of true religion is even more clearly spelled out. Mornay paraphrases Lactantius at several points on the existence of one and one only God who is acknowledged "even by the very confession of the false Goddes themselves, which have gone about to deface his name by al meanes." Of particular interest is Lactantius's story of the oracle of Apollo approached at Colophon by Theophilus, who asked "whether there was a God or no, and what he is," and Mornay quotes the last three lines "englished" of Lactantius's twenty-one Greek verses:

> The selfebred, bred without the helpe of Moother,
> Wise of himselfe, whose name no wight can tell,

> Doth dwell in fyre beyond all reach of thought;
> Of whom we Angelles are the smallest part.[22]

If Milton knew this piece of Sidneiana, he hardly would have questioned in it the topic of "true religion" and the existence of a God who is "selfebred," dwelling in fire beyond thought. But he may have inquired into the practical method of attaining to such "angelic" status and the experiential knowledge of God—at least before his decision to marry brought about a major change in his approach to divine things.

The Sidney legend contributed to Milton's development of the phoenix in the simplicity with which it identified Sidney as such a rare bird. Thus Matthew Roydon in his "Elegie, or friends passion for his Astrophill" in *The Phoenix Nest* stated the metaphor: Sidney was the Arabian bird that flew to England, "And in a Caedar in this Coast / Built vp her tombe of spicerie."[23] Moreover, Sidney's sister, Mary Herbert, the Countess of Pembroke, drew an equation between the phoenix and the condition of angels. In the dedicatory poem to Sidney's translation of the Psalms, which she completed, Mary addresses her brother as an "Angell spirit" and pays her "debt of Infinits"

> To thy great worth; exceeding Nature's store,
>   wonder of men, sole borne perfection's kinde,
>   Phoenix thou wert, so rare thy fairest minde
> Heav'nly adorn'd, Earth justly might adore,
>   where truthfull praise in highest glorie shin'de.

The righteousness of adoring or not adoring such a creature, as the Countess's hyperbole suggests, has everything to do with its angelic transparency to the singular divine glory and with its singing of the divine praises. Almost anticipating Milton's conflation of the phoenix with angels and virgins in *Damon's Epitaph*, Mary goes on to say,

> Thy Angell's soule with highest Angells plac't
> There blessed sings enjoying heav'n-delights
>   thy Maker's praise.[24]

So, too, as Milton renegotiates the worthiness of Sidney's character and reputation in order to determine the meaning of his poetic vocation, the phoenix-angel becomes the complex figurative measure of the difference between praise and idolatry.

The problem the Sidney legend posed for Milton was that of the origin and destiny of the poet and his capacity to generate the future. Either poetic genius manifests a spiritual regeneration in the image of the only-begotten Son of God, which reproduces, in turn, other sons and daughters of God through the poet's word, or the poet reveals in speech a deceptive and idolatrous autogenesis. The first brings immortality; the second is illusory and brings perdition. Spiritual regeneration in the sacred Phoenix—*divina avis, unica terris* (*Epitaphium Damonis*, lines 187, 138)—signifies Diodati's quasi-divinization as one of the unique "sons" of God, the new kind of corporeal "angel" joining the circle of the Lamb and repopulating heaven. Significantly, *Damon's Epitaph* is the *only* poem, however, in which Milton alludes directly to the sacred Phoenix, basing its representation on Lactantius. Elsewhere Milton either does not name the phoenix, except through its metonymic attributes, or his naming of it indicates ambivalence or poses the antithesis between regeneration and autogenesis, between participation in the life of the only-begotten Son and an illusion of self-begetting. Thus the apparently heroic origin announced by an angel in flames, "As in a fiery column charioting / His Godlike presence" (*SA*, 25–28), and a destiny "Like that self-begott'n bird" of classical myth (*SA*, 1699) may actually be damnation in faint praise for Samson. In any case, the expression of this phoenix discloses Miltonic ambivalence toward the naming of the hero in an antithesis that Manoa completes with a near tautology. "*Samson* hath quit himself / Like *Samson*," Manoa says, suppressing the lamentation of the Semichorus that would poetically regenerate the hero, and the antithesis informs critical debate, too (*SA*, 1709–10).[25]

As we might expect, the image of the phoenix possesses great cultural complexity in Milton insofar as he combines its elegiac expression in the Sidney legend with the erotic figure in Petrarch's *Rime sparse*, with the sacred symbol of the creative Exemplar in Torquato Tasso's *La Sette Giornate Del Mondo Creato*, and with the received native tradition of the Old English *Phoenix*, also based on Lactantius, in romance. Petrarch alludes to the phoenix three times, denoting the full scope of love from fixed self-absorption to the Desire who is Christ, the absent presence informing the *Rime*. These phoenix metaphors—of the "new" self and its desire in *Rime* 135, of Laura and her beauty in *Rime* 185, and of an apparently celestial being that turns out to be an apocalyptic vision of death in *Rime* 323—bear multiple significances as they cross-reference in the *Rime* and contain within their design the antitheses Petrarch works into his paradoxes.[26] Tasso, however, simply presents the sacred Phoenix on the fifth day of creation as an Italian version of Lactantius's allegory: God's one immortal Son destined from birth to rise from the dead is the androgynous and remarkably fecund Exemplar of the abundance of living things.[27] Certainly the Old English *Phoenix* was similarly androgynous, echoing the classical myths of female initiation as well as Lactantius's

Christianization of a sexually transcendent figure, but it underwent a sea change through medieval romance into Chaucer's complex figures of Nature, the garden, and Temple of Venus.[28] From here one may trace a native tradition to Spenser and Milton, but not without attending as well to the masculine emphasis in the elegiac definition of spiritual fruitfulness in the phoenix of the Sidney legend.

Between 1639 and 1649, the entries in Milton's "Commonplace Book" reflect his rereading both of Sidney and of Lactantius. The key to Milton's later treatments of the phoenix lies in these allusions between Diodati's death and King Charles's execution. Several of the antiprelatical tracts echo the aesthetics of Sidney's *Defence*, as well as Petrarch's poetic ideal, until metonymic features of the phoenix seem to coalesce in Milton's dismissal of human androgyny in his discussion in *Eikonoklastes* of the King's purported use of Pamela's prayer from the *Arcadia* before he died. Ruth Wallerstein once observed that the elegy leads us deeply into the temper of the seventeenth century. Milton's phoenix of the 1640s states the question of all elegy in this respect, especially in view of the fact that in the Italian Renaissance the exemplar of beauty vanquished before its time was the female Laura but in England the archetype was the male Sidney.[29] Either there is resurrection from the dead for the elect because of the saving power of the only-begotten Son of God who took on human flesh, died, and rose, or there is utter vanity in human life as an erotic movement toward dust and ashes. In the latter case, no one is more deluded than the irresponsible King supposedly praying a fictive woman's pagan prayer or the literary man who thinks his expenditure of words will guarantee the spiritual revolution of his century and make him live forever.

The Gospel versus "Painted Feathers"

Having praised the Lactantian idea of an inbred wisdom in *Of Reformation*, Milton in *Animadversions* locates the power of his evangelical ministry of the Word not in priesthood but in angelic status. He explains that it is not ordination and jurisdiction "that is Angelicall but the heavenly message of the Gospell, which is the office of all Ministers alike; in which sense *John* the *Baptist* is call'd an *Angel*, which in Greeke signifies Messenger, as oft as it is meant by a man," and "that the whole Booke soares to a Prophetick pitch in types, and Allegories" (*CPW*, 1:714). In 1641 in *The Reason of Church Government*, Milton continues to inscribe the evangelical identity of the poet-prophet not in the authority of the visible Church but in the pattern of the Word made flesh; this time, however, he makes his point through a negative example of the phoenix. The power of the poet is an "inspired guift of God, rarely bestow'd," he explains (*CPW*, 1:816), and the idea of rarity, an attribute of the phoenix, is the verbal clue that the image is in the workings of Milton's composition. Several pages later, excoriating prelates who "make of none effect the crosse of Christ" and nullify "the power and end of the Gospel," Milton's metaphor slashes at Anglicans: a prelate who does sustain the cross and Gospel is as rare in Milton's experience as the "Phenix" (*CPW*, 1:825) and certainly much less truthful than the poet who stands ready to take over the task of the spiritual regeneration of God's people. In case we think we have removed ourselves completely from the pale of the Sidney legend, we need only recall Roydon's "Elegie" alluding to "The lineaments of the Gospell books" in Sidney's assuring face: "I trow that countenance cannot lie, / Whose thoughts are legible in the eie" (lines 15–19, 4).

Even if Sidney helped to send Milton into the blaze of the Gospel, when Sidney spoke of such high matters he referred, however, not to cross, Gospel, and prophecy but to "that lyrical kind of songs and sonnets; which Lord, if He gave us so good minds, how well it might be employed, and with how heavenly fruit, both private and public, in singing the praises of the immortal beauty: the immortal goodness of that God who giveth us hands to write and wits to conceive" (*Def.*, 116). This sentiment is most Petrarchan of Sidney, and in *An Apology* Milton also changes its significance and its expression. On the basis of Petrarchan poetic imagination, Sidney and Milton seem to part ways in their visions of the poet's androgyny.

In *Rime* 135, Petrarch says that the poet's erotic desire, which fuels his poetry, makes him a "strange" and "new" thing, an extranatural creature—*Qual piu diversa et nova / cosa fu mai in qualche strania clima, / quella, se ben s'estima.*[30] Sidney composed a sonnet sequence exploring a similar mystery and morality of love, developing Petrarchan antitheses and paradoxes.[31] Milton never composes such a sequence; nor does he use the lyric to explore the erotic. Milton's sonnets occasionally idealize a lady but quickly adapt the elegiac to the praise of heroes and martyrs, even in the case of his "late espoused Saint" whose holiness is decidedly based on the mortal transformation of her flesh into immortal spirit. So, too, in *The Defence*, Sidney morally defines the uniqueness of the poet. He credits forms "such as never were in nature, as the Heroes, Demigods, Cyclops, Chimeras, Furies, and such like" (*Def.*, 78), and promotes an androgynous coupling of the poet-architect-statesman and "the mistress-knowledge, by the Greeks called ἀρχιτεκτονική' which stands (as I think) in the knowledge of a man's self, in the ethic and politic consideration with the end of well-doing and not of well-knowing only" (*Def.*, 82–83). Sidney allegorized the pair of poet and Lady Poesie, a form of Sophia or practical wisdom exercised in conscience.[32] Milton expounds the difficulty of bringing self-knowledge to right action in the opening of *An Apology*, breaking androgyny down to a clearer emphasis on manhood per se.

Almost talking back to Sidney, Milton writes, "If, Readers, to that same great difficulty of well doing what we certainly know, were not added in most men as great a carelessnes of knowing what they, and others ought to do, we had bin ere long ere this no doubt but all of us much farther on our way to some degree of happiness in this kingdome" (*CPW,* 1:868). At midpoint in *An Apology*, Milton explicitly attaches himself to Dante and Petrarch, those "two renowners of *Beatrice* and *Laura*," but to defend his chastity and his art (*CPW,* 1:890), he proceeds, then, to explain than he sees the lack of chastity in a man as a greater fault than in a woman because the man *in his body* is "both the image and glory of God" and the woman is the glory of the man (*CPW,* 1:892). Milton's transference of the adjunct of a poet into a metonymy for him makes the poet's very being a speech-act of singular desire. The "true Poem" (*CPW,* 1:890) so unites chastity to the notion of Solomonic wisdom in such a man that the poet *alone* is the arbiter of heroism, civilization, and faith, and manhood alone expresses Milton's ideal self-knowledge on behalf of society.

Marriage, divorce, and remarriage intensify gender difference in Milton. At the end of the 1640s, the phoenix appears again in a negative, adjunctive form in Milton's complicated use of the figure to criticize King Charles. From a Protestant literary perspective, Sidney's poetic art in general and his romance in particular are deliberately sophisticated pictures of unregenerate human sinfulness. Milton responds aesthetically, then, to the didactic purpose of Sidney's invention of a lusty star-lover and to the ethical and political malaise of irresponsibility, court intrigue, cross-dressing, misrule, arranged marriages, and Stoicism in Sidney's romance.[33] The *Arcadia* is a "vain amatorious Poem," he says in *Eikonoklastes*, but "a Book in that kind full of worth and witt" (*CPW,* 3:362). This is a nice literary distinction separating the decorum of Sidney's execution of the genre from the indecorum of the King's behavior at his execution, when he supposedly used the book for his prayers.

Most commentators say that Milton is not attacking Sidney, but he does associate the King's lack of spontaneity in prayer with an insult to the Holy Ghost and he teases the Sidneian idea not "that poetry abuseth man's wit, but that man's wit abuseth poetry" almost to the point of abuse (*Def.*, 104). The repetition of words such as "Countesses *Arcadia*" and "Arcadian" and the listing of titles of French, Spanish, and Portuguese romances of the Renaissance characterize the effeminacy of a King who reads books for ladies, praying a fictional princess's prayer at his last hour. Milton does not mention Sannazaro, the author of the Italian *Arcadia* that launched the fashion of pastoral romance, perhaps because Sannazaro's shepherds, like Milton's poet, prefer melancholy to romance and the delights of language to love.[34] With this omission and these assertions, one must also notice such phrases as "the polluted orts and refuse of *Arcadias* and romances," "Sir Philip and his Captive Shepherdess," "Phillipic prayer," and "*Arcadian* prayer"—locutions mixed in with more serious sentences expressing Milton's horror at the cult of Thammuz, acts of irreverence, and idolatry (*CPW*, 3:362–67). These great faults are pinned, apparently far from the spirit of *Areopagitica*, on the trope of the King's "idoliz'd Book" (*CPW*, 3:364).

Developing a metonymy to target the reputed behavior of the King, Milton parodies Charles as a courtly phoenix. This is a prince who, if he had "borrowd much more out of Prayer-books than of Pastorals" would still have appeared "in painted Feathers, that set him off so gay among the people," dragging them further into idolatry (*CPW*, 3:365). The phoenix distinguished from other birds by "the variation of its plumage" was established by Tacitus and appears in "parti-colored wings" in *Epitaphium Damonis* (lines 188, 138) and with "colors dipt in Heav'n" in *Paradise Lost* (5.283).[35] Here Milton applies a sense similar to the one in *The Reason of Church Government* when he criticized bishops and priests for thinking "by these gaudy glisterings to stirre up the devotion of the rude multitude" (*CPW*, 1:827–28).[36] In this image of Charles, Milton gives us the image of Petrarch's Laura and her necklace of "gilded feathers" of *Rime* 185—*Questa fenice de l'aurata piuma*—and the apocalyptic image of death in disguise in *Rime* 323. *Una strania fenice* seems a form celestial and immortal, Petrarch says, until it comes to "the uprooted laurel." *Ogni cosa al fin vola*, "Everything comes to an end."[37]

The total effect of Milton's treatment of the execution as it was portrayed in *Eikon Basilike* is the reduction of the existence of Charles to a kind of fiction of nonrule. Such reduction is comparable to "the ruin of royal sovranty" described in "an Oligarchie of nobles abusing the countnance" in the *Arcadia* (*CB*, *CPW*, 1:463). The idea so enigmatically represented in Milton's prose—that the King who prays wrong before dying has probably loved wrong, ruled wrong, and read the wrong books (or the right ones incorrectly), bringing himself in the fashion of romance to an ordeal he cannot escape except by the divine intervention he does not seek and by the moral rectitude he does not possess—is the antithesis of the Sidney legend. Charles is hardly a man.

In his *Life of Sidney*, Fulke Greville drew on the essential point of the phoenix myth to express the paradox of the decay of the dying Sidney's flesh and the vigor of his spirit conveyed by his worthy philosophizing and religious faith, "the fire of this Phenix hardly being able of any ashes to produce his equall."[38] Since Greville's polemical biography was available in manuscript drafts, and at Cambridge, earlier in the seventeenth century than its publication in 1652, decades after Greville had composed it and after he himself died, it is not impossible that Milton knew it earlier on. Whether or not the *Life* was part of a political enterprise to produce an image of an *active* Puritan "saint" and help fuse Protestant factions together in the wake of the execution of King Charles, it proposed the Christian manner of Sidney's death, which contrasts vividly to the death of Charles portrayed by Milton. Greville's sense of Sidney's "Architectonical art" of self-mastery, seeking not merely the ends of writing but the purpose of making "himself and others, not in words or opinions, but in life and action, good and great," expresses a Protestant affirmation of self-centering that encourages Milton's individuality.[39] The well-born Sidney, striding across the gap of socio-economic class difference because of the quality of his mind, clarifies for Milton the Londoner, university man, and revolutionary, the common ground of the Protestant intellect—"regenerate reason" (*CPW,* 1:874)—established in grace even against the follies of heroism, desire, and literary idolatries. Sidney's death triumphantly manifests the exercise of good by evil.

We may surely locate, therefore, a literary-aesthetic bond between Sidney and Milton in a certain poetic strategy based on Lactantian moral principles and designed to cultivate acts of discernment in writers and readers alike. In passages recorded in the "Commonplace Book" between 1639 and 1641, Milton explains that God permits evil because "the good is made known, is made clear, and is exercised by evil," so that, as Lactantius says, "reason and intelligence may have the opportunity to exercise themselves by choosing the things that are good, by fleeing from the things that are evil" (*CPW,* 1:363). Scholars have long observed the poetic importance of this principle in Milton's development of the necessary trial of virtuous chastity in *A Mask*; in the worthlessness of a cloistered virtue in *Areopagitica*, since "reason is but choosing" (*CPW,* 2:527); and in the design of tests of virtue in Abdiel and in Adam and Eve in *Par-*

adise Lost, the former standing though free to fall and the latter falling though free to stand. Recently, Dennis Danielson has recognized the Lactantian "principle of contrariety" in the " 'soul-making' theodicy" of the poem, too.[40] Inadequately developed in Milton scholarship, however, is the awareness of Sidney's expression of a similarly Lactantian moral argument in *The Defence* in the idea that "in the actions of our life who seeth not the filthiness of evil wanteth a great foil to perceive the beauty of virtue" (*Def.*, 96) and in the aesthetic technique of antithetical kinds of poetic imagery. The *eikastic* kind figures forth "good things," and the *phantastic* infects the fancy "with unworthy objects" (*Def.*, 104). The definition of these terms occurs in the context of Sidney's refutation of the charge that poetry "abuseth man's wit, training it to wanton sinfulness and lustful love" (*Def.*, 106), and Sidney's aesthetics demand the recognition that the truth of poetic fiction lies *between*, not *in*, these kinds of images. Contrariety, antithesis, and even paradox mediate the truth of the imagination that can be glimpsed but not univocally expressed, *especially* in the defence of the Christian tetragrammaton, Love.[41]

When Milton made entries from the *Arcadia* in his "Commonplace Book" in a sequence on the topics of lust, chastity, "death self-inflicted," drunkenness, and courage (*CPW,* 1:369–74), he interspersed with them entries from the writings of Lactantius, too. Saint Jerome had lamented to Saint Paulinus of Nola that Lactantius's apologetics were almost too intense. "Would that he had been as ready to teach our doctrines as he was to pull down those of others!" he cries.[42] Yet when Sidney exclaims, "Alas, Love, I would thou couldst as well defend thyself as offend others," almost parodying Jerome's remark, we encounter again a moral staple in the education of English schoolboys (*Def.*, 103). Milton combines Lactantius's condemnation of pederasty and homosexuality with his own consideration of the degeneracy brought to a people through lechery and unlawful union and of bizarre methods for protecting chastity, such as the self-mutilation of nuns (*CPW,* 1:369–70).[43] A certain difference of tone must be perceived in Sidney's gesture toward the defence of Love and Milton's anatomy of forbidden desires and equally forbidden cures, to which he will add in *The Doctrine and Discipline of Divorce* the questionable literalism of making oneself a eunuch for the sake of the kingdom of heaven by taking "*Origen*'s knife" and becoming one's "own carver" (*CPW,* 2:334). Not without good reason, the problem posed by Sidney's reputation as a phoenix is finally too great to be resolved by Milton in prose. Milton restructures the ambivalence of likeness to the self-begotten bird and regeneration in the only-begotten Son in his great poems.

Son, Samson, "Spirits Masculine," and the Sacred Phoenix

The Son of Milton's *Paradise Regained* is never named as a sacred Phoenix, but his character fulfills both the Lactantian moral principle and the poetic paradigm of Tasso. Tasso's "happy bird" is not touched by the delights of Venus and is "unmarked by sex" (*cui non distingue il vario seso*).[44] Satan and his cohorts despair of finding a woman to tempt the Son, so different is he from Solomon and all men who have grown "from the daily Scene effeminate" (*PR*, 2.208 and 4.142), and a *masculine* angelic spirit comes to tempt him instead by sounding him out in words and images. Milton's Jesus is uniquely chaste, however, because he is uniquely transparent to the will of God. The sacred Phoenix in Tasso is so imbued with light and radiance it is functionally invisible, veiled, and this is the divine glory in Jesus that Satan cannot quite grasp.[45] Driven into the sun of the desert by the Spirit, which is the same scene as the "torrid heat" that parches "the temperate Clime" of Eden at the end of *Paradise Lost* (12.634–36), the Son "divinely taught" (*PR,* 4.357) makes the only heroic journey a man must ever make—back through the angelic flames to the knowledge he possesses within himself, the "true wisdom" not deluded by any "false resemblance" (4.318–24) and solely revealing "What makes a Nation happy, and keeps it so, / What ruins Kingdoms, and lays Cities flat" (4.359–63). Yet the English poet qualifies the Italian. Obviously Milton alters the divine Exemplar of Tasso by his representation of the scriptural historicism of Jesus, who is distinctly a *man* and the human child of a mother, unlike the "selfebred . . . without the helpe of Moother" of Lactantius's oracle cited by Mornay.

The character of Jesus allows Milton to distill the central points of the Christological arguments of antiquity to a simple article of faith. Whether this special creature is God becoming man or man becoming divine or merely human or solely divine are the questions asked by Satan and are dismissed as such by the poem as a whole. Milton's good angels here celebrate the Incarnation, the undoing of Satan's rebellion and effort at sabotage, and the reversal of the Fall of humankind in language that is no anamorphic mirror but a simple reflection of clear-eyed faith in the true Image. In a few lines not unlike those sketching in the Arian controversy over the Holy Spirit at the beginning of book 3 of *Paradise Lost*, Milton sketches in all that one needs to know in faith of centuries of debate over the hypostatic union of divine and human natures in Jesus:

> True Image of the Father, whether thron'd
> In the bosom of bliss, and light of light

> Conceiving, or remote from heaven, enshrin'd
> In fleshly Tabernacle, and human form
> Wand'ring in the Wilderness
>
> (*PR*, 4.596 – 600)

Milton's theological options and poetic faith in *Paradise Regained* are antitheses of the interrogation of sexual nature of the too sexed hero in *Samson Agonistes*. Samson sees himself as the "prime cause" of his suffering because he gave up his "fort of silence to a Woman" and was yoked by "foul effeminacy" (*SA*, 236 and 410). He has dissipated his wisdom in speech, and it is death, not self-containment or love, that fulfills him. In accusing himself of having dissipated his wisdom in speech, wasting the procreative power of his divine secret much in the way he has wasted his seed in his liaison with Dalila, Samson portrays Milton's autobiographical judgment of himself. That is, Milton sees his involvement with the English Revolution and his compromising of his poetic gift in politics and in marriage, divorce, and remarriage in the 1640s as Samson-like trials of virtue in which he finds himself wanting. The Sidneian Milton thus out-Plutarchs Plutarch, the author of the lives of the heroes who recognized that garrulity and curiosity are forms of incontinence. Failure in oral self-control is an adultery or autoeroticism. This *acrasia*, also related to drunkenness, makes it as difficult to count the cities and empires ruined through revelations of secrets, which "water down" one's power of prophecy, as it is to number the men lost in amorous pleasure. Apollo Loxias or "Apollo the oblique" is, on the contrary, self-contained in his brief, enigmatic speech, and so is Milton's Jesus in *Paradise Regained*.[46] We are far from the oracle of the self-bred who dwells in fire beyond thought here.

Or are we? Particularly in *Samson Agonistes*, the poem in which the Sidneian hero is most apparent, does Milton's inscription of the uniqueness of the sacred Phoenix in human, not angelic characters, produce a profitable interpretive ambivalence. The failure of a sexed self-begetting in human procreation controls the dialectic between the only-begotten and death self-inflicted in this poem. The Sidney legend throws more light on Samson as the protagonist of his own elegy than our debate on his stature as either a "saint" or a tragedian has so far. E. G. Fogel noted the relationship between Sidney's *Arcadia* and the virtues and vices of Milton's Samson decades ago, and we may refine it by recognizing the *eikastic* and *phantastic* sustained carefully by Milton's rhetoric.[47] In the long choric simile at the end of the poem, Samson is compared to the "self-begott'n bird" as a fallen hero who "His fiery virtue rous'd / From ashes into sudden flame"

(1699, 1690–91). Yet the praise paradoxically marks Samson as *merely* a man and *only* a legend, for it centers a rather gorgeous rhetoric on a "fame" that survives "her body" as a rare "secular bird" for "ages of lives" (1699–1707). Manoa speaks more plainly, identifying Samson for his human individuality and just that: Samson is like Samson, born a hero and finishing a hero (1709–11). Given what we know of Milton's critique of the heroic tradition, this mirror similitude of names is less a logical tautology than a statement of Samson's originality, completely absorbed in his heroic destiny. This is self-containment turned inside-out, a parody of the virginal condition of Milton's Jesus.

John Milton has constructed *Samson Agonistes* in two rhetorics as his own elegy. The story of a man whose birth was announced by an angel in flames, "As in a fiery column charioting / His Godlike presence" (*SA*, 25–28), is one demanding readers to debate which kind of angel, good or bad, was involved. Yet having fulfilled his name in action, Samson's name is synonymous with "hero" in the syntax of his father's utterance. His enfleshed character is a word that has become a deed, like Sidney's, and a "true Poem," like Milton's, in this correspondence. When Manoa pronounces approval of his son, promising to enroll Samson's actions "In copious Legend, or sweet Lyric Song" to enflame "valiant youth" and inspire the lamentations of virgins over the loss of a prospective bridegroom, we may, indeed, hear Milton's version of the vanity of human wishes he learned from the Sidney legend. The moral elegance of *Samson Agonistes* as a poem depends on the ambivalence in which it may be read either as a *phantastic* companion to the *eikastic* image of *Paradise Regained*, with the poet's truth standing not in one or the other but between the two, or as an antithetical statement all on its own, in which Samson is saved in spite of himself by a truly terrible Love of God and tragedy turned to devastating *opera buffa*. Manoa dismisses the rich tropes of the Semichorus bespeaking the Latinate figure of the bird "In the Arabian woods embost" (1700), but the funeral speech of the Semichorus is as decorous for the sensual character of Samson as the *Arcadia* is "full of worth and witt" in its kind. Samson is a myth, a Petrarchan strange and new thing, an *eikon heroica* made to be broken. Manoa himself, consequently, promises lyrics for a mortal man, the son of his flesh. Roydon's poem for Sidney explains why lamentation and lyric are important and why, perhaps, Milton denies the active expression of both at the end of *Samson Agonistes*. The "generall sorrow" among "creatures of kind" is the force that "Fir'd the Phoenix where she laid" ("Elegie," lines 22, 7), and Milton does not desire to feed the fire of the heroic tradition. Either the suppression of elegiac commemoration and consolation at the end of this elegy indicates the end of the hero, the heroic tradition, and the idea of the poet as a hero, or it indicates Milton's profound desire to observe the nature of sacred utterance, which ought to be invented truly and spontaneously under the influence of the Holy Spirit as a form of prayer or not spoken or written at all.

If the sacred Phoenix appears, unnamed, in *Paradise Regained*, it does so not in the easy paradox of the androgynous bird but in the discomfiting solitude and sexual transcendence of the Son, a self-contained man not drawn to woman. If the sacred Exemplar appears in *Samson Agonistes*, it appears not merely in the judgment of the tragic isolation of man and woman and of father and son, hero and people, but also in the dialectic between a false phoenix and the sacred One in the very diction of *Samson Agonistes*.[48] The poetic *speech* that destroys and regenerates is the sacred thing, the inspired power of the unique Word, and it can move through the poet's brilliant construction of false appearances as silently and invisibly as the two-edged sword severing the genders—masculine, feminine, androgynous—as creatures from the total difference of the Creator.

Milton does not arrive at the truly Petrarchan image of the lovers at the end of the twelve-book *Paradise Lost* without having his narrator explore the entire universe of engendered creatures ambivalently similar to and different from the Creator. Nor does Milton arrive at the "new" androgyny of gender difference in his greatest poem without having Adam confront the angels and know homoerotic desire, at least imaginatively, for "Spirits masculine" (*PL*, 10.888–95) as tellingly as he fears the loss of boundaries of the self in face of Eve. The truth of divine Love in this poem lies neither in one gender, masculine or feminine, nor in angelic diversification of gender, including androgyny, but through them all. Multiple *phantastic* and *eikastic* sexual imageries merely represent a sacred fire beyond thought. Although I have attended to Sidneian allusions in *Samson Agonistes*, therefore, Milton's transformation both of the erotica in Sidney's sonnets and romance and of the military heroism at Zutphen may constitute an even greater literary presence in *Paradise Lost* as Milton infuses the romance of Adam and Eve, and sexuality itself, with the significance of a cosmic contention. The passion of Milton's Sidney is, in great measure, the suffering of sexuality in a world of Reformation threatened by abortion and unmanning—the unpeopling of the kingdom by expulsion of religious dissidents and the despoiling of manhood and grace that might "effeminate us all at home" (*Ref, CPW,* 1:588). Married love has to succeed in such an historical context.

Milton's angels are troublesome regarding gender precisely because they are neither absolute, as the Son is, nor dissolute, as Samson is.

"For Spirits when they please / Can either Sex assume, or both," Milton explains, since their pure essences are not compounded by "cumbrous Flesh" (*PL,* 1.423–28). This explanation comes, however, in the context of the narrator's description of the deformation of numberless "bad Angels" (1.344) into the gods and goddesses of idolatry. The angelic rebellion appears poetically, in part, as a fall from the transparency Tasso assigns to the head of the sacred Phoenix to the opacity that grows in Satan, his legions, and their ability to take various shapes. The question of angelic gender thus helps to structure the design of *Paradise Lost* around the "bright" or "obscure" angelic exercise of "love" or "enmity" (1.429–31), providing multiple *eikastic* and *phantastic* ambivalences for interpretation in the poem as the test par excellence of wedded love.

Not surprisingly, when we meet the phoenix in *Paradise Lost*, its image is diversely related to angelic and human characters. Of multiple angels, for instance, Milton gives us Petrarch's three in reversed order. Satan is not named as a phoenix but is seen parodically and metonymically acting like one in his unnatural flight across the "Coast" of the paradise of fools toward "the coast of Earth beneath" (3.487 and 739) through the "purer air" like that blown "from the spicy shore / Of Araby the blest" (4.162–63). He flies up to the Tree of Life and sits there "Like a Cormorant" (4.196). Uriel, whose name means "fire of God," does not sit but *stands* watchfully in the sun (3.622–23), and Milton designates him, too, by one of the metonymic adjuncts of the phoenix—his "beaming sunny Rays, a golden tiar / Circl'd his Head" in "brightness" (3.625–26). Raphael possesses the name outright—"A *Phoenix* gaz'd by all," who sails between worlds like the Arabian bird (5.268, 271–72). He is highly erotic in character because Milton's vision of "that sole Bird / When to enshrine his reliques to the Sun's / Bright Temple, to Egyptian Thebes he flies" (5.271–72) brings the journeys of *eros* and immortality into poetic focus. Milton's Raphael pulls into *Paradise Lost* the Ovidian context in which the phoenix is one of several explanations of sexuality and generation yet remains "ever alone of its kind."[49] The effect of Milton's multiplication of angel-phoenixes is change in the meaning of its usual classical designation, *unica*, from only one phoenix to many individualities. The true uniqueness of the sacred Phoenix Milton reserves to human nature, and Raphael's individuality is the subject of Adam's wonder in book 5 and gender inquiries in book 8, when Adam discusses sexuality and generation with the angel to gain self-knowledge—Sidney's theme.

Milton's description of Raphael's dress is a description of his androgynous "body"—for "six wings he wore," two of which are "Girt like a Starry Zone" around his waist and skirting "his loins and thighs with downy Gold" (5.277–82). Three books later, when Adam's questions about astronomy help Eve to decide to leave the conversation, this starry zone turns out to be the same as sexuality. The iconography of Raphael when he first appears indicates androgyny in a Petrarchan way; the colors of this feathered beauty have parallels not with the morbid celestial figment of Petrarch's *Rime* 323, but with the image of Laura in her scarlet dress with cerulean border in *Rime* 185, and Raphael occupies the center of Milton's poem as Laura's phoenix sonnet does the center of the *Rime—Purpurea vesta d'un ceruleo lembo.* The dress veiling Laura is, of course, sprinkled with roses— *sparso di rosi.* Raphael's third pair of wings covers his feet with "Skytinctur'd grain" (5.284–85), and when Adam asks about angelic love-making in book 8, the angel answers with a smile that glows "Celestial rosy red, Love's proper hue" (8.618–20). Nowhere does Milton describe Raphael's head and face, having assigned the first pair of wings to his shoulders and breast (5.279–80). Rather than describing Raphael's angelic face, which is presumably transparent with light and almost invisible, Milton gives us the attributes of his personality in his speech, in an allusion to his smile, and a reference to his "contracted brow" (8.560). The gilded head of Petrarch's false phoenix in *Rime* 323 (*l'capo d'oro*) does not occur here, and the gilded feathers of the necklace around Laura's white neck (*Questa fenice de l'aurata piuma /. . . collo candido gentile*) have been moved to the "downy Gold" of Raphael's loins and thighs (5.277–82).[50] The mystery of angelic nature and gender is revealed only in speech in his intercourse with Adam and Eve and in Adam's effort to understand himself by understanding angelic love.

The fact that God has instructed Raphael to go and converse with Adam "as friend with friend" (5.229) is usually read in the Spenserian context of Red Cross Knight's vision of the angels travelling up and down Jacob's ladder "As commonly as friend does with his friend" in *The Faerie Queene* (1.10.56), and the Ladder is Christ. This reading is certainly appropriate, but Milton's description also bears reference to Sidney's *Arcadia,* changing the homoerotic expression of the phoenix in Sidney's imagery of Pyrocles when he has disguised himself as Zelmane the Amazon. Pyrocles' first pseudonym is Diaphantus, which indicates transparency to light, but he has disguised himself after falling in love with Philoclea's portrait and going in search of a way to meet her. Mucidorus (Palladius) finds him in the woods and recognizes him by his singing voice, much as Milton later describes how Raphael "in *Adam's* Ear / So Charming left his voice" (8.1–2).[51] The visual appearance of Pyrocles (Diaphantus) is considerably altered in

Sidney's parody not so much of Petrarch's Laura but of the lady of Petrarchist poetry. *This* phoenix is more opaque than transparent, and its head is described, beginning with the hair "drawn into a coronet of gold richly set with pearl, and so joined all over with gold wires and covered with feathers of divers colours that it was not unlike to an helmet, such a glittering show it bare." Upon "her body," Sidney says, "she ware a doublet of sky-colour satin, covered with plates of gold," and the "nether part of her garment" is cut to reveal some of the skin of the small of the leg and "the foot dressed in a short pair of crimson velvet buskins" (130–31). The passages that follow are even more to the point for understanding Milton's Raphael, for the reunited friends conduct a complex dialogue on the themes of love and friendship along lines both feminist and antifeminist having to do with one's preference for solitude or society. Milton considerably rewrites these commonplaces in the discourse of his faceless angel and Adam, developing the whole into a complex series of *eikastic* and *phantastic* imageries and a scene for the making of choices among erotic alternatives.

Milton mediates choices of love in the literary choices between the oral conversation of men, which rests on the fulcrum of the passion known between master and boy described by Socrates, and the reading of romances by men and women or by women alone.[52] The first can move to erotic pleasure in language, if not in touch, and the second does conventionally move from reading to the orality of kisses. Eve departs from the scene of Adam's "Studious thoughts abstruse" not because she is "not with such discourse / Delighted, or not capable her ear / Of what was high" (8.40–50), but because she chooses an expression of speech and love having its literary roots in romance in the legends of Heloise and Abelard, Paolo and Francesca, and Astrophil and Stella and in lessons punctuated by kisses. From Adam's lip "Not Words alone pleas'd her" (8.55–57). The three couples in these literary predecessors, alas, undergo permanent separations from each other's erotic love because of their transgressions, and the chosen departure of Eve at this point innocuously anticipates the later separation scene followed by transgression. Adam's conversation with Raphael, meantime, raises the question not so much *whether* "Words alone" pass between them—for Raphael makes the Socratic choice where his student at the end of book 8 probably could not—as to *what* actually transpires between any two speakers engaged in intimate dialogue.

When Sidney's Pyrocles faints under the chiding of Mucidorus, the latter falls down by him and "kissing the weeping eyes of his friend" beseeches him not to be troubled by the vehemence of his earlier remarks. The two are an image of "them that most dearly love."[53] In

Milton's scene, however, no such event happens. Rather, Adam's story (8.205, 252, and 522) is almost equally divided between his self-affirmation as a "son" of God and his wonder at Eve. We meet Petrarch and the sonneteers here in an Adam in need of a hermeneutics to "read" Eve as much as Sidney's Astrophil needs to read the starry zone of his Stella. "Who will in fairest booke of Nature know, / How Vertue may best lodg'd in beautie be," Astrophil begins. " 'But ah,' Desire still cries, 'give me some food.' "[54] The immortal Raphael, like the beauties of Sidney and Laura both, exemplifies interpretation in his stories, merely overseeing Adam's fledgling self-knowledge.

Adam tells the angel new experiences of "Transported touch," "passion," and "Commotion strange" (8.530–31). God has presented Eve to Adam as "thy other self" (8.450), but Adam's gender hierarchical language erects superlatives on the absolute nature of Eve—in whom all that is fair in the world is "summ'd up" (8.472–73), "wisest, virtuousest, discreetest, best" (8.550)—that obscure, perhaps, the conduct of his relationship with her. In other words, this man-to-man talk moves toward *phantastic* language not unlike Astrophil's, and Adam's fancy is as infected with his own inventions as Eve's was when Satan injected his bad dream into her ear. Raphael's effort to teach Adam a few *eikastic* points on bringing the superlatives into proportion—Adam should weigh Eve with himself and consider the nature of the ladder of love (8.561–94)—does not really help Adam, who has to learn the "oblique" and the "right" for himself as a man, not an angel (*Def.*, 96). When Adam responds by idealizing his passion in procreation and the kind words and actions of every day establishing his and Eve's "Union of Mind" as "both one Soul" (8.604), neither self-knowledge nor the question of desire is resolved. Two great differences between Sidney's sonnet and Milton's dialogue are, of course, the emphasis on the moral innocence of Adam compared to Astrophil and the presence of a pedagogue. Yet we should expect that the quality of Raphael's narratives of the war in heaven and the creation and the failure of these narratives to keep Adam and Eve from falling also have bearing on Milton's judgment on the nature of Petrarchan and Sidneian literature. Reason is but choosing, and each reader is responsible to bring knowledge with him or her to the text.

The Masks of God Coming "In His Majesty"

Elsewhere in *Paradise Lost*, Milton does not use the word "phoenix." He presents instead the genealogy of the Word historically descended from "our first parents." The language appropriate to the only-begotten Son is the diction of incarnational paradoxes in book 3, but it is also the Miltonic narrator's appropriation of the Word of God throughout the poem as he travels up and down the whole universe from hell to heaven's throne in conjunction with the Word. The action of the only-begotten Son appears twice in *Paradise Lost* in the image of his operation of the *merkavah*, the chariot-throne of paternal Deity, to defeat the rebel angels and to create the world in books 6 and 7.[55] This theophany also occurs a third time in the disguise of another kind of vesture entirely. The holy eroticism that deserves the "lovely name of Love" (*Def.*, 103), as Sidney put it, reveals Milton's transformation of Petrarch's descriptions of the strangely regenerative self, the beautiful woman, and the vision of mortality into an image of a divinely human sexuality at the end of *Paradise Lost*: the dynamism of the sacred Phoenix appears in the inward motions of the erotic desires of man and woman.

Greville had described the "high pinnacle" of Sidney's aspirations as he planned the trip to America and the confirmation of the Protestant League by gazing at "the present Map of the Christian world" beneath him.[56] Adam and Eve, having been strengthened in the repeated revelation of the *protoevangelium*, prepare to travel as exiles and religious pilgrims to their new world. Led "Down the cliff as fast / To the subjected Plain" (12.639–40), they leave behind almost all vestiges of a Sidneian imagination with their humility. "The World was all before them, where to choose / Thir place of rest" (12.645–46), and they are about to be in its midst knowing the mixture of good and evil in human affairs that had, according to Greville, forged Sidney's will to action. Greville demurs from interpreting Sidney's "Heroicall design," surrendering what happens in the synchronicity of the frustrated American voyage and the death-summons to the Netherlands to the hiddenness of God's secret judgments.[57] Milton, having assigned conscience to Adam and Eve as their "Umpire" and "guide" before the Fall for their "safe" arrival at their divine destiny (3.194–97), now assigns "Providence" as "thir guide" (12.647). Poetically he does much more: the concluding scene of *Paradise Lost* is a blazing consummation in which fire colors the entire utterance. The divine mandate to depart from Eden is, indeed, like Sidney's, a death-summons, and here Milton does allude to the "dreadful Faces" of the angels (12.644).

Yet when we see Adam and Eve once again being visited by avian creatures, this time the "bright array" of the Cherubim preceded by the sword of God blazing "Fierce as a Comet" (12.627–34), we are gazing not merely on Michael but on the sacred Phoenix, the Word beginning his historical entrance into time through human flesh. The imagery tells us that we are again witnessing the manifestation of the only-begotten Son in the wheels-within-wheels of the *merkavah*. All of Eden is "Wav'd over by that flaming Brand" (12.643) as the lamenting pair go out looking for "Thir place of rest" (12.647). The fire is also *within* them, however; it *is* their erotic desire henceforth, for Milton has sexualized and gender-divided in them the historical presence of the Word. Quite literally, Adam and Eve have burned their own nest and themselves in it; they are utterly changed. They are also on their way through history not to any Temple of the Sun but to "A paradise within . . . happier far" (12.587). Eve is the parent almost treated singly (*phoenix unica*) from whose seed the sacred Phoenix will come in the flesh, the only-begotten Son entering history through the Virgin Birth of Mary, for whom Eve is prototype and in whom the woman clothed with the sun in the Book of Revelation is also signified.[58] These three women circumscribe all of human history that is important to know—creation, incarnation, doomsday—as Milton reinstates the feminine.

Petrarch had interlaced his image of the phoenix with images of the nest, the sun, and the laurel tree, and so does Milton. Matthew Roydon had done the same in regard to Sidney: "It cannot sinke into my mind, / That vnder branches ere can bee, / Of worth and value as the tree" (lines 29–31, 7). In *Paradise Lost*, Milton takes the Tree of Life and transposes it into a phoenix nest. God has commanded both the descent of the Cherubim to expel Adam and Eve and guard the Tree in case man would steal the fruit "And live for ever, dream at least to live / For ever" (11.95–96) and also the Cherubim's dispensation of new hope. "As I shall thee enlighten," God says to Michael, speaking of the Promised Seed, "intermix / My Cov'nant in the woman's seed renew'd" with the dismissal from Eden. "So send them forth, though sorrowing, yet in peace . . ." (11.115–17). Certainly these lines phrase the necessary mix of good and evil for moral instruction discussed by Lactantius, Sidney, Greville, and Milton. As in Petrarch's experience of Laura's death, too, but in reverse motion, the Tree stays in Eden, and the "Tree" goes with Adam and Eve in the consolation of the Word and of the flesh. In their sexuality, the changed Adam and Eve, one new phoenix, carry the burning nest between them for the regeneration of the race, and love is "thir rest."

Clearly it is Milton, not Sidney, who transforms the austerities of Lactantius into the authorized Christian gods and goddesses of a new age. Milton creates enfleshed divine icons whose wounds of imperfection—flesh, gender, sin, death—bear within them the glories of grace, the revelation of an Incarnation surpassing the condition of the angels. Yet Sidney showed Milton the way to such lyricism when, in the

Defence, he described those "notable *prosopopoeias*" of the poets who "maketh you, as it were, see God coming in His majesty" either to judge or to expose the arrival in the world of the Word made flesh (*Def.*, 77). Milton did not defend himself from imagining any aspect of the Apocalypse, and his God comes in glory either to reside with the lovers Milton pictures or to judge them. Likewise, the poet's participation in this theophany discloses the symposium of Sidney's "heavenly poesy" in which a writer such as Milton can sing like David, showing himself "a passionate lover of that unspeakable and everlasting beauty to be seen by the eyes of the mind only cleared by faith" (*Def.*, 77). In 1630 in "The Passion," Milton's composition of an image of the unique heroism of Christ broke down on the boundaries of flesh and spirit suffered in death. "O what a Mask was there, what a disguise!" (19, 62), Milton exclaimed. But by the end of his life, Milton had, indeed, formed in Lycidas, the uncouth Swain, Adam and Eve, Satan, Raphael, Uriel, Michael, the Son, Samson, and Dalila the many "masks" of God in whose actions the divine, inexpressible Love may be seen terribly or joyfully, even through the tarnishings of the "common errors of our life" (*Def.*, 95).

The "Phoenix" of Lofty Hymns

Lactantius had argued for the articulation of the Word, the utterance of divine truth in the Son. Milton's problem with the King's purported use of Pamela's prayer from the *Arcadia* has to do with such spiritual indecorum, a displacement of speech. Yet Pamela, too, was God's creature; Milton saw a little of himself in her character, her plea for protection of her chastity and mercy for her lover.

Early in the eighteenth century, about thirty years after Milton died, John Dennis expressly used the figure of a phoenix in a metonymy applied both to Milton and to a passage in *Paradise Lost*. In 1704 in *Grounds of Criticism*, Dennis presents Milton as an "Original" and not a "Copyist," disagreeing with Dryden on several points, and praising the poet as the first epic poet "who in the space of 4000 years, resolved for his country's honour and his own to present the world with an Original Poem, that is to say, a Poem that should have his own Thoughts, his own Images, and his own Spirit." Most especially Dennis admires Milton's imagination of human speech before the Fall, notably the "incomparable Hymn" in book 5: "A Hymn, which tho it is intirely taken from Scripture, for it is apparently the 148th Psalm, yet will always stand alone, the Phoenix of lofty Hymns."[59] Psalm 148, of course, is a praise of divine creativity in the evidence of the creation, and it was a standard if not ritual option for morning "Orison" (*PL*, 5.153–208). Milton first marks its spontaneity as a "fit" strain, "Unmeditated" eloquence flowing from the lips of Adam and Eve "in Prose or numerous Verse, / More tuneable than needed Lute or Harp" (5.145–61).[60] In the Geneva Bible, however, this Psalm is glossed not on the innocence of original creation, but for the special pertinence it has to God's Church and "the power he hathe giuen to the same after that he had chosen them and ioyned them unto him."[61] This is a hymn for regenerate sinners, a post-lapsarian song of praise and gratitude for the divine election. So, too, Milton disposes the Psalm in the context of the perceived taint of "evil" felt by Eve and Adam in her narrative of a devilish dream, which a "sad" Adam reasons them out of (5.94–135). Only after the morning prayer does Milton's narrator clear the two of them from the sense of being tainted: "So pray'd they innocent, and to thir thoughts / Firm peace recover'd soon and wonted calm" (5.209–210). Prayer alone heals the disjuncture in their conjunction, restoring it to the love of God.

What Dennis wants to praise for its rarity and originality, Milton attaches to the view that prayer—and poetry—is the inspired gift of the Holy Spirit. In the mouth of the condemned King, Pamela's prayer offends against the very essence of such a concept. The prayer is Stoic, fictional, and written. Sharing the idea of the poet as "maker," Sidney and Milton shared even more profoundly an anthropology of the poet as a special creature made, reformed in grace, and recreated according to the pattern of the only-begotten Son who speaks the Word in the breathings of the poet. Uniqueness, not physical or moral sonship to any previous poet, makes Milton a "true Poem," a strange creature not formed in nature but embracing within his imagination all that is so formed. The poet himself is a hymn to divine creation.

Beyond the explicit use of the word "phoenix" or the bird's attributes, Milton's variegated use of the figure conceals other, less verbally denoted appearances of the phoenix in dynamically realized poetic patterns, too. The significance of the phoenix helped Milton to trace on a colossal scale the device that Puttenham called "proportion in figure" and Herbert composed hieroglyphically in the quadruple "triquet" of "Easter-Wings."[62] Since Milton's poems reconstruct the apocalypticism of Ezekiel's wheels and Saint John's visions, giving new meaning to the theophanies of the divine chariot within the spirals of nature, the recognition of Milton's transformation of the Petrarchan phoenix of desire and Tasso's sacred Phoenix in the context of the Sidney legend should contribute to our knowledge of the subsequent English literary tradition.[63] After all, Romantic poets reconceived this phoenix, too, in Blake's visions and in Keat's Hyperion until Yeats composed his turning gyres between the two world wars of our own century.

Certainly Milton loved Diodati and criticized himself for leaving alone to die the one to whom he had confessed as late as 1637 that God had instilled in him "a vehement love of the beautiful" (Letters, *CPW,* 1:326–27). Quoting Pauline gender hierarchies in *An Apology* and struggling with them in the divorce tracts, perhaps Milton floundered when he identified woman more as man's "glory" while the man in his body is "the image and glory of God which is in himselfe" (*Apology, CPW,* 1:892). We shall debate the effect on portrayals of Eve and Dalila a long time. Yet whether or not the older Milton may truly be said to have gathered the ashes of his rational civilization around him, as if it were his own autogenesis, dismantling finally his own male ego in the image of Samson's "death self-inflicted," it was from the phoenix nest he moved in the image of spiritual regeneration, and his God was a consuming fire. *Nam Christus ignis verus est,* "For Christ is the true fire," Prudentius said.[64] So, too, Sir Philip Sidney taught Milton about himself. In face of that historical icon, we sever Milton's religious faith and longing from his eroticism at the risk of putting out the eyes of his poems and stopping up the flame of his voice. Similarly, we deny the many names of love Milton explored in his poetry at the risk of silencing Love itself, the Word known in its utterance in human history, its articulation in human bodies. The classical phoenix came every five hundred years according to legend, Milton's once and for all time, everywhere. What a mask, what a disguise, for this poet to have claimed for England the new source of the Exemplar Tasso had described symbolically as unique: "And there she builds her nest—her tomb and nest, / where, father to herself as well as son, the bird will perish and once more have life."[65]

Notes

1. *The Defence of Poesie,* in *Miscellaneous Prose of Sir Philip Sidney,* ed. Katherine Duncan-Jones and Jan van Dorsten (Oxford: Clarendon Press, 1973), 110. All references to *The Defence* are to this edition and will be cited by page number.

2. Hyder Edward Rollins quotes Philip and discusses the Sidneian "Phenix" in his edition of *The Phoenix Nest* of 1593 (Cambridge: Harvard University Press, 1931), ix–x. John Buxton pursues the Shakespearean use of the figure in "Two Dead Birds: A Note on 'The Phoenix and the Turtle'" in *English Renaissance Studies Presented to Dame Helen Gardner,* ed. John Carey (Oxford: Oxford University Press, 1980), 44–55, and in regard to the Sidney legend since Sidney's wound in the thigh made him like Adonis, in "Shakespeare's *Venus and Adonis* and Sidney," in *Sir Philip Sidney: 1586 and the Creation of a Legend,* ed. Jan van Dorsten, Dominic Baker-Smith, and Arthur F. Kinney (Leiden: E. J. Brill, 1986), 104–10. On the medieval

and Italian conflation of *eros* and hero and its consequent development in English poetry, see Thomas P. Roche, Jr., *Petrarch and the English Sonnet Sequences* (New York: AMS Press, Inc., 1989), 107ff.

3. These are phrases extracted from the series of Astrophel elegies published with Spenser's in 1595, especially "An Epitaph upon the right honourable Sir Philip Sidney Knight," which may be found in *Spenser, Poetical Works*, ed. J. C. Smith and E. de Selincourt (Oxford: Oxford University Press, 1912), 559. In addition to *Sir Philip Sidney: 1586 and the Creation of a Legend* cited in note three, see two other collections of essays revealing the growth of Sidneiana before and during the 1986 anniversary: *Sir Philip Sidney, An Anthology of Modern Criticism*, ed. Dennis Kay (Oxford: Clarendon Press, 1987) and *Sidney in Retrospect: Selections from ELR*, ed. Arthur F. Kinney et al. (Amherst: University of Massachusetts Press, 1988).

4. William A. Ringler, Jr., "Sir Philip Sidney, the Myth and the Man," *Sir Philip Sidney: 1586*, ed. van Dorsten, 3–15, counts eleven editions of Sidney's work through the seventeenth century, 400 printed allusions to Sidney before 1625 (the year Milton went up to Cambridge), and 207 purely literary allusions to Sidney as compared with 72 to Shakespeare and 103 to Spenser (13 and 14 n. 34).

5. Dennis Kay, "Sidney–A Critical Heritage," *Sir Philip Sidney, An Anthology of Modern Criticism*, 3–41, provides a superb overview of the development, rise, fall, and revival of Sidney's literary reputation. Kay says that at the end of the nineteenth century, Sidney's art became "the exclusive preserve of the learned and those curious in old writings" (38)—exactly the condition, Miltonists should notice, in which Christopher Hill found interest in Milton in the mid–twentieth century as he prepared to write *Milton and the English Revolution* (New York: Viking Press, 1978), 3. In Kay's opinion Virginia Woolf's recognition that all the seeds of English fiction lay in the *Arcadia* helped to launch the recovery of Sidney's reputation (40–41). See also Yvor Winters, "The 16th Century Lyric in England: A Critical and Historical Reinterpretation," *Poetry* 53 (1939): 258–72, and *Poetry* 54 (1939): 35–51, who significantly refueled Dryden's image of a witty, Petrarchist Sidney, obscuring the recognition of the Protestant moral genius in Sidney's poetic theory and practice for decades. S. K. Heninger, Jr., *Sidney and Spenser: The Poet As Maker* (University Park, Penn.: Pennsylvania State University Press, 1989), 303–5, considerably clarifies the teleological differences in "wit" as used by Sidney and Dryden.

6. Kay, "Sidney–The Critical Heritage," 31–32, observes that the last edition of Sidney appeared in 1739 and Pamela was transformed into Samuel Richardson's *Pamela* the following year. See also Edmund Leites, "Pamela and the Hierarchy of the Sexes," *The Puritan Conscience and Modern Sexuality* (New Haven: Yale University Press, 1986), 118–39.

7. *The Last Days of Elia* (1833) as quoted in *The Romantics on Milton: Formal Essays and Critical Asides*, ed. Joseph A. Wittreich, Jr. (Cleveland, Ohio: Case Western Reserve University Press, 1970), 301–2. In the same volume cf. Coleridge's remarks on Sidney and Milton, 230, and Hazlitt's, 390.

8. *Sir Philip Sidney* (London: Macmillan, 1886), 200. Kay, "Sidney—A Critical Heritage," mentions Symonds's opinion that Sir Edmund Gosse gave the male coteries of poets in "the phoenix nest" built up after Sidney's death a homoerotic interpretation, posing the homosexuality of Sidney's bond with his mentor, Languet (38). Symonds himself assigns the letters between Languet and Sidney the quality of romance (27–28).

9. *Sir Philip Sidney As a Literary Craftsman* (Cambridge: Harvard University Press, 1935), 16.

10. Milton's allusions to the *Arcadia* may be found in his "Commonplace Book,"

CPW, 1: 371–72 and 462–63; to "Countrymen's *Arcadia's*" in *Areopagitica*, *CPW*, 2: 524–25; and among references to various Renaissance *Arcadias* in *Eikonoklastes*, *CPW*, 3: 362–67 and 547. Ralph A. Haug, ed., *The Reason of Church Government*, *CPW*, 1: 746–861, makes a concerted effort to acknowledge intellectual and verbal echoes of Sidney's *Defence* in Milton's treatise; see especially 1: 811–18.

11. Dryden's remarks occur in the preface to *Fables Ancient and Modern* (1700) found in *Essays*, ed. W. P. Ker, 2 vols. (1900; rpt. New York: Russell and Russell, 1961), 2.247. Quilligan comments on the slow arrival of Spenser–Milton critical studies in her book, *Milton's Spenser: The Politics of Reading* (Ithaca: Cornell University Press, 1983), 19–20, from the title of which I have clearly stolen the phrasing for consideration of "Milton's Sidney." Quilligan also briefly examines Sidney's theory of "right reading" in *The Defence* with regard to Milton's *Areopagitica* as another example of an oration "written to be read" (31–36).

12. A. S. P. Woodhouse, *The Heavenly Muse: A Preface to Milton*, ed. Hugh MacCallum (Toronto: University of Toronto Press, 1972), 16, cited by Wittreich to begin his argument about the "line of vision" in " 'A Poet Amongst Poets': Milton and the Tradition of Prophecy," *Milton and the Line of Vision*, ed. Joseph A. Wittreich, Jr. (Madison: University of Wisconsin Press, 1975), 97–142.

13. "Sidney and Milton: The Poet As Maker," *Milton and the Line of Vision*, ed. Wittreich, 57–95, especially 57.

14. *A Milton Encyclopedia*, ed. William B. Hunter et al., 9 vols. (Lewisburg, Penn., Bucknell University Press, 1978–83), 7:195–99.

15. Cf. Oscar Wilde, "Two Biographies of Sir Philip Sidney," *Pall Mall Gazette*, 44 (1886), 5, on Sidney's life as his own best poem.

16. *The Compact Edition of the Oxford English Dictionary*, 2 vols. (Oxford: Oxford University Press, 1971), 2.565–66, s.v. "pattern." See also the headnote to the "October" aeglogue of Spenser's *Shepheardes Calendar* in *Spenser, Poetical Works*, 456.

17. Cf. the remark George Gifford attributes to the dying Sidney in "The Manner of Sir Philip Sidney's Death," *Miscellaneous Prose*, ed. Duncan–Jones and van Dorsten, 171, as Sidney responds to the suggestion that he take comfort from his former life in which he glorified God: " 'It is not so,' said he, 'in me. I have no comfort that way. All things in my former life have been vain, vain, vain.' "

18. 1 Cor. 15: 20 and Rom. 8: 29, both in the translation of *The Geneva Bible, A Facsimile of the 1560 Edition*, intro. Lloyd E. Berry (Madison: University of Wisconsin Press, 1969). See especially Hugh MacCallum, *Milton and the Sons of God: The Divine Image in Milton's Poetry* (Toronto: University of Toronto Press, 1986), 11 and 24–58, on Milton's development of Christology out of Scripture and out of his dialogue with dogmatic theology, and Michael Lieb, "The Kenotic Christology," *The Sinews of Ulysses: Form and Convention in Milton's Works* (Pittsburgh, Penn.: Duquesne University Press, 1989), 38–52, on Milton's notion of God's divestment of divinity in the Son's investiture in the flesh.

19. Cf. Thomas Wilson on Homer's *Odyssey* as the "lively paterne of the mind," *The Arte of Rhetorique* (1560), ed. G. H. Mair (Oxford: Oxford University Press, 1909), 195. For a description of Sidney's plans and his fatal obedience, see Greville's *Life of the Renowned Sir Philip Sidney* (1652), Facsimile Reproduction with an Introduction by Warren W. Wooden (Delmar, N.Y.: Scholar's Facsimiles and Reprints, 1984), 82–91 and 126–34.

20. *Lactantius and Milton* (Cambridge: Harvard University Press, 1929), 123–33.

21. Ibid., 199–200.

22. *A Woorke concerning the trewnesse of the Christian religion . . . Against Atheists, Epicures, Paynims, Jewes, Mahumetists, and other Infidels*, trans. Sir Philip Sid-

ney and Arthur Golding, in *The Complete Works of Sir Philip Sidney*, ed. Albert Feuillerat, 4 vols. (Cambridge: Cambridge University Press, 1912), 3: 249–50.

23. Roydon's poem is in *The Phoenix Nest*, ed. Rollins, lines 26–28, p. 7.

24. In William A. Ringler, Jr., ed., *The Poems of Sir Philip Sidney* (Oxford: Clarendon Press, 1962), 267–69. Any citations of Sidney's poems will also be from this edition. See especially Margaret W. Hannay, *Philip's Phoenix: Mary Sidney, Countess of Pembroke* (Oxford: Clarendon Press, 1989) on the literary relationship between the brother and sister.

25. See Michael Krouse, *Samson and the Christian Tradition* (Princeton: Princeton University Press, 1949), 108–18, on "saint" Samson, the Stoic *agon*, and the early Christian theme of ascetic "wrestlers" with the devil; Merritt Hughes's comments on Krouse's book, *Complete Poems*, 540–42; Mary Ann Radzinowicz, *Towards Samson Agonistes: The Growth of Milton's Mind* (Princeton: Princeton University Press, 1978), 290, on Samson's discovery of the inadequacy of his conception of God; and Joseph A. Wittreich, *Interpreting "Samson Agonistes"* (Princeton: Princeton University Press, 1986), 244–45, on the "tarnished Samson" overlaid with political significance and engaged in the wretched exchange of wrong for wrong.

26. *Petrarch's Lyric Poems: The Rime sparse and Other Lyrics*, ed. and trans. Robert M. Durling (Cambridge: Harvard University Press, 1976), 272–3, 330–31, and 504–5, respectively, the first being cited in the epigraph.

27. *Creation of the World*, trans. Joseph Tusiani and annotated by Gaetano Cipolla, *MRTS* 12 (Binghamton, N.Y.: Center for Medieval & Early Renaissance Studies, 1982), lines 1232–39, p. 135, a line of which is also cited in the epigraph.

28. Carol Falvo Heffernan, *The Phoenix at the Fountain: Images of Woman and Eternity in Lactantius's Carmen de Ave Phoenice and the Old English Phoenix* (Newark: University of Delaware Press, 1988), 18, 161–64, on androgyny and an English turn toward emphasis on the masculine, and 102–23 and 136–39 on the phoenix in the romance tradition and Chaucer. Heffernan reads the phoenix myth in anthropological and literary terms as a myth of female initiation portraying the sequences of menstruation, conception, and birth.

29. *Studies in Seventeenth–Century Poetic* (Madison: University of Wisconsin Press, 1950), 5. Cf. Milton's statement in *An Apology* (*CPW*, 1:889) that the sound and matter of elegy were agreeable to nature's part in him.

30. *Petrarch's Lyric Poems*, trans. Durling, 272–73.

31. See Thomas P. Roche, Jr., "*Astrophil and Stella*: A Radical Reading," *Spenser Studies* 3 (1982): 139–91, and "Autobiographical Elements in Sidney's *Astrophil and Stella*," *Spenser Studies* 5 (1984): 209–29.

32. For a full discussion, see M. J. Doherty, *The Mistress-Knowledge: Sir Philip Sidney's Defence of Poesie and Literary Architectonics in the English Renaissance* (Nashville, Tenn.: Vanderbilt University Press, 1991). On Sidney and androgyny, see also Constance Jordan, *Renaissance Feminism: Literary Texts and Political Models* (Ithaca: Cornell University Press, 1990), 127, 220–40, and 247–48.

33. Commenting on Milton's phrase, "Countrymen's Arcadia's," in *Areopagitica* (*CPW*, 2:524–25), Annabel Patterson has discussed Sidney's intentionality from a political perspective, arguing that Milton recognized political allegory in the *Arcadia* and its contradictory interpretations. See *Censorship and Interpretation: The Conditions of Writing and Reading in Early Modern England* (Madison: University of Wisconsin Press, 1984), 24ff.

34. I am indebted to David M. Toomey for this observation.

35. Tacitus describes the phoenix in *The Annals*, 6, 28, trans. John Jackson (London: William Heinemann, 1937), 4:201.

36. The comment is made about liturgical vestments and practices. See Thomas N. Corns, *The Development of Milton's Prose Style* (Oxford: Clarendon Press, 1982), 72, on the links between Catholicism, things Roman, press censorship, and Milton's depiction of Charles in *Eikonoklastes*.

37. *Petrarch's Lyric Poems*, ed. and trans. Durling, 330–31 and 504–5. See Leonard Barkan, *The Gods Made Flesh: Metamorphosis & the Pursuit of Paganism* (New Haven: Yale University Press, 1986), 206–15, on Petrarch and the passionate exposition of the self and 214 on the apocalypticism of *Rime* 323.

38. *Life of Sidney*, 149–52.

39. *Life of Sidney*, 21. In his introduction, Wooden dates the composition of Greville's *Life* to 1609–14, noting its status as "political hagiography" and observing the existence of an early manuscript version found at Trinity, Cambridge in the nineteenth century (v–vi). See Thomas N. Corns's analysis of Milton's prose, especially *Eikonoklastes*, for its "ambivalences and contradictions" in appealing to various Protestant factions, in his essay, entitled from *Samson Agonistes*, " 'Some rousing motions': the plurality of Miltonic ideology," *Literature and the Civil War*, eds. Thomas Healy and Jonathan Sawday (Cambridge: Cambridge University Press, 1990), 110–26.

40. *Milton's Good God: A Study in Literary Theodicy* (Cambridge: Cambridge University Press, 1982), 164–201.

41. The terms are drawn from Plato's *Sophist*, from the Protestant humanist Scaliger, and most of all from *Platonis Opera Quae Extant Opera*, 3 vols. (Geneva: Henri Estienne, 1578) and the commentaries by the French Calvinist, Jean de Serres. For a discussion of this edition of *Plato* and its importance in Sidney's *Defence* and probably in Milton's thinking, too, see M. J. Doherty, *The Mistress–Knowledge*, chapter 4.

42. Letter 58, *The Principal Works of Saint Jerome*, trans. W. H. Fremantle in *A Select Library of Nicene and Post-Nicene Fathers*, 2d series, ed. Philip Schaff and Henry Wace (1892; rpt. Grand Rapids, Mich.: Wm. B. Eerdmans Publishing Company, 1979), VI:122.

43. Homoeroticism is an old *topos* in Milton studies that probably needs to be reexamined in categories other than the modern Freudian ones. A good historical source with which to begin the discussion is Marsilio Ficino, *Commentary on the Symposium*, trans. Sears Reynolds Jayne, *University of Missouri Studies* 19 (1944): 207, 217, and 233–34. But see also Jean de Serres's revision of the ladder of love for Protestants in his commentary on the *Symposium* in the 1578 *Plato* (III. 170ff.) and, in the same place, his condemnation of pederasty and the very idea of the "man–woman" or ἀρρενοθῆλυν as a *phantastic* kind of love. Steven Ozment briefly addresses the subject in his discussion of marriage and ministry in *The Age of Reform, 1250–1550: An Intellectual and Religious History of Late Medieval and Reformation Europe* (New Haven: Yale University Press, 1980), 389–96. Edward Le Comte, *Milton and Sex* (New York: Columbia University Press, 1978), dismisses Robert Graves's suggestion that Milton was latently homosexual and sublimated his desire in chastity, but states that "a carefully developed theory of youthful ambivalence would be entitled to . . . unprejudiced consideration." William Kerrigan, *The Sacred Complex: On the Psychogenesis of Paradise Lost* (Cambridge: Harvard University Press, 1983), 49–50, draws a similar conclusion, finding traces of "homoerotic feeling" in Milton's friendship with Diodati but denying that homosexuality could have been Milton's solution to the oedipal complex. John T. Shawcross, *With Mortal Voice: The Creation of Paradise Lost* (Lexington, Kentucky: University Press of Kentucky, 1982), 178 n.3, takes a different psychological approach

that frames the question of gender definition, anti–feminism, and homoeroticism more suitably for Milton's poetry. Shawcross remarks that not enough is yet known about "the received mythic notions of female inferiority and of sexual characteristics of worthiness and unworthiness . . . or Milton's own sexual orientation" to draw strong conclusions.

44. *Creation of the World*, trans. Tusiani, lines 1488–94, p. 141, and *Opere*, ed. Bartolo Tommaso Sozzi, 3d ed. (Turin: Union Tipografico–Editrice, 1974), II. 677. Cf. Claudian, *Epigram de Phoenice* and the poem on consulship, ed. and trans. M. Platnauer, 2 vols. (London: William Heinemann, 1956), 1.101 and 2.230.

45. *Creation of the World*, lines 1147–59, p. 140.

46. Plutarch's comments are discussed by Guila Sissa, *Greek Virginity*, trans. by Arthur Goldhammer (Cambridge: Harvard University Press, 1990), 60–62.

47. "Milton and Sir Philip Sidney's *Arcadia*," *Notes and Queries* 196 (1951):115–17. See also William Riley Parker, *Milton, A Biography* (Oxford: Clarendon Press, 1968), 1: 317–18, for an effort to date *Samson Agonistes* to the mid–1640s, and John T. Shawcross, *Paradise Regained: Worthy T'Have Not Remain'd So Long Unsung* (Pittsburgh, Penn.: Duquesne University Press, 1988), 14–16 and 111–12 on the interpretive problems of such a dating.

48. Joseph A. Wittreich, Jr., calls upon Milton's "female readership" to retrieve *Paradise Regained* and *Samson Agonistes* from the "male establishment" by examining misogyny and patriarchy in them in his book, *Feminist Milton* (Ithaca: Cornell University Press, 1987), 118. My argument here is that Milton himself conducts such an interrogation of male sexuality and its cultural dominance by considering the potentially idolatrous emulation of Sidney by younger poets and distinguishing his own work from theirs. We need to consider the homoerotic and the androgynous as well as the feminist and antifeminist Milton. See Dominic Baker-Smith, "Sidney's Death and the Poets," *Sir Philip Sidney: 1586*, ed. van Dorsten, 83–103, on Sidney's patronage of university men and the origin of Cambridge and Oxford commemorative volumes of elegies on the occasion of Sidney's death and funeral. On androgyny in *Samson Agonistes*, see Jackie Di Salvo, "Intestine Thorn: Samson's Struggle with the Woman Within," *Milton and the Idea of Woman*, ed. Julia Walker (Urbana: University of Illinois Press, 1988), 211–20, especially 227.

49. See *Metamorphoses* 15.393ff., trans. Frank Justus Miller (London: William Heinemann, 1916), 2.393, and *Amores* 2.6.54. For a biblical view of Raphael the seraph in Isaiah, see Jon S. Lawry, *The Shadow of Heaven: Matter and Stance in Milton's Poetry* (Ithaca: Cornell University Press, 1968), 190–94 and 221–32.

50. *Petrarch's Lyric Poems*, ed. and trans. Durling, 330–31 and 504–5.

51. *The Countess of Pembroke's Arcadia*, ed. Maurice Evans (Harmondsworth, Middlesex, England: Penguin Books, 1977), 1. 12, 129–32.

52. See Ficino's discussion of the Socratic choice to procreate souls through educating young men and building up civilization rather than physically loving them, in the *Commentary on the Symposium*, trans. Jayne, 233–34.

53. *Arcadia* 1. 12, pp. 138–39.

54. *The Poems of Sir Philip Sidney*, ed. Ringler, 201.

55. See Michael Lieb, *Poetics of the Holy, A Reading of Paradise Lost* (Chapel Hill: University of North Carolina Press, 1981), 228–35 and 291–303.

56. *Life of Sidney*, 91.

57. Ibid., 90–91 and 134.

58. On the *merkavah* in this scene and its relation to the ideology of holy war, see Lieb, *Poetics of the Holy*, 307. On the "seed of Woman," see Diane Kelsey McColley, *Milton's Eve* (Urbana: University of Illinois Press, 1983), 213–18, and Dayton

Haskin, "Milton's Portrait of Mary As a Bearer of the Word," *Milton and the Idea of Woman*, ed. Walker, 169–84.

59. In *Milton, the Critical Heritage*, ed. John T. Shawcross (London: Routledge and Kegan Paul, 1970), 128–36.

60. On this Psalm and the fact that Adam and Eve's eloquence is prompt while Milton's is "promoted," see John Leonard, *Naming in Paradise: Milton and the Language of Adam and Eve* (Oxford: Oxford University Press, 1990), 244–47.

61. *The Geneva Bible*, p. 266ᵛ. See Mary Ann Radzinowicz, *Milton's Epics and the Book of Psalms* (Princeton: Princeton University Press, 1989), 146–48 and 153–54.

62. See *The Arte of English Poesie* (London, 1589), Facsimile Edition introduced by Baxter Hathaway (Kent, Ohio: Kent State University Press, 1970), 104–14. Herbert's "Easter-Wings" recapitulates twice in its form the theme of the paradox of the fortunate fall; cf. Milton's comments, *CG, CPW,* 1:807, on choosing a poetic subject and having enough time "to pencill it over with all the curious touches of art, even to the perfection of a faultless picture."

63. See Joseph A. Wittreich, Jr., *Visionary Poetics: Milton's Tradition and His Legacy* (San Marino, Calif.: Huntington Library, 1979), 213, on prophecy as Milton's "gift" to the Romantic poets.

64. *Peristephanon Liber II*, trans. H. J. Thompson (London: William Heinemann, 1953), 2:130. See Milton, *CB, CPW,* 1:471–72, on Prudentius and the divine source of human nobility, and *Ref, CPW,* 1:611, on Prudentius and the martyrdom of Saint Lawrence. See Hartwell, *Lactantius and Milton*, 99–110, on the Logos as an uttered word, not a mental thought, and on the audibility of the Word coming from the mouth of God (108).

65. *Creation of the World*, trans. Tusiani, lines 1351–53, p. 138.

Of Prelacy and Polity in Milton and Hooker

P. G. STANWOOD

"To be of no Church is dangerous. Religion, of which the rewards are distant, and which is animated only by faith and hope, will glide by degrees out of the mind, unless it be invigorated and reimpressed by external ordinances, by stated calls to worship, and the salutary influence of example.... [Milton] grew old without any visible worship ... [and] omitting public prayers, he omitted all."[1] The words, of course, are unmistakably Dr. Johnson's as he balances what is presumably "normal" against the odd or exceptional. However inadequate or incomplete his judgment, Dr. Johnson does call us to think of what is important. What was Milton's doctrine of the church and the structure of his ecclesiastical system? How can one function as his own church in the absence of a worshipping community? These are issues for which Milton provides answers, which could not have pleased Dr. Johnson; they are the logical end of an extreme protestant sensibility, whose uncompromisingly stated principles seem to continue the Reformation ideals of individual liberty and freedom of conscience.

While Milton addressed these concerns throughout his life and reflects them in almost everything he wrote, my wish is to consider especially the early church related tracts and the later, posthumously published *De Doctrina Christiana*. I shall explore Milton's well-known ecclesiological beliefs in the wider context of the thought of Richard Hooker (1554–1600), the greatest of Anglican theologians and apologists, an influence impossible to ignore.[2]

We need to begin by describing the foundation on which Hooker erects his systematic theology. Then we shall be able to see what features of his doctrine of the church Milton inherited—and rejected. But we will be better instructed if from Hooker's standpoint we look back to Thomas More (1478–1535) before we look forward to Milton; for the tradition of natural law and the liberty of right reason unites them all in spite of their very different lives and objectives. The following brief sketch of More's difficulties, and Hooker's probable solution to them, may serve to foreshadow Milton's reaction to the conditions of his time.

The general outline of More's trial and execution is well known. But the fundamental issues involved in More's resistance to King Henry might be examined more closely: What did More and the King mean by authority? What connections were there between the royal and ecclesiastical "regiment," and between them and the natural law? Neither More nor his judges really disagreed on the inviolability of the law, but their contention was over its interpretation and jurisdiction. In simple terms, More might refuse to take the Oath of Supremacy on grounds that it forced him to make a decision in an area where he denied competence; the King, of course, took a contrary position, claiming the aptness of his right to force judgment. Yet both King and subject implicitly appealed to the same, unchanging natural law.

The natural law, or the bringing into accord man's reason with God's will, lies at the heart of More's dilemma whether to submit or not to the King. To what extent might the King justly claim ecclesiastical as well as secular authority? Both depend on God's rule, but in a way which More could not reconcile. The large issue of authority troubled More over many years, and his works are filled with descriptions of government, with appeals to reason, to right judgment, to God's ordering of men's affairs, to faith governed by tradition. His last work recalls, often most poignantly, all of these concerns. In *De Tristitia* (1535), More writes of Malchus, whose name is the Hebrew word for "king," who can be taken as a figure of reason:

> For in man reason ought to reign like a king, and it does truly reign when it makes itself loyally subject to faith and serves God. For to serve Him is to reign. . . . And so whenever the rational mind rebels against the true faith of Christ and devotes itself to heresies, it becomes a fugitive from Christ . . . led astray by the devil and wandering down the byways of error.[3]

But Christ takes pity on those who err and instructs them who are confused. More had spent his life trying to accommodate his own reason with faithful service to God and the King whose very sovereignty he saw as a figure of God's dominion.

On the interpretation of scripture, More relies on the church informed by reason; for the spiritual, like the temporal sphere, depends on and reflects the patterns of natural law. Again in *De Tristitia*, More also appeals to tradition in his condemnation of contemporary folly, in lines that anticipate Hooker's views:

Nowadays, first in one place, then in another, there are springing up from day to day, almost like swarms of wasps or hornets, people who boast that they are "autodidacts" . . . and that, without the commentaries of the old doctors, they find clear, open, and easy all those things which all the ancient fathers confessed they found quite difficult. . . . But now these modern men, who have sprouted up overnight as theologians professing to know everything, not only disagree about the meaning of scripture with all those men who led such heavenly lives, but also fail to agree among themselves concerning great dogmas of the Christian faith. (445–47)

But let us, More continues prophetically, with God's grace find our way out of exile, "united in the true faith of Christ and joined in mutual charity as true members of Christ" (449).

More's appeal to authority typically embraces both king and church within the rule of reason, although he could not finally reconcile the one with the other. But it was possible for Richard Hooker to build this bridge while accepting the same plans and enlarging them—even as Milton would later avoid or even ruin the bridge in his determination to exalt the role of reason. Hooker's description of the natural law is extended and detailed in a way which both More and Milton would have understood but not have imagined necessary. Hooker, More, and Milton do not disagree in any important way about the natural law; but Hooker, in writing so extensively about it, vindicates both "protestantism" and the royal supremacy, yet retaining the wisdom of "holy and ancient men" and the prescriptural and apostolic church. Milton, of course, was to declare the sanctity of the individual conscience in a state governed by reason where the visible church is known by the true believer on the authority of the Holy Spirit.

Hooker starts first of all with the abstract law, with God himself who is that law which man may know through right reason. He is careful to distinguish the different, yet interlocked, kinds of law; for all men are subject to many laws, which ask for a variety of responses. There are thus eight kinds of law:

[1] The lawe which God with himselfe hath eternally set downe to follow in his owne workes; [2] the law which he hath made for his creatures to keepe, [that is,] the law of naturall and necessarie agents; [3] the lawe which Angels in heaven obey; [4] the lawe whereunto by the light of reason men find themselves bound in that they are men; [5] the lawe which they make by composition for multitudes and politique societies of men to be guided by; [6] the lawe which belongeth unto each nation; [7] the lawe that concerneth the fellowship of all; [8] and lastly the lawe which God himselfe hath supernaturally revealed.[4]

Each law is distinct yet the law altogether rests in the "bosome of God":

> Her voyce [is] the harmony of the world, all thinges in heaven and earth doe her homage, the very least as feeling her care, and the greatest as not exempted from her power, but Angels and men and creatures of what condition so ever, though ech in different sort and maner, yet all with uniforme consent, admiring her as the mother of their peace and joy. (1, 142; book 1.16.18)

Hooker is here implicitly arguing for another, and ninth, law that harmonizes all the rest, toward which God providentially moves all people. But the disjunction and conflict between the law of "politique societies" and the law of God forms the line of the dilemma that More failed to resolve. Milton saw no need in his ideal faith to harmonize the opposing demands of the positive law with the natural law, for Providence was already working its rule of conformity to God's will.

Having established his work on the natural law, and assuming man's informed reason, Hooker turns to the authority of the scriptures, of the church and its "proceedings," its ceremonies and its government, and finally to the authority of the king or "Civil Governour" in matters civil and ecclesiastical. Pursuing the details that follow from his general discussion of the natural law in book 1, Hooker's argument about the jurisdiction of kings, in book 8 *Of the Laws of Ecclesiastical Polity*, is immensely complicated. Although all authority derives from the natural law and from God himself, "all men are not for all thinges sufficient." The prince may not act for the bishop, nor the bishop for the prince, yet both are subject to the universal law:

> And therefore publique affayres being devided, such persons must be authorized Judges in each kinde as common reason may presume to be most fitt. Which cannot of *Kings* and *Princes* ordinarily be presumed in causes meerly Ecclesiasticall, so that even *Common* sense doth rather adjudge this burthen unto other men.[5]

Hooker argues that the king is supreme while nevertheless he points out his limitations both in the spiritual and political realm.

Protestantism in one sense is defined by the nature and source of authority, generally independent of "superior" or traditional judgment, whether of the church or of anyone acting as its interpreter or head. More saw authority in terms of tradition and the wise rule of an ecclesiastical judge. How could the King claim to be that judge simply by saying so? For More the royal supremacy threatened the apostolic church by undermining its authority; he could not, as Hooker afterwards was able to do, distinguish between "lawes positive" and open to change, and "lawes naturall [which] do alwayes binde" (1, 130; book 1.15.1). The issue was not one that worried Milton, whose mind was untroubled by any desire to mediate or compromise.

Yet Hooker did not reconcile the traditional church, avoiding the supposed protestant extremes of Calvin or Luther, with a secular head of state. He was no Erastian, however, nor was he really a mediator, nor was he particularly conciliatory. But he was able to describe those principles that create possible kinds of desirable actions. Some later observers have regarded Hooker as "judicious" and a "compromiser." But he was judicious in the special sense of astutely defining God's rule of law and society's practical relation to it. The sense of compromise is missing from Hooker, in any current use of that term; for he dismissed the arguments of his opponents. While the king is supreme in his jurisdiction, and the bishop in his, authority derives from right reason tuned by the law of God—not according to compromise, but just understanding.[6] These basic ideas remained the same for Hooker as for More; but Hooker was better able to see and explain them. Milton essentially followed the same course, determined to uphold "the honest liberty of free speech" and meanwhile to put down *Prelatical jurisdiction*" in a free commonwealth "where no single person, but reason only swaies" (*CG, CPW,* 1:804, 830, and *Way, CPW,* 6:427).

In a rare effort to compare Hooker and Milton, Joan S. Bennett sees a close link between the two ideologies. Both men are unwilling to give up individual "consent" or "liberty"; and both hold to some form of church and state or holy society (or community). Milton "radicalizes" the external form of Christian humanism, which was, Bennett says, "originally aristocratic."[7] Milton's free commonwealth is thus the heir of Hooker's "politique society," his worldview being effectively the same as Hooker's. Reason, deriving from the positive law (the personal and particular terms necessary for realizing the natural law amongst men), must be the ground of action; and order must be the end of reason and right government.

It is true that Hooker and Milton may seem alike in the ways, albeit somewhat factitious, noted here; yet Hooker's description of the natural law and his devotion to right reason lead him to define a Christian commonwealth that is different from Milton's notion of a properly constituted society. In his *Treatise of Civil Power in Ecclesiastical Causes* (1659), for example, Milton argues that the only just rule of the state in religion is to protect Christians from intimidation or constraints aimed at coercing them in their consciences. No other rule but the holy scriptures, illuminated by the Spirit, can rightfully persuade us:

And these being not possible to be understood without this divine illumination, which no man can know at all times to be in himself, much less to be at any time for certain in any other, it follows cleerly, that no man or body of men in these times can be the infallible judges or determiners in matters of religion to any other mens consciences but thir own.[8] (*Civil Power*, *CPW*, 7:242–43)

In appealing against the restoration of the monarchy, Milton urges that the happiness of a nation depends not on a single, regal person but on a representative council, freely chosen by persons who are impelled by reason; they will understand that the ideal work of kingship is the government of Christ, the universal Lord, for they will be suitably instructed:

To make the people fittest to chuse, and the chosen fittest to govern, will be to mend our corrupt and faulty education, to teach the people faith not without vertue, temperance, modestie, sobrietie, parsimonie, justice; not to admire wealth or honour; to hate turbulence and ambition; to place every one his private welfare and happiness in the public peace, libertie, and safetie. (*Way*, *CPW*, 7:443)

Such an education might need the direction of an archangel; but Hooker, recognizing human limitations, is more practical, more realistic, and more determined to make "conveniency" determine domestic, political, and ecclesiastical organization. Although Hooker, like Milton, is dedicated to right reason and its engagement, he stops short of an "ideal" commonwealth or ecclesiastical structure, accepting tradition and remaining content with custom. Milton appears, on the contrary, eager always to push ever harder against any organization that might compromise the purity of his beliefs or any constraint upon the thoroughgoing operation of "rectified reason."

Because of his difference, Milton helps us better to understand Hooker's grand description and view of church and state, and to recognize more clearly those ideas that would not fade with time; for it is untrue that Hooker launched his great work into a world that forever turned away from its principles. Hooker knew that he was not only defending but creating the reformed English church, established by law among men:

Though for no other cause, yet for this; that posteritie may know we have not loosely through silence permitted things to passe away as in a dreame, there shall be for mens information extant thus much concerning the present state of the Church of God established amongst us, and their carefull endevour which woulde have upheld the same. (1: 1; preface,1.1)

Hooker did not expect his huge treatise to pass unnoticed, nor did it; he intended his design to be comprehensive and he begged comparison by his very title with such works of antiquity as Cicero's *De Legibus*. Milton's tracts seem in contrast much more of their time, in spite of their high principles; for Hooker's idealism, unlike Milton's, is tempered always with pragmatism.[9]

One must not be misled, moreover, into thinking that Milton and Hooker would really have agreed on the work of the Holy Spirit who inspires the understanding of fallen man. The inner law responds to the leading of the Spirit in diverse ways, including prophecy and prayer, and so Milton's rational Christianity is neither an obvious nor direct descendant of Hooker. John R. Knott, Jr., offers a helpful distinction:

> Hooker, always moving toward the 'plainer ground' of reason, looked for 'some judicial and definitive sentence' and regularly found it in the pronouncements of the established church, which he insisted that everyone accept. Milton's sense of the dynamic operation of the Spirit in the lives of individual Christians prevented him from accepting the kind of consensus of rational men that was such a powerful ideal for Hooker. . . . Milton's own evolving understanding of the truth of the Spirit led him to the ultimate iconoclasm of rejecting all forms of worship and governance established by visible churches.[10]

Milton argues this point with special force in *Considerations Touching the Likeliest Means to Remove Hirelings out of the Church* (1659). Here he sees the ideal church as needing little formal guidance, any necessary ministers being self-chosen, self-dedicated, and ordained by their responsiveness to the Spirit, and distinguished from other Christians only "by thir spiritual knowledge and sanctitie of life" (7: 319).

Milton wrote several tracts specifically concerned with church government and ecclesiastical questions. Among these are five of his earliest prose works, written close together, beginning with *Of Reformation Touching Church-Discipline in England* (1641); *Of Prelatical Episcopacy* (1641); *Animadversions Upon The Remonstrants Defence Against Smectymnuus* (1641); *The Reason of Church-government Urg'd against Prelaty* (1642); *An Apology Against a Pamphlet call'd A Modest Confutation of the Animadversions upon the Remonstrants against Smectymnuus* (1642). These works have much in common, sharing especially concern for the nature of the church, its organization, its relationship to the state, and to the individual. I shall consider especially *Reason of Church-government*, for not only does Milton set out in it his views on the episcopacy with sharp clarity, but he also describes his own abiding belief in liberty of conscience. In this tract Milton incidentally refers to Hooker—the only explicit reference to his works.

The immediate occasion of *Reason of Church-government* was the publication in 1641 of a little volume called *Certain Briefe Treatises, written by diverse learned men, concerning the ancient and Moderne government of the Church.* Archbishop James Ussher (1581–1656) collected the treatises included in the volume, most of them being composed many years earlier. The second or subtitle page of this book is helpfully descriptive: *A Summarie View of The Government both of the Old and New Testament: whereby The Episcopall Government of Christs Church is vindicated; Out of the rude Draughts of Lancelot Andrewes . . . Whereunto is prefixed (as a Preamble to the whole) a Discovery of the Causes of the continuance of these Contentions touching Church-government: out of the fragments of Richard Hooker.* Hooker's "Preamble" is an anomalous work, being neither tract nor sermon, but rather a fragment of some longer work, either lost or unfinished. It has almost nothing to say about church government, but it briefly urges that the church should struggle to find peace in a time of disturbance. Thus it acts as a general preface to the other, more specifically argued treatises on the appropriateness of episcopal government.[11] Milton, in fact, does not refer to Hooker's *Causes of the continuance of these Contentions* but instead to the *Laws*, book 3, and the supposed inconsistency of interpretation of 1 Tim. 1:5 and 6:14.[12] Hooker's third book would certainly have been important to Milton when he wrote *Reason of Church-government*, for it deals mainly with the Presbyterian assertion that the scriptures specifically affirm a nonepiscopal form of church polity.

Milton's concern for church government and his response to Ussher's compilation must be put into context. The 1640s had seen the publication of numerous works in support of the episcopacy, among them *Certain Briefe Treatises*, and many other books and treatises in favor of its reform or abolition. These years would lead, one must remember, to Archbishop Laud's execution in 1645, and finally to the King's death in 1649. Milton, along with many others, contributed to the flood of controversial literature, strongly taking up sides. Hooker, of course, could not engage fully in these arguments, even as a distinguished though dead authority; for book 6, on the role of lay elders, is a mere fragment, book 7, on the rule of bishops, did not appear until the Restoration, and book 8, the last, and climactic statement on regal dominion, is incomplete. Thus Hooker's full statement on the doctrine of the church and its relationship to the state could not have been known to Milton in the years when he was writing his episcopal treatises, though Milton would likely have preserved his own views even with all of Hooker's before him.[13]

Milton believes that right reason leads to the conviction that episcopacy has no scriptural foundation. Church discipline and order naturally is "platform'd in the Bible," an idea Milton shares with his episcopal opponents; but Milton understands that discretion, that is, discernment or prudence, will teach what this platform means, for church discipline is beyond man's vulgar invention or faculty to frame—"it is the worke of God as father, and of Christ as Husband of the Church" (*CG, CPW,* 1:750, 756). The argument is shifting, as it so often does in Milton, from practical to theoretical, from common to idealized values.

Simplicity is the rule, Milton argues, for "if the religion be pure, spirituall, simple, and lowly, as the Gospel most truly is, such must the face of the ministery be" (*CG, CPW,* 1:766). Nor should Bishop Andrewes argue on behalf of the episcopacy by referring to the Old Testament; for indeed, as workers in the "ripe age of the Gospel," we ought to be free from the law (*CG, CPW,* 1:763). A "priesthood" depending on hierarchy or on ordination (to deacon, priest, and bishop) is plainly wrong, for "every Minister sustains the person of Christ in his highest work of communicating to us the mysteries of our salvation, and hath the power of binding and absolving" (*CG, CPW,* 1:767). But in *Reason of Church-government,* Milton seems willing to accept a church depending on presbyters and deacons, rejecting at the same time the contention that presbyters are also bishops. His willingness to countenance the presbyterian model would soon pass, however, a change that may have occurred between 1642, the date of the last of the early antiprelatical tracts, and about 1644, the publication of *Areopagitica,* though the particular circumstances of this alteration of belief are uncertain. For the present, Milton zealously tries to root out the claims of the traditional episcopacy and the "fair forwardnesse" of the altars of the prelates, such as Andrewes, who would "missificate" (i.e., celebrate Mass).[14] Although spoken to a different time, Hooker's portentous judgment in book 7 of the *Laws* about episcopacy and the claims of the Presbyterians is cogent: "O Nation utterly without knowledge, without sence! We are not through error of mind deceived, but some wicked thing hath undoubtedly bewitched us, if we forsake that Government, the use whereof universal experience hath for so many years approved, and betake our selves unto a Regiment, neither appointed of God himself, as they who favour it pretend, nor till yesterday ever heard of among men" (3: 148; book 7.1.4).[15] Of course, Milton could not hear, nor, if he had heard, would he have understood how to change his course.

Milton's dislike of certain bishops can be explained partly through contemporary events leading up to the Civil War and the establishment of the Commonwealth.[16] But he also was responding to his own strong belief in voluntarism, which would lead him to define no denomination, to seek no organized church, but rather to celebrate the free motion of the Holy Spirit in man. For him all formal structures, devices, distinctions, ordinances, and orders of the church were to become irrelevant, to be relegated to the *adiaphora*, the nonessentials of religion and worship. His cry in *Areopagitica* reveals his true and abiding conviction: "Give me the liberty to know, to utter, and to argue freely according to conscience, above all liberties" (*Areop*, *CPW*, 2:560).

Yet Hooker (and others) argued that there are good reasons for supporting the episcopacy, such as its ability to put down disagreeable schismatics. Milton turns this positive notion around, insisting that faction and prelacy exist together, that the pyramidal organization of the traditional church encourages ambition and dissension. The calling of councils for dealing with schism thus exalts one authority (the bishops) and dismisses another (the piety of the generality of people). However, "the timeliest prevention of schisme is to preach the Gospell abundantly and powerfully throughout all the land, to instruct the youth religiously, to endeavour how the Scriptures may be easiest understood by all men" (*CG*, *CPW*, 1:791). The bishops have willfully acted against Christian believers by violating their independence and liberty of conscience, for surely, Milton argues, the terms for fighting falsehood are to allow its encounter with truth. This view is very familiar to all of Milton's readers: "vertue that wavers is not vertue, but vice revolted from itselfe, and after a while returning." Sects and schisms, indeed, are but "as the throws and pangs that go before the birth of reformation" (*CG*, *CPW*, 1:795).[17] Milton has thus managed to condemn the episcopacy for attempting to root out schism while breeding it, even encouraging a particularly virulent kind of its own. But schism, by which Milton means sectarianism as well as common disagreements about religion, may be good so long as it can flourish. In such a way, error can burn itself out or truth can demonstrate its purity. The fundamental point is that Milton decries external authority or coercion of any sort.[18]

Milton's fervent dislike of authority is the corollary of his belief in right reason leading to mankind's perfectibility, an ideal that he cherished to the end of his life. Even the title of *Reason of Church-government* intends a pun, for "reason" implies both explanation and fit response. The chapter headings in the second book particularly point to what Milton sees as the obvious use of "the reason and end" of the gospel, which is opposed to "prelatical jurisdiction," but tunes the mind in harmony with God.

Milton's *Reason of Church-government* is the third of the major tracts written within about a year on a similar subject. We should, therefore, remember that Milton is continuing, not starting his battle against what he perceives as a threat to the reformation of the English church and also to the English nation itself. *Of Reformation*, the first of these vigorous treatises, bristles with phrases such as "ignominious bondage" (of the old pre-Reformation Church), with its "new-vomited paganism of sensual idolatry" (*Ref, CPW,* 1:535, 520). There he had also railed against the episcopacy:

> And it is still *Episcopacie* that before all our eyes worsens and sluggs the most learned, and seeming religious of our *Ministers*, who no sooner advanc't to it, but like a seething pot set to coole, sensibly exhale and reake out the greatest part of that zeale, and those Gifts which were formerly in them, settling in a skinny congealment of ease and sloth at the top: and if they keep their Learning by some potent sway of Nature, 'tis a rare chance; but their *devotion* most commonly comes to that queazy tempter of luke-warmnesse, that gives a Vomit to God himselfe. (*Ref, CPW,* 1:536–37)

But "the very essence of Truth is plainnesse, and brightnes; the darknes and crookednesse is our own." Milton insists again and again on the obviousness of truth; he teaches that "the deep mistery of the Gospel, is the pure simplicity of doctrine"; and he appears to wonder how anyone can doubt his description of it (*Ref, CPW,* 1:566, *CG, CPW,* 1:826).

The argument of *Church-government* is basically simple although it is stated with many permutations. The essential idea is that "the lordly form of prelaty" frustrates the message of the gospel and the spread of Christ's kingdom in the English church and state. Milton abhors the tyranny of tradition, irrationality, intemperance, pompous authority, ritual without substance. He writes an extremely lively prose, severely contentious. He is in this kind of tract adopting the strategy common in his day: one attacks from a superior moral ground, appealing to high principles which the other side is supposed viciously to have tried to corrupt. Milton's speech is strident, unbending, and righteous; but so was the speech of his opposition. He apparently enjoys taking the offensive and plowing his opponents under a siege of outspoken language. But Milton is not being gratuitously vituperative; his purpose is to reform and improve the church and state, a point set out with great power in the splendid preface to the second book where he typically urges "the honest liberty of free speech" in order that "the call of wisdom and virtu may be heard every where" (*CG, CPW,* 1:804, 819).

Milton's church polity and discipline is obviously quite different from Hooker's, for Milton abandons serious analysis in favor of sweeping condemnation of existing structures. Hooker would preserve what might be useful, yet he does not hesitate to cast spears at the enemies of "naked truth" (1: 34; preface,7.1). While dedicated to right reason, Hooker recognizes its earthly limitations, and he sees the need to interpret absolute truths in human society. Near the end of book 1 of the *Laws,* Hooker portrays his antagonists, including Thomas Cartwright and the Admonitionists, in a sketch that describes a general type, to which Milton could, at a later election, belong:

> How commeth it to passe that we are at this present day so rent with mutuall contentions, and that the Church is so much troubled about the politie of the Church? No doubt if men had beene willing to learne how many lawes their actions in this life are subject unto, and what the true force of ech law is, all these controversies might have dyed the very day they were first brought forth. It is both commonly sayd, and truely, that the best men otherwise are not alwayes the best in regard of societie. The reason wherof is for that the law of mens actions is one, if they be respected only as men; and another, when they are considered as parts of a politique body. Many men there are, then whom nothing is more commendable when they are singled. And yet in societie with others none lesse fit to answere the duties which are looked for at their handes. Yea, I am perswaded, that of them with whom in this cause we strive, there are whose betters amongst men would bee hardly found, if they did not live amongest men, but in some wilderness by themselves.... By following the law of private reason, where the law of publique should take place, they breede disturbance (1: 139–40; book 1,16.6).

Milton's doctrine of the church, indeed, would suit well an independent, isolated "community" of one, situated in a wilderness. But Milton's church, while depending on no community, nevertheless promoted reason and intended peace.

This doctrine, which we have generally seen, especially in *The Reason of Church-government*, is fully described in *De Doctrina Christiana,* Milton's long treatise, composed in Latin, of systematic theology. This work, begun probably in the 1640s and completed in about 1670, was not published until 1825. It contains Milton's carefully formulated views on most theological issues, including his well known "heresies": Milton denies the coeternity and coequality of the three-personed Godhead; he denies creation *ex nihilo*; he affirms that matter is inherent in God.[19] But more important to the present discussion, he defines the nature of the church: "The marks of the visible church are pure doctrine, the true external worship of God, true evangelical charity, insofar as it can be distinguished by man, and the correct administration of the seals," that is, the sacraments (*CD, CPW,* 6:563).[20] In this chapter, Milton further declares, in typically protestant fashion, that there can be no head of the visible church except Christ himself, that worship may be conducted individually where there is no convenient church, that any believer can be a minister so long as he has certain gifts (of preaching, etc.), that extraordinary ministers are the prophets, apostles, and evangelists, especially inspired by God to reform the church. In the subsequent chapter, "Of the Holy Scripture," Milton asserts that the scriptures are absolutely clear to those who believe in them—there is the "external scripture" of the written word, and the "internal scripture" of the Holy Spirit which is given to every man: "the pre-eminent and supreme authority . . . is the authority of the Spirit . . . and the individual possession of each man" (*CD, CPW,* 6:587). Finally, where there is a particular church, Milton directs independent congregations to require a covenant among the gathered people, and a promise of concern and dedication for each new person who comes to enter that church.

Milton must have had the first five books of Hooker's *Laws* easily available to him when he was writing in the early 1640s, and he was aware, as we have seen, of one of the detailed arguments of book 3; and the direction of Hooker's argument and much of its detail is perfectly clear in these books. But Milton was not interested in Hooker's ecclesiology, nor in his ambitious design to explain the nature of the Christian church and the position of the Church of England within it. That Milton and Hooker believed in the primacy of reason is no matter here, for the end of their believing is so different. Hooker's principal teaching about the church was ignored not only by Milton, indeed, but also avoided by most of his contemporaries. We should summarize these basic tenets of Hooker's ecclesiastical system, which were unfortunately obscured in the sectarian conflicts of the earlier seventeenth century.[21]

In book 3 of the *Laws,* Hooker identifies the church as the visible body of persons who profess "*one baptisme* wherewith they are all initiated. The visible Church of Jesus Christ is therefore one, in outward profession of those thinges, which supernaturally appertaine to the very essence of Christianitie, and are necessarily required in every particular christian man" (1: 196; book 3,1.3). The statement is crucial to Hooker's exposition of the church; for he carefully separates the issues of faith from the concerns of church polity, which, while important, are not absolutely essential to the well being of the church.

Hooker eloquently affirms what he terms the "foundation" of the faith in many places, especially in the early *Discourse of Justification,*

Works, and how the Foundation of Faith is Overthrown (1586). I cannot here adequately trace Hooker's complex argument by which he demonstrates his belief that the Church of Rome has erred in misinterpreting the doctrine of salvation by faith through works. We cannot be "justified," Hooker says, through any inherent quality in ourselves, but solely through the merits of Christ. The Church of Rome, however, teaches justification by inherent grace. Of course, we must do works; but for our own part we must distinguish sanctifying grace as something different in nature from "the Righteousness of Justification." Hooker links "our belief" with truth, and with the foundation of faith; Roman belief "overthrows" the foundation, though it does not deny it:

> Salvation therefore by Christe is the foundacion of christianitye. As for workes they are a thing subordynate, no otherwise necessary then becawse our sanctificacion cannott be accomplished without them. The doctrine concerning them is a thing builded upon the foundacion, therfore the doctrine which addeth unto them the power of satisfying or of merittinge addeth unto a thing subordinated, builded upon the foundacion, not the very foundacion it self, yett is the foundacion consequently by this addition overthrowne.[22]

Again and again, Hooker urges that "salvation onely by Christe is the true foundacion, whereupon indeed Christianitye standeth." Nothing else matters so much as this one truth, for all doctrines must be tested against it. Milton would surely have agreed with such Gospel truths, but the fine distinction between their "overthrowing," on the one hand, and their "denial," on the other, could easily have seemed ambivalent and even compromising.

Hooker's view of episcopacy, as his conception of so many features of the church, evidently satisfies neither conservative nor liberal attitudes. On the rule of the church within the state, Hooker writes elaborately. Since Christ is in fact the head of the church, then kings must have a subordinate role in the administration of the church, which is not absolutely essential to its existence:

> I am not of opinion, that simplie always in *Kings* the most, but the best limited power is best, both for them and for the people; the most limited is that which may deale in féwest thinges, the best that which in dealing is tyed unto the soundest perfectest and most indifferent rule; which rule is the law. I meane not only the law of nature and of *God* but very nationall or municipall law consonant therunto. Happier that people, whose lawe is their *King* in the greatest thinges then that whose *King* is himself their lawe. (3: 341–42; book 8, 2.12)

The same rule is also true of the episcopacy, for both "regiments" belong to the category of positive law. Hooker elsewhere defends the role of bishops because of the antiquity and the conveniency of their office. They may quite properly claim apostolic descent; but their authority belongs to the positive, not to the natural law, and their government belongs to order, not to faith. While there must always be a church on earth, no man should presume that its government must remain forever the same. What does persist is the rule of faith, available to us through reason in harmony with the natural law, and in this way scripture may be opened to us.

Thus we return to Hooker's description of the natural law, now recognizing its function within his intellectual and ecclesiastical system:

> Now if nature should intermit her course, and leave altogether, though it were but for a while, the observation of her own lawes: if those principall and mother elements of the world, wherof all things in this lower world are made, should loose the qualities which now they have, if the frame of that heavenly arch erected over our heads should loosen and dissolve it selfe: if celestiall spheres should forget their wonted motions and by irregular volubilitie, turne themselves any way as it might happen: if the prince of the lightes of heaven which now as a Giant doth runne his unwearied course, should as it were through a languishing faintnes begin to stand and to rest himselfe: if the Moone should wander from her beaten way, the times and seasons of the yeare blend themselves by disordered and confused mixture, the winds breath out their last gaspe, the cloudes yeeld no rayne, the earth be defeated of heavenly influence, the fruites of the earth pine away as children at the withered breasts of their mother no longer able to yeeld them reliefe, what would become of man himselfe, whom these things now do all serve? See we not plainly that obedience of creatures unto the lawe of nature is the stay of the whole world? (1: 65–66; book 1, 3.2)

This expressive statement embodies the Renaissance view of order and degree out of which Hooker—and later Milton—constructs his doctrine of the church.[23] For the one, that leads to a visible hierarchy—not the *esse* of the church, but its best and living tradition; for the other, that means reforming the conscience of the true believer by means of the Spirit "that dost prefer / Before all Temples th' upright heart and pure" (*PL*, 1.17–18).

According to his church polity, Milton insists on the "church of one," favoring a kind of organization (or really absence of one) that in fact contains the elements of its own opposition and ruin. The comprehensive religious and political commonwealth proposed by Hooker assumes a community of believers, impossible in Milton's system that leads to the fracturing of that community. Milton wrote of the representative, ideal type: the poet singer of *Lycidas*; the Lady in *Comus*; the figures of Adam and Eve leaving Paradise; the invincible Samson; and most of all, the figure of Christ himself, who, having struggled against Satan, stands alone. These are the individuals, sustained by grace and guided by Providence, through whom Milton expresses his understanding of community—independent and suffering, yet finally working out their own salvation.

Yet we should not be misled into thinking that such lonely figures finally embody Milton's church. In one sense, they are perfect expressions of it, for they have achieved that stage of intense enlightenment which we should all aspire to have; but they are, of course, in a realm of achieved spirituality hardly available to others. Milton principally saw "lewd Hirelings" in the church of his time (*PL,* 4.193); and doubtless he might also have applied to that church the sad circumstances of his own life, of one "fall'n on evil days,"

> and evil tongues;
> In darkness, and with dangers compast round,
> And solitude.
>
> (*PL,* 7.26 –28)

These poignant lines express the direness that many sensitive persons discover in their lives, disappointed by the unbending meanness of a persistently disorganized world. Like Milton, Hooker, too, impatiently attacked what he regarded as vice and folly, only to be ignored or misunderstood.

While their doctrines of the church are quite different, we should not leave Hooker and Milton on different worlds, unattached to each other. Hooker urged a kind of structure that Milton rejected, but they are united at least in their desire to elevate the "Sanctity of Reason," and to celebrate faith. Hooker's splendid view of all the elements of the world at work together might be usefully compared to that "inmost seat of mental sight" (*PL,* 11.418) in which is revealed to Adam the course of human history, culminating finally in "Eternity, whose end no eye can reach" (*PL,* 12.556). Hooker's ideal of the Christian community, with its fixed positions, might seem distant indeed from Milton's insistence on the particular conscience of a right believer. But I would suggest that Hooker admits process and development in the midst of continuity and changelessness, a paradox no stranger than Milton's need to welcome company into his solitude. Both Hooker and Milton embrace those who not only need but also can give advice.

Notes

1. Samuel Johnson, "Milton," in *Lives of the English Poets* (London: J. M. Dent, 1925), 1: 92.

2. See Peter Munz, *The Place of Hooker in the History of Thought* (1952; rpt. London: Routledge & Kegan Paul, 1970); W. D. J. Cargill Thompson, "The Philosopher

of the 'Politic Society': Richard Hooker as a Political Thinker," in W. Speed Hill, ed., *Studies in Richard Hooker: Essays Preliminary to an Edition of His Works* (Cleveland, Ohio: Press of Case Western Reserve University, 1972), 3–76, rpt. in Cargill Thompson, *Studies in the Reformation,* ed. C.W. Dugmore (London, 1980); Robert Eccleshall, "Richard Hooker and the Peculiarities of the English: The Reception of the *Ecclesiastical Polity* in the Seventeenth and Eighteenth Centuries," *History of Political Thought* 2 (1981): 63–117; and H. R. Trevor-Roper, in *Catholics, Anglicans, and Puritans* (London: Secker & Warburg, 1987).

3. See St. Thomas More, *De Tristitia Christi*, trans. and ed. Clarence H. Miller (New Haven: Yale University Press, 1976), 14, i, 509–11. Subsequent references occur in the text.

4. See Richard Hooker, *Of the Laws of Ecclesiastical Polity: Preface, Books I to IV*, ed. Georges Edelen (Cambridge: Belknap Press of Harvard University Press, 1977), 1: 134; book 1,16.1. The Folger Library Edition of the Works of Richard Hooker. Subsequent references to the preface, and to books 1–4 are to this edition and cited in the text, but see n. 5, below.

5. See Hooker, *Laws: Books VI, VII, VIII*, ed. P. G. Stanwood (Cambridge: Belknap Press of Harvard University Press, 1981), 3: 430; book 8,8.8; later quotations from books 6–8 are cited in the text.

6. See Arthur Stephen McGrade's just assessment in his introduction to Hooker's *Laws* (preface, book 1, book 8), in Cambridge Texts in the History of Political Thought (Cambridge: Cambridge University Press, 1989): "Hooker's breadth of vision was unique among sixteenth-century religious writers. He was master of vast intellectual resources for placing the most divisive issues of the day in a larger, less divisive historical and doctrinal context. But he also took sides. The *Laws* is decidedly 'partisan' in the sense that it is written to refute the positions of presbyterians, militant liturgical reformers, and Roman Catholics on a host of specific issues, some relatively unimportant, others momentous" (xxx).

7. See Joan S. Bennett, *Reviving Liberty: Radical Christian Humanism in Milton's Great Poems* (Cambridge: Harvard University Press, 1989), 13. The historical and theological situation is helpfully summarized by Don M. Wolfe in his introduction to vol. 1 of the *Complete Prose Works of John Milton.* See also C. A. Patrides, *Milton and the Christian Tradition* (Oxford: Clarendon Press, 1966); Peter Lake, *Puritan and Anglican? Presbyterianism and English Conformist Thought from Whitgift to Hooker* (London: Allen & Unwin, 1988); Christopher Haigh, ed., *The English Reformation Revisited* (Cambridge: Cambridge University Press, 1987). A good presentation of a natural law position similar to that discussed in the present essay is by J. M. Finnis, *Natural Law and Natural Rights* (Oxford: Clarendon Press, 1980). Milton writes of the natural law in *De Doctrina Christiana*, I.xxvi, in *CPW*, 6:513–20: "The unwritten law is the law of nature given to the first man. A kind of gleam or glimmering of it still remains in the hearts of all mankind. In the regenerate this is daily brought nearer to a renewal of its original perfection by the operation of the Holy Spirit" (516). Hooker sees the natural law as universally and continuously available to all regardless of the individual's state.

8. See Michael Fixler's excellent essay on "Ecclesiology," in *A Milton Encyclopedia*, ed. William B. Hunter et al., 9 vols. (Lewisburg, Penn.: Bucknell University Press, 1978–79), 2:190–203.

9. Hooker's church polity is normative, I believe, for the Anglican communion. The fact that so many Laudian churchmen ignored or misrepresented his message, and that Milton may have misunderstood it does not change its essential meaning or significance. See Patrick Collinson, *The Elizabethan Puritan Movement* (Oxford:

Clarendon Press, 1967), on the later sixteenth century from the standpoint of Hooker's opponents; and *The Religion of Protestants* (Oxford: Clarendon Press, 1982), which demonstrates the continuity of the church from Elizabethan through Jacobean times. See also C. J. Sisson, *The Judicious Marriage of Mr. Hooker and the Birth of The Laws of Ecclesiastical Polity* (Cambridge: Cambridge University Press, 1940), which, with David Novarr's *The Making of Walton's Lives* (Ithaca: Cornell University Press, 1958), helps to describe the circumstances of Hooker's great enterprise and its immediate fate.

10. See John R. Knott, Jr., *The Sword of the Spirit: Puritan Responses to the Bible* (Chicago: University of Chicago Press, 1980), 122–23.

11. See my discussion of the provenance of Hooker's work along with an edition of it in Hooker, ed. Stanwood, 3: 451–61, supplement 1. See also the historical sketch by Don M. Wolfe in his introduction to the episcopal tracts in *CPW,* 1:193–203.

12. See Hooker, ed. Edelen, 1: 256–58; book 3,11.11–12. Milton further discusses 1 Timothy in *Of Prelatical Episcopacy* where he also dismisses the claim that bishops were known in apostolic times (*CPW,* 1:630–34).

13. See Hooker, ed. Stanwood, 3, xiii–xxvi, 462–538. Hooker lived to see the publication of the preface and books 1–4 (1593) and book 5 (1597); the last three ("posthumous") books first appeared with the *Works* in 1662, but a small part of book 6 and most of book 8 were published (probably through Archbishop Ussher's intervention) in 1648 although manuscripts of book 8 had been circulating in the early years of the seventeenth century. See "Publishing History," in Edelen's edition (with the collaboration of W. Speed Hill), 1: xiii–xxvii. See also Rudolph Almasy, "Richard Hooker's Book 6: A Reconstruction," *Huntington Library Quarterly* 42 (1979): 115–39.

14. Milton alludes to the controversy on the position of the altar, or "holy table" (*CG, CPW,* 1:771). Should the altar be in the east end and treated reverently, or set among the people in the midst of the church?

15. See also McGrade, ed., *Laws:* "Hooker's own appeal is to a judgement of conscience, for he sees that unless his own party and opposing parties can live together in good conscience, there will be no law or community left to defend" (xxx).

16. The very complicated political and ecclesiastical history of this period is impossible to summarize briefly. But an outline of major events appears in C. V. Wedgwood, *The King's Peace 1637–1641: The Great Rebellion* (London: Collins, 1955), especially 85–125. An important recent study about the Caroline period is by Kevin Sharpe, *The Personal Rule of Charles I* (New Haven: Yale University Press, 1992).

17. Cf. the Elder Brother's speech in *Comus* (381–84):

> He that has light within his own clear breast
> May sit i'th' center, and enjoy bright day,
> But he that hides a dark soul and foul thoughts
> Benighted walks under the midday Sun.

18. For the sake of both church and state, Milton appealed to the "purity" of the scriptures and to the early apostolic church and the first Council at Jerusalem (*ca.* A.D. 49; see Acts 15). He was thus a "puritan" in this special sense of desiring the church to be governed according to a reformed model, whence an appropriate political democracy would necessarily follow.

19. See Maurice Kelley's introduction to *De Doctrina Christiana, CPW,* 6:3–116; and see W. B. Hunter, C. A. Patrides, and J. H. Adamson, *Bright Essence: Studies in*

Milton's Theology (Salt Lake City: University of Utah Press, 1971). Cf. Hunter's revisionary argument for "The Provenance of the *Christian Doctrine*" in *Studies in English Literature* 32 (1992): 129–66.

20. The lines are quoted from book 1, chap. 29, "Of the Visible Church."

21. See Paul Avis, *Anglicanism and the Christian Church: Theological Resources in Historical Perspectives* (Minneapolis: Fortress Press, 1989), especially chap. 4, "Architects of Anglican Ecclesiology: Richard Hooker," and also W. J. Torrance Kirby, *Richard Hooker's Doctrine of the Royal Supremacy* (Leiden: E. J. Brill, 1990). I am also generally indebted to many discussions with my colleagues who have worked on the Hooker edition, particularly to John E. Booty, A. S. McGrade, and W. Speed Hill.

22. See Hooker, *Tractates and Sermons*, ed. Laetitia Yeandle and Egil Grislis (Cambridge: Belknap Press of Harvard University Press, 1990), The Folger Library Edition of the Works of Richard Hooker, 5: 154, 149.

23. Hooker has adapted a passage from Arnobius, a Christian apologist of the early fourth century, author of *Disputationem Adversus Gentes*. See Lee W. Gibbs on "The Source of the Most Famous Quotation from Richard Hooker's *Laws of Ecclesiastical Polity*," *Sixteenth Century Journal* 21 (1990): 77–86.

The Craftsmanship of God:
Some Structural Contexts for the
Poems of Mr. John Milton (1645)

MAREN-SOFIE RØSTVIG

The generally accepted view of Milton's *Poems* (1645) is that in it Milton explores "the appropriate roles for poetry and the poet," which permits him to "invent, publicize, and defend his own identity as poet-prophet."[1] To this unity of purpose, however, must be added the unity created by Milton's grouping of some of his poems according to genre and chronology, or according to the principle of juxtaposition as shown in the companion poems. When more than two poems are involved, the issue becomes one of intertextuality, and Joseph Wittreich has argued that to make "arrangements mirror a dialectical interplay between poems" is a distinctly Miltonic device.[2] Contexture is yet another key concept: a contexture exists when contexts "are provided for each poem by the larger frame within which it is placed."[3] In what follows I hope to define some of Milton's arrangements more precisely than has been done so far, and to relate these arrangements to the textual structures found in individual poems. Spenser was an adept at combining highly structured poems into highly structured collections,[4] and Milton was no less adept, although the 1645 *Poems* cannot be said to constitute an integrated collection like *The Shepheardes Calender*; there are, instead, framing poems and ordered progressions within the frames.[5]

Spenser's poetry will provide points of reference, and so will Giles Fletcher's *Christs Victorie, and Triumph* (1610).[6] Behind these two, though, looms the father figure of Augustine; it is unlikely (to put it mildly) that Milton would have been ignorant of the biblically based structural poetics advocated by Augustine in so many of his works,[7] and I believe that he was aware of the circumstance that it conditions the form of Augustine's spiritual epic, the *Confessions*.[8] Milton was also bound to be familiar with the structural exegesis of the Psalms as exemplified by Cassiodorus whose *Expositio Psalmorum* was the authoritative textbook for the Middle Ages and the Renaissance. Whoever reads Cassiodorus knows that he considered as meaningful the textual arrangement of individual psalms (such as Psalm 119, the accepted pattern for Nativity hymns), groups of psalms, and the Psalter as a whole.[9] These, then, are the contexts I shall adduce.

1

By 1645 Milton was a mature poet; sixteen years had passed since he wrote *On the Morning of Christs Nativity*, eleven since *Comus*, and seven since *Lycidas*. Milton's collection of that year is odd in some ways. Why, for example, omit "On the Death of a Fair Infant" (printed in 1673), and why include the unfinished "The Passion"? And why give a separate title-page to *Comus* (dated 1645), to the sequence of largely Latin poems, and to the *Epitaphium Damonis*? Some evidence of order is found in the groups organized by genre and chronology, as in the ten sonnets and the seven Latin elegies, but what about the remaining poems? And if the *Nativity Ode* was placed first because of its sacred subject, are there other examples of what we may call logical placing? But can we expect logic when two epitaphs (one on the Marchioness of Winchester and one on Shakespeare) are separated by the "Song. On *May* morning"? That we should proceed from two jesting poems on the university carrier to *L'Allegro*, and from *Il Penseroso* to the sonnet on the nightingale is more appropriate. On the other hand, we also find that poems on similar subjects do not adjoin each other, as in the case of "On Time" (item 5) and the sonnet on time ("How soon hath Time the suttle theef of youth"; item 21). And the praise of spring in *Elegia quinta* harks back to "Song. On *May* morning," the *Elegia sexta* to the companion poems, and the *Elegia septima* to Sonnet IV. Another linkage (often noted) is between the *Epitaphium Damonis* (last in the second sequence) and *Lycidas* (last in the first). Yet another observation is that Psalm 114 figures in both parts, in one paraphrased in English, in the other in Greek.

Let us begin the quest for answers by surveying the items that constitute the collection. There are three parts: (1) 26 poems in English and Italian concluding with a pastoral elegy; (2) *Comus*; and (3) 26 poems in Latin and Greek concluding with a pastoral elegy.[10] The numerical balance between the first part and the last is exact, even including the number of languages used, and *Comus* functions admirably as a centerpiece, expressing as it does Milton's main theme of the conflict between purity and corruption, harmony and discord. This conflict informs the *Nativity Ode* as well as *Lycidas* (items 1 and 26) and the concluding *Epitaphium Damonis*. We find the same antithesis in the companion poems, whose placing as items 13 and 14 makes them the halfway point in the first sequence, Janus-like looking backward in the direction of the joy of the Nativity and forward to the elevated seriousness of *Lycidas*. These observations suggest that the 1645 *Poems* may have been arranged so that a poem could gain an added dimension from a consideration of its placing within the whole. That some degree of balance is entailed is equally obvious.

Since the reading experience is one of great variety, a search for relevant contexts must begin with the classical *sylva* (or *silva*) as exemplified by the group of Latin poems that Milton entitled *Sylvarum liber*.[11] As Julius Caesar Scaliger defined it, a sylva is above all characterized by variety, and according to Quintilian the poems should be "expressed spontaneously and with warmth." The term refers to the crowded character of the subjects or to their roughness. Among the subjects considered suitable for a sylva, Quintilian mentions praises of a place or a person, and among genres epithalamia, birthday odes, panegyrics, hymns, elegies, epigrams, invocations, and palinodes.[12] The list is as valid for Milton's *Poems* as for Ben Jonson's *The Forrest* (1616), and further examples are Ben Jonson's *Underwood* (1640) and Andrew Marvell's *Miscellaneous Poems* (1673).[13] However, to explain Milton's placing of the *Nativity Ode* at the head of his collection and his overall strategy as well, we must also adduce the Psalms as glossed by theologians like Augustine and Cassiodorus. In some ways the Psalms resemble a sylva: some are very short, others very long and thematic variety is great, ranging from praise and blame, penitential confession (a kind of palinode), and sound doctrine to prophetic vision. Then, too, there are identifiable groups such as the fifteen Psalms of Ascent, the seven penitential psalms, psalms that have the same superscription, and psalms that consider the same topic. One scholar who has seen the relevance of the Psalms to early seventeenth-century poetry is Alastair Fowler who relates the fifteen poems in Ben Jonson's *The Forrest* to the fifteen Psalms of Ascent. In Ben Jonson's collection an "inner structure of ascent" matches the external structure of the fifteen items that take us from earthly to heavenly love.[14]

To Cassiodorus (480?–575), the Psalms formed a highly unified collection where each psalm is placed exactly where it must be to preserve the same order which we find in the Bible as a whole and in the created universe (God's works in space and time). The sum total of psalms (150), like the number of the Psalms of Ascent (15), shows that they take us from time to eternity, from the Old Testament to the New, and they do this because 70 + 80 = 150, just as 7 + 8 = 15, and 7 is the number of time as 8 is of eternity (because Christ rose the eighth day in Easter week).[15] It was axiomatic that the Psalms are a summary and abridgement of the Bible, but the argument is not wholly numerical. Psalm 1 was taken to refer to Christ; Christ is the *beatus vir* and the "tree planted by the rivers of water" (Ps. 1:1–3), just as he is the Tree of Life in the midst of the Garden (Gen. 2:9) and the tree planted by the water of life in the midst of the heavenly Jerusalem (Rev. 22:1–2). Hence Christ is at the beginning and end of the Psalms and of the Bible as a whole as he is of all things (Rev. 1:8 and 22:13).[16] Another link between the beginning and end of the Bible is the union between Adam and Eve and the marriage union between Christ and his spouse (the Church) at the end of time as narrated in the Book of Revelation. Such biblical "framing devices" are far more important than anything we find in Horace or elsewhere,[17] and Milton's placing of the *Nativity Ode* first and *Lycidas* last (within the first part) therefore mirrors the overall structure attributed to the Psalms and to the Bible as a whole. Since the *Epitaphium Damonis* too concludes with an apocalyptic vision of a marriage union in Heaven, this is true also of the 1645 collection as a whole. The *Ode* celebrates the marriage between Heaven and Earth in the incarnation, *Lycidas* and the *Epitaphium Damonis* the immortal marriage in Heaven itself.

Psalm 1 is a particularly interesting context for the *Ode* since Cassiodorus saw it as the source from which all the psalms issue and to which they return in the last *carmen* which has no textual divisions because it represents our return to the state of unity in Christ our head. Thus the Psalms terminate on a note of sweet grace that somehow looks back to the beginning. The end must connect with the beginning, because Holy Writ must display harmony (*omnia conuenientia*). To Cassiodorus, Christ is at the beginning in the same way that the Monad is at the beginning of all numbers, and the multitude of numbers proceed from him in such a way that they may achieve a return—which means that they are organized according to the Pythagorean and Platonic formulas for world harmony. Hence Cassiodorus adds that numbers must be studied; the Fathers of the Church have said so, and we read in Solomon that God made everything in number, weight, and measure (Wisd. 11:21). Cassiodorus here repeats what Augustine himself says in the *De Trinitate* (IV.viii.10) and *De Doctrina Christiana* (II.xvi.25).[18] When Milton gave the first place in his *Poems* (1645) to the *Nativity Ode*, therefore, the placing defines Christ as creator and redeemer and the source of all harmony, including the harmony of his verse.

Milton was certainly not alone in looking to the Psalms for inspiration; Spenser had already done so in *The Shepheardes Calender* (1579), whose chronological scheme ("Loe I have made a Calender for every yeare") takes us from the beginning to the end of time like the Psalms. Spenser's scheme of the four seasons should be aligned not only with the ages of man as described in the *December* eclogue, but also with the ages into which world history was traditionally divided.[19] Another link between the *Calender* and the Psalms is perceived on reading what Thomas Becon, that redoubted Elizabethan clergyman, has to say about David. David was a plain and rude "minstrel" who "lacked ye chefe poynt of a Mynstrell & of a syngyng man, which is to lye & flatter," which was due to the fact that David "kept shepe to longe for to be a Mynstrell to such delycate & softe religious parsons. But Dauid was a good, playne, simple, & homely man brought vp in ye countre." He is no dissembler, but on the contrary "as playn as a pack staffe."[20] The "rudeness" of Spenser's diction may well reflect this supposed rudeness of the shepherd poet, king, and prophet. The organization attributed to the Psalms is mirrored in the *Calender*'s symmetrical structure, which is seen most clearly by focusing on the moral import of each eclogue. The wounded pride displayed in *Januarye* has in *December* been exchanged for humility, and at the center (*June* and *Julye*) pride and humility are contrasted. In between these three points other moral qualities form a pattern of recessed symmetry. Thus ambition links *February* and *November*: the tale of the oak and the briar exposes unsound political ambition, but ambition is taken in a good sense (*in bono*)[21] when Colin's muse is challenged ("Up then *Melpomene*"), at the same time that the 15 stanzas of the Lay of Dido mark an ascent to heavenly bliss. The subject of love connects *March* and *October*—the one earthly and the other the love that raises the mind above the starry sky (line 94). Compassion with a friend's misfortune connects *April* and *September*, while *May* and *August* contrast the rewards of concupiscence and innocence.

We find the same symmetrical structure in the *Epithalamion*, as Max A. Wickert has shown; instead of the progression of the months, here the unifying idea is that of a procession to and from the church and the progression of the marriage ritual.[22] The habit of composing in this way was so strong that Spenser obeyed it even when he wrote the sixteen dedicatory sonnets prefixed to *The Faerie Queene*.[23] Spenser has clarified his structural intent by referring to the sonnets as a "Pageaunt" where each person addressed is given his proper place (sonnets 8 and 9), and again as a "garlond" (sonnet 16). The linkage between the beginning, middle, and end is particularly strong. The two first sonnets honor the men who, like powerful pillars, uphold the burden of the state (the sonnets are linked by the repetition of the phrases "graue affaires" and the "burdeine of this kingdom"); the sonnets at the center (8 and 9) praise the men who have defended the realm against external enemies (8) and base rebels (9), and sonnets 15 and 16 pay homage to two noble ladies who form the procession's triumphal conclusion. It is their achievement to "triumph ouer feeble eyes" and to "tyranyse" in "subdued harts." The sonnets in between display recessed symmetry. The poet's modesty links sonnets 3 and 14, and 7 and 10: his verse is unripe fruit, unsavory and sour (3 and 14), mere wild fruit from savage soil, far from the hill of Parnassus (7 and 10). The verbal repetitions make the linking easy to observe ("wilde fruit, which saluage soyl hath bred" is repeated as "Rude rymes, the which a rustick Muse did weaue / In sauadge soyle"). However, poetry bestows immortality (4 and 13). Other linking topoi are praise of the queen (6 and 11), elevation (5 and 12; raising the mind and raising the lowly muse), and seeing the "deeper sence" of the poem and the father's image reflected in the daughter's face (2 and 15). The sonnets, then, form a pageant of honor, and in this pageant society appears as a sylva or forest of splendid individual trees much like the catalog of trees in *The Faerie Queene* (1.1.8–9). In this catalog the earthly and the heavenly king find appropriate placing: the king (the oak) is flanked by 4 + 2 trees (i.e., the ratio 2:1), while Christ (the "Mirrhe sweete bleeding in the bitter wound") is at the center of 6 + 6 trees as if in the middle of his apostles. Judas is there in the maple tree, rotten at the core.

2

Similar structures may be found in the 26 poems in English and Italian that form the first part of Milton's *Poems* (1645). The linear progression from the *Ode* to "The Passion" (item 4) is plain, and in between are paraphrases of two psalms (114 and 136) that describe the great Old Testament types of Redemption, the exodus and the crossing of the Red Sea and the river Jordan.[24] The incomplete character of "The Passion" suggests the tradition of the sylva in its aspect of a rough draft. Perhaps "The Passion" was thought to present a young poet hurried by his emotions (as suggested by Quintilian) in a direction he was as yet incapable of sustaining. The religious vein is continued in the next three poems (items 5, 6, and 7), "On Time," "Upon the Circumcision," and "At a solemn Musick." All three present God, "High thron'd in secret bliss" who "Emptied his glory, ev'n to nakednes" ("Upon the Circumcision," 19–20), and it is before his "saphire-colour'd throne" that the heavenly music sounds "everlastingly" ("At a solemn Musick," 5–16). The music of course takes us back to the *Nativity Ode*, and so does the related topos of Eternity. The harmony of Eternity (its "ninefold harmony" and "holy Song") informs the centrally placed stanzas 13–15 of the *Ode*, the centrally placed lines 11–12 of "On Time" ("Then long Eternity shall greet our bliss / With an individual kiss"), and lines 6–7 and 16 of "At a solemn Musick" ("That undisturbed Song of pure content, / Ay sung before the saphire-colour'd throne . . . . Singing everlastingly"). Joy and music are featured even in "The Passion" ("Ere-while of Musick, and Ethereal mirth . . . . My muse with Angels did divide to sing"; 1–4), and the grief of contemplating the Passion soon yields to a "holy vision" experienced in "pensive trance, and anguish, and ecstatick fit" (6:6–7). (This fusion between joy and anguish recalls Giles Fletcher's *Christs Victorie, and Triumph* III.66 on the "joyful misery" felt on contemplating the death of Christ.) The joy of being delivered by the Lord from slavery resounds through the two paraphrases of the Psalms, thus increasing the feeling that the first seven items form a substructure or "contexture" where the linkage is particularly strong between items 1, 4, and 7. One reason, then, why Milton included "The Passion" must have been that he needed it as a center-piece for this particular group of poems. The restoration of the fair music (*Ode*, "At a solemn Musick") depends on the Passion— a familiar idea expressed, for example, by George Herbert in "Easter" ("His stretched sinews taught all strings, what key / Is best to celebrate this most high day"; 2:5–6). If we listen to this music, we shall "keep in tune with Heav'n" ("At a solemn Musick," 26).

The "Epitaph on the Marchioness of Winchester" (item 8) shifts the emphasis to the fate of an individual whose death, though, is the prelude to her triumphant reception in Heaven. The feeling of linear continuity is apparently broken with the "Song. On *May* morning" (item 9), but Nature has its types as well as the Old Testament, and the "bright morning Star, Dayes harbinger" that "Comes dancing from the East" is replete with allusions to the resurrection. Giles Fletcher's *Christs Victorie, and Triumph* (1610) furnishes what may be a source: with the resurrection the early sun comes "lively daunc-ing out" (IV.1:6), and the "bright morning Starre, / . . . Springs lively up into the orient" (IV.12:1–5). All of nature is reborn in a spring that is much more than just a natural phenomenon. This is traditional enough, but Giles Fletcher's treatment of spring is sustained and memorable and occurs in the passage that furnished some of the phrases for the *Nativity Ode* (see below). "On Shakespear" (item 10) connects with the "Epitaph" (item 8) through the image of the marble tomb ("This rich Marble doth enterr"). The "languisht Mothers Womb" becomes a "living Tomb" for the unborn child, but Shake-speare does not need "the labour of an age in piled Stones," since he is already "Sepulcher'd" in the marble into which we are all turned "with too much conceaving." Hence it is we who are Shakespeare's living tombs. This witty consideration of death is taken to a point of wonderful absurdity in the two poems on the university carrier (items 11 and 12), after which follow the companion poems with their double emphasis on mirth and pensiveness. In *L'Allegro* several themes and topoi refer us back to the earlier poems: the May morn-ing is there (17–24), and so are the "Quips and Cranks" of the poems on the university carrier (25–32)[25]; the shepherds on the lawn reap-pear in all their simple rusticity (57–68), and voice and verse meet again in the "*Lydian* Aires, / Married to immortal verse" (136–37). Shakespeare puts in another appearance (132ff.), just as the "melting voice" untwists "all the chains that ty / The hidden soul of harmony" (142–44). This invocation of the soul of harmony refers us back to its solemn celebration in the *Ode*, while Orpheus in "golden slumber on a bed / Of heapt *Elysian* flowers" (145–46) forms a mythic ana-logue to the "sleeping Lord" in the last stanza of the *Ode*.

The second half—from *Il Penseroso* to *Lycidas*—gives equal prominence to the theme of harmony: Orpheus figures in *L'Allegro* (145–50), *Il Penseroso* (105–8), and *Lycidas* (58–63), and the theme of song, in voice or verse, is virtually omnipresent. In the companion poems (items 13–14) Orphic song commands Hell itself (*L'All,* 148–50; *Il P,* 108), and in *Lycidas* it becomes the "unexpressive nup-tiall Song, / In the blest Kingdoms meek of joy and love" (176–77). Sonnet I ("O Nightingale, that on yon bloomy Spray / Warbl'st at eeve") pitches the theme in a personal key, but such are the associations connected with the nightingale that the bird's "amorous power" becomes semi-divine, while the cuckoo becomes a Satanic "rude Bird of Hate" that foretells his doom. Those who listen to the song of the bird (and the song of the poet) will become attuned to the music of God's works in space (creation) and time (redemption). As Anna K. Nardo points out, Milton associates the song of the nightingale with cosmic harmony in his second Cambridge prolusion, written near the time when he composed the sonnet.[26] The ten numbered sonnets (items 15–24) divide into 6 + 1 + 3 as indicated by their subjects. Song and love are the related themes of Sonnet I (in English) and Sonnets II–VI (in Italian); Sonnet VII is the well-known personal sonnet on time ("the suttle theef of youth"), and Sonnets VIII–X are concerned with moral and religious (or public) issues. Sonnet VII, therefore, is in a pivotal position between respectively 6 and 3 sonnets, thus creating the ratio of the diapason, 2:1 (on this ratio, see below). The arrangement therefore suggests that harmony prevails between the private and the public sphere—that it is the goodness of the individual that preserves the goodness of the state, as in Sonnet X. A link between Sonnets I and X is found in the antithesis between good and evil: just as the "rude Bird of Hate" threatens the poet's quest for love in Sonnet I, in Sonnet X the good earl and his daughter are threatened by "a hostile and dishonest world."[27] In the pivotal Sonnet VII the threat is posited by time itself: despite his "late spring" no "bud or blossom shew'th." But the parallel is with a difference: while the nightingale is exhorted "now timely sing," in Sonnet VII the poet is content to wait for the desired "inward ripenes" until it is given to him by the "will of Heav'n." We see, then, how the first sonnet and the last are connected, and both in their turn with Sonnet VII.

Each subsection (Sonnets I–VI and VIII–X) has its own textual structure as well. Linear linkage is observed when we pass from the song of the nightingale (I) to the power of the lady's speech and song (II), and from there to the poet's own song (III) and to the language of which love boasts (the *Canzone* added to Sonnet III as an unnumbered item). From the subject of the foreign tongue in the *Canzone* we turn to the foreign lady and her gift of song (IV), and familiar Petrarchan images of eyes and heart link Sonnets IV–VI. In Sonnet VI the poet's dedication of himself to "the melodious lyre, and the Muses"[28] returns us to the beginning in Sonnet I with its affirmation of service to the muses and to love. This linkage between the beginning and the end suggests a symmetrical structure, which is perceived when we consider the *Canzone* as a center, flanked by three sonnets. The canzone's praise of a "lingua ignota e strana" (a language unknown and foreign) is flanked by sonnets on the English poet as a plant on foreign soil (III), and (IV) on praise of a "nova idea / Pellegrina bellezza" ("a foreign beauty of a new pattern"). This foreignness may be more than just a matter of nationality; Milton seems to be hinting at a new and altogether higher kind of speech capable of conveying more than mortal love. Perhaps this is the self-transcendence that Nardo characterizes as the theme which unifies all Milton's sonnets.[29] The idea that links Sonnets II and V is the lady's power—the power of her Orphic song (II) and the power of her eyes (V). In the English sonnets VIII–X, the center is occupied by climactic praise of an unnamed and unknown young lady ("in the prime of earliest youth") who has "shun'd the broad way and the green," instead laboring up "the Hill of heav'nly Truth." She has chosen "The better part with *Mary*, and with *Ruth*," undeterred by a world hostile to virtue. She is the "Virgin wise and pure" who will pass "to bliss at the mid hour of night" on the arrival of "the Bridegroom with his feastfull friends." This sonnet, then, bestows praise and fame, and in the preceding sonnet this power of bestowing fame is playfully used to deter the invasion of the home by hostile "Captain or Colonel, or Knight in Arms." In the concluding sonnet praise is again offered for the "noble vertues" that constitute fame.

There are interesting thematic parallels between Milton's sonnets and Spenser's sixteen dedicatory sonnets. The difference of course is marked since Milton distances himself from the idea of patronage that was so important to Spenser. Spenser addresses Lord Grey as the "Patrone of my Muses pupillage," but for Milton it is God's gifts alone that can provide "inward ripenes" (Sonnet VII). However, Milton's sequence, like Spenser's, contains praise of the man who has upheld the burden of the state (Spenser's sonnets 1 and 2, and Milton's Sonnet X); both poets express their dedication to poetry and the muses (Milton's Sonnet I and Spenser's sonnets 4, 6, and passim); both are self-conscious about their unripeness (Milton's Sonnet VII and Spenser's sonnets 7 and 10), both praise martial valor, although Milton does so ironically (Milton's Sonnet VIII, Spenser's sonnets 5, 8, 9, and 13), and both conclude with two sonnets addressed to ladies. And just as Spenser's sonnet 15 discovers the father's "goodly image" in "the diuine resemblance of your face," Milton exclaims in Sonnet X that the father lives in the daughter: "yet by you / Madam, me thinks I see him living yet." To these thematic parallels can be added more precise echoes. Milton's playful allusion to himself in Sonnet III as a strange plant that grows "weakly" in an "alien air, far from its own nourishing springtime," recalls Spenser's twice-repeated complaint that his verse is wild fruit grown in savage soil far from the hill of Parnassus (sonnets 7 and 10). Similarly Milton's Sonnet VIII addressed to "Captain or Colonel, or Knight in Arms" may owe something to Spenser's sonnet 13 to "the most valiaunt Captaine, Sir Iohn Norris knight," whose opening lines express the argument presented by Milton: "Who euer gaue more honourable prize / To the sweet Muse, then did the Martiall crew; / That their braue deeds she might immortalize / In her shril tromp, and sound their praises dew?" The concluding couplet presents the lesson that Milton uses to such good effect: "Sith then each where thou hast dispredd they fame, / Loue him, that hath eternized your name." The occurrence of these themes and topoi in both sequences is sufficiently striking to suggest that Spenser was very much in Milton's mind as he composed some of his sonnets, and as he arranged his ten sonnets in the sequence that we have in the *Poems* (1645).

As we approach the conclusion of the first sequence, "Arcades" (item 25) repeats ideas featured in the companion poems at the same time that it points forward to *Lycidas*. Thus the "Genius of the Wood" (44–45; *Il P,* 154) is active "early ere the odorous breath of morn / Awakes the slumbring leaves, or tasseld horn" (56–57), just as the speaker in *L'Allegro* oft listens "how the Hounds and horn, / Chearly rouse the slumbring morn" (53–54). The Genius enjoys being "amidst these shades alone," and "in deep of night" he listens "To the celestial *Sirens* harmony, / That sit upon the nine enfolded Sphears, / And sing to those that hold the vital shears" (61–65; cp. *Il P,* 151–54 and *L'All,* 143–50). The power of music is such that it draws "the low world in measur'd motion" after "the heavenly tune" ("Arcades," 70–72; cp. also "At a solemn Musick," 25–26). While the Genius protects the wood and brushes off "the evil dew" and heals what "hurtfull worm with canker'd venom bites" (50–53), in *Lycidas* "Canker" and "Taintworm" and untimely frost ravage flowers and "weanling Herds" (45–47), just as the "blind *Fury* with th'abhorred shears" wilfully "slits the thin-spun life" (75–76). Instead of music, there is the harsh noise made by "scrannel pipes of wretched straw" (124)—until the sudden reversal when harmony reasserts itself through the power of Christ. The suddenness of the transition echoes the suddenness with which the joy of the resurrection manifested itself, and this joy returns us to the *Nativity Ode,* thus closing the circle of the first part of *Poems* 1645.

3

Symmetrical and graded arrangements are found also in individual poems. M. Christopher Pecheux has observed that the textual structure of "At a solemn Musick" creates the ratio of the diapason,[30] and further examples are not far to seek. Song and music and "measur'd motion" are recurring ideas that may influence the structure of the poems where they prevail. The historical background for this tradition extends back to Augustine and Plato[31]; in the *De musica* VI and the *De vera religione* Augustine praises *aequalitas* structures (formed by the ratios 1:1 and 1:2). These are rational rhythms that take the mind back to God as their source, whether contemplated in God's works in space and time, or in a work of art.[32] To refer to cosmic structures is not enough; the structures attributed to the record of God's work of redemption in Holy Writ are just as important. Their interdependence is shown when theologians relate the number 12 not only to the tribes of Judah and the apostles, but also to the signs of the zodiac, just as the 4 gospels connect with the 4 elements, the 4 humors, the 4 corners of the earth, and so forth. As Bonaventura states, the Scriptures are most highly ordered, and their order is like that of nature (*Collationes in Hexaemeron,* XIV.5).[33] Augustine's *De Trinitate* IV attributes the ratio 2:1 to the works of creation and redemption as an expression of their harmony, and in Greek thought harmony included the concept of *rhythmos*, the basic meaning of which is to *join together*. Rhythmos is the principle of power which enables parts to be joined in meaningful wholes; when expressed in action it relates to *ethos*, so that any discussion of harmony must include virtue or *areté* (Plato, *Laws* 654ff.). The fact that Plato praises choral dancing shows that he accepted the old concept of *mousiké* as an ideal which fuses the arts of words, melody, and movement.[34] "At a solemn Musick" describes just such a fusion; before men fell, the love of God "their motion sway'd / In perfect Diapason" (22–23), and in "Arcades" music keeps "unsteddy Nature to her law" and the "low world" is drawn in "measur'd motion" "After the heavenly tune" (70–72). In "At a solemn Musick" this *rhythmos* is found in the division of the lines into a sequence of 16—8—4, or a twice-repeated diapason. Cassiodorus therefore thinks Platonically when he associates harmony with *obedience*. As we may read in his *Institutiones* (*Introduction to Divine and Human Readings*), musical science "is diffused through all the acts of our life if we before all else obey the commands of the Creator and observe with pure hearts the rules which he has established . . . . When we sin, however, we no longer have music."[35] Milton expresses this idea in *Paradise Lost* when Adam feels "the falt'ring measure" of Eve's footsteps after she has eaten of the fruit (9.846). The Christianization of Plato in Augustine and Cassiodorus is above all a Christianization of *mousiké*, as we may see for example in Augustine's *De Trinitate* IV. As a chapter heading puts it, "The one death and resurrection of the body of Christ harmonizes with our double death and resurrection of body and soul, to the effect of salvation. In what way the single death of Christ is bestowed upon our double death." Augustine also connects the ratio 1:2 or 2:1 with the work of creation by arguing that the number 6 (as in the 6 days of creation) is the sum of the digits in the formula $1 + 2 = 3$. Also 6 is the sum of 4 and 2.[36]

Milton was of course not the only poet to think in these terms about God and man. George Herbert's "Mans medley" plays around with the idea of man's "doubleness" in 6 6-line stanzas divided into $4 + 2$ by the contents. The subject of stanzas 1–4 is man's happy state. Unlike the beasts, man has double joys: "Mans joy and pleasure / Rather hereafter, then in present, is" (1:5–6). Also man joins two worlds, heaven and earth: "In soul he mounts and flies, / In flesh he dies" (3:1–2). A heavy *but* heralds the contemplation, in the last 2 stanzas, of the possibility of double death: "But as his joyes are double; / So is his trouble. / He hath two winters, other things but one," so that he "of all things fears two deaths alone" (5:1–3, 6). Hence "Happie is he, whose heart / Hath found the art / To turn his double pains to double praise" (6:4–6). The double praise must be for a double being (body and soul) capable of double life through the one death of Christ. The ratio 2:1 may be traced in the stanzaic pattern, too, consisting as it does of a couplet and a quatrain (aabccb), while the 6 6-line stanzas may relate to the work of creation which is Herbert's subject. Man's "doubleness" relates to the "singleness" of the creatures on the one hand, and, on the other, to the single death of Christ which ensures a double life for us.

Perhaps better known examples of the use of the ratio 2:1 are Spenser's *Epithalamion* where the change in the refrain divides the 24 stanzas into $16 + 8$, and the *Prothalamion* where stanza 7 (on the Thames which makes "his streame run slow") divides the 10 stanzas into 6—1—3, thus anticipating the arrangement of Milton's 10 sonnets. In Milton's sequence, too, item 7 marks a point of rest where the poet reflects on his own condition. In the *Prothalamion* the harmony is between the brides and the rural scene on the one hand, and, on the other, the grooms and the urban scene, in Milton's sonnets between private and public (or religious) issues. We find a similar joining together in *The Shepheardes Calender* where the last eclogue and the first have the same stanzaic pattern (unique within the sequence) at the same time that the number of stanzas—26 and 13—creates the ratio of the diapason. The harmonious ratio supports a positive interpretation of Colin's stance in *December*: just as in the octave the last note returns to the first, but in a higher key, Colin's humility in *December* expresses the elevation of his mind from the mortal to the immortal as he welcomes "timely death."

"On Time" is another poem that shows the care which Milton took to let the subject of a poem find expression in its textual structure. It has been argued that the 12 syntactical units coincide with the development of the theme so as to "present the visual image of a clock hand sweeping through its arc."[37] The circle is certainly closed when the last words in the last line (". . . O Time") hark back to the opening address ("Fly envious *Time* . . ."), at the same time that the uselessness of the flying is brought out by the contrast to those who "shall for ever sit, / Triumphing over Death, and Chance, and thee O Time." Eternity has been placed at the textual center in lines 11–12 ("Then long Eternity shall greet our bliss / With an individual kiss"), and this antithesis between time and eternity structures the whole poem, divided as it is into 10 lines on what is mere "mortal dross" (1–10) and another 10 on praise of what is divine (13–22). Related phrases are balanced with perfect precision. When the poem begins, time *runs* its futile race, and when it ends the soul *sits* in triumph; the downward movement of the heavy plummet (2–3) balances the ascending "heav'nly-guided soul" (19), "mortal dross" (5) is placed over against the "supreme Throne" (17), and "For when as each thing bad" (9) over against "When every thing that is sincerely good" (14). Just as the hand of the clock goes *down* from midnight to 6 A.M., and *up* from 6 A.M. to noon, negatives balance positives in a verbal enactment of this pattern.

Form and contents are equally glove-in-hand in "Upon the Circumcision," just as antitheses again function as a structuring principle: man's sins and transgressions are juxtaposed with Christ's atonement as foreshadowed by the pain of the circumcision. The poem consists of two 14-line stanzas, each of which is terminated by three short lines that envisage the Passion: "Alas, how soon" and "but O ere long." Each stanza, then, consists of 11 + 3 lines, where 11 is the number of transgression and contrition (because it goes beyond the just number 10) as explained by Cassiodorus.[38] The sum total of lines (14) is the number of redemption, since it is the sum of the law (10) and the gospels (4), or justice and grace. Since the contents serve as a gloss on these numbers, we must assume that the disposition is part of the invention; indeed, that the invention of the arrangement cannot be separated from the invention of the contents. Against man's transgression of, or going beyond, the great covenant, God places his own excess that functions entirely *in bono*: "O more exceeding love or law more just? / Just law indeed, but more exceeding love!" (15–16). The contrition for the transgression is the subject of stanza 1, while stanza 2 describes the exceeding love that prompted Christ's act of atonement for the transgression. A much simpler case of numerical decorum is found in the "Epitaph on the Marchioness of Winchester" whose 23 couplets on the life and death of the marchioness correspond to her age at death ("Summers three times eight save one"; line 7).

Among the Latin poems in the second part, the *Elegia sexta* has a simple but effective symmetrical pattern, while the *Epitaphium Damonis* combines symmetry with an arrangement in the ratio 2:1, like Spenser's *Epithalamion*. Although the *Elegia sexta* refers to the composition of the *Nativity Ode*, its affinity is rather with the companion poems whose bipartite structure is mirrored in the praise, first of convivial mirth with attendant harmonies in song and verse, and then of the frugal and chaste life called for in him who would sing of the deeds of gods and heroes. In the first 8 lines the topos of transcendence is put to witty use when Milton explains that no measured verse can contain the affection he feels for his friend; it must needs burst all bounds and will not "limp on elegiac feet." In the last 4 lines (note the ratio) the poetic inadequacy is equally stated: his lines have been "simply fashioned on my native pipes."[39] When we move inward from these framing passages, references to the Nativity connect lines 9–12 and 79–86, and yet another linkage is between passages on the connection between song and the gods:

> Carmen amat Bacchum, carmine Bacchus amat (14)
> Diis etenim sacer est vates, divumque sacerdos (77)

Song loves Bacchus, and Bacchus loves song, and Phoebus Apollo was not ashamed to prefer the ivy to his own laurel. In line 77, which is 14th from the end, this idea is presented in a higher key when the poet is said to be a priest, sacred to the gods. These passages connect directly with the center where Apollo is envisaged as stealing silently into the breast, penetrating the very bones with a sudden glow (43–48). It is after we have passed through this central passage that the transition is made to the poetry devoted to more serious concerns. The sacred character of the poet's task is foregrounded again in the

Epitaphium Damonis, a poem that cannot be justly assessed without a consideration of its structural felicities.

The elegy consists of 19 paragraphs or stanzas as indicated by the refrain, but the first sets the stage, as it were, so that the lament itself consists of 18 units divided into 12 + 6 (see diagrams). Para-

Epitaphium Damonis: 2–13 Summary, in English, of the contents of each paragraph.

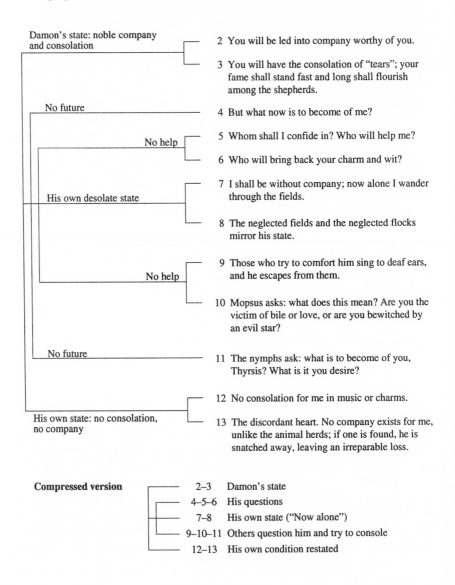

Damon's state: noble company and consolation

2 You will be led into company worthy of you.

3 You will have the consolation of "tears"; your fame shall stand fast and long shall flourish among the shepherds.

No future

4 But what now is to become of me?

No help

5 Whom shall I confide in? Who will help me?

6 Who will bring back your charm and wit?

His own desolate state

7 I shall be without company; now alone I wander through the fields.

8 The neglected fields and the neglected flocks mirror his state.

No help

9 Those who try to comfort him sing to deaf ears, and he escapes from them.

10 Mopsus asks: what does this mean? Are you the victim of bile or love, or are you bewitched by an evil star?

No future

11 The nymphs ask: what is to become of you, Thyrsis? What is it you desire?

12 No consolation for me in music or charms.

His own state: no consolation, no company

13 The discordant heart. No company exists for me, unlike the animal herds; if one is found, he is snatched away, leaving an irreparable loss.

Compressed version

2–3   Damon's state
4–5–6   His questions
7–8   His own state ("Now alone")
9–10–11 Others question him and try to console
12–13   His own condition restated

Epitaphium Damonis: 14–19 Summary of the contents of each paragraph.

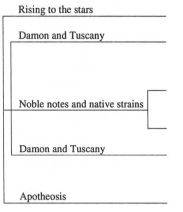

Rising to the stars

Damon and Tuscany

Noble notes and native strains

Damon and Tuscany

Apotheosis

14 If he had remained at home, he could have said
farewell: remember me as you rise to the stars.

15 I shall never weary of your memory; he
recalls happy days in Tuscany (the home of
Diodati's family), and the gifts he received, and
the love of Dati and Francini.

16 Because ignorant of his death, he thought of
Damon as still alive; his pipes broke when he
attempted noble notes.

17 But his pastoral pipe, changed, shall sound
forth a British theme in native strains.

18 He had kept Manso's gift of two cups for
Damon; he describes the figures which adorn
the cups, such as the phoenix and the heavenly
Cupid who kindles only sanctified minds.

19 You are among these and not in the Lethean
underworld; Damon's apotheosis.

graphs 2–13 on the irreparable loss display recessed symmetry, and
so do 14 –19 on the happy memories, the dedication to heroic song,
and the vision of Diodati in bliss. It is a structural *tour de force* that
the textual center by line-count (109–11) indicates the division into
the ratio 2:1 by forming the conclusion of paragraph 13; in these
lines the speaker states the human predicament: a man can hardly
find a single friend among thousands, and when Destiny gives you
one, he is snatched away at an hour when you least expect it. However, as in *The Shepheardes Calender*, the ratio of the diapason
strengthens the positive message of the conclusion.

4

If the *Nativity Ode* is associated with Psalm 1, its structure may conceivably define Christ as the source of the harmony it describes. It
may of course be said to do so through its structural numbers 8 and
27 (seen as a modified version of the 22 groups of 8 verses that constitute Psalm 119) and through its poised symmetry, but since I have
discussed these formal aspects elsewhere,[40] I shall focus instead on
the graded arrangement of the 27 stanzas as shown in my diagram.
The positive movement from the child in the rude manger to the full

and perfect bliss of the *regnum Christi* (the second coming) requires 18 stanzas, while 9 stanzas suffice for the negative movement on the cessation of imperfect types and the expulsion of the evil deities through the power of "The dredded Infants hand" (25:2). As in the first act of creation, what is "adverse to life" is purged off and like joined to like (*PL,* 7.235–42) to form a balanced universe. The positive and the negative movements relate as 2:1, thus showing the two aspects of Christ's power as creator and redeemer. Each of these

Nativity Ode: At all structural levels the ratio 2:1 shows the harmony of God's works in time and space.

In medio annorum	The CHILD in the manger Nature's reaction	2	1 2		
			3		
	Universal PEACE 8	4	4 5	12	
			6		
	Reaction of the sun and the shepherds	2	7 8		18
			9		
	The MUSIC of the angels	4	10		
The beginning: Christ as creator	The MUSIC of creation		11 12		
ETERNITY	The POWER of HARMONY		13 14 15	6	
The end: Christ as judge	MUSIC of redemption		16 17		
	Judgment Day and the Regnum Christi		18		
	Shadowy types must cease		19 20 21	6	9
	Evil powers expelled		22 23 24		
	The POWER of the "dredded Infants hand"		25 26	3	
In medio annorum	The BABE at rest		27		

major divisions accommodates substructures that keep repeating the ratio of the basic harmony of the diapason: the 18 stanzas divide into 12 + 6, the 9 into 6 + 3, and the 12 stanzas in their turn into 8 + 4. That the main line of division occurs between stanzas 18 and 19 is shown when the opening lines of stanza 18 fuse the first and the second coming, thus returning us to the beginning: "And then at last our bliss / Full and perfect is, / But now begins." The repetition of the same or related words helps to identify the substructures. In stanzas 3–6 *peace* and related words are conspicuous: "meek-eyd Peace" "strikes a universall Peace through Sea and Land" (3:2 and 8); there is "No War" (4:1), "peacefull was the night" (5:1) when "the Prince of Light / His raign of peace upon the earth began" (5:1–3), and the very stars "Stand fixt in stedfast gaze" (6:1–2). These stanzas are framed by stanzas on the response to the event by earth and the sun. In stanza 2 the earth "woo's the gentle Air" to cover her "naked shame" with the "Saintly Vail of Maiden white," and shame is the key word placed in rhyme position in stanza 7 as well, where we read that the sun "hid his head for shame" to see "a greater Sun appear." The rustic rudeness of the manger in stanza 1 similarly finds its analogue in stanza 8 in the "silly thoughts" of the "Shepherds on the Lawn." Stanzas 1–8, then, may well be conceived of as 2 + 4 + 2 stanzas, that is, as 4 stanzas framed by groups of 2. Stanzas 9–12 on the music of the angels are unified by similar or identical phrases: "such musick sweet" (9:1), "such pleasure" (9:7), "such sound" (10:1), "such harmony" (10:7), and "Such Musick" (12:1). Stanzas 13–15 envisage the power of the heavenly harmony (which is the source of the song of the angels) to restore the "age of gold" and reinstitute the reign where Mercy will be "set between" Truth and Justice. Although "This must not yet be so" (16:2), stanzas 16–18 take us to the end of time on Judgment Day when "at last our bliss / Full and perfect is, / But now begins," and now is of course the moment, *in medio annorum*, when Christ became incarnate in the child in the "rude manger." In the last 9 stanzas the power of the infant (25–27) is opposed to those who feel its manifestation (19–24). Sad and dreary sounds prevail in the 3 stanzas on the cessation of what is imperfect (19–21): "hideous humm" (19:2), "hollow shreik" (19:6), "loud lament" (20:3), and "A drear, and dying sound" (21:5). Finally the repetition, in initial position, of "In vain" (22:8, 23:4, and 24:7) connects the 3 stanzas on the expulsion of what is evil.

We observe that all thematic groupings are based on the numbers 2 and 3 and their multiples, as in Plato's *lambda* formula (2 and 3 squared and cubed).[41] It is part of this formula that the cubes are harmonized by the mean numbers 12 and 18 (8:12::12:18::18:27), and these 4 numbers were taken to represent the 4 elements harmonized by Christ, a view often expressed in comments on Ezekiel's vision of the chariot with all its groups of 4. We cannot understand Milton's subsequent use, in *Paradise Lost,* of this vision without familiarity with arithmetical theology (to use Sir Thomas Browne's term). The structure of Milton's *Ode* reveals the primacy of the ratio of the diapason in Renaissance thought concerning the harmony of creation and of God's plan of redemption, a primacy which derives from the fact that it contains within itself all the other consonances and their ratios. The structure shows, too, how the symmetrical and the graded arrangements are perfectly aligned, and the perfection of this alignment recalls *The Faerie Queene,* book 1, whose 12 cantos possess both a symmetrical structure and a division into 8 + 4, as I explain elsewhere.[42] Milton, then, based the structure of his *Ode* on the most powerful abstract image of perfect harmony known to the Renaissance, thus creating an analogue to Spenser's *Epithalamion* and providing the earliest example of the structural craftsmanship largely responsible for the successful presentation of the divine scheme of creation and redemption in *Paradise Lost.*

The complexity of the textual structures explains why different scholars have traced such different patterns; however, if one pays careful attention not only to loosely stated themes but also to the verbal texturing, I believe that the divisions indicated here must be accepted. To perceive the significance of these divisions, though, one must be familiar with the "common gloss of theologians" on Psalms 1 and 119, and on the overall structure of the Psalms.

Milton's indebtedness to part 4 of *Christs Victorie, and Triumph* provides supporting evidence, consisting as it does in structural as well as verbal and thematic parallels. Stanzas IV.1–15 describe the reaction, by nature, men, and angels, to the resurrection and ascension, and this is of course what Milton does, the difference being that the reaction is to the Nativity. Moreover, in each poem the sun responds in exactly the same way. Giles Fletcher writes about Christ, during his ascension, that he "The Sun it selfe outglitters, though he should / Climbe to the toppe of the celestiall frame, / And force the starres *go hide themselves for shame*" (IV.11:3–5; my emphasis); Christ had stayed so long below on the earth that Heaven became "Halfe envious, to *see on earth appeare / A greater light, then flam'd in his own skies*" (IV.13:3–4; my emphasis). This topos of recognizing something greater is repeated in stanza IV.15 on the ascension when "The Sunne to blush, and starres growe pale wear seene" (IV.15:4). Milton compresses all this into a few lines in stanza 7, where the sun *"hid his head for shame"* on seeing *"a greater Sun appear / Then* his bright Throne, or burning Axletree could bear" (7:4 – 8; my emphasis). The parallel is exact, the echo plain.[43] One verbal and one structural parallel connect stanza 15 in each poem: in each stanza the number of ascent (15) featured in the ordinal number is identified as such by the image of the opening of the gates of Heaven. A fainter echo is found when Milton's angels who sit "all about the courtly stable" in "order serviceable" (27:7– 8) recall Giles Fletcher's saints in Heaven, who receive Christ on having "Pitcht round about in order glorious, / Their sunny Tents, and houses luminous" (IV.31:4 –5). It is the *order* which is important, whether glorious or serviceable. The final parallel is the 27 stanzas of Milton's hymn and the concluding 27 8-line stanzas of part 4 of Giles Fletcher's poem. As I show elsewhere,[44] Giles Fletcher's 27 stanzas, like those of Milton, subdivide into the ratio 2:1; the major subdivision is into 9 + 18 (against Milton's 18 + 9), where the 9-stanza segment is further subdivided into 6 + 3 and the 18-stanza segment into 12 + 6; these 12 stanzas in their turn subdivide into 6 + 6, and the 6 stanzas into 4 + 2. Giles Fletcher's 27-stanza segment (IV.24 –50) describes the arrival of Christ in the midst of the heavenly Jerusalem and the life of bliss enjoyed by the saints in their one eternal day. The difference between Milton and Giles Fletcher is that Milton emphasizes the idea of music and harmony, Giles Fletcher the stability, permanence, and fullness of life in bliss, although he too includes song and harmony as a matter of course. The interesting point is that the number 27 has both these meanings. It applies to music and harmony because it represents the Platonic *lambda* formula, but it also signifies permanence, fullness, and stability because squares and cubes express these qualities. Biblical support was found in the fact that the heavenly Jerusalem is a cube (Rev. 21:16).[45] The abstract character of this mathematical image of a return to unity would have recommended itself to Protestants intent on avoiding the fulsome all-too-physical images favored by Roman Catholic poets.

5

We have seen that textual structures are found in individual poems, groups of poems, and the collection as a whole. In the collection as a whole *Comus* is the obvious center-piece, flanked as it is by sequences of equal length written in an equal number of tongues. The use of 4 languages suggests an alignment with the 4 elements that "in quaternion run / Perpetual circle" (*PL,* 5.181– 82), thus conveying the idea of a harmonious, balanced fullness. It is likely that the two poems in Greek were included to permit English, Italian, Latin, and Greek to form just such an image of perfection.[46] Another quaternion may perhaps be found in the sum total of poems in each of the two sequences (52); there are 52 weeks in the year, and the year is a quaternion as Augustine explains: "the day and the year both run their courses in a quaternion: the day in hours of morning, noon, evening, and night; the year in the months of spring, summer, autumn, and winter."[47]

I have already touched on some aspects of the overall structure of the collection. The poems that frame the first sequence focus on the contrast between innocence and guilt, harmony and discord; in *Lycidas* as in the *Ode* harmony is restored through the power of Christ who is the source of all harmony. At the halfway point, in the companion poems, the speaker opts for harmony as he draws a clear line of distinction between good and bad versions of Mirth and Melancholy, embracing what is good and denouncing the perverse version— as the Lady does in *Comus*. *Comus* must have been placed at the centre because it provides climactic expression of the theme of a choice of life. Choices are featured also in the *Elegia prima* and the *Epitaphium Damonis*. In the former the young Milton favors the city by the Thames (rather than Cambridge) where he can give his time to the quiet Muses and the books that are his life. In the latter the speaker emerges from his trial through grief with renewed dedication to poetry and renewed faith. His choice of British themes and of British rivers and islands harks back to his choice of the Thames and of British girls in the *Elegia prima*.

Choice clearly plays an important role. The most familiar literary and iconographical expression of this theme is found in the Choice of Hercules,[48] and I would argue that Milton's masque is his version of this famous theme. In the Renaissance Hercules became an *exemplar virtutis*, and his combat with Antaeus was interpreted as a combat with the desires of the flesh; his strength is fostered by constant contact with carnality, that is, the earth. This association may possibly explain why Comus encourages his followers to "knit hands, and beat the ground" (line 143). It became part of the tradition that dramatic representations of the Choice of Hercules would replace Hercules with the ruling monarch or prince,[49] and since the masque honors the Earl of Bridgewater, Lord President of Wales, Milton may conceivably have been prompted by this tradition to let the masque focus on the famous choice between Vice and Virtue. The earl's daughter, then, should be seen as a female Hercules. Hercules figures in the *Nativity Ode* as well, in the description of how "the dredded Infants hand" controls the "damned crew" in his "swadling bands" (stanza 25). That which Hercules in the cradle foreshadowed (as a type taken from classical myth) is realised in the life of Christ and reflected in that of the Lady as she abides faithfully by her choice. The power invested in her virginity, therefore, is a power derived from Christ. Her temptation, too, is a temptation in the wilderness as she prays: "Eie me blest Providence, and square my triall / To my proportiond strength" (328–29). In her person Christ and Hercules meet and merge in the approved Renaissance manner.

Thematic and verbal echoes forge a strong link also between *Comus* and the companion poems. Comus and his revelers have rightly been called "sinister incarnations of L'Allegro, whose 'jest and youthful jollity' become in the masque 'Tipsie dance and jollity' (line 104)." A second echo occurs when L'Allegro's invitation to trip it "On the light fantastick toe" (33–34) is changed to Comus's "light fantastick round" (143–44).[50] These passages occur in Comus's opening speech, largely written in the tetrameter couplets associated with the companion poems. Then, too, Comus hails the "Goddesse of nocturnal sport" who lives in "Stygian darknes" (128–33), just as the "loathed Melancholy" denounced by L'Allegro inhabits a "*Stygian* Cave forlorn" (1–3). Similarly the line on the "Wood-Nymphs deckt with Daisies trim" (*Comus*, 120) recalls the "Meadows trim with Daisies pide" (*L'All*, 75). Furthermore, the Lady, her two brothers, and the Attendant Spirit repeatedly voice sentiments typical of the divine version of Melancholy hailed by Il Penseroso in the line located at the center of the two poems.[51] The scales, it would seem, are tilted in her favor. The Lady's song echoes heavenly harmonies (242), and Comus recognizes its power to pacify even Scylla herself, and Charybdis (243–63)—a passage that connects with the twice-repeated description of the way in which the song of Orpheus compels Pluto to give up Eurydice (*L'All*, 148–50 and *Il P*, 107–8). Music transports the soul to ecstasy (*Il P*, 161–66 and *Comus*, 622–24). The virtue and the wisdom that characterize Il Penseroso's Melancholy are met again in *Comus*: Virtue sees "By her own radiant light," and "Wisdoms self / Oft seeks to sweet retired Solitude, / Where with her best nurse Contemplation / She plumes her feathers, and lets grow her wings" (*Comus*, 373–77). Il Penseroso's Melancholy too consorts with Contemplation—with "Him that yon soars on golden wing, / Guiding the fiery-wheeled throne, / The Cherub Contemplation" (52–54).

Milton, then, saw to it that the poems that feature his favorite themes were located so as to frame the collection as a whole and its two clearly defined sequences. Each sequence moves from a beginning to an end that marks a new beginning, but in a higher key (as in the octave). The *Ode* envisages the joy that lies in the future, "But now begins" (stanza 18), and in *Lycidas* we contemplate our immortal end when we, too, may hear "the unexpressive nuptial Song" through "the dear might of him that walk'd the waves" (173–76). The *Elegia prima ad Carolum Diodatum* and the *Epitaphium Damonis* in their turn take us from youthful exuberance to the mature poet's rededication of himself. Between these sequences *Comus* functions as a central pivot connecting the *Ode*—our beginning in Christ, our true head—with our end in Christ as described in the *Epitaphium Damonis*. Diodati's "virginal honors" (214) correspond to those of the Lady, while the expulsion of pagan deities in the *Ode* finds its analogue in the defeat of Comus and his midnight revelers. Within these frames Milton placed a plenitude of forms and themes. To the 4 languages we may add the 4 passions and the 4 humors, the 4 seasons, the 4 chief hours of the day and night, time and eternity, public and private concerns, all ages and sexes,[52] peace and war, rural and urban scenes, the humble and the great, the sacred and the profane. If the universe is God's *carmen pulcherrimum*,[53] then Milton's *carmina* form a comprehensive pageant showing life in its manifold aspects, the noblest being the harmony of voice and verse. This is why the poet-singer holds center stage on so many occasions; he, too, mediates between God and man. We may grasp the reality of an invisible Deity through these man-made *poiemata*, as we do on contemplating the craftsmanship of God in his works of creation and re-creation.[54] The same *rhythmos* pervades them all, as it does the Psalms and the Bible as a whole. What Milton presented to the public in 1645, after such mature deliberation, embodies a structural concept worthy of an epic poet; Tasso and Spenser would have recognized the *constellations* and *configurations* of his verse.[55] Milton's famous pride may perhaps have prompted this alignment between divine and human artifacts, but it is surely also possible to interpret this pride *in bono*: Milton was content to reflect the craftsmanship of God.

Notes

1. Neil Fraistat, "Introduction. The Place of the Book and the Book as Place," in *Poems in Their Place. The Intertextuality and Order of Poetic Collections*, ed. Neil Fraistat (Chapel Hill: University of North Carolina Press, 1986), 12.

2. Joseph Wittreich, Jr., " 'Strange Text!' *Paradise Regain'd . . . To which is Added Samson Agonistes*," *Poems in Their Place*, 165. See the important recent analysis of Milton's volume by John K. Hale, "Milton's Self-Presentation in *Poems . . . 1645*," *Milton Quarterly* 25.2 (May 1991): 37–48. See also C. W. R. D. Moseley, *Milton: The English Poems of 1645* (Harmondsworth, England: Penguin Books, 1992).

3. Fraistat, 3. Fraistat proposes that the term "contexture" be used to refer to

"the contextuality provided for each poem by the larger frame within which it is placed, the intertextuality among poems so placed, and the resultant texture of resonance and meanings."

4. See for example the following studies: Charlotte Thompson, "Love in an Orderly Universe: A Unification of Spenser's *Amoretti*, 'Anacreontics,' and *Epithalamion*," *VIATOR* 16 (1985): 277–335; M.-S. Röstvig, "*The Shepheardes Calender*—A Structural Analysis," *Renaissance and Modern Studies* 13 (1969): 49–75; and Marianne Brown, "Spenserian Technique: *The Shepheardes Calender*," *REAL. The Yearbook of Research in English and American Literature* 2 (1984): 55–118.

5. For a discussion of the varying degrees of integration or cohesion in collections of poems, see Earl Miner, "Some Issues for Study of Integrated Collections," *Poems in Their Place*, 18–43.

6. The text of Giles Fletcher's poem is quoted from Giles and Phineas Fletcher, *Poetical Works*, ed. Frederick S. Boas (Cambridge: Cambridge University Press, 1908), 1:1–87.

7. I present a brief account of Augustine's aesthetic principles in "Ars Aeterna: Renaissance Poetics and Theories of Divine Creation," *Mosaic* 3 (1970): 40–61, rpt. in *Chaos and Form*, ed. Kenneth McRobbie (Winnipeg, Canada: University of Manitoba Press, 1972), 101–19.

8. For a detailed structural analysis of the *Confessions*, see Chap. 2 of my book on *Configurations: a Topomorphical Approach to Renaissance Poetry* (Oslo, Copenhagen, and Stockholm: Scandinavian University Press and London: Oxford University Press, 1994).

9. See *Configurations,* Chap. 3.

10. For the text of Milton's *Poems* (1645) I have used the facsimile edition published by Scolar Press in 1970. The lines beginning *Haec ego mente* placed after *Elegia septima* (Part 2, p. 39) have not been considered as a separate item. If they should be so considered, then the structure will be 26 + *Comus* + 26 + *Epitaphium Damonis*.

11. Part 2, pp. 44–76 (ten items including "Ad Patrem" and "Mansus").

12. See Alastair Fowler, "The Silva Tradition in Jonson's *The Forrest*," in *Poetic Traditions of the English Renaissance*, ed. George de Forest Lord (New Haven: Yale University Press, 1982), 163–80. Fowler cites Quintilian (*Instit. Orat.* 10.3.17–18) and Scaliger (*Poetics libri septem*, 1561, p. 150) in notes 6 and 7.

13. See Annabel Patterson, "Jonson, Marvell, and Miscellaneity?" in *Poems in Their Place*, 95–118.

14. Fowler, "The Silva Tradition," 173.

15. From the comments on Psalm 70 in Cassiodorus, *Expositio Psalmorum* published in the Corpus Christianorum Series Latina, vols. 97 and 98 (Turnholt, 1958), 639–40. The *Exp. Ps.* was frequently reprinted in the Renaissance, either *in toto* or in excerpts together with other famous commentaries, or as part of the *opera omnia*.

16. The statement that "I am Alpha and Omega, the beginning and the ending, saith the Lord" (Rev. 1: 8) was taken to mean that the nature of God is circular (i.e., unending); the alphabet too was conceived of as a circle, since we return to the beginning when we reach the end. This is often stated in comments on the alphabetical composition of Psalm 119 (Vulg. 118), which provided the formal pattern for Nativity hymns. It was a theological commonplace that Christ always is at the beginning, middle, and end; see, for example, Bonaventura, *Collationes in Hexaemeron*, Collatio I. The Latin text with a translation into German is found in the edition published by the Wissenchaftliche Buchgesellschaft (Darmstadt, 1964). Giles Fletcher bases his poetics on this idea: Christ, himself without beginning or end like

the circle, but who gives beginning to everything, must teach him "how to begin, and how to end" the story of "The love, that never was, nor ever can be pend" (*Christs Victorie, and Triumph*, I.1–3).

17. See Matthew S. Santirocoo, *Unity and Design in Horace's Odes* (Chapel Hill: University of North Carolina Press, 1986); reviewed by Roger A. Hornsby, *Philological Quarterly* 67 (1988): 265–67.

18. Cassiodorus, *Expositio Psalmorum*, pp. 1329–32 (from the comments on Ps. 150). For Augustine the following texts have been used: *On the Trinity*, trans. Arthur West Haddam (Edinburgh: T. & T. Clark, 1873) and *On Christian Doctrine*, trans. D.W. Robertson (Indianapolis, Ind.: The Liberal Arts Press, 1968).

19. See my essay on *The Shepheardes Calender* (note 4).

20. Thomas Becon, *Workes* (London, 1564), I, fol. 150. Giles Fletcher similarly describes David as one who was wont to "comb rough speech" (*Christs Victorie, and Triumph*, IV, 45: 4).

21. It was an exegetical commonplace (also applied to the interpretation of classical myths) that the same word (or *signum*) may occur *in bono* or *in malo*. See Augustine, *De Doctrina Christiana* III.xxv.35–36. The context must decide whether the meaning is good or bad.

22. Max A. Wickert, "Structure and Ceremony in Spenser's *Epithalamion*," *ELH* 35.2 (1968): 135–57. It is indeed obvious that "stanzas 12 and 13 provide an emphatic and mathematically exact midpoint, and that the two halves on either side of this midpoint invite some sort of matching." The poem's second half is "a mirror-inversion of the imaginative order of the first half" (137).

23. These sonnets are not numbered, but I have done so to avoid having to use the long superscriptions. Spenser arranged his sonnets strictly according to the heraldic rules for precedence; see Carol A. Stillman, "Politics, Precedence, and the Order of the Dedicatory Sonnets in *The Faerie Queene*," *Spenser Studies* 5 (1984): 132–48. The omission of seven sonnets from the first issue of the first edition "was due to some minor oversight of the printer, the poet, or an intermediary. The mistake was soon discovered and rectified by inserting the missing dedications in strict accordance with the heraldic rules for precedence" (146). My analysis supports this conclusion.

24. On the typology of the exodus, see Jean Daniélou, *From Shadows to Reality* (London: Burns & Oates, 1960).

25. See H. Neville Davies, "Milton and the Art of Cranking," *Milton Quarterly* 23:1 (1989): 1–7.

26. Anna K. Nardo, *Milton's Sonnets & The Ideal Community* (Lincoln: University of Nebraska Press, 1979), 30.

27. Nardo, *Milton's Sonnets*, 51.

28. All translations from the Italian given in quotation marks are from Douglas Bush's edition of Milton, *Poetical Works* (London: Oxford University Press, 1969); otherwise they are my own.

29. Nardo, *Milton's Sonnets*, 29. In her discussion of Sonnets I and VII Nardo refers to the "dynamic tension between self-concern and a desire for self-transcendence which will become one of the unifying themes of his sonnets and continually reappear in his major works."

30. M. Christopher Pecheux, "'At a Solemn Musick': Structure and Meaning," *Studies in Philology* 75 (1978): 331–46. Footnote 1 lists earlier analyses of the poem. Both E. M. W. Tillyard [*Milton* (London: Chatto and Windus, 1930), 64], and P .L. Heyworth, "The Composition of Milton's *At a Solemn Musick*," *BNYPL* 70 (1966): 450–58, divide the 28 lines into 16 + 8 + 4. As Pecheux puts it, "In a poem

on music which abounds in musical terms such a structuring into eight and its multiples suggests the musical octave, which was for the Renaissance the ultimate harmony—a symbol of the divine and human harmony which is the theme of the poem" (333). However, the wedding of voice and verse may also be related to the first Hebrew poem, in Exodus 15 (believed to be the first recorded poem). In this song of triumph music and poetry were one, as in the Psalms of David. The musical accents given to the Hebrew text "encode the perfect union of words and music imparted to the cosmos by the Tuneful Voice engaged in the act of creation." My quotation comes from an unfinished study, in manuscript, of *Renaissance Poets, Hebraists, and Musicians. Theories on the Origin of Poetic Form* by Seth Weiner (University of California, Los Angeles), 170. Weiner quotes Gioseffo Zarlino who argues that every poet and musician ought to know these accents since they form the basis for setting texts to music; Zarlino connects these accents, logically enough, with the Pythagorean and Platonic formulas for world harmony. Zarlino published his famous *Istitutioni Harmoniche* at Venice in 1558, his *Supplimenti Musicali* in 1588, and his *Opere* at Venice in 1589. Weiner refers to the *Supplimenti*, book 8, chap. 13. I have been unable to get hold of Hans Walter Gabler, "Poetry in Numbers: A Development of Significative Form in Milton's Early Poetry," *Archiv* 220 (1983): 54–61, which argues that the four short lines have been located so as to create significant proportions.

31. Other important sources are Martianus Capella, *The Marriage of Philology and Mercury*, trans. William Harris Stahl and Richard Johnson with E. L. Burge (New York: Columbia University Press, 1977), and Macrobius, *Commentary on the Dream of Scipio*, trans. William Harris Stahl. Records of Civilization, Sources and Studies, Vol. 48 (New York and London: Columbia University Press, 1952). Capella is relevant particularly for Spenser's *Epithalamion* and for Milton's *Nativity Ode* (when considered as a sacred epithalamion on the marriage between Heaven and Earth).

32. See my essay "Ars Aeterna" (note 7). Augustine summarizes his structural aesthetics in the following words: "In all the arts that which pleases is harmony, which alone invests the whole with unity and beauty. This harmony requires equality and unity either through the resemblance of symmetrically placed parts, or through the graded arrangement of unequal parts" (*De vera religione* xxx.55; my trans.). I cannot recommend the translation by J. H. S. Burleigh (Chicago: Henry Regnery Company, 1964), since it suffers from serious terminological inaccuracies. The Latin text with excellent translation into French is found in vol. 8 of the *OEuvres de Saint Augustin* (Paris: Desclée, de Brouwer et Cie., 1951), 22–191. Ficino's *Theologia Platonica* XIII.5 contains almost all of the *De vera religione* xxix.53–xxxix.73, and the chapter that follows contains extracts from the *De musica* VI. Ficino does not acknowledge his borrowings, but weaves them into his own discourse. In these chapters (XIII.5–6) Ficino presents an authoritative version of Augustine's important argument that beauty is harmony (i.e., proportioned arrangement), and harmony a reflection of the unity of God; hence, the art of creation, whether human or divine, consists in the imposition of unity by means of harmonious proportions. For a modern edition of Ficino's important work, with French translation, see Marsil Ficin, *Théologie Platonicienne de l'Immortalité des Ames*, trans. Raymond Marcel (Paris: Société d'Edition "Les Belles Lettres", 1964). For Augustine's *De musica*, see vol. 7 of the *OEuvres* (Paris: Desclée, de Brouwer et Cie., 1947).

33. "[Scriptura] ordinatissima est, et ordo eius est consimilis ordini naturae in germinatione terrae" (*Collationes in Hexaemeron*, p. 432). The sentence that follows anticipates Milton's *PL,* 5.470–90 on the scale of being: the order proceeds like the

plant which begins with the root and the shoots, and continues with leaves and flowers and fruit. The progress is similar in man: "primo est sensualis . . . deinde fit animalis . . . deinde rationalis . . . deinde intellectualis, cum fit sapiens" (XIV.10). To these four phases corresponds the salvation promised by the patriarchs, the Law, the prophets, and Christ (XIV.11).

34. See Ove Kr. Sundby, "Musiske Perspektiver i Platons Dialog *Lovene*," *Studia Musicologia Norvegica*, vol. 5, 67–104.

35. Cassiodorus, *An Introduction to Divine and Human Readings*, trans. Leslie Webber Jones (New York: Octagon Books, 1966), 190 (from II.v.2).

36. Augustine, *On the Trinity*, pp. 112–15 (IV.iii.5–6).

37. R. Darby Williams, "Two Baroque Poems on Grace: Herbert's 'Paradise' and Milton's 'On Time,'" *Criticism* 12 (1970): 180–94 as cited by Pecheux, 334.

38. See his comments on Psalm 11.

39. The English translation is quoted from the translation by Douglas Bush in his edition of the *Poetical Works*.

40. M.-S. Röstvig, "Elaborate Song: Conceptual Structure in Milton's 'On the Morning of Christ's Nativity'," in *Fair Forms*, ed. M.-S. Röstvig (Cambridge: D. S. Brewer Ltd., 1975), 54–84 and 206–12. The overall structure of the hymn is seen as a sequence of 12-3-12 stanzas that coexists with a division into 1–9–7–9–1. Another point concerns the transition from 7-line stanzas in the introduction to 8-line stanzas in the hymn, which is taken to reflect the transition from the world of time (as expressed in line 1) to the realm of eternity as represented by the incarnate Deity.

41. Even orthodox theologians, both Protestant and Roman Catholic, shared the view expressed for example by Augustine, that the 6 numbers in the Platonic formula correspond to the Mosaic account of creation in 6 days; Plato was *Moses Atticus*, Moses in Attic garb. Ficino's *Commentarium in Timaeum* argues in similar terms.

42. For an extended analysis, see *Configurations*, Chap. 6.

43. The Carey-Fowler edition of *The Poems of Milton* (London: Longmans, 1968), p. 104 note on 80–84 refers to Spenser, *The Shepheardes Calender*, April 73–78, where the sun blushes to see "another Sunne belowe." Giles Fletcher's version of this topos, though, is much closer to Milton's. Another possible echo from Giles Fletcher is Milton's line 13 ("Forsook the Courts of everlasting Day") and Giles Fletcher's "So him they lead along into the courts of day" (IV.19: 8) and "So him they lead into the courts of day" (IV.20:1).

44. "Golden Phrases: The Poetics of Giles Fletcher," *Studies in Philology* 88.2 (1991): 169–200.

45. See the chapter on the number 27 in Pietro Bongo, *Numerorum mysteria* (Bergamo, 1591); this handbook on the meaning of biblical numbers, licensed by the Roman Catholic church with a warm recommendation, incorporates a great deal from Cassiodorus's *Expositio Psalmorum*. It appeared in many editions, and such was its currency that Carnelius à Lapide (early seventeenth–century exegete) will often insert a *vide Bongo* when he touches on the meaning of a given number.

46. On Milton's use of quaternions, see my essay on "Images of Perfection" in *Seventeenth-Century Imagery*, ed. Earl Miner (Los Angeles: University of California Press, 1971), 1–24, and especially 12–14 and 21–23.

47. *De Doctrina Christiana* II.xvi.25.

48. See Erwin Panofsky, *Hercules am Scheidewege* (Leipzig, 1930), published as vol. 30 in the Studien der Bibliothek Warburg. For the literary tradition, see G. Karl Galinsky, *The Herakles Theme. The Adaptations of the Hero in Literature from Homer to the Twentieth Century* (Oxford: Basil Blackwell, 1972). See esp. Chap. X on Her-

cules as *Exemplar virtutis*. St. Augustine compared Agnes to Hercules (p. 189; source not cited).

49. Galinsky notes that a dramatization of the Choice figured in the entry of Charles VIII into Vienna in 1490, and that other adaptors "replaced Herakles with their ruling monarchs" (199).

50. Annabel Patterson, " 'Forc'd Fingers': Milton's Early Poems and Ideological Restraint," in Claude J. Summers and Ted-Larry Pebworth, eds., *"The muses common-weale": Poetry and Politics in the Seventeenth Century* (Columbia: University of Missouri Press, 1988), 14.

51. Lines 12–13 are at the center of the two poems; 163 lines precede and follow. I owe this observation to H. Neville Davies.

52. The description of panegyrical processions (for example in honor of a new consul) would use the phrase "all ages and sexes."

53. Augustine, *De civitate Dei* 11:18.

54. My allusion is to one of Augustine's favorite biblical passages, Romans 1: 20 ("For the invisible things of him from the creation of the world are clearly seen, being understood by the things that are made, even his eternal power and Godhead; so that they are without excuse").

55. The terms are George Herbert's (see "The H. Scriptures. II").

Myth, Masque, and Marriage:
Paradise Lost and Shakespeare's Romances

STELLA P. REVARD

Eden, that happy garden state where married love was first instituted, is a touchstone for Shakespeare as he seeks in his trio of late romances—*The Tempest, Cymbeline*, and *The Winter's Tale*—to portray both blissful young love enjoying its innocence and wedded love about to be tainted by Eden's inevitable serpent. What is metaphor in Shakespeare becomes means for Milton, for his aim is not just to suggest *a* blissful Eden but to delineate Eden itself, not Edenic marriage, but marriage in Eden, not sin's first temptings, but original sin. What Shakespeare does as he dramatizes young men and women seeking to experience in their love what the world's parents first felt is crucial for Milton in *Paradise Lost* in two ways. Shakespeare is both a poetic and a conceptual model. In *The Tempest, Cymbeline*, and *The Winter's Tale* he displays a whole range of dramatic devices and poetic comparisons to celebrate first love—masques, mythic allusions, and complex imaginative machinery that evoke love's delights—devices and delights that Milton deftly adapts for his Eden as he tries to suggest the essence of Adam's and Eve's marriage. But it is more than dramatic and poetic machinery that binds Milton to Shakespeare. In every one of Shakespeare's late romances marriage is the crucial issue on which depends not just the personal happiness of the young couple, but also the success or failure of the society in which they live. Not until the young couple in *The Tempest* are united, not until the married couples in *Cymbeline* and *The Winter's Tale* resolve their differences can we be assured that the societies about them are on the mend. In *Paradise Lost* sin enters Eden when the human marriage falters and recovery can only take place when that marriage begins to regenerate. So important is the marriage relation for both Milton and Shakespeare that they make it in a sense the necessary means for healing comfort and renewal, the necessary bridge to a world of peace and harmony. Shakespeare has long been recognized as an important poetic and dramatic influence on Milton. Nowhere is this more so than when he lays down for Milton many of the Edenic similes, metaphors, and mythic patterns by which the later poet will construct the world of Eden before and after the fall.[1]

The allusions to the perfect garden state and to Adam and Eve that abound in Shakespeare's last plays create both a nostalgia for Eden and a sense of our irrevocable displacement from it. Again and again the playwright seems deliberately to compare the prelapsarian joys of the first human couple with those his young lovers experience. Ferdinand and Miranda in their island paradise and Florizel and Perdita in a pastoral Bohemia play the parts of perfect young lovers who seem for a moment untainted by the fall. Ferdinand is the first young man that Miranda has seen and she reacts to him with Eve-like wonder. Miranda whom Ferdinand at first thinks goddess of the island excels every woman, "so perfect and so peerless . . . created / Of every creature's best" (3.1.47– 48); like Milton's Adam he considers her heaven's best gift.[2] Not only Eden, but also the world of classical myth invades the sphere of Shakespeare's lovers. Like Ferdinand, Florizel in *The Winter's Tale* applies mythic superlatives. Perdita is the goddess Flora, a beauty more rare and chaste than any god ever courted. To Posthumus in *Cymbeline* Imogen is "more fair, virtuous, wise, chaste, constant" than any other lady in the world (1.4.59– 60), matchless as the diamond she bestows on her husband. Posthumus, as both Jachimo and the gentlemen of the English court describe him, is a "god" among men, "more than a mortal seeming" (1.6.171), "a creature such / As, to seek through the regions of the earth / For one his like" (1.1.19–21). These "godly" creatures have enjoyed a golden age idyll in the English court and as friends and play-fellows have fallen in love. Shakespeare emphasizes their special qualities through two more mythic comparisons to the incomparable and rare. Imogen is like the Arabian bird, the phoenix, peerless and without rival; Posthumus, the foster child of the king, is also in a sense a foster child of Jupiter himself—an eagle among men, whom Jupiter in the final scenes of the play restores. In *Paradise Lost* Milton follows Shakespeare's lead by mixing mythic and Edenic superlatives to describe Adam and Eve as gods of the garden. Eve is alternately the goddesses Aphrodite, Juno, Ceres. Adam plays the part of Jupiter to Eve's Juno, as he delights in her beauty and presses "her Matron lip / With Kisses pure" (4.501–2).

In *The Winter's Tale* the Eden myth takes on a more ominous color. It is true that the royal couple of Sicily seem to be experiencing the joys of Eden as the play first opens. But in Leontes' diseased imagination,

Eden is already forfeited. Even as Polixenes jests with Hermione, the innocence of Eden becomes a thing of the past. Polixenes equates his own and Leontes' boyhood joys and male bonding with Edenic innocence before sexual experience, describing himself and Leontes as "twinn'd lambs" who did not know the "doctrine of ill-doing," and so had escaped the taint of hereditary sin. In jest he tells Hermione that it was their wives who first tempted them and brought them to sin, to which Hermione counters that it was not sin, "If you first sinn'd with us, and that with us / You did continue fault, and that you slipp'd not / With any but with us" (1.1.84–86). But the hint of sexual lapse is enough to effect a fall. Leontes, observing at a distance Hermione and Polixenes in conversation, is inwardly stung by the Edenic serpent. What is introduced as jest becomes deadly serious and the paradise of Sicily is forfeited. In *Cymbeline* too, Eden is just as quickly lost, as the lovers are separated and Posthumus goes into exile.

The allusions to Eden that Shakespeare employs are more than decorative imagery. In all three plays he is seriously looking at the place of marriage not only in the divine plan for man and woman, but also in the social and political order that surround them; hence, he creates in these plays heroes and heroines, whose marriages or potential marriages remind us of God's institution of marriage as a sacrament and as the first true social institution in paradise. Because Shakespeare describes the young couples of these plays as "Adams" and "Eves," they can become models for Milton's own first couple.

Milton twice narrates the account of the marriage of Adam and Eve, first in book 4, when Eve recalls how she met Adam and he wooed her, next late in book 8 of *Paradise Lost*, immediately before he turns his notes to tragic, when Adam narrates the account of his marriage to the listening Raphael. In book 8 Milton not only gives us a different narrator, but also embellishes the account of the wedding with suggestive poetic and mythic details, making it resemble a formal masque-like pageant, such as often appears in Shakespeare's late plays. In this marriage masque, Eve the bride assumes a central place. Adam describes how she appears "not far off," adorned (like Pandora) "with what all Earth or Heaven could bestow / To make her amiable." She is "Led by her Heav'nly Maker, though unseen, / And guided by his voice" (8.481–86). "Grace was in her steps, Heav'n in her Eye, / In every gesture dignity and love" (488–89). Adam tells briefly how he greeted and wooed Eve and how Eve accepted his "pleaded reason" (510). Now, joining her, Adam takes his place in the masque-like procession, leading Eve to the Nuptial Bower. While Eve blushes like the dawn goddess, Aurora, the Deities of heaven assemble and, taking their places in the masque, bless the wedding couple:

                              all Heav'n,
And happy Constellations on that hour
Shed thir selectest influence; the Earth
Gave sign of gratulation, and each Hill;
Joyous the Birds; fresh Gales and gentle Airs
Whisper'd it to the Woods, and from thir wings
Flung Rose, flung Odors from the spicy Shrub,
Disporting, till the amorous Bird of Night
Sung Spousal, and bid haste the Ev'ning Star
On his Hill top, to light the bridal Lamp.

                                        (8.511–20)

At first inspection, this seems only a poetic pastoral in which Adam as narrator has made the elements of nature assume personality and act as attendants for the bride and bridegroom. But when we consider its place in the narrative and its significance as the first wedding, it becomes more. The gods of nature are present in this theogonic masque. Hesiod's Uranus, the eldest god of the universe, appears with his constellations. Gaia or Earth, the primal mother and spouse to Uranus, presides and gives gratulation. She is the very goddess who in book 9 at the onset and completion of original sin will twice groan. The spring winds, the Gales and gentle Airs, are those deities, Zephyr and his company, whom the narrator in book 4 tells us led on, with Pan, eternal spring (4.264–68). Other nature presences serve as attendants for the masque: an amorous Bird of Night—no woeful, fallen Philomela—sings the marriage song, and, in place of the planet Venus, an androgynous Evening Star—Hesperus—lights the bridal lamp. The marriage masque brings heaven down to earth. Delicately poised before the catastrophe in book 9, it affords a last look at marriage in its prelapsarian beauty.

Before exploring the implications of this marriage masque to the coming tragedy and exploring further Milton's views of the married state, I want to consider how Milton is poetically anticipated by some Shakespearean marriage masques. One is a Whitsun pastoral in which the future bride takes the part of Flora and her intended spouse a lowly shepherd; their sheep-shearing is "a meeting of the petty gods" (*The Winter's Tale*, 4.4.4). Perdita is the Whitsun queen and Florizel's wooing of her takes on the mythological trappings of Jupiter's courting of Europa, Neptune's of Theopane, and Apollo's assumption of a shepherd's disguise to serve Admetus and Alcestis. Through these references Shakespeare tells his audience that what passes in this shepherd's pageant predicts the future wedding of Perdita and Florizel, a wedding that will bring the eternal spring back to Sicily that has been banished through Leontes' mad transgression. The other pageant is staged on an Edenic isle by a paternal father-ruler, who also invokes the attendance of the deities of sky and earth to grant their blessings to a woman and a man. The play is *The Tempest*, the father-ruler Prospero, the couple an Eve-Miranda and an Adam-Ferdinand, and the deities, Juno, Ceres, and Iris, spirit-actors called up by Prospero's potent rod, to solemnize the betrothal of his daughter before the whole company must return to a "real" and quite fallen Milan. Both the play *The Tempest* and its marriage masque Milton admired and had imitated before when he created the scenes for Sabrina and her watery deities in his own masque, *Comus*.[3]

When he came to compose the marriage masque for *Paradise Lost*, Milton once more was mindful of Shakespeare and his pastoral melodies. But more important, he had learned from Shakespeare's play the importance of dramatic placement. Milton's masque, like Shakespeare's, occurs at a dramatically significant moment and functions not only as a moment of lyrical pageant, but also to anticipate the climax of the action. Further, it is not just from *The Tempest* that Milton could have learned the importance of a well-placed masque. In both *The Winter's Tale* and *Cymbeline*, masques highlight dramatic action and initiate movement from an idyllic setting back to the real world. The pastoral masque in *The Winter's Tale* celebrates the flower-maiden Perdita's coming of age and anticipates her betrothal to Prince Florizel; the statue masque at the conclusion restores Hermione to the court and reunites her with her husband and daughter. In *Cymbeline* the funeral masque marks the end of Imogen's pastoral interlude with her brothers and prepares us for the scene at the end of the play when she will be reunited with them. Finally, the masque of Jupiter restores Posthumus to Imogen. These masques are quite different from those that occur in the earlier comedies. The masque of Hymen that concludes the festive *As You Like It* is functional, bringing the comedy to a happy conclusion with the multiple weddings; the masques of the later romances, as we shall see, are deeply significant symbolic enactments.

The masque in *The Tempest* comes at the conclusion of the sequences of testing to which Prospero has subjected Ferdinand; it immediately precedes those final sequences in which Prospero confronts the two sets of conspirators—Caliban, Stephano, and Trinculo on the one hand and Antonio, Sebastian, and Alonso, on the other. Before he bestows Miranda on Ferdinand, Prospero, like God later in *Paradise Lost*, must test the sincerity of the would-be bridegroom and the quality of his love.

> All thy vexations
> Were but my trials of thy love, and thou

> Hast strangely stood the test. Here, afore heaven,
> I ratify this my rich gift.
>
> (4.1.5–8)

Like Eve, Miranda is Heaven's last best gift; accordingly, their marriage must be approved by Heaven. So, as he gives Miranda, Prospero issues a strong injunction to obedience and restraint. He enjoins Ferdinand to respect Miranda's virginity until "All sanctimonious ceremonies may / With full and holy rite be minister'd" (4.1.16–17). Should Ferdinand violate this one condition, curses and not blessing will attend the marriage.

> No sweet aspersion shall the heavens let fall
> To make this contract grow; but barren hate,
> Sour-ey'd disdain, and discord shall bestrew
> The union of your bed with weeds so loathly
> That you shall hate it both.
>
> (4.1.18–22)

Like Milton's Adam in paradise, Ferdinand in this lesser Eden owes his continuing happiness to obedience to his lord's single prohibitive command. To violate the command means to lose Eden, wife, all. For both Milton and Shakespeare, the state of paradise is intimately bound up with the commitment to marriage.

Shakespeare in Ferdinand and Milton in Adam create young idealistic heroes who not only respect, but almost worship the women they take in marriage. Marriage is the testing ground for such idolizing sentiments. Milton's Adam does not live up to his professed devotion when sterner tests intervene. In *The Tempest*, however, Shakespeare does not put Ferdinand to further trials than carrying wood and maintaining faith in a game of chess. What the return to Milan and Naples offers we can only guess and hope. The enactment of the marriage masque, however, gives us ground for hope.

The celebration of the marriage masque in *The Tempest* is both a glance back at the paradisal beginnings of the human race and a hopeful glance forward to its restoration through grace. Prospero has his spirits impersonate two goddesses of the classical pantheon who are closely associated with marriage and fertility—Juno and Ceres—and one goddess—Iris—whose function is to negotiate between them. The goddesses are summoned not just to celebrate a "contract to true love" (4.1.84), but also to assure the ensuing social blessings that accompany stable marriage, particularly when that contract of true love is also a political contract. Ceres' and Juno's blessing is not only on Miranda and Ferdinand, but on the society that will surround this young couple when they return to Italy as rulers of Naples and Milan.

As the masque begins, wanton love is banished. Iris tells us that she met Venus and Cupid speeding to the island with the intention of working "some wanton charm upon this man and maid" (4.1.95); she intercepted them, however, and sent them off. Wanton love has no more place in this Shakespearean Eden than it will have in the Eden of *Paradise Lost*. In the Marriage Hymn of book 4, Milton specifically commends the Heavenly Eros, while banishing wanton Cupid, who inspires passion that is "loveless, joyless, unindear'd"—the bought smile of harlots and casual fruition (4.765–67). True fruition in *Paradise Lost*, as in *The Tempest*, is connected with Juno and with Ceres, the goddesses of Shakespeare's masque, and the goddesses in *Paradise Lost* to whom fruitful Eve is compared, as she cultivates her garden and her happy marriage.[4] For both Milton and Shakespeare, Ceres is the goddess associated with fertile nature and fruitful motherhood, Juno the goddess, queenly in eminence, who governs proper marital relationships. Eve is likened to Pomona and Ceres "in her Prime" when she sets out with rude gardening tools to put her flower beds in order (9.393–95). She is compared to Juno and Adam to Jupiter as the god smiles on his wife when "he impregns the Clouds / That shed *May* Flowers" (4.500–501). Juno is queen of the universe and mother of all. From her comes the ruling majesty and fertility of which all women, whether queens of Eden or of Naples and Milan, must partake to assure the continuance of society and social order.

Shakespeare's Ceres and Juno descend to Prospero's Eden in order to bless Miranda as a latter-day Eve, on whom the future of two Italian kingdoms depends. Iris's invocation of Ceres sets the tone, for she describes the goddess in terms of those productive landscapes with which she is associated:

> Ceres, bounteous lady, thy rich leas
> Of wheat, rye, barley, fetches, oats, and pease;
> Thy turfy mountains, where live nibbling sheep,
> And flat meads thatch'd with stover, them to keep;
> Thy banks with pioned and twilled brims.
>
> (4.1.60–64)

Ceres returns the invitation with compliments to Iris, Juno's messenger and the goddess of the rainbow, which depicts Iris's own association with fertility. Iris diffuses "honey-drops, refreshing show'rs" (4.1.79) upon those flowers that Ceres makes grow and together with Juno, the Queen of the Sky, renews the earth. In the formal blessing of the couple, Juno and Ceres promise prosperity and honor, both for the couple and for their children. Juno's blessing is more specifically concerned with dynastic honors, Ceres' with abundance and plenty.

Juno promises "Honor, riches, marriage-blessing, / Long continuance, and increasing, / Hourly joys," and Ceres adds "Earth's increase, foison plenty, / Barns and garners never empty; / Vines with clust'ring bunches growing, / Plants with goodly burthen bowing" (4.1.106–8, 110–13).

"This most majestic vision," as Ferdinand describes it, has intimations both of the blessings conferred on earth in the first Edenic golden age and of those blessings promised when the Age of Gold shall return in the end. Ceres concludes by conferring an eternal summer upon the young couple: "Spring come to you in the farthest / In the very end of harvest!" (4.1.114–15). So delighted is Ferdinand with his rare father-in-law and wife that he calls Prospero's island paradise and wishes to live there forever. But even in this would-be Eden everything is not as idyllic as it seems to the young prince. As the reapers and the nymphs of the brooks are joining in a final celebratory dance, reality intrudes. A demi-devil, free in paradise, is plotting to destroy Prospero's Edenic kingdom and to lay his hands upon the Eve-like Miranda. Prospero remembers Caliban and his fellow conspirators and, breaking off the masque, turns his attention to thwarting their plot. The spirits melt into air; the magical moment fades; and Prospero is troubled with man's mortality: "the great globe itself, / Yea, all which it inherit, shall dissolve, / And like this insubstantial pageant faded / Leave not a rack behind" (4.1.153–56). Edenic dreams, like the dream of life itself, are insubstantial—"We are such stuff / As dreams are made on; and our little life / Is rounded with a sleep" (4.1.156–8).

As the masque ends with the reminder of Caliban's devilish conspiracy and Prospero's weary reflections on man's mortal destiny, we understand that we have been witness to more than an entertainment or interlude in the drama. More is promised by the descending deities than the future happiness of an agreeable young couple. The marriage masque that Prospero arranges must not only bring Prospero back to Milan, but also must restore a world gone badly awry. Prospero's island paradise is no more pastoral never-never land, but a deliberate evocation of the primeval world of Eden. There, Prospero, like God in Eden, has brought together man and woman under his watchful eye, and the marriage that he ordains between them and that he causes the deities of power and fertility to bless is a kind of cosmic hymenaeal that reminds us of the first match with which the world began. Shakespeare is rewriting the Eden story. In his paradise, Miranda, nurtured and educated as a more perfect Eve, is guarded from the attempted ravishment of the demi-devil Caliban and waits in innocence for the coming of an Adam, whom she and her father regenerate. Ceres and Juno descend to deliver the keys of the kingdom into the hands of a new Eve and Adam, whose marriage perhaps will make something better of the world. As act 5 of *The Tempest* amply illustrates, this marriage must do more than to expedite the politics of Miranda's and Prospero's return to Italy. It must reknit friendships, heal relationships, bring brother to brother, father to son, and even offer grace to a demi-devil. The match made in heaven has earthly work to do.

The final act of *The Tempest* may not take us back to Milan, but it does take us from the pastoral world that nurtured Miranda's and Ferdinand's love back to the real world of hate, treachery, and attempted murder. Grace in the figure of Prospero's forgiving presence and in the manifestation of the match of love between the two young people must work the miracle of restoration. A cosmic design transcends the mere magic that set events in motion at the beginning of the play. As Prospero himself recognizes, he only brought Ferdinand to Miranda; it was "grace" that bred affection between the two. She herself, like Eve in Eden, chooses Ferdinand for his goodness and nobility; to her he is a "thing divine" (1.2.419); he chooses her for her "noblest grace" (3.1.45). Prospero recognizes that the meeting between them is a "Fair encounter / Of two most rare affections" and he prays that "Heavens rain grace / On that which breeds between 'em" (3.1.74–76). The divine design of this marriage Ferdinand also recognizes. In act 5 he confesses to his father that "immortal Providence" gave him Miranda as his bride and restored him to a "second life" (5.1.189,195). If the marriage masque in act 4 symbolically reenacts God's blessing on first marriage in Eden before the fall, the revelation of Miranda and Ferdinand to the entire company symbolically confers the promise of restoration after the fall. Alonso spontaneously asks for forgiveness, and Gonzalo, rejoicing in the betrothal of Ferdinand and Miranda, pronounces what can only be Shakespeare's comedic echo of the *felix culpa*:

> Was Milan thrust from Milan, that his issue
> Should become kings of Naples? O, rejoice
> Beyond a common joy.
>
>   (5.1.205–7)

The distribution of grace that we witness in act 5 touches all levels of society and all the persons in the play. The concord of paradisal marriage promises to bind together the family first of all, for with the new love of husband and wife comes also the reknitting of brotherly love. "Abel" will pardon the plotter "Cain," as not only Sebastian, but even Antonio, is forgiven. The offer of grace next makes friends of those who were servants aspiring to overthrow the allegiance of vassal to lord. Stephano and Trinculo are taken back to their own company and forgiven by their masters; even Caliban learns to be wise and to seek for grace, repenting that he ever took a drunkard for a god or worshipped a dull fool (5.1.295–98). The demi-devil who conspired against his lord suffers no worse a fate than landing in the mire. Shakespeare's comedy extends grace even to those villains whose conspiracy images the conspiracy of Satan against God.

Shakespeare uses a similar pattern of restoration and return in *The Winter's Tale*. As the betrothal of Ferdinand and Miranda makes possible the brave new world of the final act of *The Tempest*, so in *The Winter's Tale* Perdita's betrothal to Florizel creates a new order of grace. Leontes can at last find forgiveness and release; Sicily gains a new prince and princess to replace those that have been lost; the Sicilian Eden blooms again and a new social order seems possible with the marriage of the young people whose constant love redeems the sins of their elders.

The marriage masque in *Paradise Lost*, like that in *The Tempest*, occurs at a strategic moment in the action, permitting the audience for a moment to look forward and backward. Milton, like Shakespeare, is not just celebrating an idyllic dream—one that will shortly be lost forever. The qualities he celebrates in the masque—grace, dignity, love—are those which will be sorely needed to effect renewal after loss, restoration after rebellion and betrayal. In the postlapsarian world that succeeds the lost Eden, marriage must assume a central place as a new order comes into being. When Milton's Father-God ordained marriage, he created an institution that would outlast mankind's golden days in Eden. In fact, as the hopeful masque of the next to the last act of *The Tempest* confers blessings that look beyond the stay in the magic isle, so the masque that brings woman to man in book 8 of *Paradise Lost* looks to marriage in a postlapsarian world.

When Milton outlines the order of paradise in book 4 of *Paradise Lost*, he also sets forth both prelapsarian order and the postlapsarian wished-for ideal. Adam and Eve who in Eden are rulers of the garden, endowed with its abundant fertility, become the governors of the world that succeeds in the wake of fallen paradise. They are the heads of a family of humankind that does not yet exist in the prelapsarian Eden, but one that takes its pattern from what is said about the marriage relationship in Eden. Both the marriage masque of book 8 and the marriage hymn of book 4 stress that marriage is an institution that has a heavenly origin. Its heavenly origin, however, does not abrogate its earthly purposes nor ignore those earthly hurts that it can heal. Marriage as an institution bridges the ideal and the real world, works not just for the man and woman who found it, but for the family and the society that exist about it. It is the reason why both Shakespeare and Milton present marriage masques at the ninth hour of their dramas, not simply to idealize young love as man and woman first make their commitment to one another, but to show how the grace shed on them can renew and restore all about it. Consider, for example, the terms Milton uses in book 4. He begins by describing a cosmic mystery; he concludes by describing a real institution with purposes that address our world and not merely an idealized Eden long gone. On the one hand, we have marriage as a "mysterious Law," a thing befitting holiest place, a "Perpetual Fountain of Domestic sweets," whose bed is undefiled and chaste (4.750, 759–60). On the other hand, we have marriage as a practical social contract—the "true source / Of human offspring," the "sole propriety" among all other things left common, a practical solution to adulterous lust, which is "driv'n from men / Among the bestial herds to range" (4.750–54). Marriage as it exists in Eden with Adam and Eve as yet the only human beings cannot be concerned with offspring, property rights, and adultery; yet these are the issues that Milton raises when he extols wedded Love. The marriage hymn certainly idealizes the love of the prelapsarian couple, who embracing sleep, are lulled by nightingales, and on whom the flowery roof sheds roses that the morn repairs. But it also does much more. Marriage may begin with nightingales and roses, but we, as Milton's postlapsarian audience, know it takes more to sustain. Marriage, though ordained in paradise, has express use in the post-paradisical world. As it is ordained, it bridges Heaven and Earth, but as it survives the fall, it bridges Eden and after-Eden. It will bring Adam and Eve out of paradise, hand in hand, as it will bring Miranda and Ferdinand and all the company of Naples and Milan back to Italy. If marriage is, as Adam describes it in book 8, the "sum of earthly bliss" (8.522), there is a potential danger in taking that bliss for granted. For Adam, Eve has not just "Innocence and Virgin Modesty," "Honor" and "obsequious Majesty," but a Beauty that seems to disarm him of rational control. Yet, as Raphael reminds Adam, true marriage must value highest the rational quality in human love if the institution that came down from heaven as a heavenly gift is to show the way back to heaven. Raphael invokes the so-called platonic ladder to illustrate this point:

> Love refines
> The thoughts, and heart enlarges, hath his seat
> In Reason, and is judicious, is the scale
> By which to heav'nly Love thou may'st ascend.
>
> (8.589–92)

It is not the first time in *Paradise Lost* that Milton has referred to the platonic ladder. In fact, it is highly significant that the other occasion was when Eve describes in book 4 how she accepted Adam as spouse. As she consents to marriage, Eve affirms that those heavenly qualities of love (grace and wisdom) that she recognized in Adam excel the appeal of pure earthly beauty.[5] In this affirmation, she echoes Plato, takes the first step up the platonic ladder, and also anticipates what Raphael tells Adam in book 8. If marriage is made possible when love makes its descent from heaven, it endures because the married lovers set their minds and hearts on that rational love that makes possible a heavenly reascent: a Platonic climb to God. Raphael's cautionary words are timely, for Adam's and Eve's choices in book 9 will be far from heavenly. The reascent to Heaven involves more than either calculate.

As we look beyond book 8 of *Paradise Lost* both to the catastrophe in book 9 and to the aftermath of the fall in books 10 through 12, the other two of the trio of Shakespearean romances become important both for their portrayals of marriage under stress and for their hopeful optimism that through a recommitment to marriage a world troubled by strife and deceit may be renewed. In *The Winter's Tale* and *Cymbeline* Shakespeare tests the power of marriage to survive when evils, within and without, threaten it. Hence, if we would understand more fully what Milton inherited from Shakespeare and his view of marriage and domestic life, we would do well to investigate how the serpent enters the Shakespearean Edens of these two last plays.

Both *Cymbeline* and *The Winter's Tale* involve the testing of marriages that at first appear perfect. In these plays Shakespeare explores an experience that neither his earlier comedies nor his tragedies looked at—the shattering of a relationship and its restoration after breach and distrust. Although his late romances give glimpses of so-called prelapsarian Adams and Eves in couples such as Ferdinand and Miranda and Florizel and Perdita, they also look at "postlapsarian" Adams and Eves, who sin and are forgiven. Hence, the experience of an Imogen and a Posthumus, a Hermione and a Leontes, has as much meaning and implication for *Paradise Lost* as that of a Miranda and a Ferdinand or a Perdita and a Florizel.

In both *Cymbeline* and *The Winter's Tale*, Shakespeare deliberately exiles his married couples from Eden. In *Cymbeline* first Posthumus, then Imogen, must leave the court, must go, in effect into exile, where each undergoes trial before they are restored to the court and to each other. In *The Winter's Tale* Leontes' jealousy is provoked by an innocent friendship that only he suspects as adulterous; thus Leontes loses his wife and an innocent Edenic Sicily. In *Cymbeline* Jachimo is

the subtle Italian devil, working separately on husband and wife, as
Satan on Adam and Eve, whose evil undermines Posthumus's and
Imogen's marriage. Although unable to shake Imogen's confidence in
her husband or to seduce her, indirectly Jachimo succeeds in using the
wife to destroy the husband. Taking advantage of Imogen's gullibili-
ty, he places his trunk in her chamber to observe her sleeping and to
gather the evidence he needs to persuade her still more gullible husband of her infidelity. Thus husband and wife succumb to the effects
of Jachimo's machinations, for he succeeds in driving a wedge of distrust between the two. Posthumus is the more guilty in that he readily
falls victim to despair, abandoning his wife, plotting her death and his
own would-be suicide. In his despair, he is very like Milton's Adam,
who, believing Eve irrevocably lost, succumbs to the hopelessness of
the situation, consigning both himself and his wife to death. Only in
the pastoral wildernesses of Britain and of Bohemia do the lost
heroes, Posthumus and Leontes, find grace. Once more masque and
myth play a significant role, for through these devices Shakespeare
attempts to bridge the real and the ideal worlds and restore two lost
paradises.

The masques of *Cymbeline* and *The Winter's Tale*, like that of *The
Tempest*, combine Christian and classical motifs. Not only are they
fertility pageants that confer blessing, but also Christian ceremonies
that bring life from apparent death and offer a renewed grace. In
Cymbeline Shakespeare brings both wife and husband back to life
through masque ceremonies. The first of these is celebrated over the
body of Imogen, who as the disguised Fidele is supposed dead; the
second is a cosmic debate conducted over the sleeping Posthumus by
Posthumus's dead parents and Jupiter that decides whether Posthumus
will be spared and reunited to Imogen. The funeral masque in *Cymbeline* is both a celebration of human mortality and the promise of
rebirth. It begins as Belarius enters with Imogen's body and her
brothers promise to strew her bier with flowers—primrose, harebell,
eglantine, flowers which are compared to Imogen herself. Emblems
of spring, they promise the rebirth of earth and assure the audience
that Imogen like the flowers will also awake. The song that the brothers sing reminds us of the common mortality of the human race.
Mean and mighty, as Belarius comments, have one dust; "All lovers
young, all lovers must / Consign to thee and come to dust"
(4.2.274–75). Yet the very song that seems to mark the end of Imogen
and the hope of young married lovers has hardly ended when Imogen
begins to awaken to life. Belarius and her brothers have laid the head-
less body of Cloten next to her, conferring on him also the last rites
due to man. Imogen, mistaking Cloten for Posthumus, since he is

wearing Posthumus's clothes, forgives, as she laments his death, that very husband who has plotted her death.

Implicit in the pastoral ceremony and in the strewing of flowers is the recollection of the Proserpina myth; this story of death and rebirth is deeply significant for both Shakespeare and Milton. As Stevie Davies has shown, it plays a significant role in *The Winter's Tale* and *Paradise Lost*, where Shakespeare's and Milton's heroines actually enact the parts of Ceres and Proserpina.[6] In different ways, Perdita, Hermione, and Imogen play the role of Proserpina. All three are victims of circumstance; all three "die," only to be brought back to life with the spring. Perdita is a flower maiden, like Proserpina, but she plays a comic and not a tragic part in her masque of flowers. It is significant that Shakespeare exploits the ceremonious aspects of a Whitsun masque or pastoral not only in the scene where Florizel woos Perdita, but also in that where she, like a Whitsun queen, greets visitors by presenting them with flowers. She foils the designs of those "other-world" visitors—Polixenes and Camillo—when she artfully bestows her gathered flowers, for they, of course, would nip her young love in the bud. When she wishes, moreover, that she had the flowers of the spring—flowers that the frighted Proserpina let fall from "Dis's waggon"—she rewrites the Proserpina story. She would make garlands of these flowers for lovers and would strew her "sweet friend" "o'er and o'er":

> like a bank, for love to lie and play on;
> Not like a corse; or if—not to be buried,
> But quick and in mine arms
>
>   (4.4.130–32)

At this point, however, she breaks off, saying that she plays, as she has "seen them do / In Whitsun pastorals"—and our masque is at an end. This masque of flowers has redeemed our Perdita-Proserpina from tragedy, just as she has transformed the symbolic flowers from tragic emblems to emblems of reviving love.

But this is not the only masque in which Perdita plays a part. Assuming the role of a revived Proserpina, she is restored to her mother at the end of act 5. Hermione, in turn, the Sicilian queen, relinquishes the tragic aspect of Proserpina that her death has mimicked— a death at the hands of a husband only too like to Pluto—and now assumes the role of Ceres to greet her restored daughter. As Hermione becomes once more an Eve-Ceres, she gives back to Sicily its lost fruitfulness. How neatly this masque works in tandem with the fertility masque of *The Tempest*, where a fully realized Ceres confers a wedding blessing on a betrothed maiden, so like to the Perdita Hermione now blesses:

> You gods, look down
> And from your sacred vials pour your graces
> On my daughter's head

(5.3.123–25)

As we shall consider more fully later, Shakespeare also makes the closing masque of *The Winter's Tale* the occasion of Hermione forgiving her death-dealing husband, just as Imogen has her Pluto-Posthumus. This marks a significant change in the Proserpina story. Shakespeare's Hermione and Imogen embrace their would-be killers, thus not only re-making their marriages, but bringing life, and not death. It is a change that has an impact on Milton and his delineation of a Proserpina-Eve.

As the flower catalogue from *Lycidas* demonstrates, Milton remembered Perdita's flowers when he strewed the laureat hearse for Lycidas. As he alludes to Proserpina in book 4, his lines have haunting echoes of Shakespeare's. Extolling the delights of Eden, he compares it to that "fair field of *Enna*, where *Proserpin* gathering flow'rs / Herself a fairer Flow'r by gloomy *Dis* / Was gather'd, which cost *Ceres* all that pain / To seek her through the world" (4.268–72). Milton couples the violence of Proserpina's rape with the pain of Ceres' bereavement. Both the innocence of the fragile flower and the fruitfulness of earth are struck barren in one moment—prologue to Eve's ravishment by the god of the underworld in book 9 and Adam's grief at the fall of the blossom: "Defac't, deflow'r'd, and now to Death devote" (9.901). Milton's reworking of the Proserpina myth makes Adam both parent and spouse at Eve's fall.

Before we consider how these scenes of restoration in *Cymbeline* and *The Winter's Tale* affect those in *Paradise Lost*, we must look more closely at Posthumus's role as the erring husband. In many ways Posthumus in *Cymbeline* is a more important counterpart to Adam than Imogen to Eve. He is a man guilty both of overidolizing his wife and overcondemning her. Moreover, he rapidly changes from an idolater to a violent misogynist. Disillusioned with his wife, he turns against all women; he regrets the very role that women must play in procreation—"Is there no way for men to be, but women / Must be half-workers?" (2.5.1–2). Women for him are the sum of evil; he asserts that "there's no motion / That tends to vice in man, but I affirm / It is the woman's part" (2.5.21–22). Adam's misogyny is similar. Critics usually credit Milton's immediate source for Adam's words as those of Euripides' Jason and Hippolytus. We cannot overlook the possibility, however, that he may also be echoing Shake-speare's Posthumus, a misogynistic counterpart, whose situation more closely resembles Adam's.[7] Like Posthumus, Adam is rejecting a creature he once adored, blaming all future womankind in Eve, as he accuses her of bringing evil into the world. Like Posthumus, he regrets that God did not "find some other way to generate / Mankind" (10.894–95) except by means of women. Woman is the source of all evil; the present mischief would not have occurred without her and more shall befall because of her, "innumerable / Disturbances on Earth through Female snares" (10.896–97). Posthumus's misogynistic thoughts lead him to order Pisanio to kill Imogen. He does not learn to forgive his wife, until he turns his eyes into his heart and sees the greater evil there. Then, even though he still thinks Imogen guilty, he begins to move towards regeneration, forgiving first the wrongs he supposes she has committed and then trying to make reparations by fighting for his native Britain. Correspondingly, Adam does not forgive Eve, until he too recognizes his greater guilt (10.955–58).

The second masque of *Cymbeline* comes at the crucial moment in Posthumus's career when he is on the path to restoration. Like the masque in *The Tempest*, this masque brings the gods to earth to confer blessing and renewal on human beings. The supreme classical god, Jupiter in the form of an eagle, is central to the proceedings that take place in Posthumus's prison cell as he sleeps. Posthumus, sick at heart, welcomes his imprisonment as punishment and prays for death, supplicating the gods to take his life in exchange for Imogen's. His soliloquy looks forward to Adam's guilty reflections after the fall when he can find no way out of his sinful state but to hope for his own dissolution in death. Like Posthumus, he wishes that his death might pay all and that he linger no longer in suffering. Both Posthumus and Adam are not quite ready to accept the grace that will be extended to them. While Posthumus sleeps, the apparitions of his mother and father and his two brothers appear and bewail the unjust dealings of the gods toward Posthumus, the entire family of the Leonati, and mankind in general: "No more, thou Thunder-master, show / Thy spite on mortal flies:" (5.4.30–31). They cry out that Posthumus deserves the favor of the gods, not their scorn. Why, says his father, did the gods permit Jachimo to taint Posthumus's heart with needless jealousy? Why indeed, we might ask, did God permit Satan to invade paradise, tempting Eve and causing Adam to fall with her? In this scene, Shakespeare has raised the debate to a cosmic level and poses questions analogous to those Milton, attempting to justify the ways of God to man, sets before us in *Paradise Lost*. Why should God create a man, confer favor on him, only to cast him down? Both Shakespeare and Milton pose the question, and both Shakespearean and Miltonic Gods answer. To the outcry of the indignant ghosts, Jupiter replies with a thundering vindication of his justice. Descending on the eagle, he asserts that he cares for human life, and though he may test those he loves, he ultimately brings relief: "Whom best I love, I cross; to make my gift, / The more delay'd, delighted" (5.4.101–2). Is this once more a Shakespearean version of the *felix culpa*? Jupiter assures the ghosts that Posthumus shall indeed be lord of Imogen and "happier much by his affliction made" (108). In token of his promise, he drops a tablet with a prophecy on Posthumus's breast. Posthumus awakes, reassured by his dream, and finds the tablet. Like many scriptural prophecies, the tablet is enigmatic. Although reassured by it, Posthumus cannot yet comprehend its meaning. Yet it is the means not only to bring him back to favor, but also back to his wife Imogen.

In *Paradise Lost*, Milton introduces a similar dramatic device. Included in the Son's judgment of Adam, Eve, and the serpent is also the prophecy of the bruising of the serpent's head, a prophecy Adam and Eve cannot fully comprehend until Michael explains how Jesus, the seed of woman, will destroy Satan, thus bruising the serpent's head. When they first begin to be reconciled to one another in book 10, they recall the prophecy, but they must await Michael's account of the coming Messiah in book 12 before they understand its full import, thus understanding God's design for them and for the world. Such also is the case with the prophecy in *Cymbeline*; Shakespeare saves its decipherment until the final moments of the play, when the soothsayer, taking the role of the priest, unravels its meaning. Until he is reunited with Imogen and the two have exchanged forgiveness and plighted faith once more, he is not ready spiritually to receive the gift of the god. Then he will understand that he has, as the tablet tells him, without seeking found and been embraced by a "piece of tender air" (mulier = mollis aer), that is, by his own wife, who hangs about his neck like fruit, restoring the true fertility to his Britannic paradise.[8] On the decipherment of this prophecy depends not only the reconciliation of Posthumus and Imogen, but also the restoration of peace and prosperity to the kingdom of Britain.

Oracles, dreams, masques—features so intrinsic to Shakespeare's late romances—are the pagan equivalents to devices that Milton will Christianize in his epic enactment of man's fall from and restoration to grace. The oracle in *The Winter's Tale* is a close counterpart to that delivered to the hero of *Cymbeline*. It not only convicts Leontes of guilt and vindicates Hermione, but also promises that restoration of the paradisal bliss he once enjoyed. Perdita will bring the golden days back to the Sicilian Eden as the daughter is returned to her parents, at the very moment the wife is also restored to her husband, Leontes in *The Winter's Tale*, like Posthumus in *Cymbeline*, having undergone penance. The pagan oracles delivered in these plays by Jupiter and Apollo are shadowy counterparts of the Christian promise that is central to the Eden story and so also to *Paradise Lost*. In the wise Apollo who sends Cleomines and Dion back from Delphos, in the thundering Jupiter who descends on an eagle, Shakespeare has created counterparts to the Christian God. Milton may very well have Shakespeare's dramatic patterns in mind when he describes in book 10 the God who looks down upon the grieving Adam and Eve and sends the Son to judgment and who in book 11, having sent prevenient grace upon them, dispatches the angel Michael to enlighten them further through dream and vision. Shakespeare has used in his theatre the dramatic devices of oracle, dream, and pageant to instruct his audience on the means that grace may use to intervene in human life. In the final books of *Paradise Lost*, oracles, dreams, and visions enlighten erring sinners and bring them to repentance.

As the fall from grace both in *Paradise Lost* and in Shakespeare's romances coincides with a spouse fatally violating the marriage vow, restoration begins with the remembrance of love and the recommitment to marriage. In all cases, it is the woman who first forgives her spouse, and returning to him, renews the marriage. Here, once again, masque is important. A marriage masque marks the moment in *The Tempest* when young love is triumphant and when Prospero is about to work the reforming transformations of act 5; a masque in *The Winter's Tale* is the means that restores Hermione to her husband and brings the events in Sicily to a happy conclusion. In the ceremony that appears to bring the statue of Hermione back to life, Shakespeare combines several mythic accounts—the story of Pygmalion, who prayed to the gods that the perfect woman he had fashioned in stone might come to life; the story of Proserpina who returned from the dead to bring spring back to her native Sicily; and the story of Eve, whom God created and gave to her husband Adam as the last best gift of paradise. In this last scene of *The Winter's Tale*, when Leontes views the statue of his wife, Shakespeare creates a spell of suspended animation—all the characters move as though in a trance. Music accompanies the pageant. Dream is about to become reality. Shakespeare gives us the impression that he has taken us back to the very dawn of life when in the garden of Eden at Adam's request a wife was fashioned for him and brought to life. Slowly, Hermione appears to wake, to breathe, to move, to descend from the pedestal, to extend her hand to Leontes, to embrace him, and finally to speak. As this transformation occurs, music sounds as the enabling medium to bring about the miracle. Is this Proserpina shaking off the numbness of death, a Galatea coming to life? Or is this Eve come again in a renewed paradise?

Milton's description of the birth of Eve immediately precedes the wedding masque of book 8 that I have described at the beginning of this essay. It occurs in a waking dream, where Adam witnesses the fashioning of the human being like the creation and adornment of a living statue. As such, it has relevance to the statue scene in *The Winter's Tale*. In *Paradise Lost* God forms and molds the creature Eve in his hands as though he would fashion a work of art. After her creation, Eve disappears from view and Adam waking longs to "find her, or for ever to deplore / Her loss" (8.479–80). Like Leontes, who at Paulina's direction awaits the restoration of the perfect wife, Adam recognizes in Eve all that is perfect in womankind. To be complete, he must find and wed her and no other. Then, far off, he sees Eve being led to him, and his waking dream becomes reality. Leontes' experience in *The Winter's Tale* prefigures many of the elements Milton employs in book 8 of *Paradise Lost*. At Adam's and Leontes' request, a creature comes to life, a creature adorned with all the gifts of nature. Eve comes to Adam, as Hermione descends to Leontes. The scene that rejoins the married lovers in *The Winter's Tale* reenacts the marriage ceremony that first joined them.

More is happening in the masque in *The Winter's Tale*, however, than the reenactment of a wedding. When Hermione embraces Leontes and "hangs about his neck" (5.3.113), she initiates the reconciliation between the two. As with Imogen in *Cymbeline*, the embrace mends a marriage and marks the fulfillment of the oracle. Once more Shakespeare anticipates a comparable moment in *Paradise Lost*. Like her counterparts in Shakespeare, Eve is the first to forgive. In book 10, embracing Adam's feet, she humbly begs pardon; he relents and raises her up with peaceful words. Together they seek reconciliation with God. At the conclusion of the epic, moreover, when Eve has awakened from her prophetic dream, she initiates the final action for the human race. Addressing Adam, she urges him to lead on, confident that the prophecy that they have been told will be accomplished through her: "By mee the Promis'd Seed shall all restore" (12.623). As in *Cymbeline* and *The Winter's Tale*, a woman demonstrates how, through mending a marriage, a shattered society or a shattered world may once more also be made whole.

In his late plays, Shakespeare saw the marriage relationship as both the symbol of worldly concord and the place where insinuating evil might most easily wreak havoc. When it did, it was not just a private woe. The whole society stood or fell as the Edenic marriages he depicts in *Cymbeline*, in *The Winter's Tale*, and in *The Tempest* stood or fell. For him also, the symbol for offered grace involved first of all the restoration of the marriage relation. After man and wife were once more one, society could hope also to be healed. We can hardly exaggerate the effect that Shakespeare's dramatic description of married bliss or woe had on Milton. His Eve and Adam look back to the heroes and heroines of Shakespeare's romances. They share their perfections and their flaws; they are described often through the mythic allusion and dramatic devices that Shakespeare used to create vivid characterizations. Most important of all, Milton shared with Shakespeare the belief that love took its most noble form and aspect in married love and that married lovers, as they loved and forgave one another, offered the world the best hope for the return of the golden age.

Notes

1. For commentary on Shakespeare's views on marriage in the later plays see, for example, Kay Stockholder, *Dream Works: Lovers and Families in Shakespeare's Plays* (Toronto: University of Toronto Press, 1987); Lisa Jardine, *Still Harping on Daughters: Women and Drama in the Age of Shakespeare* (Sussex, England: Harvester Press, 1983); R. A. Foakes, *Shakespeare: From the Dark Comedies to the Last Plays;—From Satire to Celebration* (London: Routledge and Kegan Paul, 1971); Hallett Smith, *Shakespeare's Romances: A Study of Some Ways of the Imagination* (San Marino, Calif.: Huntington Library, 1972); D. L. Peterson, *Time, Tide, and Tempest: A Study of Shakespeare's Romances* (San Marino, Calif.: Huntington Library, 1973).

The most recent and fullest commentary on marriage in *Paradise Lost* is in James Turner, *One Flesh: Paradisal Marriage and Sexual Relations in the Age of Milton* (Oxford: Clarendon Press, 1987). Many writers on *Paradise Lost* deal in some way or another with the marriage of Adam and Eve. See Joseph H. Summers, "The Two Great Sexes" in *The Muse's Method* (Cambridge: Harvard University Press, 1962), 87–111; John N. King, "Milton's Bower of Bliss: A Rewriting of Spenser's Art of Married Love," *Renaissance and Reformation* 10 (1986): 289–99; Gary M. McCown, "Milton and the Epic Epithalamion," *Milton Studies* 5 (1973): 44–55; William Haller, " 'Hail Wedded Love,' " *ELH* 13 (1946): 79–97; John Halkett, *Milton and the Idea of Matrimony: A Study of the Divorce Tracts and "Paradise Lost"* (New Haven: Yale University Press, 1970); Roland Mushat Frye, "The Teachings of Classical Puritanism on Love in Marriage," *Studies in the Renaissance* 2 (1955): 148–59; Peter Lindenbaum, "Lovemaking in Milton's Paradise," *Milton Studies* 6 (1974): 277–306.

2. Citations of Shakespeare are from *The Riverside Shakespeare*, ed. G. Blakemore Evans (Boston: Houghton Mifflin Co., 1974).

3. The cadences of Iris's invocation of the naiads at the end of the masque scene clearly affected the young Milton when he came to write the poetry for Attendant Spirit's invocation of Sabrina. Iris calls the naiads from the brooks:

> Ye nymphs, call'd Naiades of the winding brooks,
> With your sedg'd crowns and ever-harmless looks

> Leave your crisp channels, and on this green land
> Answer your summons

$$(4.1.128-31)$$

The Attendant Spirit, clearly susceptible to the music of Shakespeare's lines, echoes Iris's song.

> By all the Nymphs that nightly dance
> Upon thy streams with wily glance,
> Rise, rise, and heave thy rosy head
> From thy coral-pav'n bed,
> And bridle in thy headlong wave,
> Till thou our summons answer'd have.

$$(883-88)$$

For discussion of the relationship of *The Tempest* and *Comus*, see, for example, John Guillory, *Poetic Authority: Spenser, Milton, and Literary History* (New York: Columbia University Press, 1983), 75–76; Mary Loeffelholz, "Two Masques of Ceres and Proserpine: *Comus* and *The Tempest*," *SQ* 10 (1959): 177–83; Edith Seaton, "Comus and Shakespeare," *Essays by Members of the English Association* 31 (1945): 68–80; Paul Stevens, "The Meaning of Magic in the Mask," in *Imagination and the Presence of Shakespeare in Paradise Lost* (Madison: University of Wisconsin Press, 1985); Harold Toliver, *Transported Styles in Shakespeare and Milton* (University Park: Pennsylvania State University Press, 1989). For a comprehensive review of the critical issue of Shakespeare's influence on Milton, see John T. Shawcross, "Shakespeare, Milton and Literary Debt," *John Milton and Influence: Presence in Literature, History and Culture* (Pittsburgh: Duquesne University Press, 1991), 5–38.

4. For Milton's connections of Eve with mythic figures, see, for example, Diane McColley, *Milton's Eve* (Urbana: University of Illinois Press, 1983), esp. 66–67. Also see Stevie Davies, *The Feminine Reclaimed: The Idea of Woman in Spenser, Shakespeare and Milton* (Lexington: University Press of Kentucky, 1986).

5. For commentary on the Platonic implications of this scene in book 4, see Marc H. Arnold, "The Platan Tree in *Paradise Lost*," *PLL* 11 (1975): 411–14.

6. For a discussion of the Ceres-Proserpina myth in both Shakespeare and Milton, see Davies, 154–65, 231–47.

7. See Hughes, note to *PL,* 10.888.

8. For commentary on this scene and the marriage emblems throughout *Cymbeline*, see Peggy Munoz Simonds, "The Marriage Topos in *Cymbeline*: Shakespeare's Variations on a Classical Theme," *English Literary Renaissance* 19 (1989): 94–117.

Lachrymae Christi: The Theology of Tears in Milton's *Lycidas* and Donne's Sermon "Jesus Wept"

MARGO SWISS

1

In 1519 Erasmus wrote to Justus Jonas concerning the recently deceased John Colet. In his letter Erasmus cites the founding of St. Paul's grammar school as one of the most notable of Colet's achievements: "he [Colet] constructed a new school, dedicated to the boy Jesus, a magnificent building, in St. Paul's Churchyard."[1] As a "Pigeon of Paules" one hundred years later, John Milton, himself dedicated to Christ's ministry at his baptism,[2] lived on Bread Street, only a short walk from the cathedral close. Though probably not so early as 1617–20 as Donald Clark speculated, Milton did attend St. Paul's some time before February 1625 when, it is known for certain, he entered Christ's.[3] Numerous authorities attest to the nurturing connection between the cathedral and its adjacent school.[4] The influence of cathedral life must have been felt directly by Milton, whose father, the elder John, had been a working associate of John Tomkins, organist at St. Paul's (1619–38).[5] Whether or not we go one step further to endorse Clark's claims for the influence of St. Paul's on Milton's early poetry, we can at least concede that his father's working relationship with Tomkins, the proximity of St. Paul's, and Milton's years at Paul's, with its academic and liturgical links to the cathedral, must have affected the young poet for a formative period. The most remarkable of St. Paul's associates during these years was of course Dr. John Donne, Dean (1621–31). Even before receiving the deanery of St. Paul's, Donne's sermonic prowess was well known to Londoners. During his incumbency, his fame prompted the publication of certain sermons on special occasions, and more sermons app─

after his death, preceding his son's eventual release of the three folios of 1640, 1649, and 1660.[6] If Milton read some of Donne's sermons, it is to date unproved. It is probable, however, that as a "Pigeon," Milton would sometimes have listened to the impressive voice and witness of his cathedral Dean.

Until the last decade scholars have generally cautioned against linking Donne and Milton. George Reuben Potter and William John Roscelli both minimize the Donnean influence, returning us, for all intents and purposes, to Sir Walter Raleigh's statement that "as for the great Dean of St. Paul's, there is no evidence that Milton was touched by him, or for that matter, that he had read any of his poems."[7] However, other observations have been made which encourage the search for links between these two major writers.[8] Frederic Tromly's analysis of Donne's "Death Be Not Proud" and Milton's "On Time," for example, argues for a direct influence of Donne upon Milton. The most comprehensive study of Milton and Donne to date, Thomas Sloane's *Donne, Milton, and the End of Humanist Rhetoric*, also demonstrates this connection by situating both authors in their shared humanist context.[9] In the light of these more recent tendencies, then, I offer the following intertextual reading of Milton's *Lycidas* and Donne's sermon "Jesus wept" and will do so within the context of the theology of tears as described by the Catholic literature of tears and the Protestant literature of contrition.

2

Milton's own theological definition of Holy Baptism in *De Doctrina Christiana*, book 1, has often served as a gloss on salient passages of *Lycidas*: "Under the gospel the first of the sacraments commonly so called is BAPTISM. AT BAPTISM THE BODIES OF BELIEVERS WHO PLEDGE THEMSELVES TO PURITY OF LIFE ARE IMMERSED IN RUNNING WATER. THIS IS TO SIGNIFY OUR REGENERATION THROUGH THE HOLY SPIRIT AND ALSO OUR UNION WITH CHRIST THROUGH DEATH, BURIAL AND RESURRECTION" (*CD*, *CPW*, 6:544). As is well known, this act of immersion and regeneration describes the progress of Lycidas's body from one lost at sea under "perfidious" (100) auspices to one fully glorified in union with Christ at the poem's close. Although scholars have traced the implications of the aquatic motives in *Lycidas*, few, if any, have examined the source of this effusion, the strenuously extracted "melodious tear" (14) of the poet-priest-shepherd who weeps in the ancient tradition of Theocritus, Moschus, Bion, and Virgil, but who just as surely weeps in the tradition of Christ Himself.

In writing *Lycidas* in 1637, Milton crafts his pastoral on Greek and Virgilian models, as well as on the earliest Christian precedents of Petrarch, Boccaccio, and Sannazaro.[10] As ministerial designate of Christ, the priestly celebrant functions for the last time in the sacerdotal role which Milton enunciates on several occasions in his early poetry. In ritualized fashion, he incorporates into his text themes familiar to Renaissance elegists to disclose Christ's regenerative power through a variety of scriptural allusions and religious *signa*. In addition to these familiar contexts, however, it is my contention that the poem's subtextual structure is informed by another tradition based on the three scriptural accounts of Christ's weeping: at the death of Lazarus (John 11:35), over the future of Jerusalem (Luke 19:41), and at his own passion and death (Hebrews 5:7). These accounts of Christ's weeping constitute a significant substructure in *Lycidas*, comprising the lament for a friend, the indignant lament over the religious establishment, and the lament over Christ's sacrifice and death. This formation obviously amplifies the poem's Christian allusions and emphasizes its unity. *Lycidas*'s three-part structure, first observed by Arthur Barker in 1941, therefore assumes a still more significant logic when viewed in the context of Christ's weeping.[11]

The poetic celebrant initiates his lament in *Lycidas* by sacramentally expressing his "melodious" offering. This ritualized mode of weeping signifies the speaker's participation in what the theology of tears repeatedly describes as a kenosis of Christ-like weeping. The literal emptying of self that occurs during the act of religious weeping constitutes a true humiliation, which mimetizes Christ's self-emptying in his own weeping.[12] When we apply this principle to *Lycidas*, the lachrymal expression of line 14, first, transcends the speaker's initial protests of unpreparedness; second, in light of kenotic theology, the poet's reluctance mirrors Christ's own human anxieties about ministry. In effect, the representative authority, which the speaker so ably commands throughout the poem, derives paradoxically from this preliminary gesture of Christ-like humiliation.

The poet's priestly "tear" in the opening of *Lycidas* works efficaciously to redeem the pagan genre of the pastoral and its corrupt constituents: the postlapsarian land and seascape, the evil *ecclesia*, and what, for Milton, had become the *murder* of Edward King. Kenotically expressed, the "tear" flows through the aquatic network from smaller to larger bodies: from wells and springs (15–16), through rivers (55–106), and finally to the sea (154 ff.), regenerating, as it proceeds, the whole world of the speaker's attention. Just so, writes John Donne in "Sermon 13" (4:324–44), did Jesus weep. Preaching at Whitehall in Lent (1622/3), Donne addresses the briefest of ser-

texts, "Jesus wept." He recounts Christ's weeping in a manner that connects his sermon with the tradition of tears and, thus, aligns it intertextually with Milton's three-part mourning for Edward King:

> The teares of the text are as a Spring, a Well, belonging to one houshold, the Sisters of *Lazarus*: The teares over Jerusalem, are as a River belonging to a whole Country: The teares upon the Crosse, are as the Sea belonging to all the world. (326)

Donne, like Milton, traces the effect of *Lachrymae Christi* from minimal signification (for Donne a "spring, a Well," for Milton a unique "tear") to an ubiquitous transformation. As Donne explains,

> and though literally there fall no more into our text, then the Spring, yet because the Spring flowes into the River, and the River into the Sea, and that wheresoever we find that Jesus wept, we find our Text, . . . in all these three lines, as he wept here over *Lazarus*, as he wept there over Jerusalem, as he wept upon the Crosse over all of us. For so often Jesus wept. (326)

Assuming the priestly mind of Christ in *Lycidas*, Milton, as a kenotic agent, patterns his lament after the three-fold grieving of Christ. Milton would certainly have known the scriptural accounts of Christ's weeping which informed Donne's text.[13] Further, he, like Donne and other seventeenth-century writers, would have been acquainted with the tradition of Christian tears so generally extensive in eastern and western Churches.[14]

Several notable religious writers have endorsed tears. In his *Confessions* Augustine speaks of the "business of weeping," and defines lachrymal work to have been essential to the process of his own conversion.[15] For writers who speak of them, Christian tears are themselves a spiritual good work; the liturgy of tears is a veritable vocation, to which all are called individually and corporally, as Augustine's account suggests. Besides the *Confessions*, two influential handbooks of the late sixteenth and early seventeenth centuries were Thomas à Kempis's *Of The Imitation of Christ* and *Saint Bernard, His Meditations: or Sighes, Sobbes, and Teares, upon our Saviours Passion*. Thomas Rogers's translation of *Imitatio* first appeared in 1580, and became the authoritative edition in the period. The *Imitatio* occurred in various reprintings, as did *Meditations*, in its fourth edition by 1631. These two texts were among the most widely circulating books of the time and valorized the tears of Christ as paradigms of Christian grief expression. Like Augustine before him, Thomas à Kempis credits godly sorrow with being central to his own vocation. Christ replies to the weeping soul saying, "Lo, because thou callest for me, I am come: thy teares, thy groning, thine humilitie, and hartie sorow have mooved me so to doe."[16] Christ's own grief eminently qualifies him as a respondent to the sorrowful penitent since, as Bernard concludes, "never was there sorrow like unto this [Christ's] sorrow."[17] Remarkably congruent with Milton's rhetorical question at the opening of *Lycidas*, "Who would not sing for *Lycidas*?" (10), and his subsequent expression of a single "tear" is Bernard's reflection on Christ's tears over Jerusalem, at the prospect of which Bernard asks "who could not, nor would not shed one teare"? (19). In the *Spiritual Exercises*, whose influence on seventeenth-century poetry Louis Martz has long ago shown, Ignatius Loyola also emphasizes *Lachrymae* and defines them as a primary "Spiritual comfort: this is the name I give to any interior movement experienced by the soul. . . . The name also applies to the shedding of tears leading to love of God, either out of sorrow for sin or for the sufferings of Christ our Lord, or for other reasons directly concerned with His service and praise."[18]

In the eastern Church tears are even more strenuously advocated. *Penthos*, or "compunction," is central to the religious life, as John Chrysostom explains in his *De Compunctione*: "As in the natural order we weep for the dead, so should we weep—to put it no more strongly—for our salvation. It is with such desire and courage that we all should keep the eye of our soul trained to this end; everything should serve us as a reminder of it."[19] With equal rigor in *Regulae Brevius Tractate* Basil writes: "Compunction of this sort is a gift of God, either to awaken desire, so that the soul having once tasted the sweetness of this sorrow should strive to maintain it, or for showing that the soul with more serious application can remain in compunction at all times and places, and so render inexcusable all who lose it through indolence."[20] Gregory of Nyssa, in his *De Vita S. Patris Ephraem Syri*, celebrates the latter's compunctious gifts in a language equivalent to Donne's own in "Jesus wept." Of Ephrem, Gregory writes: "When I start to remember his floods of tears I myself begin to weep, for it is almost impossible to pass dry-eyed through the ocean of his tears. There was never a day or night, or part of a day or night, or any moment, however short, when his vigilant eyes did not appear bathed in tears."[21] Gregory's emphasis on tears, like Donne's and all who plead for *Lachrymae*, is best summarized by Origen's blatant call "to mourning, to weeping, to tears."[22]

Of the advocates cited above, five (Augustine, Bernard, John Chrysostom, Basil, and Gregory of Nyssa) are referenced in Donne's sermon "Jesus wept," together with Jerome, Ambrose, Epiphanius, and Justus Martyr. Of this catalog William Riley Parker assures us of Milton's having read Augustine and Jerome.[23] In addition, Milton himself claims, in the last part of *Tetrachordon*, to have consulted Justus Martyr, Tertullian, Origen, Lactantius, Basil, Epiphanius, and Ambrose (*Tetr, CPW,* 2:693–98). Moreover, Thomas à Kempis and Ignatius (cited above) would have been known by all educated Christians of the period. Milton and Donne therefore demonstrate a shared familiarity with a significant number of lachrymal advocates, many of whom Donne finds pertinent to his sermonic commentary on Christ's weeping. For example, Augustine, the authority cited first and most often by Donne in "Jesus wept," played a formative role in Milton's Christian education at Cambridge and after.[24] On the subject of religious tears generally, Louis Martz has observed the prevalence of "the literature of tears" which "flooded Europe during the sixteenth and seventeenth centuries." In *The Poetry of Meditation* Martz notes as well how two major documents of Catholic tear literature enjoyed repeated publication: Southwell's *Saint Peter's Complaint* "was printed in London no less than eleven times between 1595 and 1636, to say nothing of two continental and two Edinburgh editions during the same period." Similarly, his *Marie Magdalenes Funeral Tears* "saw eight editions in London and two on the Continent between 1591 and 1636."[25]

In addition to these Patristical and Jesuitical influences, English reform theologians contemporary with Donne and Milton prescribed their own occasions and modes of weeping. In an era of recurrent plague, religious persecution, and civil strife, "godly sorrow" was frequently invoked as an antidote for "sinne" or as a prevenient agency against the impending execution of God's vengeance. In 1623, the same year Donne preached "Jesus wept," William Whately published his sermon *Charitable Teares.* Like Donne, Whately began with a plea for communal weeping:

> Intercede to God for her [England] with a bended knee, and a broken heart, and moystned eyes. Not thy money, not thy toyle, not thy fighting, not thine hazard, but thy sorrowes are called for.[26]

As unusual as it may seem to twentieth-century readers, Whately's subsequent claim that national penitence could alter the course of England's history was typical of the potential attributed to godly grieving. Tears were themselves perceived as mighty political instruments for the establishment of Christ's kingdom on earth. Other contemporary endorsements for the private and public efficacy of *Lachrymae* include the following: William Hunnis, *Seven Sobs of a sorrowfull soule* (1583); *The Teares of our Saviour in the Garden* (1601); Nathaniel Cannon, *The Cryer* (1613) and *Lacrimae: Lamenta-*

tions over the Dead (1616); William Leighton, *Teares or lamentations of a sorrowfull soule* (1613); Richard Stock, *Churches Lamentation for the losse of the godly* (1614); *Christs Teares over Jerusalem* (1624); Daniel Featley, *Ancilla pietatis* (1625) and *House of Mourning* (1640); John Featley, *A Fountain of Teares* (1646) and *Teares in Time of Pestilence* (1665); John Quarles, *Fons Lachrymarum* (1648). It is interesting to note that two authors in this list enjoyed liturgical associations with All Hallows Bread Street, Milton's boyhood parish. Richard Stock and Daniel Featley (whose influence upon the boy Milton William Riley Parker has stressed) were both rectors of All Hallows.[27] As seventeenth-century Christians, Milton and Donne evidently shared a common knowledge of *Lachrymae*, as surely as their contemporaries, Richard Crashaw, George Herbert, and Henry Vaughan returned repeatedly to them in their poetry. In short, their intensive reading of Scriptural and patristic material and the proliferation of lachrymal writing of the time would have ensured Donne and Milton's knowledge of this tradition especially as pertaining to its paramount source, Christ's weeping.

3

Because Donne employs the same tradition of *Lachrymae*, his sermon provides an illuminative commentary on the progress of Milton's priestly "tear" and therefore on the structure of *Lycidas*. As he begins, Donne does not equivocate; "My vicarage," he declares, "is to speake of his [Christ's] Compassion and his teares. Let me chafe the wax, and melt your soules in a bath of his Teares" (324). Donne's intention is not merely to be rhetorically persuasive. If *Lachrymae Christi* are expressed faithfully, "soules" will "melt" and be "bath[ed]" in "the manifold benefits of godly teares" (342). Donne's exordial predicate "melt" adumbrates the eventual effects of Milton's "melodious tear" in *Lycidas*. Modeled on Christ's three laments, Milton's poetic liturgy will also advance in its third section the exhortation to "melt with ruth" (163).

As it reiterates Donne's predicate, Milton's phrase also reflects the currency of metaphors of mollification as obligatory to godly sorrow. For example, in his *Meditations* Bernard laments Christ's passion as "a most ruthfull Spectacle forcible enough to have drawn streames of teares out of the dryest eie, and to have incited a multitude of heavie groanes out of the *hardest heart*" (282). In meditating upon Christ's own tearful eyes, Bernard, himself tearful, observes "how soone doe they dissolve the Ice, and melt the frost of our hard hearts" (209–10).

In his more overtly political plea for England's welfare, William Whately exhorts the hearts of his readers to "be filled with ruth, for the faults that fill this Kingdome [England]" (03). Of numerous instances of mollification detailed throughout the genre, one of the most useful in contextualizing the "melodious tear" of *Lycidas* must be John Quarles's Royalist lament in *Englands Complaint* (1648). Quarles's mournful condemnation of civil strife, though leveled from a Royalist perspective, is ironically compatible with Milton's intentionality in composing his elegy:

> Let every word you write
> Be Truth, and then let every word invite
> A *tear*; each *tear*, a *sigh*; that every *Eye*,
> That reads, may melt into an *Elegy*.[28]

Read in the context of paradigms of mollification, Donne and Milton's identical use of the predicate "melt" provides a poetic analogue for Christian kenosis to the extent that the audience, along with the personae of both texts, is invited to participate in a corporate "melt[ing]" into *Lachrymae Christi*. Tears in this instance are regenerative as they manifest a new creation. By our "spirituall teares," writes Donne, "there is a Firmament established in us" (340). Pastoral efficacy in *Lycidas* also assumes a new dimension as the communal weeping of poet, poetic personae, and reader eventually cooperate in the holy work of Lycidas's induction into Heaven.

In the first section of *Lycidas*, the offering of the "melodious tear" for the untimely deceased, Edward King, corresponds to the first occasion on which Christ wept at the death of a friend. What Donne defines as Christ's "humane teares" compared to "a Spring, a Well, belonging to one houshold, the Sisters of Lazarus," resonate suggestively with Milton's "Sisters of the sacred well" (15). The voice and music of these female attendants, once invoked, absorb the celebrant's frugal offering to "[b]egin" (via its aquatic complex) the procedure of regeneration the whole poemscape eventually witnesses. The poet's first tear(s) are therefore like those of Christ for Lazarus. They are wept, as Donne explains (via Bernard), "as a man may weepe; for these teares were *Testes naturae, non Indices diffidentiae*, They declared him to be true man" (328).[29] Taking Christ as his model, the celebrant of *Lycidas* humanely laments his dead friend. Immediately, he draws a parallel between himself and Lycidas by first composing the place of his own committal (19–24) and, second, by reconstructing a pastoral version of their Cambridge association (25–36). Yet just as he weeps for King, it is usually affirmed, Milton laments for himself. His claim to have enjoyed an association with King consists, poetically at least, of that "self-same hill" in Cambridge on which they were simultaneously nurtured and in the speaker's hope that "[his] destin'd Urn" will, in its time, be similarly "favor[ed]" by poetic tribute. Thus, the projected wish that some Christian poet of future time may salute his burial parallels a passage from Donne's sermon.

Still speaking in connection with Christ's "humane teares," Donne cites S. Ambrose's words, "*Ad monumentum hoc digneris accedere Domine Iesu,*"

> Lord Jesus be pleased to come to this grave, to weep over this dead *Lazarus*, this soule in this body: And though I come not to a present rising, a present deliverance from the power of all sin, yet if I can feele the dew of thy teares upon me, if I can discern the eye of thy compassion bent towards me, I have comfort all the way, and that comfort will flow into an infallibility in the end. (336)

Ambrose's Latin text also bears citing:

> Utinam ergo ad hoc monumentum meum digneris accedere (*Joan* xi, 34), Domine Jesu, tuis me lacrymis laves, quoniam durioribus oculis non habeo tantas lacrymas, ut possim mea lavare delicta? Si illacrymaveris pro me, salvus ero;[30]

What is noteworthy here is the double repetition of the verb "*lavare*" to delineate the desired effect of Christ's tears. To be "lave[d]" (175) by *Lachrymae Christi* will also be the destiny of Lycidas's body in the third section of Milton's elegy. In that it corresponds to Ambrose's predicate, a traditional one in tear theology, Milton's use of this Latinate derivative helps to establish further his role as a priestly exponent of *Lachrymae*. When applied to *Lycidas* (18–22), Donne's citation of Ambrose's plea highlights Milton's firm resolve "to sing for *Lycidas*" (10) and adumbrates the provident authority with which he will guide and direct the course of his elegy. Moreover, in composing King's "tribute," Milton conscientiously prescribes his own future life and death in Christ, as both poet and glorified son of God. This premonitory event demands a heroic perseverance to be ultimately honored and redeemed by *Logós*. The Word proceeds, "flow[s]," like Christ's tears, in nonviolent repudiation of "the power of all sin," in its course to bestow (as Ambrose prays) "comfort all the way." The consolatory triumph of its closing lines leads the reader to agree with G. W. Pigman III that in writing *Lycidas* "Milton has questioned the efficacy of pastoral, its assumptions and values, . . . but rather than abandoning it despondently, [he] transcends it."[31]

In keeping with the affective imperative of his text and the genre of godly sorrow generally, Donne gives preferential emphasis to Christ's coming "neare to an excesse of passions" in lamenting Lazarus over "a privation of naturall affections" (328–30). In effect, he roundly condemns that "sin lower, that is, . . . *To be withoute naturall affections*" (330). Christ Himself wept unashamedly. "And then," Donne rhetorically asserts, "who needs be ashamed of weeping"? (331). As if he had taken his cue from Donne, the poet of *Lycidas* invites all nature to join in his lament. Echoing Moschus's pathetic fallacy, the celebrant interrogates the various pastoral personae—"the Nymphs" (50), "the Waves", "the winds" (91), and *"Hippotades"* (96)—to assuage his grief.[32] This conventional interrogation in *Lycidas* is, of course, characteristic of human grieving and invokes the customary hypothesis that, had some prevenient agencies been present, death might have been averted. Both Milton and Donne feature this contingency in their respective renderings of "humane teares." Milton asks, "Where were ye Nymphs when the remorseless deep / Clos'd o'er the head of your lov'd *Lycidas*?" (50–51). And a few lines later the inevitable, "Had ye been there—" (57). Similarly, Donne explains that, at the death of Lazarus, Christ grieved: *"Quia Mortuus*, and he wept in this respect too, *Quia non adhibita media*, because those means which in appearance might have saved his life, by his default were not used" (334). As Milton does (50–51 and 57), so Donne, through the personae of Martha and Mary (John 11), twice repeats the charge, *"Lord if thou hadst been here, my brother had not dyed"* (334).

Like the priestly Donne, the poet-priest of *Lycidas* is about to celebrate the mystery of a resurrection that transcends the sorrow of untimely death. Orpheus's "gory visage" (62) survives dismemberment as surely as Lycidas's "sacred head" (102) will eventually be "mounted high" (172). Lycidas will be resurrected from an ocean grave as surely as Lazarus will be raised from the dead. All three personae (Orpheus, as a type of Christ, Lycidas, and Lazarus) are recipients of what Donne describes as divine "Compassion." They are also manifestations of the *"Miraculum in Miraculo"* (327). Basil's definition of the miracle of resurrection is cited by Donne in connection with Lazarus's fate and may be appropriately applied to Lycidas. Though the resurrection of each is imminent, each is nonetheless authentically mourned at his death hour, focusing thereby that same emotional spectrum from grief to joy epitomized in Christ's own death and resurrection. In his humanity, Christ weeps, says Donne,

Etsi suscitandus; Though he knew that *Lazarus* were to be restored, and raised to life again: for as he meant to declare a great good will to him at last, so he would utter some by the way; he would do a great miracle for him, as he was a mighty God; but he would weep for him too, as he was a good natured man. (335)

Under similar circumstances, Milton offers his elegiac lament for Edward King though he knows that the process of his mourning will culminate in Lycidas's full apotheosis and glorification.

As the first part of his elegy concludes and in compliance with pastoral conventions, Milton pauses to address the problem of worldly fame. His famous distinction between mortal and heavenly commendation (64 – 84), though echoing Virgil's *Eclogue VI*, also reiterates Donne's reflections on the vanity of man's achievement viewed from a heavenly perspective. The familiar *"Quis homo,"* recurrent in Donne's sermons, issues in "Jesus wept" in a catalog of worldly achievers ("Lieutenants," "Kings," "religious Counsellors," "zealous Prelates") who have been "thrown all by one hand of death, into one Cart" with "vulgar, ignorant, wicked, and facinorous men" (334). The inevitable levelling of "counsellors" and "Prelates" in Donne's terse critique of vainglory figuratively prepares the way, in Milton's text, for the eventual repudiation of the English prelates. The frank disclosure of "that fatal and perfidious Bark / Built in th' eclipse and rigg'd with curses dark" (100–101) initiates Milton's rebuke of King's assassins and composes the place of Lycidas's drowning.

4

In the second section of *Lycidas* the sinking of the "sacred head" evocatively reenacts the dying of Christ and fuses securely the identities of Christ and Lycidas. Still speaking of Lazarus's death, Donne represents Christ's death in a pictorial rendering that serves as a prose equivalent to lines 100–102 in *Lycidas*:

> When our Saviour Christ had uttered his *consummatum est*, all was finished, and then their rage could do him no more harm, when he had uttered his *In manus tuas*, he had delivered and God had received his soul, yet how did the whole frame of nature mourn in Eclipses, and tremble in earthquakes, and dissolve and shed in pieces in the opening of the Temple, *Quia mortuus*, because he was dead. (333)

Christ's utterance from the cross under the explicit "eclipse" of the sun illustratively amplifies Milton's three lines. The intimate association between Christ and the deceased friend, once established in both texts, facilitates the weeping. Tear(s) wept for a friend (King/

Lazarus), associated with wells and springs, dissolve into the running water of rivers or riverlike bodies. In *Lycidas* the flow advances from the *"Deva"* (55), *"Hebrus"* (63), *"Arethuse"* (85), and *"Mincius"* (86), to, finally, the *"Camus"* (103). In Donne's sermon, Christ's "humane teares" for Lazarus move into "rivers" wept "in contemplation of a Nationall calamity foreseen upon a whole people" (336). This progress of "humane" or personal tears into the fluvial bodies introduces the second occasion of grieving in both texts: for Donne, Christ's grief over the holy community of Jerusalem and, for Milton, his own lament over the English Church.

Of the gospel sources of Christ's prophecy over Jerusalem, Donne references Luke 19:41 for its explicit allusion to Christ's tears. Another source, Matthew 23, though lacking reference to a weeping Christ, nevertheless concludes in the most cordial emotion:

> Hierusalem, Hierusalem, which killest the Prophets, and stonest them which are sent unto thee, how often would I have gathered thy children together, as the henne gathereth her chickins under her wings, & ye would not![33] (Matthew 23:37)

The provident Mother-Christ,[34] though affective and generically compatible with *Lachrymae*, is nonetheless punitive: in Luke 19 He overturns the tables of the money changers and in Matthew 23 He castigates the scribes and pharisees with the same righteous indignation that characterizes Milton's attack upon the English prelates. The "Blind mouths" (119) of *Lycidas* find their precedents in the "blind guides" (Matthew 23:16) of Christ's prophecy over Jerusalem. In Matthew's account the epithet "blind" occurs five times in connection with the Jewish establishment: "ye blind guides" (16 and 24), "Ye fooles and blind" (17 and 19), "thou blind Pharise" (26). As perversions of the priestly ideal, Milton's "blinde mouths" are an Anglican variation on the pharisaical figure whose corrupt incompetence proves "fatal and perfidious" to capable men, potential, good shepherds like King and Milton himself.

Christ's indignant lament over Jerusalem, attended to by both Donne and Milton, was a popular focus for writers of the lachrymal genre. In 1624, shortly after Donne's sermon, there appeared a poem, *Christs Teares over Jerusalem: Or A Caveat for England*, which makes explicit the subtextual parallel between Jerusalem and England in the second section of *Lycidas*:

> When Christ our Lord drew nigh
> unto Jerusalem,

Foreseeing all the miseries
    the which should fall on them:
And casting of his lookes,
    upon that beauteous Towne,
Alas, very griefe the bitter teares
    from his faire eyes fell downe.
Repent faire England now,
    repent while thou hast space,
And doe not like Jerusalem
    despite Gods promised grace.[35]

In his *Lacrimae: or Lamentations* Nathaniel Cannon explicates Matthew 23 and invokes the same fluvial metaphor used by Donne and Milton in connection with this second occasion of Christ's tears. In his "Epistle Dedicatorie," Cannon pleads that his readers be "even amongst those whose hearts bleed, and whose eyes gush out with rivers of teares, to see the abominations of these our latter and worser daies." Following Christ's example who "wept over Hierusalem, and often would . . . have gathered her together as a hen doth her chickens, but shee would not," Cannon advises that "Good Christians do the like, they mourne and melt into teares, to heare, to see, to understand, how God is provoked, his holy name blasphemed, his word neglected, his Sacraments condemned." The pastoral commission from Christ to Peter in John 21:17, declared in the Collect for the consecration of a Bishop in *The Book of Common Prayer*, is that the sheep be fed.[36] Milton, like Cannon, therefore laments the effectual violation of the pastoral ideal in that "The hungry Sheep look up, and are not fed" (125).

In the context of such deprivation, "The Pilot of the *Galilean* Lake" (109), with his much debated dual persona (Christ-Peter), serves as a consolatory agent. The "Pilot" persona, one who guides and rescues lost souls at sea, prefigures the eventual retrieval of Lycidas's body and soul and his glorification in Christ's nuptials. This redemptive event, to be celebrated later in the poem, is embodied in the fused identities of Christ/Peter inherent in the "Pilot" persona and in Lycidas's association (however transitory) with them. In keeping with the lachrymal motives of the text, King, like Peter and every man, is united with Christ in his capacity as religious weeper. In his sermon Donne also develops the lachrymal connection between Christ and all men through the widely used *exemplum* of Peter:[37]

And if Christs looking upon *Peter*, made *Peter* weep, shall not his looking upon us here, with teares in his eyes, such teares in such eyes, springs of teares, rivers of teares, seas of teares, make us weep too? *Peter* who wept under the waight of his particular sin, wept bitterly: how bitterly wept Christ under the waight of all the sins of the world? (338)

In his prophetical capacity, Christ knew how Peter would deny him.[38] Like Peter, every man suffers the frailty of his human nature. Every man sins and weeps; every man, like Peter and Lycidas, is nevertheless a potential recipient of Christ's Grace. All are elevated, as Peter (Matthew 14:31), through the "Might" of Christ who, in "walk[ing] the waves" (173), literally transcends the element that would consume him.

Christ's triumphant "Might" in *Lycidas* is exercised not only in his capacity to console but also in his prerogative to judge. The tears over Jerusalem, which provide the Christian source for Milton's righteous rebuke of the prelates, exemplify both modes of response: Christ's love and his judgment. Christ's prophecy over the holy community projects judgment as surely as do his eschatological prophecies. Donne comments on the lament over Jerusalem in a manner instructive for Milton's intention in the middle section of *Lycidas*:

> Jesus wept, *Inter acclamationes*, when all went well enough with him; [at his triumphal entry into Jerusalem] to shew the slipperinesse of worldly happinesse, and then he wept *Inter judicia*; then when himselfe was in the act of denouncing judgements upon them, Jesus wept, To shew with how ill a will he inflicted these judgements, and that themselves, and not he, had drawne those judgements upon them. (337)

Nothing could be closer to Milton's meaning in his attack upon the clergy. The same indignation is voiced by Bernard in his meditation on Christ's prophecy over Jerusalem. Reflecting with outrage on those "who were eager to lay *violent hands* upon [his] poor Iesus, as *ravenous wolves* are greedy to devoure a tender Lambe" (230), Bernard extols Christ as the prototype of all Christian persecution to follow.[39] Ultimately, then, "The hungry sheep" of Milton's account endure a violation similar to Christ's own at the hands of Jerusalem's authorities. *"The chiefe Priests"* of the Hebraic establishment who, as Donne reminds us, *"consulted how they might put Lazarus to death, because by reason of him, many believed in Iesus* John (12:10)" (327), correspond to the "Blind mouths" of the state Church whom Milton claims are responsible for Lycidas's death. The parallel between Lycidas and Lazarus is direct. As a living testament to the Resurrection, each stands adversarily against his religious establishment. Milton's hatred of religious intolerance, detailed in the prose tracts, is vehemently foreshadowed in his account of Lycidas's martyrdom. In parallel with Christ's lament for Jerusalem "which killest [her] Prophets, and stonest them which are sent to [her]," Milton condemns the prelates for their murder of Camus's "dearest pledge" (107). He attacks the English bishops in the tradition of the Old Testament prophets whom Donne also cites in typological connection with Christ's prophetical vision of Jerusalem:

> *Onus visionis*, O the burden of the judgements that I have seene upon this, and this people! It was a burden that pressed teares from the Prophet Esay, *I will water thee with my teares, O Heshbon*: when he must pronounce judgements upon her, he could not but weep over her. (337)

Milton's vision of clerical evil, beginning with the bereavement of Camus, followed by the "worthy bidden guest" being "shove[d] away" (118) from corporal communion and the graphic account of the unnourished sheep awaiting the predatory descent of "the grim Wolf" (128), compose a place informed as much by sorrow as by indignation.[40] The retributive "engine" that will stand against the Laudian hirelings suggests the "sharp two edged sword" brandished from Christ's mouth in Revelation 1:16 and resonates with the metaphorical reference to God's Word as a "two edged sword" in Hebrews 4:12. The poetic celebrant of *Lycidas*, in Christ-like fashion, sheds his tear(s) and wields the sword of his word(s) to judge and purge what has lapsed. Donne's summation of Christ's prophetical weeping serves as an appropriate closure and gloss on Milton's indignation over the prospective effect of Laud's regime. Matching the aquatic procedure in *Lycidas* (from "humane" to "prophetical teares," from "a spring, a well" to "rivers"), Donne writes of Christ's tears:

> Many such little Brookes as these fall into this River, the consideration of Christs Propheticall teares; but let it be enough to have sprinkled these drops out of the River; That Jesus, though a private person, wept in contemplation of publique calamities; That he wept in the best times, foreseeing worse; That he wept in their miseries, because he was no Author of them: That he wept not till he tooke their miseries into his consideration: And he did weep a good time, before those miseries fell upon them. (338)

So, too, did John Milton weep his elegy condemning ecclesiastical corruption and anticipating England's "miseries" five years before the outbreak of Civil Wars that would ravage his country for nearly a decade.

5

As Christ's death opened the way to resurrection and glorification, so Lycidas's death is delineated in sacrificial terms. In the third section of *Lycidas*, Milton's "melodious" offering swells grandly into the "unexpressive nuptial Song" (176) of Christ's espousal. Having passed from a well, through rivers, the poet's "tear" reaches the "sounding Seas" (154) of the poem's third section and correlates with Christ's third occasion of weeping at his own passion and death. Milton's graphic vision of King's lost body, that "Visit'st the bottom of the monstrous world" (158), parallels the death, deposition, and temporary entombment of Christ's body. And, further, the speaker's grief at his confrontation with this reality, though soon to be transcended, is modeled on what Donne defines as "his [Christ's] third teares, his pontificall teares, which accompany his sacrifice; Those teares we call the Sea" (338). Like Christ, *Deus absconditus*, temporarily separated from God during his crucial agony and entombment, Lycidas, lost at sea, seems to have been "Denied" the "moist vows" (159) of the poet-priest. Yet in the hope of Resurrection, which is his *raison d'être*, the poet "Look[s] homeward" (163). The poetic celebrant and his reader become, like Michael, lachrymal intercessors on Lycidas's behalf who will ideally "melt" with compassion into the "seas" of Christ's tears. *Lachrymae* transform the creature (the dead, the water) into redeemed agents since, as Donne explains,

> water is in nature a thing indifferent, it may give life, (so the first living things that were, were in the water) and it may destroy life, (so all things living upon the earth, were destroyed in the water) but yet though water may, though it have done good and bad, yet water does now one good office, which no ill quality that is in it can equall, it washes our soules in Baptisme; (340)

Thus Lycidas is "baptized" by those same waters in which he has drowned; he is, to repeat Milton's doctrinal definition, in "UNION WITH CHRIST THROUGH DEATH, BURIAL AND RESURRECTION." Similarly, the lachrymal "seas" wept on his behalf are for the weeper(s), as for Lycidas, a second Baptism; they are the water of life that heals man's dis/eased aridity.[41] In his book, *The Religious Symbolism of Salt*, James Latham explicates the traditional sacredness of salt with its well-known healing properties.[42] His account helps establish the sacredness of human tears whose saltiness is also evidence of man's affinity with the sea, that repository of all life, which, by Judaeo-Christian definition, is God's since "he made it" (Psalm 95.5).[43] God will ultimately claim and vindicate his own. Under Christ's baptismal auspices, Lycidas's drowned body (wherever it may actually be) is "waft[ed]" (164) safely into the third movement of the poem.

As witnesses to the imminent "Miraculum in Miraculo," the "woeful Shepherds" are commanded to "weep no more" (165). The poet's exhortation, a Theocritan echo of *Idyll* I, ends the poem's lament; weeping for all worldly evils is assumed by Christ in his final pontifical lament. Mortal weeping in *Lycidas* must cease because Christ has performed, and is performing in the eternal present of the Christian text, the perfect and sufficient act of weeping at his own passion and death. Donne insists that Christ's tears, like man's *in extremis*, exert an optimum efficiency, that they are, then, the "holiest water." *Lachrymae Christi* and those of godly men have the power to torment the anti-Christ, says Donne, "more then the fires of hell" (342). Although he urges the necessity of tears, Donne is also intent to remind us how Christ "[did] regulate and order" the course of weeping. Weeping must be performed "in the right place" (341), and so, as though in compliance with Donne's counsel, the Christ-like celebrant of *Lycidas* "regulate[s] and order[s]" the process of weeping in his elegy. The bereaved shepherds must "weep no more" because "*Lycidas* . . . is not dead" (166). He is regenerated, "lave[d]" (175) by Christ's "pontificall teares" which are to him at once baptismal, unctuous, and communal. Donne exclaims: "To how many blessednesses must these teares, this godly sorrow reach by the way, when as it reaches to the very extreme, to that which is opposed to it, to Joy? for godlie sorrow is Joy" (342–43). Tears of bereavement become the tears of *ecstasis*; they are the matrix of sanctification and finally of glorification. Aware of the joyful paradox of *Lachrymae*, Donne persists in his celebration. "So equall, so indifferent a thing is it, when we come to godly sorrow, whether we call it sorrow or joy, weeping or singing," (343) says Donne.

The mysterious progress from godly sorrow to joy is articulated by numerous writers of the genre. In his *Churches Lamentations for the Losse of the godly* (1614) Milton's former rector, Richard Stock, himself mourning Lord John Harington, expresses the same paradox of godly grief celebrated by Donne and Milton. Citing verbatim Bernard's words at the death of his beloved Gerard, Stock observes, "*I confesse it turnes my mourning almost altogether into singing, whiles being intent upon his glory, I forget almost my owne misery.*"[44] This medieval precedent serves both Stock and Milton who sorrow less for their own bereavement than for the loss of a godly man from the world. Yet like Stock and Bernard before him, Milton's lament in *Lycidas* does indeed proceed to joy; its "weeping," like Donne's, will culminate in "singing." While "all the Saints above, / In solemn troops, and sweet Societies" (178–79) offer their harmonious tribute on the particular occasion of Lycidas's reception into heaven, they simultaneously perform the choral liturgy, offered incessantly before God's throne. As it is enjoyed by its central participants, the nupital communion of Christ and Lycidas is but an individual focus for a corporal process in which all heaven is eternally engaged.[45]

The immediate consequence of the nupital union, as explained by Milton and Donne in the third sections of their respective texts, is that all weeping shall cease. As Christ has wept the definitive tears of his passion and death, so in his resurrected and glorified state He can "wipe the tears for ever from his [Lycidas's] eyes" (181). This gesture of lachrymal effacement terminates all previous modes of weeping, of "humane," of "propheticall," and now of "pontificall teares." The scriptural promise of St. John in Revelation 7:17 concludes the process of weeping in both *Lycidas* and "Jesus wept." Donne's fitting closure is directly applicable to Lycidas's condition at the end of the poem:

> Weep these teares truly, and God shall performe to thee, first that promise which he makes in *Esay, the Lord shall wipe all teares from thy face*, all that are fallen by any occasion of calamity here, in the militant Church; and he shall performe that promise which he makes in the Revelation, *The Lord shall wipe all teares from thine eyes*, that is, dry up the fountaine of teares; remove all occasion of teares hereafter, in the triumphant Church. (344)

Milton's Christ-like lament for Edward King in *Lycidas* persists in efficacious refutation of the long-standing charge that the poem contains "little grief."[46] The subjective, roundly polemical tenor of Samuel Johnson's response to *Lycidas* and its defaming effect upon the poem's reception history have been steadily corrected, and would "sink," one hopes forever, beneath the weight of critically responsible analysis.[47] This essay is intended to provide another alternative in that corrective process, especially as it concerns the poet's credentials as an authentic exponent of Christian grief. To this end Donne's sermon, "Jesus wept," through its correspondence with *Lycidas*, offers intertextual evidence that Milton is articulating his lament within the theological context of *Lachrymae Christi*, widely known to seventeenth-century readers. Like Donne's sermon, Milton's elegy advances to and attains its resolution through the three scriptural occasions of Christ's weeping. These milestones in "Christ's Compassion" formally authorize Christian bereavement over the human vicissitudes systematically presented in both texts: personal bereavement, worldly commendation or the lack of it, corruption of the religious institution, and the prospect of corporal death. The works' corresponding attention to *Lachrymae Christi* is demonstrated in the similar three-part structuring of textual material and their parallel thematic constituents: tears at the death of a friend, over the religious establishment, and in response to Christ's passion and death. Although proof for the direct influence of Donne's sermon on Milton's *Lycidas* has yet to be established, the antiphonal alignment of these two texts discloses a useful context in which to reconsider the poet's own prefatory claim "to bewail a learned Friend." Milton's pronouncement can be received unapologetically, not only within the critically illuminated tradition of elegy, but also within the theology of tears, an orthodox, well-documented and, for the seventeenth century, prominent mode of Christian grief expression.

Notes

1. Erasmus's letter is translated and quoted by Samuel Knight in *The Life of Dr. John Colet* (London, 1724), 110. An abbreviated version of this essay was delivered in Florence, Italy at the Third International Milton Symposium in June, 1988.

2. William Riley Parker, *Milton: A Biography* (Oxford: Clarendon Press, 1968), 1: 6.

3. John Shawcross has suggested to me that the date of Milton's entry into Paul's was not so early as 1617–20 [argued by Donald Lemen Clark in *John Milton at St. Paul's School: A Study of Ancient Rhetoric in English Renaissance Education* (1948; rpt. New York: Archon Books, 1964), 27].

4. For discussions of St. Paul's School and its cathedral, see Sir Michael McDonnell, *A History of St. Paul's School* (London: Chapman & Hall, 1909); *The Early Lives of Milton*, ed. Helen Darbishire (London: Constable, 1932); Arthur Barker, "Milton's Schoolmasters," *Modern Language Review* 32 (1937): 517–36; Harris F. Fletcher, *The Intellectual Development of John Milton* (Urbana: University of Illinois Press, 1961), 1:154–431.

5. Clark, 35.

6. For a discussion of the publication of Donne's sermons, see "Introduction," *The Sermons of John Donne*, eds. George R. Potter and Evelyn N. Simpson (Berkeley: University of California Press, 1962), 1:1–82. All subsequent citations from Donne's sermon are from this edition and are noted by page number in the text.

7. Sir Walter Raleigh quoted in George Reuben Potter, "Milton's Early Poems, the School of Donne, and the Elizabethan Sonneteers," *Philological Quarterly* 6 (1927): 396. For another consideration of Milton and the Metaphysical poets, see William John Roscelli, "The Metaphysical Milton (1625–31)," *Texas Studies in Language and Literature* 8 (1966): 463–84.

8. For example, Barbara Kiefer Lewalski made this suggestion in her summary remarks at a seventeenth-century division meeting during the MLA conference in New York City, December 1981; John Shawcross advanced a similar suggestion in his concluding address at the Second International Milton Symposium at Christ's College, Cambridge in August 1983.

9. Frederic B. Tromly, "Milton Responds to Donne: 'On Time' and 'Death Be Not Proud,'" *Modern Philology* 80 (May 1983): 390–93. For Thomas O. Sloane's study, see *Donne, Milton, and the End of Humanist Rhetoric* (Berkeley: University of California Press, 1985).

10. James H. Hanford, "The Pastoral Elegy and Milton's *Lycidas*," *Milton's Lycidas: The Tradition and the Poem*, ed. C. A. Patrides (New York: Holt, Rinehart and Winston, 1961), 27–55. Other studies of the pastoral elegy and its development in English are John W. Draper, *The Funeral Elegy and the Rise of English Romanticism*

(New York: New York University Press, 1929); Avon Jack Murphy, "The Critical Elegy of Earlier Seventeenth-Century England," *Genre* 5.1 (1972): 75–105; Ellen Zetzel Lambert, *Placing Sorrow: A Study of the Pastoral Elegy Convention from Theocritus to Milton* (Chapel Hill: University of North Carolina Press, 1976); G. W. Pigman III, *Grief and English Renaissance Elegy* (Cambridge: Cambridge University Press, 1985).

11. Arthur Barker, "The Pattern of Milton's *Nativity Ode*," *University of Toronto Quarterly* 10 (1940–41): 171–72.

12. For the retrieval of the neglected tradition of religious tears, see Maggie Ross, *The Fountain & the Furnace: The Way of Tears and Fire* (New York: Paulist Press, 1987). Maggie Ross is the pseudonym of an Anglican nun (Sr. Martha Reeves) whose studies on the lachrymal tradition are the most comprehensive to date. Another book-length study of tears in a specific period is Fred Kaplan, *Sacred Tears: Sentimentality in Victorian Literature* (Princeton: Princeton University Press, 1987). Neil Hertz has also written an illuminating essay, "Wordsworth and the Tears of Adam" in *The End of the Line: Essays on Psychoanalysis and the Sublime* (New York: Columbia University Press, 1985), 21–39. Hertz's reading of Adam's tear flood in *Paradise Lost*, book 11, bears some relevance to the compassionate expression of the poet-priest in *Lycidas*. Louis Martz has written on Donne, Herbert, and tears in "Donne and Herbert: Vehement Grief and Silent Tears," *John Donne Journal* 7.1 (1988): 21–34. Mark C. Taylor has offered a contemporary theo-philosophical study which considers theoretical issues raised by the convergence of such disciplines as philosophy, literature, art, architecture, and theology. See *Tears* (Albany: State University of New York Press, 1990). For three other recent essays on tears in the poetry of the period, see Claude J. Summers, "Tears for Herrick's Church," *George Herbert Journal* 14, 1–2 (Fall 1990-Spring 1991):51–71; Joan Hartwig, "Tears as a Way of Seeing," in *On the Celebrated and Neglected Poems of Andrew Marvell*, eds. Claude J. Summers and Ted-Larry Pebworth (Columbia: University of Missouri Press, 1992), 70–85; John LeVay, "Crashaw's 'Saint Mary Magdalen, or The Weeper,'" *Explicator* 50.3 (Spring 1992): 142–44.

13. A helpful supplement to reading Donne's sermons is *John Donne and the Theology of Language*, eds. P. G. Stanwood and Heather Ross Asals (Columbia: University of Missouri Press, 1986). Paul Harland has provided an approach to the sermons generically compatible with this essay: "Imagination and Affections in John Donne's Preaching," *John Donne Journal* 6.1 (1987): 33–50. Achsah Guibbory stresses the centrality of memory in Donne's preaching in "John Donne and Memory as 'the Art of *Salvation*,'" *Huntington Library Quarterly* 43 (1979–80): 260–74.

14. Aside from Maggie Ross's study (already cited), there has been a scattering of twentieth-century articles on the subject of religious tears. These include: "Larmes," *Dictionnaire d'Archeologie Chrétienne et de Liturgie*, 8, part 1 (1928): 1393–1402; Henry Bars, "A La Source des Larmes," *Vie Spirituelle* 39 (1934): 140–50; Lev Gillet, "The Gift of Tears," *Sobornost* (Dec. 1937): 5–10; Fr. Ambroise Gardeil, "La Béatitude des larmes," *Vie Spirituelle* 57 (1938): 129–36; Dietrich Von Hildebrand, "Bienheureux Ceux Qui Pleurent," *Dieu Vivant* 18 (1951): 79–90; Sr. Sylvia Mary, "St. Symeon the New Theologian and the Way of Tears," *Studia Patristica* 10, Part 1 (1970): 431–35. For a general summary of tears, see also "Larmes," *Dictionnaire de Spiritualité Ascétique et Mystique Doctrine et Histoire* 9 (1976): 287–303. Most thorough and recent of the French writing on tears is Anne Vincent–Buffault, *Histoire Des Larmes XVIIIᵉ–XIXᵉ siècles* (Paris: Rivages, 1986). This study concerns "Larmes" in the French literature of the eighteenth and nineteenth century and is not related to the tradition of religious tears. On tears in the eastern Church, Irénée Hausherr has writ-

ten *Penthos: The Doctrine of Compunction in the Christian East*, trans. Anselm Hufstader (Kalamazoo: Cistercian Publications, 1982).

15. Augustine, *Confessions*, trans. Vernon J. Bourke (New York: Fathers of the Church, 1953), book 8, chap. 12, p. 224. For Augustine on tears of bereavement and the invitation to communal weeping, see *Confessions*, book 9, chap. 12, pp. 255–59.

16. Thomas à Kempis, *Imitation of Christ*, trans. Thomas Rogers (London, 1580), 165.

17. *Saint Bernard, His Meditations: or Sighes, Sobbes, and Teares, upon our Saviours Passion*, trans. W. P., 4th edition (London, 1631), 291. All subsequent references to *Meditations* are from this edition and are cited by page number in the text.

18. *The Spiritual Exercises of Saint Ignatius*, trans. Thomas Corbishley (Wheathampstead, Hertfordshire: Anthony Clarke, 1963), 107–8. Ignatius describes his own remarkable gift of tears in his *Autobiography* and *Spiritual Diary*, both of which are explicated by Joseph de Guibert, S. J. in *The Jesuits, Their Spiritual Doctrine and Practice: A Historical Study* (Chicago: Loyola University Press, 1964), 21–73. See also Louis L. Martz, *The Poetry of Meditation: A Study in English Religious Literature of the Seventeenth Century* (1954; rpt. New Haven: Yale University Press, 1962). *Passim*.

19. John Chrysostom, *De Compunctione* in *Patrologiae, cursus completus . . . Series graeca*, ed. J. P. Migne (Paris, 1857–1912), 47: 409F. All subsequent references to works in this series are noted by *Pat. G.* For English citations of the *Patrologia G.* and *L.,* I am using Anselm Hufstader's translations.

20. Basil, *Regulae Brevius Tractate* 16, *Pat. G.* 31: 420D.

21. Gregory of Nyssa, *De Vita S. Patris Ephraem Syri, Pat. G.* 46: 829D.

22. Origen, *In Ieremiam, Homilia* 19, *Pat. G.* 13: 270C.

23. Parker, 1: 285. Of Jerome's many references to religious tears, two of the most noteworthy are: *Epistola* CXXII(f), *De Poenitentia* in *Patrologiae cursus completus . . . Series latina*, ed. J. P. Migne (Paris, 1879–90), 22: 890–900; and *In Ieremiam Prophetam, Pat. L.* 24: 904–10.

24. For the Augustinian influence in Milton's education, see Irene Samuel, *Plato and Milton* (Ithaca: Cornell University Press, 1947), 38–39. References to Augustine also occur in Milton's *Commonplace Book*, though these appear to have been entered by a scribe in the later 1650's. See Ruth Mohl, *John Milton and His Commonplace Book* (New York: Frederick Ungar Publishing, 1969), 36–37, 186, 192–93. For the most comprehensive study of the Augustinian influence in Milton's work, see Peter A. Fiore, *Milton and Augustine: Patterns of Augustinian Thought in Paradise Lost* (University Park: Pennsylvania State University Press, 1981). For the Augustinian and general Patristical influence in Donne's sermons, see Potter and Simpson, "The Early Fathers, Especially St. Augustine," *The Sermons of John Donne*, 10: 345–86.

25. Martz, 184. Southwell's treatise was only one of many renderings of Magdalene as a lachrymal exemplar. Others include *Complaynt of the Lover of Cryst Saynt Mary Magdaleyn* (London, 1520); *Marie Magdalens Love* (London, 1595); *Maries Exercise* (London, 1597); *Saint Mary Magdalens Conversion* (London, 1603); *Mary Magdalens Lamentations for the Loss of her Master Jesus* (London, 1601); John Sweetman, *S. Mary Magdalens Pilgrimage to Paradise* (London, 1617); Thomas Robinson, *The Life and Death of Mary Magdalene* (London, 1620).

26. William Whately, "The Epistle Dedicatorie," *Charitable Teares* (London, 1623).

27. For Parker's informative notes on Stock, see *A Biography*, 1: 9 and 2: 703; for Featley, see 1: 36 and 2: 733–34. Also helpful on Stock as an influence is Fletcher, 1: 53–72.

28. John Quarles, *Englands Complaint* in *Fons Lachrymarum* (London, 1648), 2.

29. Bernard, *Sermones in Cantica* 26, *Pat. L.* 183:1359D. Bernard's text reads: "*Et lacrymatus est*, inquit, *Jesus* (*Joan.* XI, 35). Fuerunt lacrymae illae testes profecto naturae, non indices diffidentiae. Denique et prodiit mox ad vocem eius qui erat mortuus, ne continuo putes fidei praejudicium dolentis affectum."

30. Ambrose, *De Poenitentia, Pat. L.* 16: 431.

31. Pigman III, 124. For another study related to dying and grief up to and including Milton's time, see Nancy Lee Beaty, *The Craft of Dying: A Study in the Literary Tradition of the Ars Moriendi in England* (New Haven: Yale University Press, 1970). Several other approaches to grief in *Lycidas* are Michael West, "The *Consolatio* in Milton's Funeral Elegies," *Huntington Library Quarterly* 34 (1970–71): 233–49; Barbara Currier Bell, "'Lycidas' and the Stages of Grief," *Literature and Psychology* 25 (1975): 166–74; Barbara A. Johnson, "Fiction and Grief: The Pastoral Idiom of Milton's *Lycidas*," *Milton Quarterly* 18.3 (Oct. 1984): 69–76; Robert E. Bourdette, Jr., "Mourning Lycidas: 'The Poem of the Mind in the Act of Finding What Will Suffice,'" *Essays in Literature* 11 (Spring 1984): 11–20; Robert Leigh Davis, "That Two-Handed Engine and the Consolation of *Lycidas*," *Thoreau Literary Quarterly* 20 (May 1986): 44–48. None of these views of grief in Milton's poem engages with the theology of tears, with the exception of Johnson's useful reminder of Michael's being sometimes conceived as a lachrymal intercessor on man's behalf (26).

32. Ellen Lambert comments evocatively on the interrogation of nature in a pastoral elegy. "Now in the pastoral elegy, when we invite nature to turn her order upside down or weep with us, what we are asking for is not a display of anger, or a promise of revenge, or even (primarily) a display of grief, we are asking for a demonstration of love" (*Placing Sorrow*, xxvii).

33. For Biblical quotations I am using *The Geneva Bible: The Annotated New Testament, 1602 Edition*, ed. Gerald T. Sheppard (New York: The Pilgrim Press, 1989).

34. For a comprehensive treatment of the tradition of a maternal Christ, see Caroline Walker Bynum, *Jesus as Mother: Studies in the Spirituality of the High Middle Ages* (Berkeley: University of California Press, 1982). *Passim*.

35. *Christs Teares over Jerusalem: Or A Caveat for England, to call to God for Mercy, lest we be plagued for our contempt and wickednesse* (London, 1624), lines 1–12. Using London for his focus of comparison with Jerusalem, Thomas Nashe even earlier wrote his version of *Christs Teares over Jerusalem* (1593).

36. Nathaniel Cannon, "Epistle Dedicatorie," *Lacrimae: Lamentations over the Dead* (London, 1616). I am citing from *The Book of Common Prayer 1559. The Elizabethan Prayer Book,* ed. John E. Booty (Charlottesville, Va.: University Press of Virginia, 1976), 233.

37. Bernard provides his account of Peter's role as an example of Christian penitence: "Let remembrance of the words wound my heart, and awake my sleepie conscience, that my soule may be cast down with true sorrow, and that I may weepe, yea weepe bitterly with sorrowfull *Peter*, Luke 22.62 for my sinnes, that I may be made partaker of the benefit of thy comfortable mercie, and obtain remission of my grievous transgressions, by true Repentance as he did" (*Meditations*, 201).

38. Two studies of Milton's prophetical function in *Lycidas* are Joseph Wittreich, *Visionary Poetics: Milton's Tradition and His Legacy* (San Marino, California: Huntington Library, 1979), 79–182; and John C. Ulreich, Jr., "'And by Occasion Foretells': The Prophetic Voice in *Lycidas*," *Milton Studies* 18 (1983): 3–23. For prophecy in Donne's sermons, see Patricia M. Howison, "Donne's Sermons and the Rhetoric of Prophecy," *English Studies in Canada* 15 (June 1989): 134–48.

39. Peter Sacks offers another useful context for Milton's "ravening wolves" in his reconstruction of London's combative atmosphere in 1637. He argues for the immediate influence of Puritan persecution on Milton's attack on the clergy. Sacks cites *A Breviate of the Prelates intollerable usurpations* (1637), a polemic written and circulated by Prynne, Bastwick, and Burton who were publicly tortured for their efforts. The document, says Sacks, "denounced the wolfish clergy for preying upon instead of nourishing their congregations, and they prophesied the vengeance of God upon the nation. The language and the stance prefigure part of Milton's poem, and the fate of the three men must have harshly sealed their influence on the poet" [*The English Elegy: Studies in the Genre from Spenser to Yeats* (Baltimore: Johns Hopkins University Press, 1985)], 92.

40. That God himself, like Christ, suffers and grieves at the lamentable effects of sin at large in the world is a significant feature of lachrymal theology. Just as Christ wept on three occasions, God is held to exhibit, according to John Featley, a "long-suffering" by which "he call[s] to repentance" and "wooe[s] transgressors" (*Teares in Time*, 64). For discussions of the theology and philosophy of divine pathos as expressed through the prophets, see Abraham J. Herschel, *The Prophets* (New York: Harper & Row, 1962), 2:1–47. God as a suffering deity has been considered by Gerald Vann, *The Pain of Christ and the Sorrow of God* (London: Aquin Press, 1947) and, more recently, by Terence E. Fretheim, *The Suffering of God: An Old Testament Perspective* (Philadelphia: Fortress Press, 1984). Finally, Samuel Terrein provides a detailed consideration of the divine involvement of God with his creation in *The Elusive Presence: The Heart of Biblical Theology* (San Francisco: Harper & Row, 1978). The actual process of weeping as it occurs in Old Testament text has been addressed by Flemming Friis Hvidberg, *Weeping and Laughter in the Old Testament* (Amsterdam: E. J. Brill, 1962). The Hebraic utterance of *Hôy* as recurrent in Hebrew prophetical Scripture is treated by Waldemarr Janzen, *Mourning Cry and Woe Oracle* (Berlin, New York: Walter de Gruyter, 1972).

41. A useful discussion of water symbolism in the seventeenth century is Donald R. Dickson, *The Fountain of Living Waters: The Typology of The Waters of Life in Herbert, Vaughan, and Traherne* (Columbia: University of Missouri Press, 1987). *Passim.*

42. James E. Latham, *The Religious Symbolism of Salt. Théologie Historique* #64 (Beauchesne: Paris, 1982). *Passim.*

43. Beyond the obvious presence of salt in human tears, Dr. William H. Frey, a biochemist, details other constituents. Dr. Frey's study of "psychogenic lacrimation, emotional tearing" provides new insight into the process of weeping. See *Crying: The Mystery of Tears* (Minneapolis, Minn.: Winston Press, 1985).

44. Richard Stock, *The Churches Lamentation for the Losse of the godly* (London, 1614), 102.

45. Michael Lieb has provided a sensitive reading of *Lycidas* as epithalamic: "Milton's 'Unexpressive Nuptial Song': A Reading of *Lycidas*," *Renaissance Papers* (1982): 15–26.

46. Samuel Johnson, "from 'The Life of Milton,'" in *Milton's Lycidas: The Tradition and the Poem*, 56.

47. For a succinct summary of the reception history of *Lycidas* preparatory to a reading of the poem's legitimate grief expression, see Bourdette, Jr., "Mourning Lycidas," 11–13.

Milton: The Truest of the Sons of Ben

JOHN CREASER

Jonson is not seen as a major presence in the work of Milton. The two authors show least affinity in their greatest writing: the satirical, loveless comedies of Jonson are as alien to Milton's aspirations as the sublimity of Milton's epics is beyond Jonson's reach. Moreover, we inherit an image of Milton as an Elizabethan poet who happened to be born five years after the Queen's death, not as a poet born into a Jonsonian era, because "the Tribe of Ben" was either content to practice a "poetry of limitation" or fell short in work of laureate ambition.[1]

Yet Jonson is a substantial presence in the creative consciousness of Milton. As Shelley writes in the Preface to *Prometheus Unbound:*

> One great poet is a masterpiece of nature which another not only ought to study but must study. He might as wisely and as easily determine that his mind should no longer be the mirror of all that is lovely in the visible universe, as exclude from his contemplation the beautiful which exists in the writings of a great contemporary.[2]

Milton was inevitably in some measure a Jonsonian, and arguably he is the truest of the Sons of Ben—even though he is a Jonsonian writer for only a short period.[3]

The Jonsonian presence in Milton's earlier work is strong and unmistakable. His first published poem, "On Shakespeare" (written 1630–31, published 1632), is an eclectic exercise in which Spenserian diction meets the ingenuity of a Marino, but, prefaced to the Second Folio, it is obviously elicited by Jonson's great tribute in the First Folio, whose Horatian topos of the *monumentum aere perennius* it also exploits. "An Epitaph on the Marchioness of Winchester" (1631), an elegy on a lady commemorated by Jonson himself, is Jonsonian in prosody and style, in its subdued and yet sustained poignancy, and in its respectful but self-serving celebration of aristocracy. The more fluid tetrameters of *L'Allegro* and *Il Penseroso* (c. 1631) descend at least in part from the sophisticated grace of tetrameters in Jonson's entertainments, though they transcend even Jonson himself in that grace. *Arcades* (1632?) adopts a form of aristocratic entertainment that Jonson had made his own, and is specifically indebted to the *Entertainment at Althorp*, while *Comus* (1634) owes its very existence to Jonson's development of the Stuart court masque.

In these few years of early maturity, Milton is working through a response to the creative example of Jonson, not only in form and style but also in perceiving the poet's social role as offering praise, advice, and consolation to potential patrons among the nobility. Moreover, parallels of form and attitude occur throughout the two bodies of work. In the *Nativity Ode* of Christmas, 1629, Milton marks his coming of age as man and poet by assimilating the full amplitude and elevation of the Pindaric ode into English verse; his sole predecessor was Jonson's "To the Immortal Memory and Friendship of That Noble Pair, Sir Lucius Cary and Sir H. Morison," written only a few months earlier. Jonson also wrote "A Hymn on the Nativity of My Saviour." Each poet addresses great men of the day in his verse; each is at his most attractive in urbane poems of social invitation, based on models in Horace or Martial. *Sejanus* and *Catiline* are the most powerful attempts to re-create classical tragedy in an English guise before *Samson Agonistes*.

There are also striking affinities of temperament. Each is a painstaking craftsman whose verse projects an assimilated meaning rather than discovers meaning in exploratory writing. Each seeks to establish a discriminating readership, and professes to be, with Horace, *contentus paucis lectoribus*. Each perceives that the highest exercise of virtue is for stubborn and lonely men, and each follows Hebrews chapter xi in extolling the solitary patriarchal exemplars of faith.[4] Neither joins fully in either the Petrarchan, the anti-Petrarchan, or the devotional strains of writing that were then so creative. The power of love is less of a central inspiration to them than to most Renaissance poets, despite Milton's early Ovidianism and the great utterances of human love in *Paradise Lost* and elsewhere, and even though Jonson in his later years wrote with rueful sympathy of erotic experience. Neither is a poet of meditation; "To Heaven" is a telling exception in Jonson, and although religious faith permeates all Milton's writing, he is little inclined to pray in verse. Milton respects the privacy of prayer and does not intrude on supplication that seems to be true communion with the divine. Leaving aside exalted invocation and exhortation, words of genuine prayer are not represented, except for the regular morning orisons of Adam and Eve, which, though "unmeditated" (*PL*, 5.149), are ritualistic in tendency and based on

Psalms and a Canticle. Their words of penitence by the Tree after the
fall are not recorded. Nor are the words of Samson as he stands
reflectively between the pillars, even though this requires Milton to
deviate from his biblical source, whose Samson prays there for
vengeance and for death. It is significant that when Milton earlier
invents a prayer for "speedy death" (*SA,* 650) by Samson, that prayer is
a mere self-indulgence.

But Jonson's main value for Milton lies in the ambition, scale, and
variety of his literary undertaking. First, although much of his work
is in forms then seen as light and ephemeral, Jonson created a literary
canon that he had printed and presented as a body of classic texts.
More than any previous English author, he established the primacy of
print over manuscript, or, for plays, over live performance. Milton
accepted this primacy, became our second major poet committed to
circulation by print rather than orally or in manuscript, and, especially in his later years, did what he could under political constraints to
establish his oeuvre.

Second, Jonson—more than Milton's "original" Spenser or the
equally learned poet Donne—opened the way for Milton to a creative
neoclassicism. In the words of Thomas M. Greene, he "invented a
classical idiom for his language, just as more broadly he invented a
classical temper, a moral style or set of styles, both recognizably
native and recognizably derivative from Latin."[5] His classicism is
post-medieval not only in its depth but in its specificity. He maintains
a dialogue with the past through precise echoes and allusions, treating
classical texts as living presences in his consciousness, approaching
them not with prescriptive veneration but working them into the texture of his immediate experience, merging one model or form or genre
with others.[6] In this way he revitalizes ancient values in modern
forms.

The innovativeness of Jonson's classicism was soon recognized. In
his poem prefaced to *Volpone,* Donne says that to other men the
ancients are "cobwebby" (*araneosi*): *Tam nemo veterum est secutor, ut
tu / Illos quos sequeris novator audis* (for no one is a follower of the
ancients like you [who] hearken as an innovator after those whom you
will follow).[7] The same term *novator* (renewer, restorer) is used in the
course of Abraham Holland's verses that accompany the earliest
engraving of Jonson, done by Robert Vaughan in the 1620s: *Scenae
veteris novator audax* (daring restorer of the ancient stage).[8]

The pugnacious explicitness of Jonson's intentions in his neoclassical plays and "strange *poems*" (*Forest,* 12.81) made the originality of
what Douglas Bush has termed his "dynamic assimilation" of classical values highly visible.[9] His coordination of a firm classical ordon-

nance with the multitudinous inventiveness of Renaissance art—the strictness of control only emphasizing the fertility of creation—opened new possibilities for English verse, and here Milton is, as Bush says, his "nearest heir" (114). Already in the *Nativity Ode* there is a Jonsonian merging of models and genres; Pindaric ode and Messianic eclogue are fused with liturgical hymn and with exalted poem on the Nativity, in a prosody that combines popular song with the intricate inflections of an Italianate and Spenserian stanza. It is unlikely that even Milton could have written with such confident and harmonious eclecticism at twenty-one without Jonsonian precedent—not specifically in the Cary/Morison ode (which was presumably unknown to him) but in the tenor of all his work.

Ultimately, Milton's appreciation of the classics was to be more competitive than Jonson's. Although Jonson takes liberties with his classical authorities, he is aware of a remote excellence that he seeks to restore. Milton often keeps closer to his classical models just because his position is combative as well as appreciative; he aims to set his art above the ancients because he is Christian, as above the Roman Catholics because he is Protestant. Yet he avoids cultural provincialism through the quality of his awareness; *Lycidas* is a worthy re-creation of ancient pastoral elegy as well as a remaking of it.

Jonson's cultivation of print and his dialogue with the ancients lead to the third and most persuasive way in which the scale of his enterprise was an inspiration to Milton. He was Milton's most immediate exemplar of, in Richard Helgerson's term, a self-crowned laureate: "the great poet as the anointed spokesman of the nation," advisor of monarch or ruler in works "doctrinal or exemplary to a Nation," "he which can faine a *Commonwealth*[,] ... can governe it with *Counsels*, strengthen it with *Lawes*, correct it with *Judgements*, informe it with *Religion*, and *Morals*."[10] The laureate self-consciously presents himself as the great poet in opposition to mere amateurs or hacks, placing himself at the center of his carefully constructed body of work, a dedicated author of massive integrity.

Despite the depth of Milton's responses to the Protestant vision of Spenser or the tragic insight of Shakespeare, Jonson offered a richer model of laureate amplitude: a unique combination of great dramatist, great poet, powerful theoretician, man of learning, voice of the public conscience, and dominating personality. Other contemporaries of matching excellence are specialists by comparison, less fitting precedents for Milton's largeness of ambition.

Why, then, granted the potency of Jonson's presence and influence, was he not to mean more to Milton? Granted Milton's profound debt to the versatile practitioner of living classicism and laureate exaltation, why does Jonson in his particularity soon come to mean relatively little to the younger poet, and why is Milton able with apparent ease to release himself from the gravitational pull of Jonsonian method? Here I disagree with David Norbrook, who, writing of Milton as he was in 1637, says: "Spenser was Milton's true poet 'father,' but it was Jonson, with his massive literary authority, who had caused a more immediate 'anxiety of influence.' Milton had been struggling to avoid becoming just one more of the 'sons of Ben'; a powerful release came with his death" (269–70).

This view overlooks the confident eclecticism of Milton, even if we confine ourselves to the poems that can be dated with some confidence within his Jonsonian phase. Even after the more disciplined Jonsonian writing is ushered in by the failure of the Spenserian "The Passion" (presumably written early in 1630), the influence of Spenser and the Spenserians remains strong and benign. For example, "At a Solemn Music," which follows the Jonsonian *Arcades* in the Trinity Manuscript, is an assured and quite un-Jonsonian poem, opulent in sonority and syntax, Italianate in the complexity of its sustained prosody, and characteristic of early Milton in its fusion of Platonic exaltation and apocalyptic fervor. The leisurely expansiveness of the masque at Ludlow brings alien voices and attitudes into that most Jonsonian of forms.

Moreover, Milton's sole explicit reference to Jonson suggests no "anxiety of influence": "Then to the well-trod stage anon, / If *Jonson's* learned Sock be on" (*L'All*, 131–32). This occurs in a whimsical instance of the Jonson/Shakespeare comparison that was becoming a critical routine. By "Sock," Milton refers to the *socci* or light shoes worn by ancient actors in comedy, a meaning not acclimatized into English and introduced only recently as a self-conscious allusion by writers such as Jonson himself, in his poem to Shakespeare. Milton's is an act of playfully imitative homage, a momentary re-creation of a Jonsonian mode of erudite elevation. At the same time, the down-to-earth meaning of sock was so dominant then, as now, that it does not disappear. The reader may either consciously exclude it as irrelevant—so it becomes a present absence in the text, like a word "under erasure," an embarrassing reminder of an unwanted significance—or, more sensitively, he may consciously admit the everyday meaning as a sign of that creaturely vitality that underlies Jonson's learned artifice. The young Milton plays with relaxed finesse around the ambivalences of the master.

The affectionate, open-ended wordplay exemplifies how Milton was never under Jonson's domination; indeed, after *Comus*, the particularities of Jonsonian practice came to mean little to him. The primary reason why he was able to dislodge Jonson with such ease was that, within broad theological and theoretical assumptions widespread at the time, the attitudes of the two writers were fundamentally opposed.[11]

The distinction may be epitomized in the statement: Jonson is an artist of *being*, Milton of *becoming*. Jonson celebrates the good by naming them, and he commemorates good and bad alike by praising or vilifying what they essentially are. He has little feeling for temporal process or change. Milton's is an art of opportunity, transition, and reformation, of growing into new experience (or tragically failing to grow). If he celebrates a given individual, he will typically proffer some new and pressing *occasio*: "O yet a nobler task awaits thy hand"; "Help us to save free Conscience" (Sonnets XV and XVI).

Self-sufficiency and changelessness are Jonson's ideal, and despite the undoubted religious faith of the man, religious experience is no more central to his literary sensibility than is erotic love. In *Discoveries*, he goes beyond his source in Lipsius in equating the spiritual experience of Christian and pagan: "*Truth* is mans proper good; and the onely *immortall* thing, was given to our mortality to use. No good *Christian*, or *Ethnick*, if he be honest, can misse it" (531–33). The quality of "To Heaven" is the exception proving the rule of mere competence among his small body of religious verse. His version of *consummatum est* as "All's done in me"—rhymed with "To worship thee"—hardly suggests a deep commitment to his subject.[12]   As Katharine Maus has argued, Socratic and Augustinian modes of thought imply a psychology of radical dependence and a sense of incompleteness, and seek to find outside the self a perfection that it cannot supply from within. Jonson, on the other hand, continually cites as his standard of value those Roman authors, stoical in tendency, who appreciate the austere virtues of temperance and self-reliance, scorn human weakness, and reject philosophies of dependence.[13]

A classic essay by Thomas Greene has made familiar how the beings and characters celebrated by Jonson are "at home" gathered within themselves, serene and impregnable in the vital stillness of their own bosoms, independent of society even when they play a distinguished role within it.[14] He values integrity and sees an individual as all of a piece: wit, language, elocution, dress, social bearing, gait—all speak of the inner being.[15] He writes with such bitterness of flattery and plagiary because they impair an achieved wholeness, whether of a mind or a literary work. His fundamental commitment is to the stoical self-sufficiency of the isolated being, and despite a deep and arrogant skepticism about the worth of the many, he has strong faith in the adequacy of the few. Jonson is one of our handful of great poets of friendship, yet his vision of friendship eschews dependence. Only those so self-reliant as not to need friendship are capable of it, and what is valued is like-mindedness, not otherness.[16] Where there is no like-mindedness, there is a strong sense of exclusion.

Typically, *Discoveries* begins with a stress on the equanimity of virtue: "No ill can happen to a *good* man." It is equally typical that the self-sufficiency of the good is fundamental to the major form developed by Jonson, the court masque. The invulnerability of virtue is its working assumption, since the masquers embody ideal values. Another great formal invention of Jonson's, the country-house poem, is also an image of self-sufficiency and integrity. There the lord can "at home, in thy securer rest, / Live, with un-bought provision blest," in a household and estate where everything is "his owne," where all is in "proportion," and where hospitality is an exchange of trust, not mere charity or the buying of favors.[17] Those at home in the country house genuinely "dwell" there; the verb is one of a cluster of words of attitude and stance—of living, of standing, of rootedness, of stasis without stagnation—which shape the positive description within much of the verse.[18]

Characterization in Jonson is consequently static. There is no lack of complex psychological pressures and distortions, but typically there is no dramatized fourth dimension. It is exceptional that Morose should tell how his boyhood education "now is growne to be another nature to me" (5.3.54) and that we see Macro withering into the man of policy which the other powerful characters have already become, and it is representative that there is no real question when Mosca exclaims against Corbaccio: "What horride strange offence / Did he commit 'gainst nature, in his youth, / Worthy this age?" (4.6.89–91).

The good in Jonson are static because the ideal is, for the elite, an attainable changelessness. It is unusual to find a stress on the process of attainment, as in "An Epistle to Sir Edward Sackville" (*Underwood,* 13), where "Men have beene great, but never good by chance, / Or on the sudden" (124–25). Even here it is assumed that there is nothing of real worth until "the last Key-stone . . . makes the Arch" (136–37): "Then stands it a triumphall marke! . . . Such Notes are vertuous men!" (139–43). On the other hand, Jonson disdains even while he relishes those for whom stasis is stagnation, those incapable of solitude who seek to project transmuted and protean images of themselves onto an admiring society, while a banal and petty self lurks within. Even Volpone, the most complex and unpredictable of his rogues' gallery, reveals an inner emptiness through all his cruel manipulations. He lacks the self-reliance to tolerate repose; for him, love is reduced to love-play and requires the curious envy of observing connoisseurs. Without role-play he cannot hide from himself, and when he is trapped in a part that he cannot relish he feels his very identity threatened. He rushes to disaster because he cannot accept Mosca's advice: "Here, we must rest" (5.2.13).

Static characterization means that Jonson's art is essentially comic and satirical; it is too pessimistic for tragedy. Despite his celebration of gathered selves or of the ideal enclave of a Penshurst, the emphasis in the art often falls on negation, and there is a clear distinction between sheep and goats, however great the creative zest in the making of the goats. His nearest approach to tragedy is at the climax of *Volpone*, where for once a dynamic character lives up to his projected image of himself as magnificent and free, despite his crumpling at earlier crises. This is Jonson's Satan—a being of large powers and energies, alluring and self-destroying—even though the tragic dimension is slight because it depends on the vindictiveness of a corrupt court. The nominal tragedies of *Sejanus* and *Catiline* are of unmatched bleakness, since there is a sickening disparity between the tragic genre and the pettiness dramatized. There can be no exultation or even relief at the defeat of the protagonists; the actions of the plays merely intensify the threat to the state through enhancing the powers of Tiberius and Caesar. Cicero does at least survive as an honest Machiavel, but there is no comfort in his eloquence—his noble tirade fails in its object—and his temporary success depends on self-seeking information from a coquette and her fancy man.

The cast of Jonson's thought is authoritarian and conservative, however adventurous his art. His prescriptive critical writings turn for their authority to academic neoclassical theory. When, occasion following intuition, he commemorates Shakespeare's genius, he refashions a Shakespeare of Jonsonian pattern, author of "well torned and true-filed lines" that have been worked over and over and which now are as lances, "brandish't at the eyes of Ignorance" (68 and 70). His *Explorata or Discoveries* are very largely reaffirmations, personal assimilations of other men's wisdom. His motto, *tamquam exploratur*, alludes not to exploration but to the incursion of a spy, learning what he can of alien territory. Although a self-made man, he celebrates established standards and institutions and is scornful of social innovation, of new modes of communication and enterprise. He repeatedly mocks even James for his cheapening of the traditional honors of knighthoods and higher titles, as tending to undermine social hierarchies. When, in the country-house poem, he is formally at his most inventive, his social criticism is nostalgic in tendency,[19] and he concentrates his vision on a particular institution, seeking to reaffirm communal values that are being ignored. His tragedies are tragedies of the whole state, his masques are celebrations of kingship. While terms such as "conservative" are poor guides to the complications of actual allegiances and alignments of power and faction in the earlier seventeenth century, it is no coincidence that the writing and action of those "Sealed of the Tribe" were to be royalist.

Jonson is never more conservative than in his impatience with giving weight to the niceties of theology. "For any religion as being versed in both," summed up Drummond (*Conversations,* 690; *Works,* 1.151). Jonson finds religious controversy odious, thinks that some of those who take part in such fencing are "like Swaggerers in a Taverne," and is content to tolerate a less than immaculate Church: "In the Church, some errors may be dissimuled with lesse inconvenience, then can be discover'd" (*Discoveries,* 1046–62). He has nothing but contempt for the Puritan, seeing him as a hypocrite and heretic, unbalanced by self-confidence, who believing he has discovered certain errors in church dogma, fights against the civil authority in the name of God (*Discoveries,* 60–64).

Jonson's art is preoccupied with power, political power as in the tragedies and masques, and domination through power of language or money at the level of social relations, as in the jostling that constitutes the plot of *Epicoene.* Comedies and tragedies alike dramatize almost continuous displays of one-upmanship, at various degrees of malignity, and throughout his work the author makes countless proclamations of authority, whether social, authorial, or verbal.

Although a bricklayer by trade, a convicted killer, and a man in numerous scrapes throughout his twenties and early thirties, Jonson attached himself to the courtly elite and its values. He creates forms of literature, such as the masque, where he can represent the alliance of power and virtue.[20] Even so, he preserves a show of independence through cultivating a militant strain of conservatism, criticizing the elite which gives him his status when it seems to fall below his standards. "A Speech according to Horace" (*Underwood,* 44) censures the nobility for leaving the cultivation of chivalry to lower classes; *The Sad Shepherd* scorns the court fashion for mirthless pastoral, as well as Puritanism's "sowrer sort / Of Shepherds" (1.4.18–19).

Jonson's whole enterprise is aimed at winning an author's authority. Determined to be seen as no mere hack or purveyor of ephemeral entertainment, he appeals to neoclassical precedent and learning, and makes his claim to laureate stature. He presents his works in ambitious and well-printed texts; the very consistency of the unusual spelling of his name without its inherited "h" from 1604 onward is a printerly claim to uniqueness.[21] He attempts to extend his authority also to the theater, to overcome the exasperating uncertainties of performance and response through critical commentary surrounding or embedded in his texts. No contemporary playwright is such a palpable and commanding presence.

Jonson is perpetually seeking or demonstrating power in and through the word. He names someone in his gallery, and confers immortality; he blasts someone else with his anger. The power of conferring immortality through verse is treated very literally: "Goe on, and doubt not, what posteritie, / Now I have sung thee thus, shall judge of thee," he assures Sir Henry Neville.[22] In the plays, power invariably goes with verbal authority; the potent reserve of Caesar in *Catiline* is exceptional, and an inarticulate character, even the virtuous Celia, is merely weak, rather than a poignant source of value, like Cordelia or Virgilia.

Characteristically, Jonson's verse concentrates on forms of pointed expression, the couplet and the epigram. Couplets—"the bravest sort of Verses" (*Conversations,* 7–8)—bring incessant reminders of authorial control. In his epigrams, Jonson is both classical and innovative, for he reaches ostentatiously behind the English tradition of epigrams as short narratives and anecdotes to the terseness and witty closure of the ancient form. His smaller forms, that is, make for definitiveness.

Superficially, Jonson's epideictic verse may seem to celebrate the individuality of a series of virtuous men and women in a modestly plain and transparent style, yet we are made continually aware of the standing of the author. First, unlike the rogues and fools of the plays—and indeed unlike the friends and contemporaries addressed in Milton's sonnets—the individuals of Jonson's aristocratic elite are unindividualized, partly because little that is circumstantial or analytical is said about them, and partly because what is said makes them all sound much alike. For example, Jonson relies repeatedly on the assertion that his subject is not only great but good.[23] Another pattern is shown in Epigram 76, "On Lucy, Countess of Bedford." Jonson lists ideal abstractions that are said to be embodied in her and then abruptly takes refuge in naming her: "My *Muse* bad, *Bedford* write, and that was shee," the echo of Sidney merely emphasizing that this poem will not be heart-searching. There is much listing and talking about the presence of values, but little is established. Jonson's aim may in part be *laudando praecipere,* but one is also conscious of his pessimism; pained by the gap between the ideal and the real, he keeps tokens of mortal frailty and circumstance out of his admiring portrayals. Where there is energy of statement, it lies almost entirely in negation, in satiric denunciation of the vices that are absent.

Second, as David Riggs has written:

Jonson projected his own code of values onto his prospective patrons. He complimented them because they shared his disregard for the external marks of wealth and status, his disdain for courtly foppery, his relish of classical letters, his appreciation for the fine points of literary craftsmanship, and his commitment to an unostentatious manner of life. In short, he congratulated them for conforming to his own self-image. Jonson could thus be at once deferential and assertive. (*Ben Jonson*, 64)

In this way, the low-born but highly educated satirist protected his pugnacious sense of integrity while making his way at court.

Third, the consequence of the projection of a Jonsonian form of courtly values onto unindividualized individuals is that we have to take Jonson on trust, that we have to take his word. Carew in commemorating Donne, or Marvell in introducing *Paradise Lost*, seek to isolate and re-create distinctive qualities of their subject for our evaluation. In characteristic epigrams such as "To William, Earl of Pembroke" (102), "To Sir William Jephson" (116), and "To Alphonso Ferrabosco, on His Book" (130), the poetry is essentially vocative: the characters are named, and their attributes are listed. Nothing gives substance to the elevated abstractions but the word of the poet. As Stanley Fish has suggested, such poetry is significant not as communication or exhortation but as testimony ("Authors-Readers," 42). Even if one retorts that some of these poems are implied exhortations, silently teaching by overtly praising, it remains true that the criteria are chosen by Jonson and that their significance is little more than asserted. So the word of the poet is his bond as much for the values as for the individuals commemorated.

The riskiness of such an abstract poetic method is clear. The magniloquent assertions of Epigram 89 to Edward Alleyn are empty beside the rare, touching immediacy of the "Epitaph on Salomon Pavy" (Epigram 120). Equally telling, by contrast, is the warmth of response elicited by such exceptional poems as "To Penshurst" and "Inviting a Friend to Supper," where virtue is allowed to coincide with circumstance. The poet's relish for particularity, that zest for worldliness that informs the satiric and comic writing, now enters the idealism of Jonson's poetry of praise. Elsewhere the stress tends to fall— not always convincingly—on the austerity of the virtuous.

Even so, as Thomas Greene says of "Inviting a Friend," "The real subject has nothing to do with the accumulation of dishes; it lies in the spirit of the voice ordering this series, subtly modulated from line to line" (*Light in Troy*, 280). This predominance of the voice leads to the final reason why in Jonson's poetry of praise we are conscious of Jonson. His verse often deviates from the principles of lucidity and transparency that he repeatedly advances in *Discoveries* and in the verse itself.[24] The so-called "plain style" is frequently dense, elusive, and difficult; the verse in couplets tends to be weighty, knotty, and strenuous, requiring an effort of syntactic deliberation and discrimination from the reader, and giving an impression of deliberation and discrimination to judgments that in themselves might otherwise seem commonplace or formulaic. Wesley Trimpi, in the standard study that takes Jonson at his word, cites passages from the "Epistle to Katherine, Lady Aubigny" (*Forest,* 13) as a model of the plain style recommended by manuals of letter writing.[25] Yet the opening of the poem, from which he quotes, is a self-consciously sustained passage that meticulously refuses grammatical closure. There are thirty-one heavy stops in the Folio text of the first fifty lines, and almost every one of them is immediately overridden by resumptive phrasing. Syntax is fluid and almost unanalyzable, but the author gives the impression of knowing always where he is in the maze of language, so that the reader senses a masterly voice with a clear sense of direction. We are teased by a blend of sustained, slow unwinding and sudden, local unpredictability in the structure, and this deviousness is not expressive of content, but of an arbitrary yet authoritative control by the poet, both when the language is orderly and when it seems wayward. Despite the superficial "idiomatic purity" and plainness of diction, and despite the asserted moral earnestness, it is very much a performance.[26] Authority is transferred to the author, the social dependent. In the major work of Milton, by contrast, we are at least as aware of the authorial manipulation of syntax, but the poet is possessed by the significance of his subject, and is intent on putting his authority at its service.

*   *   *

Jonson's celebration of being is, therefore, embedded in a more personal affirmation of power. The first of these is against the grain of Milton's sensibility, and indicates why he should soon have wished to move beyond Jonsonian influence. A later consideration of the second will suggest why he was able to assimilate and elude that influence with such ease.

Milton, in his stubborn individualism, his honoring of the defiant individual, and his sense of a spiritual elite, might seem likely to be sympathetic to Stoicism: "he who reigns within himself, and rules / Passions, Desires, and Fears, is more a King; / Which every wise and virtuous man attains" (*PR,* 2.466 – 68). Yet throughout his work he is hostile to those stoical doctrines of self-sufficiency that mean so much to Jonson: the Stoic "in Philosophic pride, / By him call'd virtue; and his virtuous man, / Wise, perfect in himself, and all possessing . . . Ignorant of themselves, of God much more" (*PR*, 4.300–310). The model of genuine patience for Milton is Job, "for sensibility to pain, and complaints or lamentations, are not inconsistent with true patience" (*CD*, II.x; *CPW*, 6:740). He is not prepared to tolerate a doctrine that lessens man's dependence on the divine, and it is Satan for whom "the mind is its own place" (*PL*, 1.254).

In Milton, radical individualism is subject to divine prompting. Samson puts the "rousing motions" (*SA*, 1382) of the spirit before his life's rule in consenting to go to the temple of Dagon, and his tragic individuality fades as he becomes an agent of the divine will. The Jesus of *Paradise Regained* subordinates his human identity to patient waiting.

For all the high role that Milton gives to "self-esteem, grounded on just and right" (*PL*, 8.572), his work is pervaded by the Fall, with a consequent sense of universal frailty. He explores the limits of self-reliance, whereas Jonson insists on its adequacy, among the virtuous. *Paradise Lost* is an epic of dependence, setting the misplaced self-reliance of Satan against the due dependence of the Son and, ultimately, of Adam and Eve. Whereas the greatest moment of Jonsonian drama is Volpone's climactic affirmation of selfhood, the whole of *Paradise Lost* undercuts Satan's even greater affirmations.

Hence Milton's work is also pervaded by the necessity of the Cross. Hanford's notion that the crucifixion had no hold on his emotions and that, for Milton, a man's salvation depended on himself, is misconceived.[27] The cosmic exultation of the *Nativity Ode* pivots on the suddenly bare emphasis: "That on the bitter cross / Must redeem our loss" (152–53). *Paradise Regained*, far from being uniformly austere, is repeatedly made poignant by the Son's unconscious anticipations of the Cross that awaits him. The early failure of "The Passion" was because the subject meant so much to Milton, not so little.

Thanks to the Fall and the Cross, Milton's art can be, unlike Jonson's, both tragic and optimistic. Even after the failure of early apocalyptic hopes and the decline of the Commonwealth, Milton retains a disenchanted optimism. Samson, Satan, and Adam and Eve show that, unlike Jonson, Milton knows tragic experience from the inside, but in the human characters tragedy is transcended as they conform themselves to the divine will. Such optimism is not shallow, because the experience of waste and loss is traversed with such fullness, and also because the stress falls ultimately not on the safety of fulfilment but on the uncertainties of promise and possibility.

Jonson diminishes the consequences of his plots. Through the

eventual courage of Volpone and through his resilience in the epi-
logue, we are led to think not of his festering in gaol but of his *joie de
vivre*. The plays end not with the "ever after" of romantic comedy but
with a *plaudite* and a stress on theatricality that return us to ourselves.
Even *The New Inn*, which apparently leads to the joyous and lifelong
pairings of romantic comedy, is so arrantly theatrical in its closing
minutes that we cannot take the denouement at face value.[28] The principal exceptions are the two tragedies, but these merely suggest that
the same will continue, or worse; there is another Sejanus in Macro,
Caesar is a more menacing Catiline.

Milton, on the other hand, ends at a decisive moment that is, nevertheless, a beginning, at the turning point between two phases of action.
The Son of God is born and in his cradle. The Lady and her brothers,
"nurs't in Princely lore" (34), enter the labyrinth of the moral life,
where Comus remains a threat. The mourner is prepared for "Pastures
new." *Paradise Lost* diminishes the traditional and facile optimism of
the *felix culpa* and stresses the terrible consequences of the fall, but
also the opportunities: "The World was all before them" (12.646).

There is no sense here or elsewhere that a world-without-end victory has been gained, just as in Milton's theology election is only
conditional, and "even a genuine believer may sometimes fall
irrecoverably" (*CD, CPW*, 6:508). An ending is a new opportunity,
and a new trial. The apparent finality of the death of Samson
becomes an opportunity for his people. Even the Son does no more
than "first lay down the rudiments / Of his great warfare" (*PR*,
1.157–58). So whereas a Jonson poem testifies what someone *is*, a
Milton poem concentrates on a particular challenge and transition.
Tragedy is a failure to cross the boundary, as in the failure of Satan to
respond to his impulses of love.

All Milton's major characters are shown in process, and from this
comes his almost Shakespearean fullness. The human and angelic
figures of *Paradise Lost* are far more alive than their biblical embryos,
and nothing in western art makes Satan so vivid. God is ineffable, yet
his accommodated selves are made dramatic presences, and even they
undergo a change, from the predominance of justice to the predominance of mercy. Only when Satan loses his capacity for change does
he become merely the devil, no longer "Arch-Angel ruin'd" (1.593).
There is here a rare point of contact between the later Milton and Jonson, for, as Robert Wiltenburg has argued, Jonson's Catiline lies
behind Satan.[29] In particular, Petreius' closing narration is Jonson's
most Miltonic passage, and here Catiline—"Arm'd with a glorie, high
as his despaire," his face "a publique ruine" (5.671, 643)—most clearly anticipates the prince of hell. Yet there is little tragedy in the loss of

Jonson's single-minded megalomaniac, and in so far as Catiline feeds into the complexities of Satan, it is through Cicero and Sallust rather than Jonson. Here, as elsewhere, Milton has an altogether more expansive conception of the self than Jonson has; when he uses a favorite image of Jonson's, he has "the mind at home in the spacious circuits of her musing" (*CG*, *CPW*, 1:812–13), not a self gathered around its center.

Similarly, Milton's art is always in process, so there is more sense of development and innovation within his work than in Jonson's. The early verse is self-consciously early, promising greater things to come. He avoids "Parnassian" verse because he never repeats himself. *Paradise Lost* is no mere versification of *De Doctrina Christiana*. That attempt at meticulous systematization is one phase in the search for the ultimate work, and the poem is prepared to contradict the treatise. The poet's dramatizing of the Fall, for example, challenges and qualifies the theologian's unyielding censure of Adam and Eve.

Milton is, in every sense, a poet of reformation. Not only is his art assertively Protestant, but also from the start it reforms and re-forms its genres. The *Nativity Ode* has been accused of ignoring "the central naturalness of motherhood,"[30] when, with full support from liturgy, it cleanses the birth of High Church sentimentalities and exults in the saving power of God. *Comus* and *Paradise Lost* are the work of a thorough-going revisionist, subjecting the values of their genres to radical scrutiny.

Jonson images the moral life as the withstanding of a siege, where the truly virtuous self is unshakable. Milton has a much stronger sense of original sin—of what Comus terms the "unexempt condition" of "mortal frailty" (685–86)—but also a deeper conviction of the possibility of moral and spiritual growth: "Assuredly we bring not innocence into the world, we bring impurity much rather: that which purifies us is triall, and triall is by what is contrary." So for Milton, the moral life is dynamic; it is warfaring and wayfaring, a race "where that immortall garland is to be run for, not without dust and heat" (*Areop*, *CPW*, 2:515).

Both artists are at their most dramatic in scenes of temptation. For Jonson, resistance is a reaffirmation or an arraignment; the virtuous manifest once again what they are, the vicious stand at the bar of judgment. For Milton, life is meaningless without trial, since trial is a chance to grow. Hence God "set before [Adam] a provoking object, ever almost in his eyes" (*Areop*, *CPW*, 2:527), while the God of *Paradise Lost* tests the allegiance of his angels in a truculent speech announcing the "begetting" of the Son (5.600–615). From the first moments of consciousness, Adam and Eve are on trial—"Thus far to

try thee, *Adam*, I was pleas'd . . ." says God after their first exchange
(8.437). God keeps shifting his manifestations in order to goad his
creations into growth or decline.

Jonson is not driven into scrupulous inquiry over what he accepts
as ultimate truths. For Milton, truth is hewn into a thousand pieces
and we shall not find them all until the Second Coming: "The light
which we have gain'd, was giv'n us, not to be ever staring on, but by it
to discover onward things more remote from our knowledge." The
strenuous years at Hammersmith and Horton, and the individual
attempt at systematic theology in *De Doctrina*, are evidence of Milton's onward search, "ev'n to the reforming of Reformation it self"
(*Areop*, *CPW*, 2:550, 553).

For the conservative sensibility of Jonson, change is to be resisted.
Milton's art, on the contrary, focuses on change and especially growth,
for in essentials it is a poetry of initiation. The epitome is the baptized
Jesus, undergoing trial in the solitude of the desert and attaining a realization of his identity and destiny. The poems present a series of *rites
de passage*, preliminary ordeals from which the survivor issues with
new calm of mind, prepared for larger possibilities. In Jonson, the
recurrent image of standing tends to imply finality, prominence, and
persistence; in Milton, it implies readiness, as with Jesus' standing on
the pinnacle, or the two-handed engine that "stands ready to smite
once" (*Lyc*, 131), or the angels in God's presence who "stand ready at
command" (*PL*, 3.650). Hence Milton's inability to suppress his bitterness when he fears that he is to be one of those who "only stand and
wait" (Sonnet XIX).

Jonson's characteristic shorter form is the pointed epigram, that
crisp affirmation of authorial mastery. The theatrical self-conscious-
ness of the plays' endings also enhances a sense of closure and, with
that, of the controlling author. Milton's tendency is to open up his
inherited forms; the text of *Comus* is more substantial and the prosody
of *Lycidas* more free and irregular than in any predecessor. In his characteristic short form, the sonnet, he reacts against the strictly ordered
sequence of quatrains and final couplet favored by most English fore-
runners and adopts the Italian form, and then treats the Italian form
very freely, creating surprise and density of meaning by playing across
the formal divisions. Whereas the English sonnet tends toward an epi-
grammatic definitiveness, Milton's tendency, perhaps influenced by
some of the odes of Horace, is to end a sonnet with a swell of association. For example, a facetious plea for clemency "When the Assault
Was Intended to the City" leads to a charged image of the greatness
and suffering of Greek civilization: the power of its lyrical and dramatic verse, its architectural magnificence, the antagonism of its city-

states, and its eventual, civilizing absorption into large imperial ambitions. Milton's revision of the close of the sonnet to Henry Lawes is telling: "*Dante* shall give Fame leave to set thee higher / Than his *Casella*, whom he woo'd to sing / Met in the milder shades of Purgatory" originally read: "mildest shades." While the associative reach of the first version is already extensive, "mildest" confines the comparison to Purgatory, and implies a Purgatory that is invariably mild, although differing in degrees of mildness. But "milder" deepens the resonance of association by drawing in the altogether more terrible shades of the Inferno, and opens the possibility that not all Purgatory is mild, except by infernal standards. By contrast, the poignancy of Sonnet XXIII on "my late espoused Saint" is made the more acute by the uncharacteristic finality of the close: "I wak'd, she fled, and day brought back my night."

Such artistic forms are expressions of Milton's commitment to theological and political reformation. Whereas Jonson views historical change with distaste, Milton in his militant Puritanism looks to participate in the process of history as the work of God in the world. Where the conservative looks back with nostalgia and sees rootedness as a form of stability, Milton looks back "radically," seeking an originating purity as the basis for reform. He sought, for example, to advance "the process of restoring religion to something of its pure original state," and, as far as humanly possible, grounded himself on what he saw as the origins of that faith, the unmediated word of God. "A bold inquirer into morals and religion," he rejected the accretions of Church tradition and followed the promptings of the word into heresy, "If this is heresy."[31] As Jonas Barish has argued, the characters of *Sejanus* are at the mercy of an obsessive evil that is inexplicable because without plausible origin.[32] The fictional expansions of the sketchy biblical sources for *Paradise Lost* are in the broadest sense historical; in order to illuminate life in the present they take the form of prolonged concentration on the origins of evil, both demonic and human.

Milton puts the spirit before the letter and has little respect for established institutions. His trust in prophetic inspiration and inner illumination is graphically presented in Samson, who violates not only his personal and national pride in agreeing to play fantastic tricks before the Philistines, but also his holy vows as a Nazarite. Despite the defiant and symbolic gesture of setting out an alternative constitution to monarchy in *The Ready and Easy Way*, Milton's later works consistently put "before all Temples th' upright heart and pure" (*PL*, 1.18), and seek to foster Christian liberty through a disestablished Church and a civil power unable to impose on the individual

conscience. When, in an earlier tract such as *Of Education*, he sketches out the form of an institution, his intent is radical, for his plan
involves abolishing the universities and establishing widespread and
decentralized academies. He venerates marriage—"the houshold
estate, out of which must flourish forth the vigor and spirit of all pub-
lick enterprizes" (*DDD*, *CPW*, 2:247)—but his views on marriage and
divorce are so liberal that to many they seemed to threaten the fabric
of society.

Milton is remotest from Jonson over the institution of kingship.
Jonson came into his full powers with the crowning of a king whom he
found accessible and responsive, and Milton came to early maturity
while Charles's personal rule, despite initial years of success, fur-
thered the slow process of dividing the country. The coincidences
emphasized the authors' individual tendencies, toward a not uncritical
orthodoxy and an ultimately radical militancy. Jonson's most original work is in essentials a celebration of monarchy by divine right,
while Milton becomes the most eloquent king-hater of the period.

The antithetical tendencies of two authors with so much in common
are here at their clearest. But the discrepancy is apparent at once in
the two great odes of 1629 where the young and the ageing poet were
the first to re-create Pindaric sublimity in English verse. Although
much of the difference between the two poems stems from the diversity of theme and the ages of the authors—a young man writes of a birth
and an old man of a death—each poet is highly and typically responsive to his subject.

Jonson abstracts truth to oneself from time. The nameless "Stirrer,"
who would have done well had he died like Morison at twenty, has simply "vexed time" (27) and sunk into a living death, while the essential
selves of the celebrated pair are timeless. Their names epitomize
friendship and they become its ideal representatives (113–16). The
length of earthly life is therefore irrelevant to its quality: "in short
measures, life may perfect bee" (74). The infant of Saguntum can be
an emblem of perfection in the birth that is also a death. Cary is so
unflinching in virtue that he can be described as if already dead, as
inseparable from Morison, "two so early men" (125) who had gathered
the harvest of friendship at its very spring. Little impression is given
that Cary is still a young man with his life ahead of him. The timeless
perfection of such being is expressed, characteristically, in images of
circle, sphere, and stance, as well as through the concentration on
naming.

The one divided character in the poem is Jonson himself: a "masse
of miseries" (55) counting his days in fear, and yet also the creator of
"this bright *Asterisme*" (89), sharer of the friends' expectation of heav-

en. The division is expressed in the straddling of Jonson's name across two stanzas, and also in a duality of tense: the wretched man lives in the present, while the singer—"who sung this of him, e're he went / Himselfe to rest" (85–86)—is already historical and unchanging through his role in the perpetuation of human value.

Nothing could be less Miltonic than such an abstracting of human perfection from time. Although Milton's work reveals no marked fear of death in itself, he is from the first deeply touched by early death, because to him such untimeliness seems to cut off the full realization of the self and the putting to use of one's full talents, as required in the grim parable of Matthew 25 of which he was so highly conscious. The *Nativity Ode* has a typical stress on the positive use of time, rather than on manifestations of timeless being. It is both in years and in skill Milton's coming-of-age poem, and as he stands on the borderline between youth and early maturity he concentrates on a border in human history, a moment of peace between two dispensations, the moment when time itself misses a beat as the stars, lost in amazement, "will not take their flight" (72). It is a moment of immense promise, when the timeless puts on time to redeem time. It is a moment of dedication to future work—the poet and his art are, like the angels, "in order serviceable" (244).

The two odes are also characteristic in their classical orientation. Both are true to Pindar in elevation of style, intricacy of form, and their stress on acts of human heroism and divine condescension that penetrate the shadow of mortal existence. Jonson, aiming to restore lost excellence, here meticulously re-creates Pindaric form as it was then understood. This is a more straightforward act of imitation than is customary with him, though, in view of the strangeness of the form, an act of bold innovation. But if Jonson's is a secondary mode of creation—an exemplary exercise in form—Milton's is already tertiary, for the Pindaric form and spirit are assimilated into a fusion of kinds that is *sui generis*. Moreover, Milton is already, with his exuberant sense of conviction, setting his Christian art above pagan achievement. "Our Babe" (227) is said to out-Hercules Hercules not only because that hero was often seen as a pagan type of Christ, but because he is, as the greatest of the deified heroes and as a traditional founder of the Nemean Games, the presiding spirit of Pindar's odes.

The attitudes and art of Milton's world of becoming are therefore profoundly opposed to those of Jonson's world of being, and this is manifest as early as his first major poem. The Jonsonianism of Milton in the four or five years that followed the ode was no doubt a valuable discipline for the author of "On the Death of a Fair Infant" and "The Passion," but it seems primarily to have been part of his conscious experimentation, part of that virtuoso assumption of diverse voices that, as Helgerson suggests, is one of Milton's Caroline characteristics.[33]

Milton writes the individual practices of Jonson, as opposed to his laureate ambition, out of his system in *Comus*, a characteristic work of recuperation that sets out to reform the most Jonsonian of genres. The fundamentals of the Jonsonian masque are the intimate interaction of audience and performer, and the invulnerability of virtue. The audience consists of a specific royal and courtly community, and participates in the action through its representatives on stage and through dancing together with the performers in the final revels. The action of the masque reflects the current life of the community, but this is seen in terms of "ideal abstractions and eternal verities."[34] Since such values are beyond all threat, there can be no dramatic conflict. The association of the audience with the celestial and of the Stuarts with the divine inevitably led to accusations that masques were "tied to rules of flattery," although modern scholars have labored to defend Jonson against such blame.[35] Milton's simple and yet drastic revision is to undermine masque expectations by making aristocratic performers subject to "mortal frailty," incorporating a degree of suspense and dramatic tension into the action. Despite the assertions of the Lady and Elder Brother that her virtue cannot even be assailed, she is duped by Comus, trapped in his chair, only half-saved by the brothers, and dependent for her rescue on Sabrina, a representative of purified nature, not an aristocratic embodiment of virtue.[36] In the action, and in the Lady's egalitarian dismissal of Comus' arguments (762ff.), the horizons of the form are expanded toward moral realism, and, apart from the matchless grace of the songs and tetrameters, a Jonsonian manner is no longer adequate. Spenserian and above all Shakespearean voices now predominate, and the poetry that follows from the later 1630s onward is quite unJonsonian. *Lycidas*, a pastoral elegy that is free in form, forthright in emotion, and radical in social tendencies, is already remote from Jonson. *Mansus*, a poem to a patron, is un-Jonsonian in the affectionate particularity of its praise, and in the confidence with which it looks beyond the patron and beyond the whole genre of panegyric.

*   *   *

There remains another major reason why the hold of Jonson's work over Milton could never be strong, and why Milton could exploit or ignore it without anxiety. Jonson's creativity is at its most exuberant and relaxed in the works that meant least to Milton, the satirical comedies. Elsewhere, in critical pronouncements, in poetry, and even in the lesser plays, as well as in personal anecdote, Jonson seems often, while making a personal affirmation of power, to be protesting too much, to be straining to live up to his proclaimed values and laureate elevation. He seems to be trying, in various senses, to get above himself, above his physical, emotional, and social vulnerabilities. As suggested already, Milton has anxieties of his own: the arduous years of preparation that his laureate vision imposed on him created a marked sense of unreadiness, an unreasonable fear that he was culpably slow in development and might fall victim to the "blind *Fury*" (*Lyc,* 75) before he had put his talents to use. But Milton never wavered in his massive confidence in those talents and his laureate calling. Jonson's insecurities as man and artist, which are prominent in much of his work, simply did not engage with Milton's own.

Jonson's was a self-assertive, passionate, and volatile temperament—"passionately kynde and angry," in Drummond's phrase (*Conversations,* 687)—committed to an ethic of equilibrium and quiet. As both author and man he insists on imperturbability because he knows the subversiveness of powerful emotion too well. He is anything but stoical about the body, about alcohol, and about the attitudes of others. He is preoccupied with envy, aggressive toward rivals, and voracious for praise. Milton's admiring friendship for Jonson's enemy Alexander Gil the Younger will almost certainly have alerted him to Jonson's vulnerabilities, since Gil wrote a derisive account of them in his poem on *The Magnetic Lady* (1632).[37] They are anyway only too manifest during Milton's Jonsonian years in the controversy stirred up by Jonson's inordinate rage over the failure of *The New Inn* (1629, published 1631).

Jonson's poetry often manifests less an expression than a repression of feeling. Despite a strong authorial presence and personality, he is a reserved writer. We know his mountain belly and rocky face, but it is Milton and not Jonson who makes his vision of a lost loved one into a poem. Jonson writes love poetry once passion can be safely displaced into wryness. He writes elegies that suppress and sometimes forbid grieving, and which show a fear of the emotions.[38] The restraint can be a source of power—the emotion lying in the effort to contain emotion—but the self-defeating quality of this poetry of inhibition is revealed, by contrast, in the humanity of two untypical poems, "On My First Son" (Epigram 45) and the unique poem of religious intensity, "To Heaven" (*Forest,* 15).

These are exceptional in being poems of self-exposure rather than self-exhibition. For once the poetry is not social, not aimed at making a particular impression on a particular audience, and it reveals weariness of life, deep melancholy and self-doubt, the emotional dependence of the bereaved father, and the social and the creaturely pains of "worlds, and fleshes rage." The volatile Stoic seeks to elude a life of hope and of emotional commitment in language that contradicts itself: "hence-forth, all his vowes be such, / As what he loves may never like too much." Reverse the verbs "love" and "like" or replace either verb with the other to produce a parallel rather than a contrast, and one is left with a logical but insipidly prudent withdrawal from living, as with the source in Martial. The emotional illogic of Jonson's formulation, subordinating loving to liking, reveals the impossibility of such a withdrawal, of reducing passion to calm.

The vulnerability and attempted inhibition illuminate Jonson's preoccupation with power and control. He stresses rationality because, as Drummond observed, he is "oppressed with fantasie, which hath ever mastered his reason" (692). He stresses his integrity through a fear of inner division. He reveals persistent anxieties about his enterprise as a courtly writer, and hence about the risk of flattery. Poems of judicious praise such as "To Penshurst" and "High-spirited friend" (*Underwood,* 26) mean that Jonson is no court sycophant, yet he is right to be anxious about the morality of praise. Some epigrams, such as those on Robert Cecil, Earl of Salisbury, and on Joshua Sylvester's translation of Du Bartas, and the epitaph on Cecilia Bulstrode reveal clear discrepancies between his public and private views.[39]

There are also rancorous failures of judgment that conflict with Jonson's standing as a moral arbiter. There are real issues of principle in his rivalry with Inigo Jones, but the decades of obsessive denigration of a colleague of genius are painful to follow. Equally disquieting is the placing of Epigram 65 "To My Muse," with its denunciation of the false praise of "a worthless lord," immediately after two epigrams praising the Earl of Salisbury. The juxtaposition has the effect of slyly kicking a man who was sick and declining when the epigrams were entered on the Stationers' Register in 1612, and dead, his memory slighted, by the time the poems were published.

According to Drummond, "of all stiles he loved most to be named honest, and hath of that ane hundreth letters so naming him" (631–32). Jonson feels society as a threat, and he twice envisages withdrawal to where he will be "*Safe* from the wolves black jaw, and the dull Asses hoofe."[40] His occasional failures in humanity reflect this insecurity.

Most of his plays embody the freedom but also the menace of living in metropolitan anonymity, an essentially new urban experience to which Londoners of his day were adjusting. His work concentrates on the alienation of living among strangers, without community. Jonson's status at court, both personal and financial, was never secure. The vehemence with which he reacts to a slight in "An Epistle Answering to One that Asked to be Sealed of the Tribe of Ben" reveals his insecurity even as late as 1623.[41] He could never leave behind his origins as a bricklayer; courtiers used this familiar gibe against him after the unpopularity of *Pleasure Reconciled to Virtue* in 1619, and Alexander Gil as late as the 1630s.[42] While Aretino—cobbler's son and self-proclaimed scourge of princes—had been able to live comfortably by threatening to write against the eminent, Jonson's social impotence is such that he is unable to name those whom he wishes to attack, even when, as in the lord of Epigram 84, his target is clearly not a type but a specific occasion and individual.[43]

Jonson's poetry is at its most humane when, untypically, it is little concerned with power. The poems of self-exploration mentioned above, or of genuine affection such as "Inviting a Friend to Supper" and "High-spirited friend," seem a loosening of the bow, a relaxation of social tension. Before the last phase, his comedies tend to move not toward marriage but toward arraignment, and Jonson writes in his own person as if he feels himself to be incessantly on trial. Whereas for Milton trial is an opportunity, for Jonson it is a humiliating reminder of vulnerability and dependence. What gives him status at court also makes him aware how rootless is his position.

The resulting abrasiveness of self-presentation so common in Jonson is exacerbated by what helps to make Jonson so impressive: the gravity of his laureate ambition. This puts him under pressure because of the prominence of the laureate himself in such writing. As Helgerson has demonstrated, the laureate expressed his central ethical core in his verse and was required to live up to the ancient doctrine that the good poet must be first a good man, or, as Milton put it, "him selfe . . . a true Poem, that is, a composition, and patterne of the best and honourablest things."[44]

Moreover, Jonson faced a fundamental problem in the apparent inadequacy of the genres in which he worked best. The example of Virgil had such authority that ascent from pastoral to epic seemed the natural course. A laureate who was a satirist, an epigrammatist, a professional playwright, and a scriptwriter for court entertainments seemed a contradiction. Jonson is therefore put in the position of making high claims for his work—his epigrams, for example, are described in the dedication as "the ripest of my studies"—and of separating himself disdainfully from the audiences and playwrights of the very theaters for which he wrote.[45]

There is consequently a frequent sense of strain in Jonson's self-presentation, and this obscures the actual freedom of intuitive creativity in the plays. In practice the drama assumes exactly the sophisticated and agile audience that Jonson's laureate aspirations prevent him from acknowledging to be there in the commercial theater of his day.[46]

Because of the evident sense of strain in Jonson, Milton could be inspired by him without being overawed. Milton has a strong sense of vocation and high destiny from his early years, and carries conviction in his professions of laureate sublimity even before he has come of age, in the prescient lines on "some graver subject" ("At a Vacation Exercise," 30). Milton was oppressively aware "that God even to a strictnesse requires the improvment of these his entrusted gifts," and knew some fear that they might be left unrealized, but he never doubted the "vital signes" of those gifts (*CG, CPW,* 1:801, 809). He was too strong a poet to be drawn into Jonsonian anxieties, and as early as *L'Allegro* he was able to excel Jonson in Jonsonian modes of writing.

Milton was consequently a Son of Ben for only a few years, but this is precisely why he was the truest of the Sons. In the words of the master: "Yet wee must adventure" (*Discoveries,* 1923).

Notes

1. Warren L. Chernaik, *The Poetry of Limitation: A Study of Edmund Waller* (New Haven: Yale University Press, 1968). For the use of the term "laureate" throughout this essay, see Richard Helgerson, *Self-Crowned Laureates: Spenser, Jonson, Milton, and the Literary System* (Berkeley: University of California Press, 1983).

2. David Lee Clark, ed., *Shelley's Prose* (London: Fourth Estate, 1988), 328.

3. The most sustained and useful comparisons of the two authors occur in the course of general studies of the period, such as: Helgerson, *Self-Crowned Laureates*; David Norbrook, *Poetry and Politics in the English Renaissance* (London: Routledge and Kegan Paul, 1984); and Isabel Rivers, *The Poetry of Conservatism, 1600–1745* (Cambridge: Rivers Press, 1973). See also A. H. Tricomi, "Milton and the Jonsonian Plain Style," *Milton Studies* 13 (1979): 129–44; Judith Scherer Herz, "Epigrams and Sonnets: Milton in the Manner of Jonson," *Milton Studies* 20 (1984): 29–41; Robert B. Hinman, "'A Kind of *Christmas* Ingine': Jonson, Milton, and the Sons of Ben in the Hard Season," in *Classic and Cavalier: Essays on Jonson and the Sons of Ben,* eds. Claude J. Summers and Ted-Larry Pebworth (Pittsburgh, Penn.: University of Pittsburgh Press, 1982), 255–78.

4. Compare *PL,* 11 and 12 and *Discoveries,* 1100–9, in C. H. Herford and Percy and Evelyn Simpson, eds., *Ben Jonson* (Oxford: Clarendon Press, 1925–52), 8: 597, cited hereafter as *Works.*

5. *The Light in Troy: Imitation and Discovery in Renaissance Poetry* (New Haven: Yale University Press, 1982), 273.

6. Richard C. Newton, "Jonson and the (Re-)Invention of the Book," in *Classic and Cavalier,* 39 of pp. 31–55; Richard S. Peterson, *Imitation and Praise in the Poems of Ben Jonson* (New Haven: Yale University Press, 1981), xvi and 3, and passim.

7. Translation from: R. B. Parker, ed., *Volpone or, The Fox* (Manchester: Manchester University Press, The Revels Plays, 1983), 78.

8. *Works* 3, frontispiece, ix, x. Also reproduced by David Riggs, *Ben Jonson: A Life* (Cambridge: Harvard University Press, 1989), 281.

9. *English Literature in the Earlier Seventeenth Century, 1600–1660*, rev. ed., Oxford History of English Literature, 5 (Oxford: Clarendon Press, 1966), 107.

10. *Self–Crowned Laureates*, 7; *CPW,* 1: 815; *Discoveries,* 1034–37.

11. Hinman surveys these assumptions most engagingly in *Classic and Cavalier,* but does not consider how little such commonplaces illuminate the actual practice of the writers.

12. "The Sinner's Sacrifice" (*Underwood,* 1). Compare *Lycidas,* 64–84 and "Epistle to Elizabeth, Countess of Rutland" (*Forest,* 12.41): "It is the *Muse,* alone, can raise to heaven."

13. Katharine Eisaman Maus, *Ben Jonson and the Roman Frame of Mind* (Princeton: Princeton University Press, 1984), 5, 80.

14. "Ben Jonson and the Centered Self," *Studies in English Literature* 10 (1970): 325–48, reprinted in Thomas M. Greene, *The Vulnerable Text: Essays on Renaissance Literature* (New York: Columbia University Press, 1986), 194–217.

15. *Discoveries,* 948–58, 2031–61, 2142–60.

16. Maus, *Roman Frame,* 115–6; Stanley Fish, "Authors-Readers: Jonson's Community of the Same," *Representations* 7 (1984): 49 of 26–58.

17. "To Sir Robert Wroth" (*Forest,* 3.13–14); "To Penshurst" (*Forest,* 2.91, 99).

18. Examined in depth in Peterson, *Imitation and Praise.*

19. Rivers, *Poetry of Conservatism,* 49, 73, 75.

20. Maus, *Roman Frame,* 109.

21. Newton, *Classic and Cavalier,* 37; Riggs, *Ben Jonson,* 114.

22. Epigram 109. See also Epigram 89, "To Edward Alleyn."

23. See, for example, *Epigrams,* Dedication and 76, *Forest,* 13 and 14, *Underwood,* 13, 15, 24, and 83. See the statistics in Judith Kegan Gardiner, *Craftsmanship in Context: The Development of Ben Jonson's Poetry* (The Hague, Netherlands: Mouton, 1975), 177 for the marked frequency of the two adjectives.

24. *Discoveries,* 575–86, 695–705, 760–800, 1870–73, 1905–80, 2237–77; "An Epistle to Master John Selden" (*Underwood,* 14.55–60). The difficulty of Jonson's style is stressed by Richard C. Newton in " 'Ben./Jonson': The Poet in the Poems," in Alvin Kernan, ed., *Two Renaissance Mythmakers,* Selected Papers from the English Institute 1976–77, N.S.1 (Baltimore: The Johns Hopkins University Press, 1977), 165–95. See also Stanley Fish, "Authors-Readers."

25. *Ben Jonson's Poems: A Study of the Plain Style* (Stanford, Calif.: Stanford University Press, 1962), 139.

26. The phrase quoted is from Trimpi's account of "Inviting a Friend," 185–86.

27. James Holly Hanford, "The Youth of Milton," in *Studies in Shakespeare, Milton and Donne by Members of the English Department of the University of Michigan,* University of Michigan Publications: Language and Literature, 1 (1925), 127 of 89–163; Hanford and James G. Taaffe, *A Milton Handbook,* 5th ed. (Englewood Cliffs, N.J.: Prentice-Hall, Inc., 1970), 115. See also William Kerrigan, *The Sacred Complex: On the Psychogenesis of Paradise Lost* (Cambridge: Harvard University Press, 1983), 62.

28. Anne Barton, *Ben Jonson, Dramatist* (Cambridge: Cambridge University Press, 1984), 276–84.

29. "Damnation in a Roman Dress: Catiline, *Catiline,* and *Paradise Lost,*" *Milton Studies* 25 (1989): 89–108.

30. J. B. Broadbent, "The *Nativity Ode,*" in Frank Kermode, ed., *The Living Milton: Essays by Various Hands* (London: Routledge and Kegan Paul, 1960), 26 of 12–31.

31. See the Epistle prefaced to *De Doctrina Christiana, CPW,* 6:117, and *Shelley's Prose,* 328. Michael Bauman, *Milton's Arianism (Sprache und Literatur, Regensburger Arbeiten zur Anglistik und Amerikanistik* 26; Frankfurt, Germany: Peter Lang, 1987) cogently argues for the older view of Milton as an Arian heretic against the recent tendency that—following W. B. Hunter, C. A. Patrides, and J. H. Adamson, *Bright Essence: Studies in Milton's Theology* (Salt Lake City: University of Utah Press, 1971)—saves Milton for orthodoxy. I am unpersuaded by W. B. Hunter's recent attempts to deny Milton the authorship of *CD.* See "The Provenance of the *Christian Doctrine,*" *SEL* 32 (1992): 129–66, and consequent debate in vols. 32–34.

32. Jonas A. Barish, ed., *Ben Jonson: Sejanus* (New Haven: Yale University Press, 1965), 20–23.

33. *Self-Crowned Laureates,* chap. 4, e.g., 191, 195, 217, 261ff.

34. Stephen Orgel, *The Jonsonian Masque* (New York: Columbia University Press, 1965), 73.

35. See Strato in the opening lines of *The Maid's Tragedy.* Among attempts to clear Jonson of flattery, Dale B. J. Randall, *Jonson's Gypsies Unmasked* (Durham, North Carolina: Durham University Press, 1975) is often cited, but has been exploded by Philip Edwards, *Threshold of a Nation* (London: Cambridge University Press, 1979), chap. 6, especially 156. For a more thorough attempt, see Leah S. Marcus, *The Politics of Mirth* (Chicago: University of Chicago Press, 1986), chaps. 1–4. The case remains to be made as securely for Jonson as it is for Shirley by Martin Butler, "Politics and the Masque: *The Triumph of Peace,*" *The Seventeenth Century* 2 (1987):117–41. For a judicious appraisal of the literature of compliment, see Martin Butler, "Ben Jonson and the Limits of Courtly Panegyric," in Kevin Sharpe and Peter Lake, eds., *Culture and Politics in Early Stuart England* (Houndmills, Hants.: Macmillan Press, 1994), 91–115.

36. These views are developed in: John Creaser, " 'The present aid of this occasion': The Setting of *Comus,*" in David Lindley, ed., *The Court Masque* (Manchester: Manchester University Press, 1984), 111–34. For compatible views, see Cedric C. Brown, *John Milton's Aristocratic Entertainments* (Cambridge: Cambridge University Press, 1985) and Marcus, *Politics of Mirth,* chap. 6.

37. Reprinted in *Works,* 11: 346–48.

38. G.W. Pigman III, "Suppressed Grief in Jonson's Funeral Poetry," *English Literary Renaissance* 13 (1983): 203–20.

39. *Works,* 1: 57–58; *Conversations,* 29–31, 103–4, 317–21, 353–54, 646–48. Compare *Conversations,* 355–56 for a slighting reference to Sir Robert Wroth, recipient of one of his richest poems of praise.

40. "An Ode. To Himselfe," 36 (*Underwood,* 23), and *Poetaster,* "To the Reader," 239 (*Works,* 4: 324). Emphasis added.

41. Robert C. Evans, *Ben Jonson and the Poetics of Patronage* (Lewisburg, Penn.: Bucknell University Press, 1989), 176.

42. *Works,* 10: 576; 11: 348.

43. Evans, *Poetics of Patronage,* 83.

44. *Self-Crowned Laureates,* 136. For the importance of this doctrine in Jonson, see the Epistle to *Volpone* and passages from *Discoveries* cited by Helgerson, 123. For Milton, see *An Apology against a Pamphlet, CPW,* 1: 890 and cross-references.

45. *Self-Crowned Laureates,* especially 102–3, 143, 145, 152, 173.

46. These views are developed in: John Creaser, "Enigmatic Ben Jonson," in Michael Cordner, Peter Holland, and John Kerrigan, eds. *English Comedy* (Cambridge: Cambridge University Press, 1994), 100–118.

"By Art Is Created That Great . . . State": Milton's *Paradise Lost* and Hobbes's *Leviathan*

CHARLES CANTALUPO

John Aubrey describes Milton's third wife and widow, Elizabeth Minshull, as "a gent. person, a peaceful and agreable humour."[1] Aubrey also records that she "assures" him "that Mr. T. Hobbs was not one of his [Milton's] acquaintance, that her husband did not like him at all, but he would acknowledge him to be a man of great parts, and a learned man. Their Interests and Tenets did run counter to each other" (Aubrey, 203). Aubrey neither confirms nor denies her apparent effort to discourage speculation about contact or correspondence between her husband and Hobbes, although subsequent critics and scholars have chosen to support and elaborate the view that Hobbes's and Milton's "Interests and Tenets did run counter to each other." Although one should expect differences—most notably, in their opposing reactions to materialism[2]—I find that, more often than not, these two writers' "great parts" are similar. No personal encounter between Milton and Hobbes is known, and the only direct comment by one on the other's work is Hobbes's statement in *Behemoth* (1679), comparing Salamasius's *Defensio Regia* (1649) with Milton's *Defensio pro Popula Anglicano* (1651): "I have seen them both; they are very good Latine both, and hardly to be judged which is better; and both very ill reasoning, and hardly to be judged which is worst."[3] Clearly Hobbes, an author of many Latin works himself, is impressed with Milton's style, if nothing else. As Elizabeth Milton implies, her husband was impressed by Hobbes's style, too. In fact, the "great parts" of both Hobbes's and Milton's style, although they obviously differ from one another, are what make them most comparable. Furthermore, to consider Milton and Hobbes together and not "counter" is as plausible and instructive as the more usual academic pairs of Jonson and Donne or Swift and Pope.

Hobbes's masterpiece, *Leviathan* (1651), is traditionally not included in the canon of English literature, yet merely to name "Milton" is to invoke through a kind of synecdoche the canon as well as its controversies from Leavis to feminist criticism. Nevertheless, to compare Milton and Hobbes, I consider the latter, in Michael Oakeshott's words,

> a writer, a self-conscious stylist and the master of an individual style that expresses his whole personality; for there is no hiatus between his personality and his philosophy. His manner of writing is not . . . foreign to his age. . . . Hobbes is elaborate in an age that delighted in elaboration. . . . He has eloquence, the charm of wit . . . he is capable of urbanity and savage irony. . . . The *Leviathan* is a myth, the transposition of an abstract argument into the world of imagination. . . . it is an accomplishment of art.[4]

To substantiate this claim, Aubrey is again useful. His life of Hobbes attributes "copie of words" to Hobbes's writing (Aubrey, 149): a copiousness, richness, and variety of language comparable to that found in fiction and drama. In his life of Milton, Samuel Johnson's criterion is the same, praising the "copiousness and variety" of Milton's language.[5] To recognize the literary quality and quantity of Hobbes's writing is not necessarily to devalue its philosophical or political tenets, but to suggest that revaluation is required. Taking greater account of *Leviathan*'s literary possibilities, its readers may need, in Paul de Man's words, "to disregard the commonplaces about his philosophy that circulate as reliable currency in the intellectual histories of the Enlightenment. . . . he has to be read not in terms of explicit statements . . . but in terms of the rhetorical motions of his own text, which cannot be simply reduced to intentions or to identifiable facts."[6] *Leviathan* may still be thought to contain a wide range of philosophical themes like materialism, empirical rationalism, naturalistic egoism, psychological egoism, nominalism, and atheism. Similar and additional themes can be found in *Paradise Lost*. Philosophical or political themes in Milton's or Hobbes's work should not be discounted simply because the rhetoric of their expression—the tropes and metaphors—might be considered primary or at least equally significant as the themes. As there is no one historical or formal entelechy of poetry or drama, so is there none for philosophical writing. It is not a transparent medium, a Lucite container for philosophical ideas: at least not in Hobbes's and Milton's time, "an age that delighted in elaboration," as Oakeshott says.

It is an age, too, as Blair Warden has noted, when much of the best political writing is art, and the best art is political.[7] Politics is an explicit subject in all modes and genres. Much of the political writing by Bacon, Harrington, Filmer, Clarendon, Winstanley, Overton, Marvell, Dryden, Halifax, Milton, and Hobbes is enjoyable as literature.

Although such writers represent a wide range of political viewpoints, all of them would agree—especially Milton in his *Defensio* and *Defensio Secunda* and Hobbes in *Leviathan*—with Harrington's sentiments that "in the Art of Man . . . there is nothing so like the first call of beautiful order out of chaos and confusion as the Architecture of a well-ordered Commonwealth."[8] For none of these writers does rhetoric merely play, in Derrida's words, "the role of a pedagogical ornament." Nor are such writers' political and philosophical texts, again in Derrida's words (taken from Anatole France), "white mythology,"[9] that is, an anemic or pale form of mythology bled of its figurative and narrative content. If *Leviathan* is "white mythology," it is more like Melville's *Moby Dick* than a text by Kant.[10] Neither Robert Filmer nor John Bramhall would have attacked Hobbes and Milton together,[11] and *Paradise Lost* and *Leviathan* would not have fed the same Oxford bonfire in 1683 (Parker, 1:661), had they lacked figurative and narrative content.

Considering the relationship between Milton and Hobbes, both Marjorie Nicolson, in her pioneering study of 1926, and more recently, David Quint, consider the assurances of Milton's widow to Aubrey as authoritative: to the point of italicizing her suspiciously insistent statement that *"Their Interests and Tenets did run counter to each other."* Furthermore, both critics create a kind of melodrama in which the name, "Hobbes," becomes a love—or a hate—which Milton dares not speak. Quint evokes Hobbes as "the name" "which all [Milton's] various political strategies . . . converge to resist."[12] Although Nicolson offers a substantial essay and not merely a coda to justify her idea, her overwhelming question—"Was not the most significant of all replies to Hobbes Milton's *Paradise Lost*?"[13]—must remain rhetorical. Unlike Dante yet according to conventional poetic decorum, Milton does not name any contemporaries in his epic. If Milton was as intent as Nicolson contends, why would he not mention Hobbes by name anywhere in the many works of polemical prose, which never fail to mention names of his multitudinous other opponents, even when they might surely do him more real, even physical harm, than would Hobbes in response? In her own fanciful coda, Nicolson becomes even more dramatic, suggesting that Hobbes was to Milton "like the Satan of the *Book of Job*, [as] this seventeenth-century Adversary brought from the lips of John Milton his confession of faith" (Nicolson, 433). Hobbes as a type of Satan is a seventeenth-century commonplace.[14] However, to consider him Milton's own personal Satan is speculation.[15] It is like claiming that Hobbes's preface to his translations of *The Iliads and Odysses of Homer*, "Concerning the Virtues of an Heroic Poem" (1675), was actually directed at Milton: regardless of whether Hobbes would have known *Paradise Lost* either through his own reading or through William Davenant, John Dryden, and many other literary friends that both Milton and Hobbes had in common. Yet such speculation does not preclude both writers' standards serving as the most coherent, contemporary measures of each other's literary achievement. Precisely by seeing Hobbes and Milton together—and not "counter"—can we realize better than ever their true statures.[16]

What makes both writers similar is that they are distinguished now and in their own time because their writing on politics, philosophy, theology, and art is so extensive and, in Hobbes's own words, "please[s] for the Extravagancy."[17] A reader of Hobbes's text will not find innocence expressed as simply and powerfully as in *Paradise Lost*, when Milton presents Adam peacefully lost in thought about "whate'er death is" (4.425); and *Leviathan* never even comes close to Milton's imaginative conception of a person who "thought no ill" (4.320). Nevertheless, Milton never writes so simply and powerfully about foreknowledge and free will as Hobbes in *Leviathan*: "God, that seeth, and disposeth all things, seeth also that the liberty of man in doing what he will, is accompanied with the necessity of doing that which God will, & no more, nor lesse" (II.21, 263). Moreover, because both writers have different strengths does not require their being considered "counter" or "diametrically opposed." Nor should absolute opposition between them be assumed if, even in the most minute formulations, they seem contrary. Milton may call "Science" knowledge of "Causes" (9.680–82), and Hobbes may call it "Knowledge of Consequences" (I.9, 149). Milton may deem "Reason" an act of "choosing" (*Areop, CPW,* 2:527), and a state of "Sanctity" (*PL,* 8.508), whereas for Hobbes reason is "nothing else but . . . Addition . . . or . . . Subtraction" (I.5, 110) and just as likely as a lack of reason to lead to Hobbes's infamous "state of nature." Not the differences between them but the powerful expression of their differences is what makes Hobbes and Milton eminently comparable.

Hobbes's *Leviathan* exemplifies Sheldin Wolin's contention that the most powerful political theories should be considered "epic" because they propose, in a style that is elevated yet simple, a mythical or imaginary kingdom that would require a superhuman figure to rule it.[18] Yet not only *Leviathan*'s "most powerful political theories" make it epic and, other than for *Paradise Lost*, the only seventeenth-century epic in English still widely read.

For Milton and Hobbes, "by Art is Created" the unique epic significance of their respective masterpieces. The terms with which Barbara Lewalski identifies Milton's "conscious art"[19] are also applicable to Hobbes's *Leviathan*. Both writers incorporate many of the same conventional "paradigms, topoi, and allusions" when establishing the epic identity of their texts (Lewalski, ix).

Notwithstanding Milton's and Hobbes's dramatically different accounts of the power of inspiration and the muses,[20] much of what distinguishes the epic of Milton is what distinguishes the epic of Hobbes. Lewalski enumerates several rhetorical conventions used by the writer of epic to convey its truths. For example, in *Paradise Lost*, "The four proems—to Books One, Three, Seven, and Nine—are personal, self-enclosed lyrics in which the Miltonic Bard analyzes poetic prophecy and poetic creation, and defines his own role as poet prophet" (Lewalski, 27). In *Leviathan*, Hobbes defines a similar role for himself in "The Dedicatory Epistle" and the "Introduction" to his work. According to Lewalski, the first twenty-six lines of *Paradise Lost* are an "epic proposition" to claim that the poem "must necessarily contain, subsume, and endeavor to surpass the greatest poems we know" (Lewalski, 28). So too does Hobbes claim in his "Introduction" what he "set[s] down as . . . [his] own reading orderly, and perspicuously" is unique in "any language or science" (Intro., 83). Lewalski finds that the epics of Virgil and Milton move from death to life: the pain of Adam to the bliss of Christ; the exile from Troy to the establishment of Rome. The pattern of *Leviathan* is similar. It begins with the death of Sidney Godolphin and the English civil war between "those that contend, on one side for too great liberty, and on the other side for too much Authority" (Ded. Ep., 79), yet proceeds toward the establishment of "that great Leviathan called a Common-wealth, or State" (Intro., 81). As the opening lines of *Paradise Lost* recite and reenact "the Beginning" of Genesis, *Leviathan* begins with its own genesis, too: "By Art is created . . . an Artificiall Man, of greater stature and strength than the Naturall" (Intro., 81)—and this act "resemble[s] that *Fiat*, or the *Let us make man*, pronounced by God in the Creation" (Intro., 82). Milton's various claims to be inspired imply that the muse, not merely his own person, is the author of his work. Varying this formula and mentioning no muse, Hobbes hopes that the voice that verifies his work is not only his own but also "the same" that the reader will "find . . . in himself." Milton's artifice to portray his traditionally epic inspiration is extended to create a "great Argument" of "advent'rous Song" that is Christian. Hobbes, too, is concerned with "The Matter, Forme, and Power" not only "Of Man" and the "State" but also of the Christian and the "Christian Common-wealth." In addition, both writers are vulnerable to a specified kind of "darkness." In *Paradise Lost*, it is the "Stygian pool" and blindness. In *Leviathan*, Hobbes's entire text is subsumed by its own fourth part on "the Kingdome of Darknesse."

The inspiration required to fulfill epic expectations makes the writer assume the heroic proportions of his text. The greatest tension in *Paradise Lost*'s four proems is in the spectacle of Milton making himself so vulnerable to a power that can either become his own or crush him like Job. So too does Hobbes become personally involved in his text. He can only hope "to passe" "unwounded" "between the points" of "too great liberty" and "too much Authority" (Ded. Ep., 79). In less grand terms, perhaps, both writers also characterize themselves as particularly Protestant heroes. The sight of "Eremites and Friars / White, Black and Grey, with all thir trumpery" (3.474 –75) and "Wolves . . . grievous Wolves" (12.508) makes Milton throughout his work aspire to the role of a virtuous knight in Spenser's *Faerie Queene*, combating any Duessa, Archimago, or Acrasia the Papacy can muster. Hobbes's self-characterization of his heroic efforts against the Roman Church occurs throughout his works, too. For example, in *Leviathan* he contends against the arguments of the Jesuit cardinal and saint, Robert Bellarmine, who is not merely designated "a Private man" but "the Champion of the Papacy" (III.42, 609). As the proems of *Paradise Lost* present Milton's self-monitoring of his progress through the epic, so the "Dedicatory Epistle," the "Introduction," the conclusions of parts two, three, and four, and the beginning and end of *Leviathan*'s "Review and Conclusion" present Hobbes in the first person directly reflecting on his epic work.

Hobbes writes about epic in his "Answer to Sir William Davenant's Preface before *Gondibert*" and preface "Concerning the Virtues of an Heroic Poem" (1675) to his translation of Homer. Furthermore, *Leviathan* exemplifies what Hobbes writes about epic and, in comparison with *Leviathan*, no work of English literature reveals *Leviathan*'s epic stature better than *Paradise Lost*. The title of Hobbes's work alone—*Leviathan, or the Matter, Forme, & Power of a Common-wealth Ecclesiastical and Civill*—declares its epic ambition. Moreover, in its broad outline and minute particulars, Hobbes's work can be profitably considered epic. Mixing high and low, humble and sublime, Milton begins book 3 of *Paradise Lost* with an epic simile on the interplay of darkness and light. Attempting to "assert Eternal Providence" in *Leviathan*, Hobbes contends "that it is impossible" for people

> to make any profound enquiry into naturall causes, without being enclined thereby to believe there is one God Eternall; though they cannot have any Idea of him in their mind, answerable to his nature. For as a man that is born blind, hearing men talk of warming themselves by the fire, and being brought to warm himself by the same, may easily conceive, and assure himselfe, there is somewhat there, which men call Fire, and is the cause of the heat he feeles, but cannot imagine what it is like; nor have an idea of it

in his mind, such as they have that see it: so also, by the visible things of
this world and their admirable order, a man may conceive there is a cause
of them, which men call God; and yet not have an Idea, or Image of him in
his mind. (I.11, 167)

Both Milton and Hobbes could not be more intent in their desire to
"Irradiate," as Milton wrote, the "Kingdome of Darknesse," as
Hobbes wrote, that they inhabited together. As both writers tried "all
mist from thence / [to] Purge and disperse" (*PL,* 3.53–54), clearly
they differed over how or whether a writer "may see and tell / Of
things invisible to mortal sight" (*PL,* 3.54–55). However, each was
similarly intent on, in John Richetti's words, "the dramatization of his
thought by means of style" (Richetti, 27), epic style, throughout their
writing careers. According to Aubrey, among the "half a dozen"
books Hobbes kept "about him in his chamber . . . Homer and Virgil
were commonly on his Table" (Aubrey, 154). Milton's interest in writing an epic poem from the age of nineteen can be more seriously and
extensively documented.[21]

Although the most eloquent, *Paradise Lost* is unique in neither its
reliance on a narrative concerning humankind's primal beginning
nor in the poem's elaboration of a comparatively simple narrative—
Genesis's first three chapters—into a hyperextended "conceit." In
Observations Concerning the Originall of Government (1652) and
Patriarcha (1680), Robert Filmer reads Genesis as closely as Milton
and imaginatively deduces a vision of patriarchy as fanciful as the
varieties of "connubial Love" that Milton finds in the same text. In
the Diggers' first manifesto, *The True Levellers Standard Advanced:
Or, The State of Community Opened, and Presented to the Sons of Men*
(1649), Gerrard Winstanley confects an elaborate vision of pre-Nor-
man England "to justify the ways" of popular, egalitarian revolutions
against a system of private ownership and virtual caste. The "state
of nature" imagined by Hobbes in *Leviathan's* thirteenth chapter is
particularly significant in such a literary historical context, and the
trappings of epic with which Hobbes surrounds his profound, if conventional, genesis greatly increases its imaginative power. Like Milton, Filmer, and Winstanley, Hobbes bases his text on a myth about
human origins. It is a primordial condition in which "the life of
Man" is memorably described as "solitary, poore, nasty, brutish, and
short" (I.13, 186). The historical consequence when the heirs of "The
Norman Bastard William himself . . . still are . . . Imprisoning, Rob-
bing and Killing the poor enslaved English Israelites" (Winstanley),[22] the political consequences when Adam the great patriarch no
longer rules (Filmer), and the personal consequences of his "first dis-

obedience" (Milton), precipitate the "misery" of "mankind" as portrayed by Hobbes.

Seeing the "great parts" of Milton's and Hobbes's text in a contemporary context clarifies their epic style and content. More specifically, "epic" to signify a literary genre can be understood to be applicable to more than writing in verse. Lewalski notes that *Paradise Lost* is
a "poem . . . sometimes assigned to categories beyond epic: pseudo-
morph, prophetic poem, apocalypse, anti-epic, transcendent epic"
(Lewalski, 3). However, such metaepic categorizing is not necessary
when the term *epic* itself is not conceived as overly constrictive. On
the contrary, to be constrictive in one's viewpoint seems antithetical
to the spirit of epic, which is nothing if not meaning great, large-scale,
and all-inclusive. In the preface to his translation of Homer, Hobbes
observes that epic writing should display "amplitude of the subject":
which means that for him the greatest writing contains "nothing but
variety" (Molesworth, X:7). The literary quality of *Leviathan* greatly
depends on its variety. The critical mistake is for the reader of
Leviathan to think that Hobbes would not want such "amplitude of
subject" in his own epic just because it is a prose text of philosophy.[23]

The epic inclusiveness of *Paradise Lost* is unquestionable, yet the
subtitle of *Leviathan*—"The Matter, Forme & Power of a Commonwealth Ecclesiasticall and Civill"—also offers a broad and "great
accumulation of materials, with judgment to digest, and fancy to combine them." According to *Leviathan*'s subtitle, the book could include
anything. If this is not enough to suggest *Leviathan*'s epic proportions,
the book also contains a descent to the underworld. The first three
parts of *Leviathan*—"Of Man," "Of Common-wealth," "Of a Christian
Common-wealth"—attempt to "Irradiate" all significant matters in
understanding human nature, civil and ecclesiastical government, and
religious salvation. In an unconventional epic manner, Hobbes concludes his epic with the colloquy of part four, "The Kingdome of Darknesse." Eliot complains that "by his metaphor of Leviathan . . .
[Hobbes] provided an ingenious framework on which there was some
peg or other to hang every question of philosophy, psychology, government, and economics" (Eliot, 312). Obviously Eliot does not see that
Leviathan is an epic. Hobbes's "metaphor" serves the same purpose as
Milton's paradise, Dante's afterlife, Virgil's Rome, Lucretius' nature,
Homer's Trojan War, and Job's suffering.

For Milton and Hobbes, writing in prose neither precludes nor even
necessarily conceals the composition of epic. While even Hobbes
admits that in epic "if Prose contend with Verse, it is with disadvan-
tage and, as it were, on foot against the strength and wings of Pega-
sus" (Molesworth, IV:445), prose can still "match," as Milton claims

in his *Defensio* (published in the same year as *Leviathan*), "the deeds of famous men or states" and the "great and wonderful deeds performed evidently by almighty God" (*Def* 1, *CPW*, 4:i, 305).[24] Milton not only considers himself capable but claims as his duty in prose "to fix all the industry and art I could unite . . . to be an interpreter & relater of the best and sagest things among mine own Citizens throughout this Iland." Furthermore, he likens such an effort to "what the greatest and choycest wits of *Athens*, *Rome*, or modern *Italy*, and those Hebrews of old did for their country" (*CG*, *CPW*, 1:811–12). Phrases like "the best and sagest" and "the greatest and choycest" indicate epic ambition. The "wits" of "*Athens*, *Rome* . . . modern *Italy*, and those Hebrews of old" signify the epic writers who are Milton's precedents. Writing about his first *Defensio* in *Defensio Secunda*, Milton thinks, "Anything greater or more glorious than this I neither can, nor wish to, claim" (*Def* 2; *CPW*, 4:i, 559). A critical commonplace of Renaissance literary theory is that nothing can be "greater and more glorious" than epic, and Milton embraces such an epic calling from the beginning of his literary career. Yet as Parker suggests, in his first *Defensio* Milton thinks "he fulfilled himself, not only as a pamphleteer but also . . . as a poet" (Parker, 1:436), since Milton himself claims, in the words of the English translation, that he has "borne witness" to "deeds that were glorious" like "the epic poet" (*Def* 2; *CPW*, 4:i, 685). In addition, he characterizes his own efforts as a writer in nothing less than heroic terms:

> I have not borne arms for liberty merely on my own doorstep, but have also wielded them so far afield that the reason and justification of these by no means commonplace events, having been explained and defended both at home and abroad, and having surely won the approval of all good men, are made splendidly manifest to the supreme glory of my countrymen and as an example to posterity. (*Def* 2; *CPW*, 4:i, 684–85)

Milton designates himself as a writer of epic prose, but Dryden is among the first to recognize Hobbes's great parts as a writer of philosophical epic. Dryden, who himself translates some of Lucretius' *De Rerum Natura*, models his portrait of the Roman poet of philosophical epic on Hobbes, whom he calls "our poet and philosopher of Malmesbury."[25] According to Dryden, whether he is reading Lucretius or Hobbes,

> the distinguishing character . . . (I mean his soul and genius) is a certain kind of noble pride and positive assertion of his opinions. He is everywhere confident of his own reason and assuming an absolute command over his vulgar reader. . . . For he is always bidding him attend, as if he

had the rod over him; and using a magisterial authority, while he instructs him . . . he seems to disdain all manner of replies, and is so confident of his cause, that he is before hand with his antagonists; using for them whatever he imagined they would say, and leaving them as he supposes, without an objection to the future. All this too, with so much scorn and indignation, as if he were assured of the triumph before he entered the lists. (Dryden, 199–200)

Dryden's description might as easily be applied to the Milton of the *Defensio* and *Defensio Secunda* as to the poet of *Paradise Lost* when he writes of "the Sons / Of *Belial*" (1.500–501), "Limbo" or "The Paradise of Fools," "the Rites / Mysterious of connubial Love" (4.742–43), the human history of "all Earth's Kingdoms and thir Glory" (11.384), and "Th' effects which . . . [Adam's] original crime hath wrought" (11.424).[26]

The recognition that *Paradise Lost* and *Leviathan* are examples of the same genre of philosophical epic clarifies their differences. As Lewalski notes, Milton's poem contains many passages on "ontology, the nature of things" (Lewalski, 40), although the pastoral Edenic fable studded with heroic intervals clearly dominates the text. While Hobbes's epic offers examples of the heroic and mock-heroic, of rhetoric and tropes, and of passages of fable or storytelling, *Leviathan* obviously is distinguished for its lucid presentation of abstract philosophical precepts. No one should question the overwhelming superiority of Milton's use of fable when it is compared with Hobbes's practice.[27] However, when *Paradise Lost* and *Leviathan* are conceived of as *philosophical* epics, the comparison is not so one-sided. As epic, *Paradise Lost* is the superior work of formal pastoral, but *Leviathan* may be considered the superior work of formal philosophy.[28] The fifth book of *Paradise Lost* is highly discursive, for example, containing abstract explanations, via Adam and Raphael, of dreams (100–116), various aspects of the relationship between matter and spirit, body and spirit, reason, free will, and angels. Hobbes discusses these topics in *Leviathan*'s thirty-fourth chapter too. Perhaps the veracity of either Milton's or Hobbes's ontology is not so much valued by the modern reader as its performance. In Milton, one of the greatest pleasures is in savoring his archaic and even archaistic accounts of what angels can taste and eat (5.404–33), the poem's first chronological action of the Father's autogenesis of the Son and his subsequent spontaneous exultation (5.600–627), and, later in book 7, the Almighty's creation of the world with "Golden Compasses" and the power of the divine word. In *Leviathan*, Hobbes is never so literally fabulous, but the way he "couches philosophical and scientific precepts in vibrant imagery and relates them directly to the experience and observation" of the reader, in Lewalski's words, is just as marvelous as Milton's Raphael or Lucretius (Lewalski, 41).

A comparison of Milton's and Hobbes's writing on dreams in their respective epics shows the particular strengths of Hobbes. In a well-known passage of *Paradise Lost*'s fifth book (95–116), Adam attempts to explain the source of Eve's nightmare to her.[29] However, Hobbes's writing on dreams in his epic should at least be equally well known for its powerful blend of imagery and abstraction. According to Merritt Hughes, Milton's passage "summarizes the popular faculty psychology which is familiar in Spenser's allegory (*FQ*, 2.9.49–59) of Phantastes."[30] Hobbes presents more than a somewhat technical summary of received wisdom. In the first part of his epic work, writing a chapter devoted specifically to the power and importance of imagination—in English an unprecedented analysis in itself—Hobbes likens imagination to dreams. This single comparison is carried to epic lengths, filling a third of the chapter.

Hobbes's discussion could not begin more simply: "The imaginations of them that sleep, are those we call Dreams" (I.2, 90). He aims at demystifying the subject. Hobbes opposes his simple, physical concept of the "Imagination" as the product of "the Organs of Sense" to any supposed mystery about dreams. He ascribes their seeming mysterious quality to human confusion and ignorance and, what is worse, to the "mischiefe" of "crafty ambitious persons [who] abuse the simple people" with "superstitious fear . . . Prognostiques from Dreams, [and] false Prophecies" (I.2, 93). Hobbes's view may sound like materialistic or rationalistic cant; it is also an example of what Charles Hinnant has called Hobbes's "misanthropic pessimism,"[31] a conventional philosophical theme heard throughout *Leviathan*. Nevertheless, stylistically, at least, Hobbes's statement about dreams signifies more. The plainness and the reductiveness, bordering on quaintness, of Hobbes's analysis of dreams' physical causes contrast with the extravagance of his argument's allusions and examples.

Hobbes writes that in the "silence of sense," an elegant yet plain phrase, when "the Brain, and Nerves, which are the necessary Organs of sense, are so benummed in sleep" (I.2, 91), "dreames are caused by the distemper of some of the inward parts of the Body; divers distempers must needs cause different Dreams." Hobbes adopts a plain, bare, analytic approach to dreams. He contends, for example, "that lying cold breedeth Dreams of Feare, and raiseth the thought and Image of some fearful object . . . And . . . when we sleep, the over heating of the same parts causeth Anger, and raiseth up in the brain the Imagination of an Enemy." He sounds disinterested, objective, "scientific," as if he is about to present a plain, unadorned, factual analysis. However, Hobbes illustrates his strong empirical assertions and reassertions with creative if idiosyncratic allusions to classical history. To increase the heat of his argument, he fans it with political allusions too, transforming a cool, almost clinical, analytic account into a hot, entertaining polemic.

To illustrate his principles on dreams, he alludes to what "We read of Marcus Brutus." Hobbes wants to describe the effect of outside temperature on our dreams and to explain how "Our Dreams are the reverse of our waking Imaginations," and how mere dreams can be feared as "Apparitions of Visions" because "it is a hard matter to distinguish between sense and dreaming" (I.2, 90). To illustrate all of these considerations with one analogy is daunting, but epic writing is often most ambitious in its use of analogy. Hobbes writes

> We read of Marcus Brutus (one that had his life given him by Julius Caesar and was also his favorite, and notwithstanding murthered him,) how at Philippi, the night before he gave battle to Augustus Caesar, hee saw a fearful apparition, which is commonly related by Historians as a Vision: but considering the circumstances, one may easily judge to have been a short Dream. For sitting in his tent, pensive and troubled with horrour of his rash act, it was not hard for him, slumbering in the cold, to dream of that which most affrighted him; which feare, as by degrees it made him wake; so also it must needs make the Apparition by degrees to vanish: And having no assurance that he slept, he could have no cause to think it a Dream, or anything but a Vision. (I.2, 91–2)

The analogy illustrates what Hobbes calls "the fourth virtue" of epic writing and the greatest praise of heroic poetry, "the elevation of fancie" (Molesworth, X:70). Nevertheless, for Hobbes, Brutus is not heroic but *mock-heroic*. Hobbes elaborates on previous historical accounts that present the harsh conditions surrounding Brutus. He is justifiably worried about the morrow's battle at Phillipi, but Hobbes's Brutus is not complex or heroic as in Shakespeare's *Julius Caesar* or Plutarch's *Lives*. Unlike Milton with Satan in *Paradise Lost*, Hobbes does not lend any credibility to his text's villain. Commonly, Brutus the night before Phillipi is considered, in Hobbes's words, "a man full of fearfull thoughts; and whose conscience is much troubled" (I.2, 91). Such a condition could be developed into a potentially heroic or even tragic portrait. Yet he is a man of republican ideals that are opposed to Hobbes's preference for absolute sovereignty. Thus, Hobbes makes him simple and comic: simple as the previous explanation of the effects of body temperature on dreams, yet comic due to Brutus' simple-minded confusion. He is a guilt-ridden buffoon who "sleepeth, without the circumstances, of going to bed or putting off the clothes, as one that noddeth in a chayre" (I.2, 92). The ghost of Caesar appears to Brutus in part because of his guilt, yet also because he falls asleep with his socks on. Even more deflatingly, Hobbes asks us to imagine Brutus "slumbering in the cold." Such mundane details do not suggest a tragic or noble character. Comically, he has no dignity. Hobbes is aware of previous literary or historical portrayals of Brutus, but Hobbes mock-heroically deflates him.

The mock-heroic as much as the heroic distinguishes *Leviathan* as epic. The heroic is more obvious, especially in *Leviathan*'s fourth part, "Of the Kingdome of Darknesse," where (like Milton in his portrayal of hell) Hobbes displays some of his greatest artifice. Both writers' infernal vision reflects their sense of "the disorders of the present time" (R & C, 728), in Hobbes's words from the end of *Leviathan* (like Dante's *Inferno*, too, as the majority of its identifiable inhabitants appear to be Dante's contemporaries). Charles II's London appears at the beginning of *Paradise Lost* (1.496–505). Hobbes's "Kingdome of Darknesse" exists as his characterization of a contemporary England that has no Leviathan-king to rule it and a contemporary European continent bedeviled by a still powerful Papacy. To recognize that *Leviathan* is an epic is to understand why the book can contain a "Kingdome of Darknesse." Otherwise, *Leviathan*'s fourth part appears incongruous and inexplicable. In his work, Hobbes makes a conventional epic's descent into the underworld and meets its fabulous inhabitants. Unlike the epic poems of Homer, Virgil, and Dante, books of philosophy or politics do not usually contain such scenes. However, in the context of such literature or poesy, Hobbes's vision gains much significance. At the end of his political epic Hobbes leaves his readers not in the ideal kingdom of "Leviathan" but rather in the fallen "Kingdome of Darknesse": much in the way that at the end of Spenser's *Faerie Queene* the reader is left in a world where the Blatant Beast is once more "got into the world at liberty againe," where "Mutabilitie" "doth play / Her cruel sports, to many men's decay."[32] Similarly in *Paradise Lost*, pastoral Eden is left behind as Adam and Eve must find a life that is "solitary" (12.649) yet also liable to become "poore, nasty, brutish, and short" (I.13, 186).

There are limits to comparing Hobbes's "Kingdome of Fayries" at the end of *Leviathan* with pictures of the underworld in traditional epics of poetry. Hobbes's creatures of "Darknesse" are neither tragic nor heroic. He does not encounter Dido, Farinata, or Satan. Instead Hobbes meets a pope who is like "Oberon" and ecclesiastics like fairies, gorging themselves on "the Cream of the Land" (IV.47, 714). To say that *Leviathan* is in some ways epic, especially in its inclusion of an underworld, is not enough. Hobbes's epic clearly breaks down into mock-epic too.

In terms of literary history, Hobbes's "Kingdome of Darknesse" looks backward and forward, parodying medieval romance yet anticipating the mock-heroic of Alexander Pope's *Dunciad* (1728). Hobbes's satiric "Comparison of the Papacy with the Kingdom of Fayries" compares "Ecclesiastiques" with "their Cathedral Churches" to "Fairies [who] have also their enchanted Castles, and certain Gigantique Ghosts, that domineer over the Regions round about them" (IV.47, 713). As already noted, Milton also presents Roman "Ecclesiastiques," "Friars / White, Black and Grey, with all their trumpery" (4.474–75). Hobbes's images of "Cradles," "Fools," and "Elves" (IV.47, 713) eliminate any seriousness attached to words like "Metaphysiques, and Miracles, and Traditions," upon which Hobbes proceeds to focus. He is lighthearted in his references. Moreover, after Hobbes's "Kingdome of Darknesse," the greatest Protestant attacks in English on Romanism—with the supreme exception of Milton—are also humorous. Ultimately, epic and humor converge most brilliantly in the mock-heroic of Pope's *Dunciad*. It too "celebrateth the most grave and ancient of things, Chaos."[33]

Hobbes presents the heroic of *Leviathan* in a more subtle, indirect, comprehensive manner, although it is not quite as enigmatic as Milton's portrayal of Satan. The heroic drama of both epics derives from the spectacle of inexorable power—*Paradise Lost*'s God the Father and Son and the Leviathan itself—inexorably challenged. Many critics have gauged the heroic attractions of the underdog Satan in such a confrontation. His powers of evil—his appearances and his power of speech—create a vital tension that the heavenly powers, including the good angels, seem to lack. Through much of *Paradise Lost*, it is Satan who exemplifies the "meaning" if not the "Name" (*PL*, 8.5) of "hero," although he too is vulnerable to becoming mock-heroic. Nevertheless, the Leviathan of Hobbes's epic seems to partake of both a Satanic and a providential heroic. Both the literary creations of Hobbes's Leviathan and Milton's Satan register a profound ambivalence in their readers. Hobbes himself identifies the Leviathan as "great," and yet its powers can appear Satanic, if not Miltonically Satanic.

In *Paradise Lost* (1.200–210), the Leviathan appears as an image of illusion or deception, yet it is identified with Satan himself:

> that Sea-beast
> *Leviathan*, which God of all his works
> Created hugest that swim th' Ocean stream:
> Him haply slumb'ring in the *Norway* foam

> The Pilot of some small night-founder'd Skiff,
> Deeming some Island, oft, as Seamen tell,
> With fixed Anchor in his scaly rind
> Moors by his side under the Lee, while Night
> Invests the Sea, and wished Morn delays:
> So stretcht out, huge in length the Arch-fiend lay
> Chain'd on the burning Lake

This "Leviathan" probably does not allude to Hobbes's work, or Milton is being atypically indirect, dispassionate and unclear. More likely, the comparison repeats the conventional notion, stemming from Isaiah to Lydgate, Wycliff, and Barnaby Barnes, that the Leviathan is a great enemy of God (Isaiah 27:1). Hobbes's inspiration to take the "comparison" of "his Governour" to Leviathan is "out of . . . Job" (II.28, 362). The entire forty-first chapter of Job catalogs the natural, horrible aspects of the Leviathan's anatomy. The "skin with barbed irons," "the doors of his face," his "scales," fiery "mouth," smoking "nostrils," and heart "hard as a piece of the nether millstone" reveal him to be the most powerful and fearful creature in a seemingly godless world.

Allusion is a common element of epics, but more important is what the epic writer makes out of allusion. John Steadman shows that "In applying the term 'Leviathan' to the state and its head, to 'the Multitude . . . united in one Person,' Hobbes was following a minor exegetical tradition that is well established, though by no means central, in the biblical criticism of the mid–xviith century."[34] The term "Leviathan" could also be used to refer simply to "a man of vast and formidable power" (OED). However, Hobbes distinguishes his use of "Leviathan" by emphasizing its signification of a body, particularly the political body. As Milton transforms biblical and classical pastoral, Christian theology, and political republicanism into his epic *Paradise Lost*, so does Hobbes from the outset of his work transform its politics and philosophy into a kind of epic. He writes,

> For by Art is created that great Leviathan, called a Common-wealth, or State . . . which is but an Artificiall Man; though of greater stature and strength than the Naturall, for whose protection and defense it was intended; and in which, the Soveraignty is an Artificiall Soul, as in giving life and motion to the whole body; The Magistrates, and other Officers of Judicature and Execution, artificiall Joynts; Reward and Punishment . . . are the Nerves . . . The Wealth and Riches of all the particular members, are the Strength; *Salus Populi* . . . its Businesse; Counsellors . . . the Memory; Equity and Lawes, an artificiall Reason and Will; Concord, Health; Sedition, Sicknesse; and Civill war, Death. Lastly, the Pacts and

Covenants by which the parts of this Body Politique were at first made, set together, and united, resemble that *Fiat*, or the *Let us make man*, pronounced by God in the Creation. (Intro., 81–82)

Hobbes's analogy recalls the famous speech by Menenius Agrippa in Shakespeare's *Coriolanus* (1.1). However, such a metaphor is common and not epic until Hobbes expands it. Like many medieval and Renaissance writers, he would be aware of St. Paul's famous analogy that "as the body is one, and hath many members, and all the members of that one body, being many, are one body: so also in Christ" (1 Cor. 12:12). Between the lines of St. Paul's description is his insistence that the *corpus mysticum* of Christ is not an earthly, political body. Hobbes's conceit is to call this *corpus mysticum* "Leviathan." Before Hobbes, the name "Leviathan" could represent a sovereign, a society or, most popularly, the devil. However, the *corpus mysticum* of Christ and the biblical monster of Leviathan joined together through the "one spirit" of civil and ecclesiastical law are Hobbes's particular literary creation. He takes the common, prosaic notion of one absolute, sovereign king and abruptly gives it the dimensions of a mythical figure: in Northrop Frye's terms, "a superhuman being" whose powers can exist "only in stories."[35]

Both Milton and Hobbes create an absolute sovereign in their epics, Milton's republican ideals notwithstanding. No one can be more absolute than Milton's "Almighty Father" (3.56) in "the pure Empyrean where he sits / High Thron'd above all" (3.57–58) with "The radiant Image of his Glory . . . His only Son" (3.63–64). The kingdom of Milton's sovereign Father and Son is, of course, not of this world. However, *Leviathan* from its elaborate frontispiece to its descriptive introduction also has no earthly likeness, as Hobbes himself admits repeatedly in his text. Furthermore, both writers emphasize in their works, in Johnson's words about *Paradise Lost*, a "Rebellion against the Supreme King" (Johnson, 118). The rebellion of Satan, the fallen angels, and ultimately Adam and Eve correspond with Hobbes's bleak portrayal of the failures of humankind, the state, and the church in a kingdom of darkness that prevails in spite of his "Artificiall Man," "that Mortall God, to which we owe under the Immortall God, our peace and defence" (II.17, 227), the "King of all the Children of Pride," or, as Milton calls him, "the Sovran Planter" (4.61) of the Edenic state of nature. Yet if *Leviathan* is considered epic, then the fact that Hobbes's absolute sovereign is a "superhuman being" and a "stylized creation that is neither plausible nor realistic" except "only in stories" (Frye, 366) should not be unexpected. Hobbes seems to invite such a reading, from the very first opening, "stylized," neither "plausible nor realistic" paragraph of the introduction to his work. Similarly, any kingdom where the Leviathan rules must also be "superhuman" and supremely unreal, like the Eden of *Paradise Lost*. Neither Milton's nor Hobbes's ideal place is presented as an historical or chronological possibility, but as a mythical and visionary reality that can exist "only in stories," and yet regardless of "the disorders of the present," whether they be ascribed to the misrule of the Saints or the Stuarts. The political and social virtues of Milton's and Hobbes's texts have no more palpable and practical relation to contemporary English politics than does Virgil's Aeneas to Augustan Rome. As Hobbes writes to Davenant on his epic poem, *Gondibert*, the poet clearly can "not [be] acquainted with any great man of the Race of Gondibert" (Molesworth, IV:447).

As Milton characterizes his epic as something "unattempted yet in Prose or rhyme," so Hobbes, in a less stately expression, himself addresses the "Novelty" of his work. On *Leviathan*'s last page, Hobbes identifies his work's "Novelty" as "the Doctrine of this Artificiall Body" (R & C, 729). Notwithstanding that all literature is primarily concerned with "doctrine by ensample, [more] then by rule," as Spenser wrote (Spenser, II, 486), the obvious source of "Doctrine" for both Milton and Hobbes is "the holy Scripture" (III.43, 626). In the conclusion of *Leviathan*'s third part, Hobbes writes: "concerning the Kingdome of God, and Policy Ecclesiasticall . . . I pretend not to advance any Position of my own, but onely to shew what are the Consequences that seem to me deducible from . . . the holy Scriptures . . . in confirmation of the Power of Civill Soveraigns, and the Duty of their Subjects" (III.43, 625–26). Hobbes's phrase, "Consequences that seem to me deducible," severely qualifies his stated desire "not to advance any Position of . . . [his] own." The phrases "That seem to me" and "not to advance any Position of my own" indicate fairly contradictory attitudes. Nevertheless, the same sentiment—or pretense—and the same kind of contradiction can be found in writers of such different stripes as Milton, Hooker, Filmer, Bunyan, Dryden, and the countless additional contemporaries who resort to the use of Scripture in their own writing. All essentially make Hobbes's claim that "I pretend not to advance any Position of my own, but onely" to reveal the political truths that "the holy Scriptures" conceal. Milton and Hobbes are hardly alone in adopting the aesthetic of amplifying their own philosophical and political preferences through scriptural authority. However, they are unique in their epic amplifications— Milton in verse, Hobbes in prose—producing the most extensive, articulate, original, confident, and entertaining English ever written on the assumption that the correct interpretation of the language of

Scripture yields not only how to live but how to rule and be ruled. Both writers are fully aware, in Hobbes's words, "how different" is their "Doctrine . . . from the practise of . . . the world" (II.31, 407). Both writers are forced to compose their epic works in exile: Hobbes literally, in Paris; Milton virtually, at home. Nor can either writer appeal to any one party for support. No one—parliamentarian or royalist, Protestant or Catholic, high church or low, contemporary or modern—can read *Paradise Lost* or *Leviathan* and not at some time in the text be seriously offended. Both writers, like Dante before and after his *Commedia*, exist alone with their own literary kingdom. Neither has any equivalent precedents or descendants and no contemporary society to acclaim or live by its contents. Their epics are too great a "Novelty," infrequent and rare. Their "great parts" are only able to share in each other's company in seventeenth-century England, where they are, as Hobbes says of his own work, "uselesse" (II.31, 407) except as epic: the virtues of which, as identified by Hobbes, they exemplify and, ultimately, "justify . . . to men."

Both *Paradise Lost* and *Leviathan* clearly fulfill the criteria that, according to Hobbes in his essay "Concerning the Virtues of an Heroic Poem," "concur to make the reading of an heroic poem pleasant": "first, in the choice of words. Secondly, in the construction. Thirdly, in the contrivance of the story or fiction. Fourthly, in the elevation of the fancy. Fifthly, in the justice and impartiality of the poet. Sixthly, in the clearness of descriptions. Seventhly, in the amplitude of the subject" (Molesworth, X:iii–iv). Writing "On Paradise Lost ," Marvell asks Milton the rhetorical question, "Where couldst thou words of such a compass find?"[36] The same question could be posed to the author of *Leviathan*, in practice and theory a masterpiece of language: concerned throughout with, to use one of Hobbes's most frequent and favorite terms, the "signification of words," and "stylized creation" of prose unprecedented and unequaled in its portrayal of human life in a dismal, violent state of nature. By "construction" Hobbes means careful yet rhythmic syntax: the manner in which "the order of words . . . carries a light before it, whereby a man may foresee the length of his period, as a torch in the night shows a man the stops and unevenness in his way" (Molesworth, X: v). No image—it is even Miltonic—could be more appropriate than Hobbes's "light" and "torch" to describe the "great parts" of Milton's syntax and, most notably, "the length of his period." Similarly, Hobbes characterizes his own pace in *Leviathan*'s "Introduction," creating "an Artificiall Man . . . of greater stature and strength than the Naturall." Providing such an elaborate narrative to deploy his political and philosophical tenets, Hobbes's power of "contrivance" could not be more immediately obvious in the same introductory pas-

sage. Similarly, the first characteristic Marvell observes—and fears—
about *Paradise Lost* is its ready and abundant willingness to engage
"sacred Truths" through "Fable and old Song" (Marvell, 209). The
"elevation" and *flight* of "fancy," what Hobbes further calls "the greatest praise of heroic poetry" (Molesworth, X:v), is indubitable in *Paradise Lost* and only second to "light" as the analogue for poetic inspiration. The fanciful nature of *Leviathan* may not be necessarily apparent
to modern readers,[37] but Hobbes's seventeenth-century audience is
aware that Hobbes's work, in the words of Edmund Waller, claims "the
whole ocean for his theater."[38] Advisers of Charles II are criticized for
telling "him of golden Indies, fairy lands, / Leviathans, and absolute
commands."[39] Recognizing how the "great parts" of Leviathan can fly
"abroad swiftly to fetch in both matter and words," (Molesworth, X:v),
one poet asks, "What paint will draw utopias, or where / Shall the
groundwork be for castles in the air? / What colours wears the man i'
the moon? Who can / Limn . . . Leviathan?" (Lord, 60).

Neither Milton nor Hobbes could utter a single word in their
respective epics with "impartiality." However, both their claims to be
writing from such an impartial perspective go to similarly great,
rhetorical lengths. Be it prayer or pretension, to invoke a muse for
inspiration is to express a desire for a kind of divine impartiality to
"Illumine" "What . . . is dark" and "raise and support" "what is low"
if the poet remains unassisted in trying to "assert Eternal Providence." Milton also implies his own impartiality as a poet when, for
example, he has the angel Raphael recount in book 7 the creation of
the world. It is Raphael's narrative, not Milton's; thus, book 8
begins, "The Angel ended." Less sublimely, Hobbes at the beginning
of *Leviathan* claims that he is just "like those simple and unpartiall
creatures in the Roman Capitol, that with their noyse defended those
within it, not because they were they, but there" (Ded. Ep., 78).
Hobbes knows that he cannot be or even sound "simple and unpartiall." By 1651 his works are widely decried; and over ten years
before he had fled England in fear of personal reprisals against him
for his writing. He is fully aware that in 1651 a large book on "The
Matter, Forme, & Power of a Common-wealth Ecclesiasticall and
Civill," or even a minor pamphlet on any one of these topics, can only
be received negatively and tumultuously by both the exiled court in
Paris and the ruling factions in England. Still, he persists, offering a
different analogy to prove his "impartiality." He contends that "making . . . Commonwealths, consisteth in Certain Rules, as doth . . .
Geometry" (II.21, 261). Hobbes's "Geometry" in this case is no more
"simple and unpartiall" than Milton's "Hail Holy Light" (*PL*, 3.1) or
"Urania" (*PL*, 7.1).

Regardless of both writers' dubious claims of "impartiality," the "clearness of descriptions"—which the ancient writers of eloquence called *icones*, that is, *images*" (Molesworth, X: vi)—which characterizes their respective claims of "justice and impartiality" are undeniable. The icon of Leviathan towers over an entire work replete with "Images." No epic poet (other than Dante, perhaps) is more self-conscious than Milton in reminding the audience about what and how clearly he sees, including even those "things invisible to mortal sight." By "amplitude of subject" Hobbes means "nothing but variety" (Molesworth, X: vii). *Leviathan*'s "variety" and "amplitude" unmistakably make its "Matter, Forme, & Power" epic. In seventeenth-century English literature, only the art and epic, as Marvell saw it, of Milton's "Messiah Crown'd, God's Reconcil'd Decree, / Rebelling Angels, the Forbidden Tree, / Heav'n, Hell, Earth, Chaos, All" (Marvell, 209) "goe yet further" (Intro., 81) than Hobbes. Most readers today do not feel the need to apologize for and try to explain, as did Marvell, Milton's direct use of biblical narrative and his avoidance of rhyme in constructing his epic. If only the same could be said for Hobbes's use of philosophy and prose in his epic.

Notes

1. John Aubrey, "Thomas Hobbes," in *Brief Lives*, ed. Oliver Lawson Dick (Ann Arbor: University of Michigan Press, 1972), 201. Additional references are cited in text by "Aubrey" and page number.

2. In *Milton Among the Philosophers: Poetry and Materialism in Seventeenth-Century England* (Ithaca: Cornell University Press, 1991), Stephen Fallon argues persuasively that "Simple diametrical opposition . . . does not suffice as a description of the relationship between Milton and Hobbes" (130). For example, "Whatever their great differences in politics and ethics, Milton and Hobbes" share significant assumptions about materialism and "Milton participates in the same materialist project as other thinkers of his time, including Hobbes" (107). Cf. 107–10, 127–30, 166. Additional references are cited in text by "Fallon" and page number.

3. Thomas Hobbes, *Behemoth* (London, "purged from the Errours of Former Editions," 1679), 229–230.

4. Michael Oakeshott, ed., *Leviathan* (Oxford: Basil Blackwell Press, 1947), xvii–xviii.

5. Samuel Johnson, *Lives of the English Poets* (1779) (London: Oxford University Press, 1952), 2:132. Additional references are cited in the text by "Johnson" and page number.

6. Paul de Man, "The Epistemology of Metaphor," in *On Metaphor* (Chicago: University of Chicago Press, 1979), 14. As de Man further argues, "the distinction between literature and philosophy cannot be made in terms of a distinction between aesthetic and epistemological categories. All philosophy is . . . dependent upon figuration . . . although to varying degrees" (28).

7. Blair Warden, "Commentary," *Times Literary Supplement*, 21 July 1978, 20.

8. James Harrington, *The Political Writings of James Harrington*, ed. Charles Blitzer (New York: Columbia University Press, 1955), xxxviii.

9. Jacques Derrida, *Margins of Philosophy*, trans. Alan Bass (Chicago: University of Chicago Press, 1982), 221, 213.

10. Cf. John Richetti, *Philosophical Writing: Locke, Berkeley, Hume* (Cambridge: Harvard University Press, 1983), 17: "Kant's text is dense with special terminology and stripped of anecdote; it is an antitext, in a sense, and demands study rather than mere reading from its audience. Its voice is impersonal and rigorously professional, just as the thought it delivers is purified of common or ordinary experience." Additional references are cited in the text by "Richetti" and page number.

11. William Riley Parker, *Milton: A Biography* (Oxford: Clarendon Press, 1968), 1: 410. Additional references are cited in the text by "Parker" and volume and page number.

12. David Quint, "David's census: Milton's politics and *Paradise Regained*," in *Re-Membering Milton*, eds. Mary Nyquist and Margaret W. Ferguson (New York: Methuen, 1987), 144. Quint's statement recalls the conclusion of Samuel Mintz: "All that Hobbes upheld, Milton opposed" ["The Motion of Thought: Intellectual and Philosophical Backgrounds," *The Age of Milton: Backgrounds to Seventeenth-Century Literature*, eds. C. A. Patrides and Raymond B. Waddington (Manchester: Manchester University Press, 1980), 165].

13. Marjorie Nicolson, "Milton and Hobbes," *Studies in Philology* 23 (July 1926): 411. Additional references are cited in text by "Nicolson" and page number.

14. Cf. Samuel Mintz, *The Hunting of Leviathan: Seventeenth-Century Reactions to the Materialism and Moral Philosophy of Hobbes* (Cambridge: Cambridge University Press, 1962), 22.

15. Not casting Hobbes in the role of Milton's Satan, Stephen Fallon nevertheless considers "the devils" of *Paradise Lost* the "true disciples of Hobbes" (Fallon, 224) and "Milton's poetic indictment of the philosophy of Hobbes" (Fallon, 222). Cf. Fallon, 206–24.

16. D. M. Wolfe, the second, great pioneering scholar on Milton and Hobbes, constructs a plainer critical drama than Nicolson to portray "their Interests and Tenets . . . counter to each other." He sets them in binary opposition. With hyperbolic statements like "Among seventeenth-century thinkers no two critics offer more diverse or contradictory interpretations of root social issues than John Milton and Thomas Hobbes" ["Milton and Hobbes, a Contrast in Social Temper," *Studies in Philology* 41 (September 1944): 410], or "The advent of Thomas Hobbes on the English political scene in 1650 was in striking contrast, as were his beliefs, to the advent of Milton in 1641" (*CPW,* 4:i, 30), this editor of Milton creates a Manichean-like discourse of "hateful contraries." Predictably, the speech of Aubrey's Elizabeth Milton, which Wolfe cites as the words of Hobbes himself, is cited to support the conclusion that "In their analyses of human nature Milton begins with a religious concept, Hobbes with biology; Milton with reason and conscience, Hobbes with motion and sensory responses; Milton with man's aspirations, Hobbes with his limitations" ("Milton and Hobbes, a Contrast," 422–23). *Leviathan*'s first page belies such criticism. Nicolson cultivates a similarly binary, rhetorical self-satisfaction: "That Milton and Hobbes were diametrically opposed in their theories of politics we are fully aware" (Nicolson, 412).

17. Thomas Hobbes, *Leviathan* (1651), ed. C. B. Macpherson (Harmondsworth: Penguin Books, 1968), I.8, 136. All subsequent citations from *Leviathan* are from this edition and are included in the text. Quotations are followed by a Roman numeral or abbreviated title and two Arabic numbers. The Roman numeral signifies the

particular part of *Leviathan*, and the abbreviated title refers to "The Dedicatory Epistle" (Ded. Ep.), "The Introduction" (Intro.), and "A Review, and Conclusion" (R & C) of *Leviathan*. The two Arabic numbers indicate respectively the particular chapters and, in Macpherson's edition, the page.

References to Hobbes's other writings (with the exception of *Behemoth*) are from *The English Works*, ed. Sir William Molesworth (London: J. Bohn, 1839–45), and are noted by volume and page number.

18. Sheldin Wolin, "Paradigms and Political Theories," in *Politics and Experience*, eds. Preston King and B. C. Parekh (Cambridge: Cambridge University Press, 1968), 125–28.

19. Barbara Kiefer Lewalski, *Paradise Lost and the Rhetoric of Literary Forms* (Princeton: Princeton University Press, 1985), 25. Additional references are cited in the text by "Lewalski" and page number.

20. Conventionally, the power of inspiration plays a major role in epic writing. The four proems of *Paradise Lost*—beginning books 1, 3, 7, and 9—memorably expand epic convention. Hobbes's writing in *Leviathan* about inspiration just as memorably diminishes this power, although Hobbes also employs many of the same literary *topoi* as Milton. Both accounts most certainly "please for the Extravagancy," to the extent that, to use T. S. Eliot's terms in "Tradition and the Individual Talent" [*Selected Essays* (New York: Harcourt, Brace & World, 1932)], neither "has . . . complete meaning alone" (Eliot, 4). Both writers treat inspiration monumentally, demonstrating a full awareness of how inspiration's already "existing monuments form an ideal order among themselves" (Eliot, 5): with Milton positively considering himself among the likes of Moses, David, Homer, and Orpheus; and Hobbes explicitly distancing himself from "sulpherous Cavernes," "leaves of the Sibils," "Croaking Ravens," "dipping of Verses in Homer and Virgil . . . and innumerable other such vaine conceipts" by those who invoke "their own Wit, by the name of Muses; their own Ignorance, by the name of Fortune; their own Lust, by the name of Cupid; their own Rage, by the name of Furies; their own privy members, by the name of Priapus" (I.12, 174). Hobbes's burlesque as well as Milton's "advent'rous Song" and "higher Argument" are, again in Eliot's terms, "An introduction of the new (the really new) work of art" among previous and contemporary portrayals of literary inspiration (Eliot, 5). Historical examples of literary inspiration, particularly as evoked by Milton, are an "existing order [that] is complete before the new work" of Milton and Hobbes "arrives." But for this tradition "to persist after . . . [their] supervention . . . the whole existing order must be . . . altered" (Eliot, 5).

The simplest way to compare the viewpoints of Milton and Hobbes on inspiration is to consider the former's hymn to Urania at the beginning of book seven in *Paradise Lost*. In the first thirty-nine-and-a-half lines, Milton wants to reveal the power of "Urania," "the flight of Pegasean wing," "Eternal Wisdom," "Celestial Song," and "the Thracian Bard." Hobbes chooses to portray extensively and often quite literally the muse to whom Milton gives barely half a line: the "empty dream." However, even such "counter" viewpoints have distinct similarities.

21. See Parker, *Milton*, 1: 47, 69, 175, 186–87, 189–92, 209–10, 436, 509, 839, 843, 857, and Ivar Lou Myhr, *The Evolution and Practice of Milton's Epic Theory* (Folcroft: The Folcroft Press, 1969), 15–27.

22. Gerrard Winstanley, cited by T. Wilson Hayes, *Winstanley the Digger* (Cambridge: Harvard University Press, 1979), 147. For a more extensive discussion of Hobbes's portrayal of human origins in *Leviathan*, see Charles Cantalupo, "How To Be a Literary Reader of Hobbes's Most Famous Chapter," 67–79 in *The Literature of Controversy*, ed. Thomas N. Corns (London: Frank Cass & Company, 1986).

23. As John Richetti states, "The philosophical text can be treated, like any other text, as an artifact; . . . the language and literary strategies that are a part of thought can be placed in history, partly in the history of writing and partly in a larger historical network. Finally, . . . there are important affinities or similarities between those intensely realized projections of the imagination called literature and those intensely realized constructions of the intellect called philosophy" (Richetti, 11).

24. As John Diekhoff and William Riley Parker observe, Milton considers the Latin prose of both his *Defensio* and *Defensio Secunda* (1654) to be "his patriotic epic" [John Diekhoff, *Milton on Himself* (New York: Humanities Press, 1965), 239], "literary climax," and "crowning achievement" (Parker, 1: 435).

25. John Dryden, "Preface to Sylvae" (1685), *Selected Criticism*, eds. James Kinsley and George Parfitt (Oxford: Clarendon Press, 1970), 199–200. Additional references are cited in the text by "Dryden" and page number.

26. Dryden's description of Hobbes also resembles what Anne Ferry hears in the narrator of *Paradise Lost*: "the masterful personality, the strongly held beliefs and values, the controlling voice, stern, compassionate, exultant" [*Milton's Epic Voice: The Narrator in Paradise Lost* (Cambridge: Harvard University Press, 1986), 12].

27. As Johnson writes, "In this part of his work, Milton must be confessed to have equalled every other poet" (Johnson, 118).

28. As Fallon observes, "Historians of ideas have too often shortchanged both poets and philosophers . . . there is a kind of poetry in the structure and imagery of the . . . *Leviathan*, and there is philosophical originality and sophistication in *Paradise Lost*. To point to the literary sophistication of Descartes and Hobbes is not to claim that they are the equals of Dante and Shakespeare. Similarly, to point to Milton's philosophical sophistication is not to suggest that he is as rigorous a thinker as Aquinas or Leibniz" (244).

29.

> Best Image of myself and dearer half,
> The trouble of thy thoughts this night in sleep
> Affects me equally; nor can I like
> This uncouth dream, of evil sprung I fear;
> Yet evil whence? in thee can harbor none,
> Created pure. But know that in the Soul
> Are many lesser Faculties that serve
> Reason as chief; among these Fancy next
> Her office holds; of all external things,
> Which the five watchful Senses represent,
> She forms Imaginations, Aery shapes,
> Which Reason joining or disjoining, frames
> All what we affirm or what deny, and call
> Our knowledge or opinion; then retires
> Into her private Cell when Nature rests.
> Oft in her absence mimic Fancy wakes
> To imitate her; but misjoining shapes,
> Wild work produces oft, and most in dreams,
> Ill matching words and deeds long past or late.
> Some such resemblances methinks I find
> Of our last Ev'ning's talk, in this thy dream.
> But with addition strange; yet be not sad.

30. Hughes, *John Milton: Complete Poems and Major Prose*, 304, n. to 5.100–116.

31. Charles Hinnant, *Thomas Hobbes* (Boston: G. K. Hall & Co., 1977), 151.

32. Edmund Spenser, *The Faerie Queene* (1596), *The Poetical Works of Edmund Spenser*, ed. J. C. Smith (Oxford: Clarendon Press, 1909), II: 452, 454. Additional references are cited in the text by "Spenser," volume, and page number.

33. Hobbes's "Kingdome of Fayries" like Pope's "Empire of Dullness" preys upon "the Geometrician" and "Astronomer" (IV.46, 683), obliterates "the faculty of Reasoning," "*Philosophia prima*" (IV.46, 684) and "Physiques" (IV.46, 694), and replaces them with Popery, "Metaphysiques" (IV.46, 688), the "occult" (IV.46, 696) and "spiritual Darkness" (IV.47, 708). In Pope's "Empire" too [*Poetry and Prose of Alexander Pope*, ed. Aubrey Williams (Boston: Houghton Mifflin Company, 1969), 378],

> Art after Art goes out, and all is Night.
> See skulking Truth to her old Cavern fled,
> Mountains of Casuistry heap'd o'er her head!
> Philosophy, that lean'd on Heav'n before,
> Shrinks to her second cause, and is no more.

As Milton presents Adam and Eve leaving behind "that flaming Brand . . . [and] Gate / With dreadful Faces throng'd and fiery Arms" (12.643–44) that was Paradise, and as Hobbes closes his vision of *Leviathan* in "Darknesse," so does Pope let "the curtain fall" on his poem, as "Universal Darkness buries All."

34. John Steadman, "Leviathan and Renaissance Etymology," *Journal of the History of Ideas* 28 (1967): 575.

35. Northrop Frye, *Anatomy of Criticism* (Princeton: Princeton University Press, 1957), 366. Additional references are cited in the text by "Frye" and page number.

36. Andrew Marvell, "On Paradise Lost," in Merritt Y. Hughes, ed., *John Milton: Complete Poems and Major Prose* (Indianapolis: The Odyssey Press, 1973), 209. Additional references are cited in the text by "Marvell" and page number.

37. With the notable exception of Christopher Pye, "The Sovereign, the Theater, and the Kingdome of Darknesse: Hobbes and the Spectacle of Power," *Representing the English Renaissance*, ed. Stephen Greenblatt (Berkeley: University of California Press, 1988), 279–301.

38. Edmund Waller, "A Letter from Edmund Waller to Thomas Hobbes," cited by Paul Hardacre, *Huntington Library Quarterly* 11.2 (1948): 432.

39. John Ayloffe, "Britania and Raleigh," *Anthology of Poems on Affairs of State 1660–1714*, ed. George De F. Lord (New Haven: Yale University Press, 1975), 123. Additional references are cited in the text by "Lord" and page number.

Milton and Crashaw:
The Cambridge and Italian Years

PAUL A. PARRISH

On 6 July 1631, Richard Crashaw, son of a vehement antipapist preacher, was admitted to Pembroke College, Cambridge.[1] One year later, John Milton acquired his M.A. from Christ's College and soon thereafter left Cambridge for Hammersmith. Crashaw continued at Cambridge for nearly twelve years after his matriculation, achieving some notable regard as a Scholar, poet, and Fellow. In 1634 he attained his B.A. from Pembroke, and in the following year he was elected to a Fellowship at Peterhouse, where he spent his remaining university years. Crashaw attained his M.A. from Peterhouse in 1638 and spent four or five more years in the College before he left under forced exile, probably in January 1643.[2] On 8 April 1644, Crashaw's formal association with Cambridge was involuntarily ended, as he and other Royalist sympathizers at Peterhouse were ejected for not being in residence. As Milton was four or five years older than Crashaw, so his education anticipated Crashaw's by several years. On 12 February 1625, Milton was admitted to Christ's as a "lesser pensioner," six years before Crashaw's admission to Pembroke. In 1629, when Milton attained his B.A. from Christ's, Crashaw was admitted to the Charterhouse School in London. Milton's B.A. and M.A. from Christ's in 1629 and 1632 antedated Crashaw's B.A. from Pembroke and his M.A. from Peterhouse by five and six years.

These biographical relationships, of interest because they concern two poets of distinction, reveal less about the subjects than do events in the seventeen years from Milton's departure from Cambridge in 1632 to Crashaw's death in 1649. While the Cambridge years were significant in helping to shape the literary and religious life of each, especially of Crashaw, subsequent events reveal even more compellingly the forces that guided them toward very different religious and artistic accomplishments. Worth particular attention is the Italian experience of each.

Although under quite dissimilar circumstances, both Milton and Crashaw went to Italy not many years after each left Cambridge. Milton left the university in 1632 and began his Italian journey six years later in 1638; Crashaw was forced out of Cambridge in 1643 and arrived in Italy three years later in 1646. When Milton toured Italy as a young man of about thirty, he was a committed Protestant and already significantly influenced by Puritan religious and political views, but he was open and receptive to influences, whether in the land of the Pope or elsewhere, that would hasten his artistic development. In 1641, when Milton published the first of his antiprelatical tracts, Crashaw was active at Little Gidding and at Little St. Mary's Church at Peterhouse, engaged in practices that would incur the wrath of Parliament. A Puritan-inspired document from that year accuses Crashaw of worshipping the Virgin, of participating in "superstitious" practices at Little St. Mary's, and of following the "popish doctrine of private masses."[3] In the 1640s, as Milton was being drawn into the political and religious war engulfing England, Crashaw was being drawn more firmly into the arms of Rome. On leaving Cambridge in 1643, he went to Leyden, then to Paris, where he formally converted to Catholicism, and finally, in 1646, arrived in Rome. When Crashaw reached Italy, he was not much older than Milton had been, thirty-three or thirty-four years old, but he must have *felt* much older, for he was arriving with few means and in exile, as a man without possessions, family, or support. But he was also arriving as a Roman convert and should have been welcomed in a fashion the outspokenly Protestant Milton had no right to expect.

In the spring of 1649, each poet received an appointment that signified a deep commitment. In March, Milton was named Secretary for Foreign Tongues and thus began his formal service to the Commonwealth throughout the next decade. A month after Milton's appointment in England, Crashaw was assigned to the office of beneficiatus at Loreto, an assignment that, because of Loreto's shrine to the Virgin, must have pleased him. But Crashaw, unlike Milton, was not able to fulfill the expectations of the office. Shortly after his arrival in Loreto he developed a fever and died on 21 August 1649.

My aims in the remainder of this essay are to reconsider two historical contexts for both Milton and Crashaw—Cambridge and Italy— and to suggest anew how these apparently similar settings affected the two poets in such different ways. In doing so, I intend to be mindful of important artistic contexts as well, for discussions about their artistry similarly point toward meaningful likenesses in the poets while revealing even more profound differences.

Milton and Crashaw are the two English poets most often associated with the Baroque. One may cite, for example, the studies of Crashaw by Austin Warren and Marc Bertonasco, each of which elevates the "Baroque" to the title of his book.[4] In a more pointed manner, Douglas Bush, searching for an apt characterization of the Baroque in literature, concludes that it might most simply be described as "poetry like Crashaw's."[5] There are, with equal authority, studies that align Milton—especially, the later Milton of *Paradise Lost*, *Paradise Regained*, and *Samson Agonistes*—with the Baroque tradition. Roy Daniells, for example, elaborates on *Milton, Mannerism and Baroque* while Murray Roston, in a book whose title parallels Bertonasco's, writes about *Milton and the Baroque*.[6]

If we have come to expect studies such as *Crashaw and the Baroque* and *Milton and the Baroque*, we must also recognize that critics have not found it easy to connect the two poets with meaningful results. Part of the difficulty no doubt lies in the continuing uncertainty (or disagreement) over what exactly the Baroque represents; part of the difficulty is surely located in the judgment that Milton's poetry and Crashaw's are, finally, very different.

Wylie Sypher's study *Four Stages of Renaissance Style* is a wide-ranging discussion of different artistic modes, including Baroque, identified under the broad heading "Renaissance." Both Crashaw and Milton figure in Sypher's discussion of the Baroque, but they are largely separated in that discussion. Sypher calls Crashaw the "most characteristic poet of baroque piety," and he finds in *Paradise Lost* evidence of "the plenitude of baroque." Furthermore, in his discussion of Milton he identifies two qualities that would seem to open the door to a fuller consideration of ways in which Crashaw and Milton are poetically connected. Sypher sees in *Paradise Lost* an "overpowering accumulation of sensory impression" and thus connects the poem to the glorification of the senses more often identified in art and verse, including Crashaw's, associated with the Catholic Counter Reformation. Indeed, Sypher later makes that connection explicit by identifying *Paradise Lost* as the point at which Milton's "Counter-Reformation poetic imagination submerges his *anti*-Counter-Reformation ethic." In spite of these arguments about "sensory impression" in Milton and the Counter-Reformation origin of the Baroque (a conclusion challenged by some later critics), Sypher does little to bring Crashaw and Milton together in any fruitful discussion.[7]

If few connections are elaborated by Sypher, there are virtually none in Mario Praz's *The Flaming Heart*, Daniells's *Milton, Mannerism and Baroque*, or Roston's *Milton and the Baroque*, though each is intent on establishing the Baroque as an important context within which to consider the poetry of Crashaw or Milton. Praz's essay "The Flaming Heart: Richard Crashaw and the Baroque" provides the title for his book-length consideration of relations between Italian and English literature from Chaucer to T. S. Eliot. Although very much concerned with the Baroque and including a contextual discussion of the artistic environment, Praz says almost nothing about Milton. Daniells identifies the Baroque as the significant artistic tradition for understanding Milton's final poetic trilogy, and, though giving brief consideration to Crashaw as a Baroque artist, he focuses on the (apparently different) Baroque elements in Milton's verse. Roston adopts an almost impossibly broad view of what the Baroque means—"the response of the era as a whole to man's cosmic discoveries"—and within that encompassing definition, he fits Crashaw and Milton, but not together. Roston calls Crashaw the "most faithful exponent of the continental Catholic tradition." Citing an example from Crashaw's Hymn to St. Teresa, he asserts pointedly, "Milton will have none of this." Espousing a view that is in marked contrast to Sypher's, Roston argues for a dissociation of Milton, *Paradise Lost*, and the Baroque from an exclusive emphasis on the Counter Reformation. In doing so, he confirms the further distance between the "continental Catholic tradition" he identifies with Crashaw and the different Baroque tradition he identifies with Milton.[8]

Roston's comments on the Baroque echo those of Frank Warnke who, in two earlier studies, argues for a broad definition of the Baroque as a diverse period style within which numerous individual traditions can be identified. The Baroque is, he says in the introduction to his anthology *European Metaphysical Poetry*, a "generic designation for the style of the whole period" from the late sixteenth century through the first two-thirds of the seventeenth. This period style, he says, gives rise to qualities such as hyperbole, conceit, and dramatic contrast, but as a whole the Baroque contains different, even conflicting, individual styles such as Metaphysical, *préciosité*, and "High Baroque." In the revealingly titled *Versions of Baroque*, Warnke elaborates on the argument he made ten years earlier in his anthology. Within a broad understanding of the Baroque, Warnke readily includes Donne, Crashaw, and Milton, among others, as exemplifying one or more "versions" of the Baroque. The Baroque includes, for example, the "highly colored, ornate" poetry of Crashaw, as well as the "monumental creations" of Milton. In his discussion of the varying traditions within the Baroque, however, Warnke is more concerned with contrasting Crashaw (who represents the "High Baroque") and Donne (who represents the Mannerist or Metaphysical mode).[9]

A recent study of period styles in literature, John M. Steadman's *Redefining a Period Style: "Renaissance," "Mannerist" and "Baroque" in Literature*, is an extensive reconsideration of the meaning and application of the period styles associated with the sixteenth and seventeenth centuries. Steadman's references to Crashaw and Milton are, however, largely in the context of readings of earlier critics such as Sypher, Daniells, and Praz. Although acknowledging Crashaw's association with the Baroque, Steadman discusses his writings primarily in a chapter devoted to the Metaphysical poets as *concettisti*. About the alignment of Milton within artistic categories such as the Baroque he expresses some doubt, concluding that "art historical categories may serve as convenient labels for differentiating facets or phases of his style, but their utility is vitiated by their uncertain denotation."[10]

I have attempted in this brief review to account for only a few of the important studies of the Baroque in literature, with particular attention to Milton and Crashaw, but they represent, I believe, the uncertain and sometimes schizophrenic analyses of the two most important Baroque poets writing in English. It might be said about each, to paraphrase Roston, that he will "have none" of the other. Yet in their art, as in their lives, there remain intriguing intersecting points. If the intersections serve ultimately to remind us of the crossing of two paths that lead to very different points, we nonetheless profit from a clearer understanding of both the associations and the ultimate divergence.

As their artistic accomplishments intersect only to signal quite distinctive characteristics, so too their lives follow similar, yet ultimately quite divergent, paths. At Pembroke, and later at Peterhouse, Crashaw was a Scholar and Fellow at the two colleges most frequently identified with the High Anglican position. At Christ's, Milton spent seven formative years in a college whose outlook was "distinctly Puritan."[11] For Milton and Crashaw in Italy, as for other English visitors, their stay included time spent at the Jesuit English College at Rome. While we cannot draw certain conclusions, especially about Crashaw's residency there, it would appear that Milton was, for the most part, greatly respected and honored, not only in the English College and in Rome, but in Florence and elsewhere during his fifteen months in the country; Crashaw, the Roman convert, seems to have had no important impact in the College during his much longer residence there, was apparently ignored by the Pope in spite of Queen Henrietta Maria's supportive letter, and was reputed to have quarreled with others serving Cardinal Pallotta. The university and Italian settings, experienced similarly yet so diversely by these two English contemporaries, serve to remind us not only of the complex forces at work in this volatile century, but also of the intricate and unpredictable relationships between political and religious contexts and artistic sensibilities.

1

Two basic truths emerge from a study of the political side of university life in the late sixteenth and early seventeenth centuries: the two great universities, Oxford and Cambridge, were, for good and ill, inextricably linked with the political and religious developments of the country as a whole, and, as the two sides of the growing controversy became more clearly defined, Oxford was more closely identified with the Royalists; Cambridge, with the Puritans.[12] Into the latter environment came the young schoolboys John Milton and Richard Crashaw. After the succession of Elizabeth many Reformation Masters, removed or in exile during earlier troublesome years, returned to their positions and "stamped Cambridge . . . with the Puritan tradition."[13] For example, 1584 marked the establishment of Emmanuel College, the most thoroughly Puritan of all of Cambridge's colleges and one historically linked to Milton's Christ's. A story told of the event, perhaps apocryphal, is nonetheless revealing. Emmanuel was founded by a Christ's man, Sir Walter Mildmay, and the first Master, Laurence Chaderton, was also from Christ's. Queen Elizabeth is reported to have observed to Mildmay: " 'So, Sir Walter, . . . I hear you have erected a Puritan foundation.' 'No, Madam,' he answered, 'far be it from me to countenance anything contrary to your established laws, but I have set an acorn which, when it becomes an oak, God alone knows what the fruit will be thereof.' "[14] By the 1630s and 1640s all would know about the fruit, for it had a distinctly Puritan flavor.

After the succession of James, the Puritan voice from Cambridge was temporarily muted, but the stillness was short-lived. James himself received "poor welcome" at the university during a visit in 1615,[15] and various incidents from the later reign of Charles I serve to reveal the open conflicts between the University and the State.[16] The continuing opposition between Puritan and Royalist sympathizers and the steady strength of the Puritan side are dramatically revealed in the controversy over the election of a Chancellor for the university in 1626, the year following Milton's admission to Christ's. On 2 February, 1626, Charles I was crowned at Westminster Abbey. Among his supporters was George Villiers, Duke of Buckingham, who, on 8 May of that year, was impeached by the House of Commons for supporting Richard Montagu, an anti-Calvinist writer to whom Buckingham was patron. Only twenty days after the impeachment of Buckingham, the Chancellor of the University of Cambridge, the Earl of Suffolk, died, and Charles immediately proposed Buckingham as his successor.[17]

Perhaps no other circumstance prior to the Civil War so fully involved the whole of the university and, at the same time, divided Cambridge into two hostile camps. To oppose Buckingham, Puritan sympathizers nominated Thomas Howard, Earl of Berkshire, as an opponent, and the contest thus became "essentially one between the two great theological parties of the time."[18] When the votes were counted, Buckingham won by a slight majority, but, as Albert Mansbridge has rightly argued, given the power of the king's pronounced wishes and the relatively disorganized opposition to Buckingham, the results testify to the strength of the Puritan forces.[19] The votes by the colleges were not surprising. The "most vehement" of Buckingham's supporters were, for the most part, associated with Pembroke and Peterhouse, among them William Beale of Pembroke, Leonard Mawe, Master of Peterhouse from 1617 to 1625, and Matthew Wren, a Pembroke man, who had succeeded Mawe as Master of Peterhouse.[20] In Pembroke, the vote was six to one for Buckingham, in Peterhouse, five to one. At the opposite end were Sidney and Emmanuel, which supported Berkshire by six to one and twelve to four, respectively. At Christ's, though there was strong opposition to Buckingham, the final vote was nearly even.[21]

One final, climactic occasion further suggests the political and religious character of the two great universities. At the Westminster Assembly of 1643, convened to advise Parliament in the new Presbyterian form of church government, sixty-two clergymen represented Cambridge, only thirty-four coming from Oxford.[22]

As we look more closely at the residences of Milton and Crashaw, we see more clearly the very different environments they entered. The influence of a college master was at times extraordinary and there was, during the period, little interest in developing a college with wide-ranging political and religious viewpoints. As a consequence, as one historian has observed, "each college too often became a narrow exclusive community, where local antipathies and religious or political animosities were fostered and developed, and that catholic interchange of thought and feeling which it is the first function of a university to promote was effectually checked."[23] Pembroke, the college of Crashaw's undergraduate years, is a revealing example.

Under Elizabeth, Pembroke was guided by Masters such as Edmund Grindal, John Young, and William Fulke, whose sympathies were decidedly Puritan. It has been argued, for example, that the choice of Grindal as Archbishop of Canterbury in 1575/76 resulted in part from the belief of the Queen's advisors, especially Cecil, that her "policy required a leaning toward puritanism."[24] Grindal is, at the same time, an example of the "church-centred" Puritan described by Mark Curtis, for he later attacked the views of Thomas Cartwright when the latter advocated presbyterianism.[25] William Fulke was said, while Master of Pembroke, to have met often to study scripture with Chaderton, Whitaker, and other Puritan clerics at Cambridge.[26] In spite of this history, with the election of the notable Lancelot Andrewes as Master in 1589, Pembroke began to develop into "one of the strongholds of the High Church party."[27] The Laudian and Royalist temperament of Pembroke continued after Andrewes and was evident in the leadership of the Masters Samuel Harsnett (1605–16), Nicholas Felton (1616–19), Jerome Beale (1619–30), and Benjamin Laney, who was Master at the time of Crashaw's admission.[28] In 1628, two years before Laney's election, the whitewash was removed from the College chapel walls, apparently to allow the old medieval paintings on them to be seen once again.[29] Crashaw takes note of the Pembroke chapel in several poems and praises Laney's role in its beautification. In his epistles dedicatory to Laney (for a manuscript collection of epigrams and for his 1634 volume *Epigrammatum Sacrorum Liber*), Crashaw praises his Master for his efforts to beautify and embellish the College chapel and thus make religion more elegant—an aim that was anathema to a Puritan but sacred to a High Churchman (and, we might note, consistent with those features of the Baroque associated with the Counter Reformation). Under Laney, Crashaw says, religion is allowed to appear in a more pleasant form ("amaeniori facis"), adorned as a most beautiful goddess ("pulcherrima dea"). The holy house of God is restored to an appropriate luster ("nitorem") that in turn reflects favorably on Laney himself. In the poem that follows the prose preface to the volume of epigrams, Laney is commended further for his efforts to adorn religion, and Crashaw's dedicatory pieces together thus ring as a tribute to Laney's Laudian sensibilities.

John Tourney, Crashaw's tutor at Pembroke, was also a vocal supporter of Archbishop Laud. He was twice called before the Vice-Chancellor of the University during Crashaw's undergraduate years for challenging the doctrine of justification by faith only, a touchstone for orthodox Calvinist belief. Although questioned, he was allowed to go unpunished, to the great disappointment of the Puritan Samuel Ward, Master of Sidney College, who complained of the "great Abettors of Mr. Tourney" and of the increasing tolerance of "Novelties, both in Rites and Doctrines."[30] As he does for Laney and his Master at Charterhouse, Robert Brooke, Crashaw singles out Tourney for special praise in his volume of epigrams, and in a later Latin poem ("Fides quae sola justificat, non est sine Spe & Dilectione") he advances a position on the "doctrine of faith only" quite compatible with the view of Tourney and other High Anglicans.

The "leading Pembroke man of the seventeenth century" was Matthew Wren,[31] who became Master, not of Pembroke, but of Peterhouse, and thus his residences mirror and anticipate Crashaw's own. Wren's Royalist position was well known at Pembroke and he was able to exercise it even more decisively as Master of Peterhouse (1626–34). So strong was Wren's support for the Royalist cause that he was twice confined to the Tower, the second time for seventeen years.[32] The Laudian position of Peterhouse was evident earlier under the Mastership of Leonard Mawe (1617–26) and continued under both Wren and John Cosin (1643–44 and 1660). Thus, during the years of Milton's university life and continuing through Crashaw's, Peterhouse was known for its supporters of the king and the archbishop. The most visible sign of the religious position of the College, the chapel, was the primary responsibility of Wren, though it was not fully completed until the Mastership of Cosin. The chapel was dedicated in March 1632, less than a year after Crashaw's arrival in Cambridge and only four months before Milton's departure. What Wren began Cosin perpetuated, and to the chapel were added a "more elaborate ritual and unwonted ornaments," causing it to become an object of particular scorn for Puritans.[33] One contemporary observer noted disparagingly that in the chapel a "glorious new Altar" was set up, and "mounted on steps, to which the Master, Fellowes, and Schollers bowed, and were enjoyned to bow by Doctor Cosins, the Master, who set it up." He further comments on the "carved crosse at the end of every seat," the "incense pot," and the habit of all Fellows and Scholars making a "low obeysance to the Altar." He concludes that anyone venturing there might "learne and practise the Popish ceremonies and orders used in that chappell."[34] Crashaw's pleasure in the chapel denounced by the Puritans is revealed in his two Latin poems on Peterhouse. Written in 1635 or 1636, they include requests for contributions toward the completion of the chapel, which Crashaw invokes as the "sweetest House in the world" ("Domus o dulcissima rerum!").

In distinct contrast to the political loyalties of Pembroke and Peterhouse, Christ's College had been, since the time of Elizabeth, more closely aligned with efforts to purify the established Church. Perhaps no other college during the Elizabethan period, says the historian of Christ's, John Peile, "contained so many residents who were in trouble for Puritanism or for Nonconformity."[35] A. L. Rowse remarks, with characteristic overstatement, that Emmanuel was a "seminary of sedition" and in such training, Christ's "came second to Emmanuel."[36] The strength of Puritanism at Christ's in the time of Elizabeth and James is perhaps best represented by Williams Perkins, a Fellow from 1584–94, "by general consent the leading English Puritan theologian" of his day,[37] and one of his students, Williams Ames, a Fellow from 1602–10 and a radical Puritan author whose theology was an impetus for Milton's *De Doctrina Christiana*.[38] Also associated with Christ's as an undergraduate was Samuel Ward, later to be the arch defender of Puritanism from his post as Master of Sidney.

Puritanism at Christ's in the seventeenth century, under the Masters Valentine Cary (1609–22) and Thomas Bainbridge (1622–46), was "less fierce" than that under Elizabeth, but it persisted nonetheless.[39] During the battle over the election of a new Chancellor in 1626, two important opponents of the king's choice, Joseph Mead and William Chappell, were from Christ's, and we can be sure of Milton's acquaintance with them. Although the political and religious positions of each are in significant ways ambivalent, each was associated with some element of the Puritan cause.[40] Mead, described by Peile as the "most interesting of the Fellows of Christ's at this period," saw his Fellowship delayed, in part, it appears, because the Master Valentine Cary thought he "inclined to Geneva."[41] Mead's *Key of the Revelation*, published in Latin in 1627, was, because of the censorship of Laud, not translated into English until 1643, when its publication was ordered by the House of Commons.[42] Chappell, who was regarded as a Puritan "because of the strictness of his life and conversation,"[43] was, significantly, also Milton's first tutor at Christ's. Milton's contact with men such as Chappell and Mead would have assured his continuing association with some elements of the Puritanism he had encountered in his youth, and while there is evidence that he may have rebelled against some of what he saw at Cambridge, there is no evidence that he rebelled against that.

Milton's poetry from or about his Cambridge years yields little direct comment on the political or religious environment there. He comments on his rustication in "Elegia Prima," focusing on personal and artistic benefits to be derived from his forced separation from the "sedgy Cam" ("arundiferum . . . Camum"). While confirming the existence of a conflict sufficiently severe to require Milton's suspension, "Elegia Prima" is first and foremost a statement about the author's commitment to poetry, of his devotion to the "quiet Muses" ("placidis . . . Musis") and to his books:

> Tempora nam licet hic placidis dare libera Musis,
> Et totus rapiunt me mea vita libri.

Indeed, the poem is itself a conscious poetic exercise of "alternating measures" ("alternos . . . modos") written by a young poet to a devoted friend. Occasional poems from Milton's Cambridge period are largely unexceptional, as he writes on the death of the Vice-Chancellor, on the Gunpowder Plot, on the deaths of Lancelot Andrewes and Nicholas Felton (both former Masters of Pembroke) as a conscientious and maturing poet and schoolboy. Much more representative of the impact of the Cambridge years on Milton's poetry are "L'Allegro" and "Il Penseroso." Devoid of ideological or doctrinal controversy, they suggest that for Milton the artist the greatest benefit from the university was the opportunity to engage and stimulate his creative genius. "L'Allegro" and "Il Penseroso" transform schoolboy exercises on the merits of contrasting images and realities. In view of the poetry that derives most immediately from the Cambridge years, poetry that suggests a disinclination to use verse for ideological debate, it is not surprising that, when Milton gives himself almost wholly to the republican cause during the Commonwealth, he very nearly abandons the writing of poetry altogether during that time.

For a final example of the distinctive positions of the colleges at Cambridge we need again to move beyond the chronological boundaries of Milton's stay at Cambridge. As Parliament gained strength over the king, it moved to crush Royalist sympathizers, both in print and with arms. On 28 June 1641, it issued an order demanding religious practices in conformity to Puritanism. In August 1643 it passed an ordinance requiring all chapels and churches to destroy all altars, tables of stone, tapers, crucifixes, and "all other images and pictures of saints or superstitious inscriptions."[44] And in December of that year the infamous William Dowsing, acting as an agent of Parliament, led his troops into Cambridge, destroying and purifying as he went.

In view of the histories of Pembroke, Peterhouse, and Christ's, and given the principal figures associated with each, their treatment at the hands of Dowsing's forces is not surprising. Pembroke and Peterhouse, among all of the colleges, were singled out for particular destruction. By the time Dowsing paid his vengeful visit to Pembroke, most loyal royalists had fled and only a few Fellows were left. According to Dowsing's journal, his troops "broke ten cherubims, broke and pulled down 80 superstitious pictures."[45] The troops were turned loose into Pembroke and "charged by their Officers to shift for themselves . . . [they] broke open the Fellows and Scholars Chambers, and took their Beds from under them."[46] In March 1644, Laney and most of the Fellows were ejected for "offending the privileges of Parliament and other scandalous acts in the University of Cambridge."[47] And when, in 1645, Richard Vines became Master, he guided an almost empty college.[48] At the chapel of Peterhouse, by reputation the most Royalist of colleges, Dowsing's troops "pulled down 2 mighty great Angells with Wings & divers other Angells, & the 4

Evangelists & Peter with his keies over the Chappell Dore, & about a hundred Chirubims & Angells & divers Superstitious Letters in gold."[49] In the spring of 1644, Cosin, Crashaw, and all other Fellows, save one, were expelled from their positions.

By 1643, the historian of Christ's argues, the College had modified its position to a point that, while not "devotedly loyal," "neither was it distinctively Puritan."[50] Even so, Christ's suffered less from the invasion of Parliament than did several other colleges, notably Pembroke and Peterhouse. Although several Fellows were ejected, Bainbridge was allowed to remain as Master. Christ's was apparently not treated like Sidney and Emmanuel, the only two colleges that, according to Dowsing, presented nothing that "needed to be mended."[51] But it is significant that Christ's goes unmentioned in Dowsing's account, indicating that what did need "to be mended" was neither prevalent nor excessive.

The university experiences of Milton and Crashaw reinforced their very different religious and political positions, although Milton's poetic writings during a briefer stay at the university are typically less revealing of his views than are Crashaw's. Milton is most consistently the artist, experimenting and imitating and only occasionally establishing a perspective that we might identify as Puritan or radical. Crashaw responds more explicitly to his surroundings and places himself squarely on the side of believers in a fuller, lusher, and more ornate Christianity. Artistically, Milton and Crashaw are both still experimenting and exploring, a fact we readily acknowledge in Milton but one we have sometimes failed adequately to recognize in Crashaw. Although his accomplishments are, on the whole, surely less impressive than Milton's, Crashaw too gives evidence of one who is trying out various poetic modes, only one of which will flower more fully in the best of his Baroque verse.[52]

2

While the two poets were able to locate in colleges fitting the temperament of each, Italy provided no such variety. If Milton's Cambridge reinforced his religious and political views, his Italian journey would inevitably have challenged them. Crashaw, finding himself comfortable in the Laudian environment of Pembroke and Peterhouse, would surely have been even more at home, by 1646, in the comforting arms of Rome. Yet the results of the two visits contradict what might have been expected. For Milton, the Italian journey contributed significantly to his artistic development. Italy was the home of great art and, if Rome posed a religious challenge, the overall effect was nonetheless a heightening of Milton's artistic goals and a solidifying of his republican sentiments. By contrast, Crashaw, whose life and art may be viewed as measuring his progress toward Rome, found no welcome in Italy and no significant refuge for an Englishman in exile.

A. N. Wilson reflects on the political and religious dimensions of Milton's Italian experience, noting that Italy was to "hasten the direction in which his mind was moving" as it "accentuated radical and republican tendencies which had hitherto been merely latent." He concludes that it "sharpened and redefined his Protestantism."[53] In this vein, one also recalls the comments of Milton, notably in *Defensio Secunda*, that speak to the religious controversy in which he could easily have become embroiled.[54] Nonetheless, the most compelling evidence from the journey as a whole confirms that he was, as he remarks in *Defensio Secunda*, traveling abroad "at my ease for the cultivation of my mind," and Milton seems both during the time and after to have muted the controversy that could have thwarted his desire to immerse himself in the art and literature of Italy and its ancestry. His comments about cities, institutions, and individuals focus pervasively on the cultural and artistic dimension, not the religious or controversial one.[55]

Aside from his initial visit to Florence in the late summer and early fall of 1638, Milton's fall and early winter months in Rome in that year must have been among the most satisfying experiences of his journey. During that time he probably visited Lukas Holste (or Holstenius), later to be the Vatican librarian, who took him through the Vatican library; he attended a concert hosted by Cardinal Barberini, Secretary of State under Urban VIII; he met the Cardinal in a private audience; and, on 30 October, he was entertained in the English College along with three other English guests. In the heart of the Roman church, Milton responded, most evidence suggests, as one interested in art and culture, not in opposition and controversy.[56] In a letter to Holste dated 30 March 1639, Milton is effusive in his praise of the kindnesses shown to him: "Although I both can," he says, "and often do, remember many courteous and most friendly acts which I have experienced at the hands of many in this my passage through Italy, yet, for so brief an acquaintance, I do not know that I can justly say that from any one I have had greater proofs of goodwill than those which have come to me from you."[57] Much of this remarkable letter focuses on the very qualities that are at the heart of the entire Italian visit: the love of books and learning and the company of men who share that love. Milton's admission into the Vatican Museum still impresses him several months later, and he remarks on both the generous spirit and the editing skill of Holste in making the prized manuscripts of Greek authors available to others. Milton's praise of Barberini, who was known as the "Pro ctor of the English,"[58] emphasizes the Cardinal's culture and learning; for Milton and others he provided "public musical entertainment with truly Roman magnificence," and, when Milton recalls his private audience the next day, he seems still in awe of "so great a man (than whom, on the topmost summit of dignity, nothing more kind, nothing more courteous)."[59] Milton's closing tribute to the Cardinal in this letter is even more extraordinary, and it confirms precisely what it is that he so highly values in this leader of the Roman church. The Cardinal's "great virtues and anxiety to do right," he asserts, "are always present before my eyes. . . . Nor do I think that, while he is alive, men will have to miss any more the Este, the Farnesi, or the Medici, formerly the favourers of learned men."[60]

Milton's visit to the English College has been described intriguingly by Leo Miller. Each of the other three Englishmen named as guests on the evening of 30 October 1638 was a staunch Catholic, and it is therefore the more remarkable that Milton was included and that the four of them, we are told, "were magnificently received" ("excepti sunt laute").[61] Miller speculates that Milton's acceptance of the invitation would have suggested to his hosts that he "would be amenable to a call for conversion."[62] If so, Miller says, Milton may have been a "disconcerting guest." Instead of claiming a new convert, "his hosts may have found that they had exposed their seminarians to a taste of eloquent and informed heresy."[63]

If Milton was combative that evening—and the claim, though worthy, cannot be established[64]—then his conduct was not so typical of the Italian visit as a whole. Indeed, his ability to hold in abeyance his political and religious opinions is much more representative of Milton's Italian visit, for throughout that year and several months his purpose was to settle in and learn from the "home of humane studies and of all civilized teaching."[65] Wilson is therefore correct in suggesting that, given Milton's classicism and his growing allegiance to classical and Italian writers, the journey to Italy gave Milton a "heady sense of homecoming."[66]

The poetry that we can associate most directly with Milton's time in Italy praises the virtues of poetry generally and of Italian poets and poetry in particular. So it is in Milton's tribute to Giovanni Salzilli ("Ad Salsillum") and in his splendid praise of John Baptista Manso, friend of Tasso and Marino ("Mansus"). The latter, Milton says in a preface, showed him "supreme kindness" ("summa benevolentia") in Naples, and thus the English poet is placed in the company of such as

Tasso and Marino, similarly graced by the favors of this man "beloved of the gods" ("Diis dilecte"). In such company, Milton is clearly happy and content. "Epitaphium Damonis," Milton's moving memorial to Charles Diodati, also reiterates what we know was the principal goal and gain for Milton in Italy. He explains his reason for not writing his elegy immediately after Diodati's death in August 1638 by noting that he was seeking the "love of the sweet Muse" ("Dulcis amor Musae") in Florence.

Milton's stay in Italy helped to form his views and his poetry, and the greatest expression of the latter occurs some thirty years after the visit itself. Milton was thus able to take back with him the influences of both classical and Italian art and culture that would be evident, under his transforming hand, in *Samson Agonistes, Paradise Lost,* and *Paradise Regained.*[67] He went back to a full and often controversial life, and the education he received in Italy was thus both lasting and mingled with other experiences and influences during the more than three decades remaining for him. For Crashaw, Italy was also significant, but the circumstances were vastly different. Although his early poetry, such as "Musicks Duell" and "Sospetto d'Herode," reveals his acquaintance with Italian verse, the whole of his early life is very much rooted in England, and there is no evidence that, save for his expulsion, he would have found it necessary to leave the comfortable surroundings of Cambridge and Little Gidding. Furthermore, while we have sometimes been told that Crashaw's art has more connections to the Continent than to England, that understanding is in need of significant revision.[68] The influences on Crashaw are diverse, Continental as well as English, and if we sometimes fail to recognize the diversity, it is only because we choose to concentrate on a few well-known poems, not the whole of his poetic activity. Even with the few, we may neglect the English character of his art. One of the most Baroque of Crashaw's poems, "The Flaming Heart," a product of Crashaw's final years, also reveals in its language and rhythm that most English of texts, *The Book of Common Prayer.*[69] If his art continues to reveal multiple influences, it is nonetheless apparent that the eventual journey to Rome, even if in its origins forced on him, was a final and appropriate stage in Crashaw's *religious* development.

Crashaw, like Milton, might well have had a "heady sense of homecoming" (though for quite different reasons) on his arrival in Rome, but otherwise his experiences on the continent and in Italy were in pointed contrast to Milton's. Milton, in spite of his religious predisposition, had the leisure of a young man to explore intellectual and cultural opportunities throughout Italy, being entertained by dignitaries, conversing with learned scholars and poets, and being given access to some of the valued books and manuscripts of the seventeenth-century world. Although we can be sure that Crashaw communed with others during his years in Rome, including acquaintances from his years at Peterhouse, there is no evidence to suggest that his experiences were characterized by close acquaintances or intimate gatherings, and his poetry, which he continued to write and revise, is the product of one who stayed largely to himself.[70]

Crashaw's travels after his departure from Cambridge, which probably occurred in January 1643, cannot always be determined with certainty. He was in Leyden in February 1644 and may have returned to England and to Oxford some time after that. In 1645 he went to Paris where he gained the attention of the Queen, though not to an extent that enabled him to avoid a state approaching poverty. The Queen wrote Pope Innocent on 7 September 1646, urging that he receive Crashaw kindly as a recent convert, and this letter may have led to his departure for Rome, where he was in residence at the English College from shortly after his arrival on 28 November 1646, until early 1648. We know little about his activities in the English College, but he was apparently a paying guest and thus the poverty that threatened him in Paris may have been partially alleviated.[71] It also appears that the Pope was unresponsive to the Queen's September 1646 letter, for she wrote again in November 1647, characterizing Crashaw as "assaulted on the one hand by many grievous and dangerous infirmities, on the other hand with extream wants and necessities."[72] Crashaw served Cardinal Pallotta, a respected prelate of Rome, during most of 1648 and into 1649, and then received from the Cardinal a benefice at the Basilica of Loreto.[73] For Crashaw, Loreto, with its shrine to the Virgin, was a supremely fulfilling assignment and a culmination of his religious pilgrimage.[74] But this part of Crashaw's Italian experience, perhaps like other segments, was not to yield any lasting comfort for the exile. Only weeks after his arrival, Crashaw died from a fever on 21 August 1649.

In his Letter to the Countess of Denbigh (publ. 1652, 1653), Crashaw writes as an avowed convert to Catholicism, urging the apparently undecided Countess not to hesitate but to "render her selfe without further delay into the Communion of the Catholick Church." The boldness of Crashaw's appeal and the settled nature of his religious commitment from 1645 on confirm his dedication to the Roman cause. Yet, we can be certain that not all of Crashaw's experiences in Rome fulfilled his high expectations, and we are left wondering, given the absence of evidence, about what exactly he did, whom he saw, and what he learned. Would Crashaw, for example, have come into contact with some, either in the English College or elsewhere, who remembered the brilliant but also feisty and sometimes outspoken Milton? By then the celebrated visitor of 1638–39 was firmly entrenched in the republican cause, receiving the position of Secretary for Foreign Tongues on 20 March 1649, shortly before Crashaw left Rome for Loreto. One imagines that conversations might well have revealed rather exactly the ironies noted here, annoyance or disdain toward a public official who was nonetheless a recognized and admired poet. Some of that irony was surely not lost on Crashaw, by that time a little known and relatively private figure embracing a new country and church, and a dedicated but certainly less celebrated poet.

Cambridge. Italy. The Baroque. Each plays a role in shaping and defining the lives and artistry of John Milton and Richard Crashaw. But a consideration of these contexts for both poets together confirms how difficult it is to make certain associations or to establish convincing causal relations. History is the revelation of predictable outcomes as well as serendipitous or fateful coincidences and surprises. The lives of John Milton and Richard Crashaw confirm their steady progress toward two very different religious and political goals while also reminding us of the not altogether expected turns and contexts that influenced each figure's choices. The Baroque Milton and the Baroque Crashaw are, moreover, surely two very different manifestations of a seventeenth-century aesthetic. Milton and Crashaw serve finally to remind us of the complex interaction of life experiences and artistic sensibilities in these (and other) poets, interactions that are sometimes conflicting, sometimes reinforcing. In Milton and Crashaw, history and art are finally interwoven in a fashion that sets them firmly within their times while allowing their particular geniuses to emerge in decisive and compelling ways.

Notes

1. Portions of this essay were presented in earlier forms as papers at the Second and Third International Milton Symposia.

2. Austin Warren, "Crashaw's Residence at Peterhouse," *TLS,* 3 November 1932, 815. For material relating to Crashaw's life, I have drawn primarily from my book *Richard Crashaw* (Twayne's English Authors Series, No. 299 [Boston: G. K. Hall, 1980]), noting particular sources where appropriate.

It is worth noting that Milton was also a "poet of exile," as Louis Martz describes him (*Poet of Exile: A Study of Milton's Poetry* [New Haven: Yale University Press, 1980]), and experienced his own form of isolation and exile after the Restoration.

For comments on Milton's life, I have relied primarily on his *Defensio Secunda* and, though less so, on modern biographies, notably William Riley Parker, *Milton, A Biography* (Oxford: Clarendon Press, 1968).

3. *Innovations in Religion & Abuses in Government in University of Cambridge.* British Museum MS. Harley 7019, fol. 73.

4. Austin Warren, *Richard Crashaw: A Study in Baroque Sensibility* (University, LA: Louisiana State University Press, 1939); Marc Bertonasco, *Crashaw and the Baroque* (University: University of Alabama Press, 1971).

5. *English Literature in the Earlier Seventeenth Century, 1600–1660.* Oxford History of English Literature, 5. 2d ed. (Oxford: The Clarendon Press, 1962), 147.

6. Roy Daniells, *Milton, Mannerism and Baroque* (Toronto: University of Toronto Press, 1963); Murray Roston, *Milton and the Baroque* (Pittsburgh: University of Pittsburgh Press, 1980).

7. *Four Stages of Renaissance Style: Transformations in Art and Literature, 1400–1700* (Garden City, N.Y.: Doubleday, 1955), 189, 193, 194, 195.

8. Mario Praz, *The Flaming Heart: Essays on Crashaw, Machiavelli, and Other Studies in the Relations between Italian and English Literature from Chaucer to T. S. Eliot* (1958; rpt. Gloucester, Mass.: Peter Smith, 1966); Daniells, *Milton, Mannerism and Baroque*; and Roston, *Milton and the Baroque*, 30, 82.

9. *European Metaphysical Poetry* (New Haven: Yale University Press, 1961), 3; *Versions of Baroque* (New Haven: Yale University Press, 1972), 14.

10. (Pittsburgh: Duquesne University Press, 1990), 162.

11. Bryan Little, *The Colleges of Cambridge* (New York: Arco Publishing Co., 1973), 86. It is well to observe at the outset that Puritanism as viewed in the context of the university was usually not aligned with the Separatists or even, necessarily, those who advocated a presbyterian form of church government. Mark Curtis comments that "Puritanism within the universities was pre-eminently a church-centred movement. . . . Though [university Puritans] wanted the Church reformed to bring it closer to the example of primitive Christianity or to the model of the best reformed Churches on the continent, they believed in one Church and not in several Churches" (*Oxford and Cambridge in Transition, 1558–1642: An Essay on Changing Relations Between the English Universities and English Society* [Oxford: Clarendon Press, 1959], 189). As a particular instance he cites the case of Samuel Ward, master of Sidney College and a man of undoubted Puritan sympathies, who, nonetheless, went so far as to side with the king rather than Parliament because of his belief in "an established national Church" (189).

12. Curtis has rightly cautioned against the simplistic view that the two universities represented the extreme sides of the developing conflict, that "Oxford was conservative and tainted with Romanism and that Cambridge was a hotbed of radicalism" (*Oxford and Cambridge in Transition, 1558–1642,* 191). Nonetheless, as he goes on to observe, "there can be no doubt that Cambridge . . . produced more active Puritan clergymen than Oxford" (193).

In his history of the two great universities, Albert Mansbridge describes the improved conditions of university life under Elizabeth, in contrast to the volatile changes, persecutions, and martyrdoms under her predecessors. In that regard, he says, it is a "matter for wonder that both Oxford and Cambridge recovered with such rapidity in the Elizabethan age. It may have been that scholarship played but a small part in comparison with the whole range of University life. Colleges were pleasant places; there were emoluments; the sons of the gentry had to go somewhere to sense the great world . . ." (*The Older Universities of England: Oxford and Cambridge* [Boston: Houghton Mifflin, 1923], 53). But Mansbridge also comments on the continuing control and involvement of the State during the Elizabethan period and after: "over both Universities lay the menacing or, according to the time, encouraging shadow of the State, destined to materialise in energetic and ruthless action not merely once, nor twice, in an eventful century, through the middle years of which 'Cavalier' and 'Roundhead' rode or stalked, personifying the main streams of social, religious, and political aspiration in English life" (57–58).

13. Mansbridge, xix.

14. Ibid., 53.

15. Ibid., 58.

16. Two examples among many are representative. In 1629, Nathaniel Bernard, a lecturer at St. Sepulchre's Church in London, had aroused Royal opposition when he delivered a sermon in which he prayed that the queen might be led "to see Christ, whom she hath pierced with her infidelity, superstition and idolatry." The king's anger must have increased as, "three years later, when on a visit to some friends in [Cambridge], Bernard was invited to preach the afternoon sermon at St. Mary's. Untaught or undeterred by his previous experience, he now 'let fall' (to use [the Puritan William] Prynne's expression) 'divers passages against the introducers of popery and Arminianism inveighing in unmeasured terms against those who were 'bringing in their Pelagian errours into the doctrine of our Church established by law, and the superstitions of the Church of Rome into our worship of God, as high altars, crucifixes, and bowing to them'" (James Bass Mullinger, *The University of Cambridge* [Cambridge: Cambridge University Press, 1911], 3:112).

17. William Riley Parker, *Milton, A Biography* (Oxford: Clarendon Press, 1968), 1: 35–36.

18. Mullinger, *The University of Cambridge*, 3: 59.

19. Mansbridge, 58.

20. H. C. Porter, *Reformation and Reaction in Tudor Cambridge* (Cambridge: Cambridge University Press, 1958), 416.

21. Mullinger, *The University of Cambridge*, 3: 58–59.

22. Everett H. Emerson, *English Puritanism from John Hooper to John Milton* (Durham, N.C.: Duke University Press, 1968), 16.

23. James Bass Mullinger, *A History of the University of Cambridge* (London: Longmans, Green, and Co., 1888), 142.

24. *DNB*, "Edmund Grindal."

25. See n. 11; Emerson, 16.

26. *DNB*, "William Fulke."

27. Aubrey Attwater, *Pembroke College, Cambridge: A Short History* (Cambridge: Cambridge University Press, 1936), 54.

28. In spite of its dominant Royalist position, Pembroke was not without its internal conflicts. In 1619, the question of a successor to Nicholas Felton resulted in a conflict between, on the one side, Wren and other supporters of the eventual winner, Jerome Beale, the king's sub-almoner, and, on the other, Puritan sympathizers such as Ralph Brownrigg (Attwater, 67). The king himself stepped in and wrote a letter urging the election of someone "bred in your own House"; in light of the developing controversy his letter is not without its ironic moment, for he pleads for the College to "be careful to make choice of such a man as shall be neither a Puritane nor Arminian" (Attwater, 67). There is little doubt that Beale was perceived as Arminian to those of the Puritan faction, and on at least one occasion they openly challenged his right to be Master (Attwater, 69–70).

29. Attwater, 68.

30. Charles Henry Cooper, *Annals of Cambridge* (Cambridge: Warwick and Co., 1845), 3: 263–64.

31. Little, 33.

32. Thomas A. Walker, *Peterhouse* (Cambridge: W. Heffer & Sons, 1935), 54.

33. Mullinger, *The University of Cambridge*, 3:122.

34. Quoted in Walker, 55–56.

35. *Christ's College* (London: F. E. Robinson & Co., 1900), 69.

36. *Milton the Puritan: Portrait of a Mind* (London: Macmillan, 1977), 19.

37. Christopher Hill, *Milton and the English Revolution* (New York: Viking, 1978), 32.

38. Maurice Kelley, *This Great Argument: A Study of Milton's 'De Doctrina Christiana' as a Gloss Upon 'Paradise Lost'* (1941; rpt. Gloucester, Mass.: Peter Smith, 1962), 25–26.

39. Little, 86.

40. Mead opposed many of the practices advocated by Presbyterians but was Puritan-like in his view of the pope as the antichrist. Chappell's exact position is even more elusive and serves as a warning against oversimplifying the complex dimensions of the political and religious controversy. The *DNB* article ("William Chappell") notes that "a few theologians at Cambridge . . . accused him of Arminianism, a charge which was also brought against him in later life, while by most of his contemporaries he was deemed a puritan."

41. Peile, 133.

42. Hill, 33.

43. Parker, 25.

44. Cooper, 364.

45. Cited in Attwater, 73.

46. Ibid., 74.

47. Ibid.

48. Little, 33.

49. Cooper, 364.

50. Peile, 160.

51. Cited in Mullinger, *The University of Cambridge*, 3: 272.

52. See my discussion of Crashaw's various styles in *Richard Crashaw*, 34–46.

53. *The Life of John Milton* (Oxford: Oxford University Press, 1983), 76.

54. He remarks, for example, that, though his meeting with John Baptista Manso at Naples was a friendly one, Manso could not give him greater attention because Milton "was unwilling to be circumspect in regard to religion" (*Def* 2, *CPW*, 4:i, 618). That he may have been too outspoken in Rome as well is suggested by his recollection, also in *Defensio Secunda*, that, "As I was on the point of returning to Rome, I was warned by merchants that they had learned through letters of plots laid against me by the English Jesuits, should I return to Rome, because of the freedom with which I had spoken about religion. For I had determined within myself that in those parts I would not indeed begin a conversation about religion, but if questioned about my faith would hide nothing, whatever the consequences. And so, I nonetheless returned to Rome. What I was, if any man inquired, I concealed from no one. For almost two more months, in the very stronghold of the Pope, if anyone attacked the orthodox religion, I openly, as before defended it" (*Def* 2, 619). Of Milton's sensitivity to political events we also have his testimony, for as he learned in early 1639 of the growing civil crisis at home in England, those "sad tidings," he says, "summoned me back. For I thought it base that I should travel abroad at my ease for the cultivation of my mind, while my fellow-citizens at home were fighting for liberty" (*Def* 2, 619).

55. In a Latin poem to the Roman poet Giovanni Salzilli, Milton describes his journey "to the genial soil of Italy to see its cities, which their proud fame has made familiar, and its men and its talented and cultured youths." Florence he calls "that

city, which I have always admired above all others because of the elegance, not just of its tongue, but also of its wit" (*Def* 2, *CPW,* 4:i, 615), and he praises the private academy as a "Florentine institution which deserves great praise not only for promoting humane studies but also for encouraging friendly intercourse" (*Def* 2, 615–16). And while Milton knew Rome to be the home of what he regarded as the false teaching of the papacy, he remarks that the "antiquity and venerable repute" of that city kept him in its grasp for almost two months (*Def* 2, 618).

56. There is some contrary evidence, of course. Holste remarks in a letter to Nicolas Heinsius in 1653 that some Italians disliked Milton "because of his 'over strict morals'" and because he "disputed freely about religion" (William B. Hunter, Jr., gen. ed., *A Milton Encyclopedia* [Cranbury, N.J.: Associated University Presses, 1978], 4, "Holste").

57. J. Milton French, ed. *The Life Records of John Milton* (New Brunswick, N.J.: Rutgers University Press, 1949), 1: 387.

58. A. Lytton Sells, *The Paradise of Travellers* (Bloomington: Indiana University Press, 1964), 77.

59. French, 1: 412.

60. Ibid., 1: 413. Shortly after Milton's visit, in 1639, Barberini approved a plan, endorsed also by Queen Henrietta Maria, to petition English Catholics for financial support for the king, which resulted in immediate commitments of £10,000 (Sells, 79). Barberini's generosity to the English, including English Protestants, did not serve him well under Innocent X. Indeed, by the time of Crashaw's visit to Rome, Barberini had himself been forced to seek exile in Paris, much as Crashaw, for very different reasons, had been forced to the Continent and Paris from England.

61. French, 1: 393.

62. Leo Miller, "Milton Dines at the Jesuit College: Reconstructing the Evening of October 30, 1638," *MQ* 13.4 (1979):143.

63. Ibid., 144.

64. Milton says that, after his first visit to Rome, English Jesuits began to plot against him for being outspoken about religion (*Def* 2, *CPW,* 4:i, 619), but there is no suggestion that their opposition necessarily had its impetus from the 30 October dinner. Since Milton also indicates that he did not force religion into conversations and since we may believe that the satisfying meetings with Holste and the Cardinal led to the invitation from the College, it is not unreasonable to suggest that Milton was on this occasion more the humanist than the controversialist, enjoying the company of other learned men.

65. French, 1: 366.

66. Wilson, 73.

67. See for general comment the discussion and references in "Italian Influences on Milton" in *A Milton Encyclopedia.* Of particular value in determining both the cultural and poetic influence on Milton are John Arthos, *Milton and the Italian Cities* (London: John Murray, 1962), and F. T. Prince, *The Italian Element in Milton's Verse* (Oxford: Clarendon Press, 1954).

68. For comments on the relationship between Crashaw and Continental art, see, for example, the studies of Warren, Bush, and Warnke cited above. See also Louis L. Martz, "The Action of the Self: Devotional Poetry in the Seventeenth Century," in Malcolm Bradbury and David Palmer, eds. *Metaphysical Poetry* (Bloomington: Indiana University Press, 1971), esp. 117. I explore the multiple influences on Crashaw's art in *Richard Crashaw,* for example, 165–68. A recent volume of essays on Crashaw edited by John R. Roberts contains several pieces that encourage a rethinking of traditional views of Crashaw's proper artistic alliances. See *New Per-*

spectives on the Life and Art of Richard Crashaw (Columbia: University Press of Missouri, 1990).

69. See Warren, *Richard Crashaw: A Study in Baroque Sensibility*, 142; and Parrish, *Richard Crashaw*, 167–68.

70. See Kenneth J. Larsen, "Some Light on Richard Crashaw's Final Years in Rome," *MLR* 66 (1971): 493.

71. Ibid., 493.

72. George Walton Williams, ed., *The Complete Poetry of Richard Crashaw* (1970; rpt. New York: Norton, 1974), xix.

73. Larsen, 494–95.

74. Fynes Moryson's description of Loreto, based on his travels in 1594 and first published as part of his *Itinerary* in 1617, confirms the high regard a Roman, or a convert to the Roman church such as Crashaw, would have had for Loreto, although Moryson himself is quite unsympathetic to the Roman position. He describes a "certaine chamber," the shrine of the Virgin, "then which nothing is esteemed more holy among the Papists." Recounting the story of the shrine (where Mary purportedly "was borne, brought up, and saluted by the Angell, foretelling her of Christs birth, and in which Christ was conceived, and in which the Virgin dwelt after Christs ascension, accompanied with the holy Apostles"), Moryson cannot resist two side notes warning the unsuspecting reader: "Let the Reader beleeve as he list. Woe to him that beleeves. Woe to him that beleeves," and the shrine "is not more helpfull to others, then profitable to the Pope and Church men" (*An Itinerary* . . . [Glasgow: James MacLehose and Sons, 1907], 1: 213, 214, 216).

The Genius of the Wood and the
Prelate of the Grove: Milton and Marvell

DIANA TREVIÑO BENET

At different times in his life, John Milton expressed a desire for the gift of divine inspiration or prophetic powers. Eventually, he came to glory even "in his 'infirmities' as a symbol of divine inspiration" and to associate himself with St. Paul (who may have been blind).[1] Such an author positions himself as the first interpretive matter his readers must address. Even today, readers who value his accomplishments may find his stated ambitions and his eventual claims of collaboration with a heavenly muse bizarre or overweening. But in an age when politics and religion were intertwined and when opposing sides fought many of their battles through the printed word, Milton's sense of himself was a truly substantial issue. In such a context, a man's desire or claim to be a prophet, to speak in a voice with divine authority, was of tremendous significance. To some of his antagonists, Milton's claim of special enlightenment seemed variously deluded, arrogant, or outrageous. It was partly such criticism of Milton and *Paradise Lost* that led to the composition of "On Mr. Milton's *Paradise Lost*," a poem in which Andrew Marvell evaluated, though not for the first time, Milton's poetic self-presentation and his published characterization of his work.

In their own day, politics connected Milton and Marvell in actuality and in the public mind. This connection may be conveniently sketched in the circumstances leading to the composition of "On . . . *Paradise Lost*." The date of the poets' first meeting is unknown. Christopher Hill repeats a story that Marvell helped Milton in the composition of *Eikonoklastes*, which would mean that they knew each other fairly well by the summer of 1649, but the story is unsubstantiated.[2] Milton's letter recommending Marvell for state service in 1653 is the first tangible connection between them, although Marvell did not secure employment in the government until late 1657. Marvell published *The Rehearsal Transpros'd* in 1672, as a reply to Samuel Parker's *A Preface shewing what grounds there are of Fears and Jealousies of Popery*, which argued against religious toleration. Subsequently, one response to Marvell's *Rehearsal* was *The Transproser Rehears'd* (1673), whose author Marvell believed to be Parker, but who was actually Richard Leigh. Leigh attacked *Paradise Lost* as well as Marvell's satirical poetry, and declared that Marvell's *Rehearsal* included miniature versions of *Eikonoklastes* and *A Defence of the English People*: "There are many *Miltons* in this one Man."[3] Marvell defended his friend Milton in the second part of *The Rehearsal Transpros'd* (1673) and in "On . . . *Paradise Lost*" (1674). The men's posthumous fortunes were also linked. Both "were published and republished under party auspices within a decade of their deaths; they would be perceived . . . as totemic figures for a Whig literary canon."[4]

The political connection between Milton and Marvell still arouses scholarly interest, and their more strictly literary relation has also received critical attention. Carol Gilbertson has argued that Marvell's "Mower" poems are deeply influenced by *Paradise Lost*, and Judith Herz, after showing echoes of Milton's verse in Marvell's, has suggested that there may be deliberate echoes of Marvell in *Paradise Lost* and *Paradise Regained*.[5] This essay aims to command a fresh perspective on Milton and Marvell that includes poetry and politics by expanding the territory previously mapped by William Kerrigan and Joseph A. Wittreich. Milton's invocations in *Paradise Lost* and Marvell's "On . . . *Paradise Lost*," with the addition of "Il Penseroso" and "Upon Appleton House," enable us to survey Marvell's reflections on Milton's poetic identity. This approach helps us to understand more clearly how Milton's prophetic stance was interpreted in its own particular milieu.

"Upon Appleton House" and "On Mr. Milton's *Paradise Lost*" present the reactions of a sympathetic and insightful poet to Milton's public aspirations to, and claims of, prophecy. A portion of "Upon Appleton House" is given to a dramatic assessment of the visionary poet described in "Il Penseroso." *Il penseroso indolente*, the self Marvell creates as a reflection of Milton's ideal, figures in an essentially private assessment (the poem was first published in the posthumous Folio). But some twenty years after "Appleton House," probably in the summer of 1674, Marvell wrote again about Milton and his poetry. "On Mr. Milton's *Paradise Lost*" was a public statement and a drastic revision of Marvell's earlier, somewhat skeptical, opinion. In both poems, Marvell appropriates Milton's own language and imagery. In the first, he does so to imitate Milton and, thereby, to examine the ideals the elder poet seems to propose for all poets and poetry. In the later poem, however, Marvell appropriates bits of *Paradise Lost* to declare that its author is invested with a singular status, power, and authority. In the end, when one of Milton's most careful readers and extraordinary contemporaries endorses his characterization of himself as a prophet, he endorses one of Milton's most enduring political statements.

*   *   *

"Upon Appleton House" was probably written in the early 1650s; our ignorance of its date means we cannot even estimate accurately the length of Milton's acquaintance with Marvell. But Herz shows that the poem reflects Marvell's continuous adaptation of his reading of Milton's 1645 *Poems*. Like "L'Allegro" and "Il Penseroso," she points out, Marvell's poem "is a record of an ideal day's journey through a habitual landscape transformed into a landscape of the mind." As far as she goes, Herz is correct, but the relationship between the two poems is more complex. Marvell is especially enthralled by "Il Penseroso" because it treats the sources of poetry and the nature of the poet. In part, "Upon Appleton House" is a reading of, and a response to, Milton's treatment of poetry and prophecy in "Il Penseroso."[6]

Milton approaches the matter of prophecy by indirection in "Il Penseroso," and with some uncharacteristic modesty. Before its well-known ending, the poem refers several times to prophecy, vision, or the generally inaccessible knowledge that is their essence. The first reference consists of a cluster of allusions. Milton begins with the fantastic idea of "unsphering" the "spirit of *Plato*" (88–89), through arduous study, in order to learn where immortal minds reside after leaving their bodies, and to learn about the Daemons above and below the earth.[7] The poet's desire to hear what no mortal has heard before is expressed again in his wish that Melancholy might raise Musaeus, Orpheus, or Chaucer (103–15). Chaucer's place in this context particularly indicates the prophetic aspects of Milton's longings. He wishes the Muse might

> call him up that left half told
> The story of *Cambuscan* bold,
> Of *Camball*, and of *Algarsife,*
> And who had *Canace* to wife,
> That own'd the virtuous Ring and Glass.
> And of the wondrous Horse of Brass,
> On which the *Tartar* King did ride.
>
> (109–15)

Milton's allusion to "The Squire's Tale," "left half told," suggests that the contemplative man counts invention or the exercise of his imagination among his pleasures. In the romance Chaucer assigns to the Squire, all the materials are in place for a fantastic story.[8] Camball, Algarsife, and Canace are the sons and daughter of Cambuscan, a Tartar king. A stranger gives Cambuscan a sword with the power to heal where it has wounded and a flying brass horse; Canace receives a mirror that reveals truth and foretells events and a ring. The ring enables her to understand and speak the language of birds and to know the properties and powers of "every gras that groweth upon roote" ("Squire's Tale" 152). The young woman is given the various powers of a prophet and a seer in the realm of nature.

Milton emphasizes the importance of study and the imagination to himself as a poet, but he also looks toward a mysterious knowledge, the acquisition of which would be extraordinary. In his wish to have commerce with the dead, summoning Plato and Chaucer to learn from them, already the outline is discernible of a figure whose access to a different sphere yields visionary insights.[9] That different sphere is charmingly domesticated in the second reference to extraordinary powers: Milton imagines "dewy-feather'd Sleep" (146) presenting him with an effortless and perfect dream-vision. This is inspiration in its most ordinary guise, surely, but its homeliness does not diminish its mystery. The same quasi-magical power is attributed to church music that might dissolve the poet "into ecstasies, / And bring all Heav'n before [his] eyes" (165–66). These instances of an easy revelation in passivity contrast with the study and the exercise of the imagination that seem desirable to the youthful poet. Perhaps Milton hoped such gifts would be the rewards reaped naturally by the mind prepared.

Finally, as the poet looks to the future, these veiled longings for the visionary culminate in his open desire for the old hermit's recondite wisdom: someday, he hopes to "rightly spell / Of every Star that Heav'n doth shew, / And every Herb that sips the dew" (170–72). The ascent to this knowledge, which would give his utterance "something like Prophetic strain" (174), is approached in Milton's poem by the intermediate steps of study, the exercise of the imagination, the motions of the unconscious, and the flight of the emotions fired by music. Like Chaucer's Canace, the poet would be able to read the herbs, but unlike her prophecy through magic props, his power would be attained gradually, through "old experience" (173); it would be, he claims modestly, an approximation of prophecy. Milton's gradual approach to his grand hope in the poem, culminating in "something like Prophetic strain," counteracts what might otherwise be an unattractive grandiosity. Besides, the would-be prophet is practical in his willingness to bestir himself, ready to study and invent in what he hopes is preparation for an amazing but retired and modest future. If there is something funny about the youth who envisions himself as a sage hermit, there is something appealing, too, about an aspirant who hopes visions will spring from sources no more remote than sleep and music.

Milton's ideals and aspirations unfold in a landscape featuring "arched walks of twilight groves" (133). Writing about stanzas 63–64 of Marvell's "Upon Appleton House," Robert Wilcher associates the scene there depicted with Milton's "cathedral of the woods."[10] For the ethereal music sent "to mortals good, / Or th'unseen Genius of the Wood" in Milton's poem (153–54), Marvell's woodsy cathedral is filled with the sound of "winged Quires" (511), the nightingale (513), and the stock-doves (523). "[A]rching Boughs unite between / The Columnes of the Temple green" to produce an agreeable dimness similar to the shadowy twilight favored by "Il Penseroso."

Milton's dreams of prophecy and his implication that, ideally, the poet should be the assiduous seeker of vision and oracular knowledge impressed Marvell. They intrigued him to the extent that he produces, in stanzas 63 to 75 of "Appleton House," his own jocoserious version of the elder poet's ideal self to test and (ultimately) to criticize it. Marvell tests Milton's ideal self by bringing him to life. Il penseroso hopes to "rightly spell / Of every Star . . . And every Herb that sips the dew," and so Marvell casts himself as a philosopher who zips through nature's mystick book from cover to cover. His literalization exposes what might be inane or problematic about the prophetic aspirations outlined in the earlier poem. Whereas Milton hopes eventually to learn to spell nature and then to achieve something akin to prophecy, the "carless" Marvell (529) demonstrates that he is already an adept as he saunters along and reads the lesson of the hewel (stanzas 68–70). Without any effortful preparation, he is unlike the ancient hermit of Milton's imaginary future. He has more in common with Canace, who is simply gifted with prophetic powers. Marvell alludes to Milton's allusion to Canace when the "*easie Philosopher*" communicates with the birds, beginning "to call / In their most learned Original" (569–70). Like Canace and the wise hermit, also, the poet can read the leaves of plants:

> Out of these scatter'd *Sibyls* Leaves
> Strange Prophecies my Phancy weaves:
> And in one History consumes,

> Like *Mexique Paintings*, all the *Plumes*.
> What *Rome*, *Greece*, *Palestine*, ere said
> I in this light *Mosaick* read.
> Thrice happy he who, not mistook,
> Hath read in *Natures mystick Book*.
>
> (577–84)

As many readers have remarked, it is impossible to take seriously an all-encompassing prophecy derived from leaves woven by "Phancy" and interpreted by someone twittering birdcalls. Marvell finishes his comic self-portrait as seer by costuming himself rather elaborately. Embroidered by oak leaves, festooned with ivy, he stands resplendent under an "antick Cope" (stanza 74).

Marvell's "*Prelate of the Grove*" (592) owes something to Milton's "Genius of the Wood," but his getup, at once attractive and pompous, magnificent and silly, apprises us of his mixed response to Milton in the guise of "Il Penseroso." The lesson of the hewel seems to validate the lore in "*Natures mystick Book*" as well as the capacity to read it. But the philosopher who characterizes himself as "easy" and "carless" denies the importance of his insights and casts doubt on the value of the enterprise as whole. Such divination, he suggests, might be any dawdler's accomplishment. Wisdom and vision that descend upon the passive mind—such things seem altogether too "easy" in Marvell's view. With a characteristically light touch, Marvell indicates the problems attendant upon Milton's ambition. A man whose philosophy comes from nature, from stars, herbs, or birds may descend beneath his proper sphere, moving closer to "the *Fowles*, or . . . the *Plants*" (stanza 71); moreover, although such a philosopher may speak to the birds (stanza 72) and believe the trees speak to him in leaves, his prophecies may be the strange products of his own fancy (stanza 73). Indeed, since the easy philosopher speaks to the birds, Marvell implies that what moves between him and the bird on the bough is *his* meaning. This prophet may claim all the wisdom of "*Rome*, *Greece*, *Palestine*" since there is nothing to inform him that he is "not mistook."

Marvell's appearance in the green cope suggests that the priest who thinks to interpret Nature's book is an attractive figure, but that he is also slightly pompous, probably misguided, and more than a little ridiculous. The younger poet grants the sincerity of Milton's prophetic ideal but lacks faith in the truth of the singular vision. Clearly (and reasonably enough), he doubts that a man's own sense of inspiration is a reliable indication of the value or truth of his revelation. Though Marvell finally contests Milton's vatic inclinations, sympathy for his fellow author is evident in the gentleness of his affectionate parody. *Il penseroso indolente* may be foolish in his leafy costume but he is also attractive and Marvell presents him as a self-portrait, however ironic. There is no doubt, either, in "Upon Appleton House" as a whole or in this section of the poem in particular, that Marvell gives the act of reading Nature's book its due. But finally, for the reasons he indicates, he cannot accept the unfailing validity or, indeed, the relative importance of such prophecy; therefore, he questions the propriety of such prophetic ambitions for the poet.

Marvell tries on Milton's ideal guise partly because it focuses so much on activities facilitating poetic creativity: the stimulation of the intellect, imagination, and emotions, and the receptivity to vision. Everything in "Il Penseroso" moves toward the attainment of vision and its expression in "something like Prophetic strain." Any poet would have been interested, surely, in Milton's version of a poet's preparation, inspiration, and anticipated song. But Marvell tries on the green cope also because Milton's ideal unfolds in the kind of retirement that always attracted the author of "The Garden." Il penseroso and the *Prelate of the Grove* both exist "Where no profaner eye may look" (140), hidden behind the trees "where the World no certain Shot / Can make" (stanza 76). To some extent, then, Marvell's critique of "Il Penseroso" amidst the broader concerns of "Appleton House" is a regretful assessment: in the early 1650s, a poetic stance entailing self-cultivation and withdrawal to read prophecy from Nature's book seems quaint and irrelevant. Milton and Marvell live in a world of military rather than flowery regiments, of political rather than contemplative retreats.

*　　*　　*

To say [God] hath spoken to [one] in a dream, is no more than to say he dreamed that God spake to him; which is not of force to win belief from any man, that knows dreams are for the most part natural, and may proceed from former thoughts; and such dreams as that, for self-deceit, and foolish arrogance, and false opinion of a man's own godliness, or other virtue, by which he thinks he hath merited the favour of extraordinary revelation. To say he speaks by supernatural inspiration, is to say he finds an ardent desire to speak, or some strong opinion of himself, for which he can find no natural and sufficient reason. So that though God Almighty can speak to a man by dreams, visions, voice, and inspiration; yet he obliges no man to believe he hath so done to him that pretends it; who, being a man, may err, and, which is more, may lie.

—Hobbes, *Leviathan*[11]

When Marvell commented again on Milton's poetry some twenty years later, retreat and prophecy had shifted into a new configuration. By 1674, when "On Mr. Milton's *Paradise Lost*" was published with the second edition of Milton's poem, many changes had taken place. Most important, the Commonwealth had long since failed, and its architects and adherents had been cast down or destroyed by the Restoration hierarchy. Marvell had weathered the transition by sitting in Parliament from 1659, his tenure including the Convention Parliament, which recalled Charles II in 1660. For Milton it was otherwise. The former Latin Secretary of the Commonwealth, whose friendship with Marvell had now spanned over twenty years, was shunned and despised by many. Not surprisingly, then, one thrust of "On . . . *Paradise Lost*" had to be political: "the poem's first aim is public: it defends the career of a man condemned for his politics and religion, accused of sacrilege in his writings, and even mocked for his blindness, which his enemies insisted was a punishment from God for his service to the regicides."[12] Samuel Parker focused particularly on Milton's blindness in *A Reproof to "The Rehearsal Transpros'd"* and Richard Leigh attacked Milton and Marvell in *The Transproser Rehears'd*. As Wittreich informs us, Leigh preferred Milton's unrhymed Christian and epic poem to "the minor, incidental, trivial literature" of the sort he thought Marvell produced. But he inveighed against *Paradise Lost* with the charges that its use of internal rhyme violates its own principles and, most important, that the poem "supposedly full of light, is riddled with dark meanings."[13] Leigh's criticism of *Paradise Lost* as confused and confusing struck at the very core of Milton's claim, in that poem, to prophetic stature.

From our more or less secular perspective, it is difficult to understand the impact of Milton's self-definition on his contemporaries. Generally, we interpret it as a statement of his conviction, translated into religious terminology, that he is inspired, as any author might be inspired who cannot identify the source of his creative impulses. But such an interpretation ignores Milton's verbal and theological precision as well as the distinctly political tinge of the prophetic voice in his day. To a great extent, in the years leading up to the Civil War and finally to the Restoration, "the tone, manner, and authority of the Old Testament prophets" had been appropriated by the Puritans. Thomas Hobbes refuted the English Revolution in *Leviathan* (1651) by anatomizing prophecy, so clearly did it indicate a religio-political stance during this era.[14] It is not difficult to understand, then, why Milton's seventeenth-century audience would have considered his claim to prophecy paramount or why some people might have found it disturbing.

The theological significance of prophecy in *Paradise Lost* has been explored fully in the work of Kerrigan and Wittreich; "On . . . *Paradise Lost*" enables us to perceive Milton's self-presentation as an exercise in what we might call personal politics—for whatever else it may be, his prophetic role is also a political stance. Reflecting this combination of factors, Marvell's poem had a personal dimension, too. Primarily, *Paradise Lost* with its vast sacred subject must have impressed him. But the private subtext that included "Il Penseroso" and *il penseroso indolente* as well as their long comradeship particularly fitted him to respond to the personal assertion of power at the core of Milton's poem. This is no longer a poet's fantasy about spelling herbs or achieving something akin to prophecy—as Milton points out, it is impossible anyhow for him to read Nature's book (3.47–50). In *Paradise Lost*, the poet claims to be a prophet within the staggering work that must substantiate his claim. Marvell's political past, no less than his history with Milton and his work, enabled him to appreciate fully that Milton's self-portrayal, in this context and at this juncture of his life, addresses issues of status, power, and authority.

Milton's prophetic identity is constructed in the invocations of *Paradise Lost*. Together, these are generally consistent: "Sometimes the passive poet receives dictation in his sleep; other times the Muse 'inspires' the poet in the act of composition. In either case, the narrator is an agent through which a greater poet realizes himself. . . . Milton is both author and amanuensis."[15] As Kerrigan's formulation here indicates, there is throughout the invocations a consistent confusion of the work of the Muse and the poet. This blending (together with Milton's association of himself with the heroic) ultimately elevates the poet to a virtually unassailable plane. By thus locating himself vis-à-vis his audience, Milton refutes the powerlessness imposed on him by his circumstances, and Marvell affirms this authorial positioning in "Upon . . . *Paradise Lost*." Since he appropriates the language and imagery of Milton's invocations and of the reflections introducing book 9, a brief review is in order.

Bird imagery links the four sections of prefatory material in *Paradise Lost*. In book 1, the Muse is invited to sing and petitioned to instruct. The poet invokes her because his work is perilous and his intention grand; his "advent'rous Song /. . . with no middle flight intends to soar / Above th'*Aonian* Mount" (13–15). Through the "Heav'nly Muse" and Mount Sion (10–12), Milton associates himself with Moses and Achithophel, "the Oracle of God" (2 Samuel 16:23). Mount Sion was "the mounte of prophesye and reuelation" (3.30n). From the start, Milton blurs the distinction between the Muse's agency and his own: the song requested of the Muse (6) becomes the aid requested from her for *his* "advent'rous Song" (13); the knowledge of the omnipresent Spirit (17–19) becomes the mind of the poet illumined to "the highth of this great Argument" (24).

By the beginning of book 3, the Muse has favored the poet, teaching him "to venture down / The dark descent, and up to reascend" (19–20). The poet himself wanders "where the Muses haunt" (27), and nightly visits Sion (32). Though these references to wandering among the Muses and visiting Sion are figurative, the language transforms passivity into activity, ascribing to the poet the volition presupposed in agency. Again, his action and the Muse's are intertwined: the poet who wanders and visits is also a passive medium.

> Then feed on thoughts, that voluntary move
> Harmonious numbers; as the wakeful Bird
> Sings darkling, and in shadiest Covert hid
> Tunes her nocturnal Note.
>
> (37–40)

His nightly visits yield thoughts on which the poet feeds and from which spontaneous verse then flows. It is impossible to say whether the poet speaks or the Muse speaks through him. What matters is the radical effortlessness of the "numbers" arising from his dream-journeys. The poet has become a prophet, and Milton's imagery insists on his metamorphosis. *Paradise Lost* is the "voluntary" song of a "Bird [that] / Sings darkling." The poet revisits Light "with bolder wing" and has already completed a "flight / Through utter and through middle darkness" (13–16). Though he asks Celestial Light to favor him yet more by shining "inward," enabling him to "see and tell / Of things invisible to mortal sight" (51–55), the poet has already transcended his own nature.

In books 7 and 9, agency continues to be distributed between the poet and the Muse. She keeps him safe from error and guides his flight. The Celestial Patroness visits his "slumbers Nightly, or when Morn / Purples the East" and he asks her to govern his song (7.29–30). She "dictates to [him] slumb'ring, or inspires / Easy [his] unpremeditated Verse" (9.21–24). However, the brave "mortal voice" that sings "unchang'd / To hoarse or mute though fall'n on evil days" (7.24–25) is his. It is the poet who deliberately chose the all-important subject of the poem (9.25–26), challenging the tradition established by earlier epics with their descriptions of jousts and tournaments.

> The skill of Artifice or Office mean,
> Not that which justly gives Heroic name
> To Person or to Poem. Mee of these

> Nor skill'd nor studious, higher Argument
> Remains, sufficient of itself to raise
> That name, unless an age too late, or cold
> Climate, or Years damp my intended wing
> Deprest; and much they may, if all be mine,
> Not Hers who brings it nightly to my Ear.
>
> (9.39–47)

In his last prefatory appearance, the poet reminds us that the "very process of composition is the poem's great happening that contains all its other happenings."[16] Calling attention yet again to the poet and his work, the syntax of these lines encourages a productive confusion: the "Heroic name" that should be raised by the "higher Argument" would seem to be that of the poet who chose it, rejecting an "Office mean" for himself. We may discard this reading as too openly ambitious but, until the end, the poet's "intended wing" and the Muse's nocturnal voice come together to produce the flight of song: how can we know the singer from the singer?

Even this brief review demonstrates that, on the level of personal politics, Milton creates an impregnable platform that confers a unique status and a host of unique personal qualities on himself. The poet who states that "all" belongs to the Muse gives himself a "Heroic name" by the expedient of implicating himself with her and with "the better fortitude / Of Patience and Heroic Martyrdom" (9.31–32): "A good man in an evil time, 'compast round' with satanic tongues [in 7.24–28], the narrator repeats the solitary heroism of Abdiel, Enoch, and Noah."[17] At the same time that the existence of *Paradise Lost* is evidence of the single heroism that speaks out courageously against a malevolent majority in a hostile world, the poet's identification with the Muse means that he spurns any idea of human contention or accountability for himself: he is utterly removed from the sphere in which "evil tongues" have power, influence, or even relevance. So, of course, were Abdiel, Enoch, and Noah finally removed from environments too vile to contain their goodness.

Milton's invocations describe a mixture of passivity and activity in his composition and, at the same time that they honor the Muse, emphasize the singularity and courage of the poet's voice. Marvell stresses these contrary motions in "On Mr. Milton's *Paradise Lost*": he understands that the assertion that breaks through, or combines with, the self-effacement represents the need of the silenced controversialist somehow to go on asserting his righteousness and superiority against his antagonists. Before treating prophecy specifically, however, he deals with possible objections to Milton's poem in a description of his unfolding reactions as he read *Paradise Lost*. He begins by thinking of the poet's blindness as enemies like Parker did, as a defect that might produce bitterness (6–10), though the allusion to Samson suggests that God uses even the destructiveness of his servants. Marvell sketches two other reservations: that Milton might reduce the truth of Scripture to the status of fable or complicate the simple truths of faith. Such were the objections of detractors like Richard Leigh. While reading the poem, Marvell dismisses his fears. His concern that Milton might inspire imitators (17–22) is crucial, as Kenneth Gross explains, because "the earlier anxieties about Milton's relation to Scripture have been turned around and directed toward Milton's text itself . . . the poem has begun to regard *Paradise Lost* as a scriptural or sacred work in its own right."[18]

Following Milton's lead, Marvell intertwines the poet's accomplishment with the Muse's gift, activity with passivity. His initial list of reservations overcome summarizes impressive authorial feats. *Paradise Lost* represents Milton's individual "Labours," work that involved seeking out all things that were appropriate and excluding "all that was improper" (28). It is Milton who treats divine matters with total propriety (33). And yet, to complete the paradox of simultaneous agency and instrumentality, the poem is not Milton's work, either:

> Where couldst thou Words of such a compass find?
> hence furnish such a vast expense of Mind?
> Just Heav'n Thee, like *Tiresias*, to requite,
> Rewards with Prophesie thy loss of Sight.
>
> (41–44)

In the invocation of book 3, Milton asked that heaven compensate his blindness by letting him "see and tell / Of things invisible to mortal sight." He declared that he would be content if he could be equal "in renown" with Tiresias and other blind prophets. *Paradise Lost* has revealed to Marvell that Milton is distinguished by a vast mind, one furnished with conceptions and language of a magnitude and quality beyond human capacity. The matter and the words of the poem—the furnishings of Milton's mind—descended on the prophet from above, so to speak. Not incidentally, Marvell has reversed himself entirely from his original concern about the poet's blindness. Like Milton himself, he arrives at the "transformation of his blindness from an affliction to a token of divine favor."[19]

Marvell uses and compresses Milton's own language and ideas, especially from book 3, to ratify that the elder poet is everything he claims to be:

At once delight and horrour on us seize,
Thou singst with so much gravity and ease;
And above humane flight dost soar aloft,
With Plume so strong, so equal, and so soft.
The *Bird* nam'd from that *Paradise* you sing
So never Flags, but alwaies keeps on Wing.

                                             (35–40)

Milton's nightly visits to Sion, the Muses's dictation, the "voluntary" or "unpremeditated" aspect of the verse—the mystical aspects of prophetic inspiration that might evoke disbelief, outrage, or derision in Milton's detractors—are summoned up and accepted in Marvell's word, "ease." In this description, as in Milton's own, the effortlessness of Milton's writing is vital to its status as prophecy, and it receives a corresponding emphasis. A song that excels in gravity but is spontaneous, the product of no effort or intellection, cannot issue from a merely human source.

Marvell concurs with Milton's suggestion that divine inspiration changes the poet's nature. Throughout *Paradise Lost*, Milton's image for his inspired self is usually implied; as we saw above, however, it is made explicit in "the wakeful Bird / [That] sings darkling" in book 3. Marvell accepts the image and expands and literalizes it. He probably relished his own play on words, but its implications are in earnest. Milton is the bird of *Paradise* (*Lost*), according to Marvell, not only because he transcends human limitations, but also because these legendary birds transcend avian limitations: "the current belief [was] that, possessing neither wings nor feet, they passed their lives in the air, sustained on their ample plumes."[20] Through the image, Marvell confirms that Milton was inspired, and responds specifically to Milton's statement in book 7, that he approaches the second half of the poem "Standing on Earth, not rapt above the Pole" and, henceforth, "More safe [will] sing with mortal voice." Through the bird image, Marvell denies that Milton ever descended to the earth or sang with a human voice in *Paradise Lost*. Despite the prevailing lore, Marvell deliberately gives the bird of paradise wings to assure Milton that his immortal wings, so often mentioned in *Paradise Lost*, can never be "Deprest."

If readers are overtaken by a mixture of delight and terrible reverence as they realize that *Paradise Lost* is not a mere poem produced by a merely human poet, other poets should be, also. Echoing Milton's emphasis on the courage and singularity of the heroic voice, Marvell distinguishes him from other writers to substantiate his claim:

But I am now convinc'd, and none will dare
Within thy Labours to pretend a Share.
Thou hast not miss'd one thought that could be fit;
And all that was improper dost omit:
So that no room is here for Writers left,
But to detect their Ignorance or Theft.

(25–30)

Paradise Lost must strike the "less skilful" (18) with dread because it is sacred and because Milton has treated his subject with supernatural exhaustiveness: he owns and depletes his subject as if it were property on which no one else can trespass. Both the author and his matter partake of an awesomeness that should keep the uninspired at a respectful distance.

Marvell first calls Milton a *"mighty Poet"* (23) as opposed to lesser "Writers," but in the final step of his differentiation, the terms change. His comments on rhyme also compose his comment on the difference between Milton's art and his own. Some poets use rhyme to attract readers. One poet, "the *Town-Bays*" (47), uses it to keep himself jogging along, as an aid to composition. Others use it because it is the "fashion," and Marvell counts himself among these:

I too transported by the *Mode* offend,
And while I meant to *Praise* thee, must Commend.
Thy verse created like thy *Theme* sublime,
In Number, Weight, and Measure, needs not *Rhime*.

(51–54)

Poets use rhyme for various reasons, but prophets do not need it. Unlike the poet, the prophet does not have to attract readers because he is the voice of heaven. Poets might need aids to composition, but prophets do not, needing only to transcribe what is dictated. Though matters of artistic fashion may be of concern to poets, they are irrelevant to prophets. Marvell's echo of Wisdom 11:20, "thou hast ordered all things in measure, and number, and weight,"[21] is significant: heavenly prophecy is best expressed in the mode of divine creation.

Wittreich suggests that Marvell deliberately uses and refers to rhyme in this poem "not to acquiesce in Leigh's criticism of his own art but to discredit that criticism by devising a poem that, even if it employs the device of rhyme, is marvelously flexible and various."[22] This is certainly true. But in this poem, rhyme specifically represents poetry, the human endeavor posing various problems for readers and authors and admitting of more or less skill on the part of its practition-

ers. The rhyme of "commend" and "offend" exemplifies the strictures
the form imposes on the author and his matter. Clearly, the demands of
poetry can be a severe limitation for a mediocre or poor poet, though
they pose no serious difficulties for a poet like Marvell. Since Milton
is not a poet, the demands of poetry do not apply at all. As "On
Mr. Milton's *Paradise Lost*" asserts, prophecy is "sublime," a different
matter altogether.

*   *   *

In *Paradise Lost*, Milton made claims that exposed him to ridicule and
opprobrium, claims that developed from the aspirations he had
expressed earlier in "Il Penseroso." Marvell must have read the invocations, especially, with a sense of returning to old themes, ideas in the
work of his friend that he had once ridiculed, however gently and indirectly. His earlier reservations arose from the gestures "Il Penseroso"
made toward a prophecy derived from nature. Milton's ideal seemed
to identify the poet's function as oracular, his utterance as visionary.
Such a vague and general melding of poetry and prophecy Marvell
could not accept. On the evidence of his parody of Milton's natural
prophet, he was especially uncomfortable with the idea of effortless
and passive vision.

There is nothing in "On . . . *Paradise Lost*" to suggest that his attitude on this subject had altered. But by 1674 Milton had declared
himself a medium of prophecy with a heavenly origin and his claim
rested on a monumental work. According to Marvell, the conception
and scope of Milton's sacred history at once removed his matter from
the realm of poetry and his composition from the sphere of ordinary
authorship. In *Paradise Lost*, the sacred subject and the "answerable
style" came together to fulfill the aspirations and validate the claims
first glimpsed in "Il Penseroso." But the treatment equal to the enormous, magnificent, and divine subject did not produce mere poetry,
as Marvell saw it. His celebration of Milton is the tribute of poetry
to prophecy, a tribute that preserves the particular qualities of each
intact and distinct from the other. The poet declares himself convinced: Milton is a prophet and *Paradise Lost* his easy, God-given
vision.

The irony of a political outcast being someone who had once
dreamed of dwelling with Melancholy in a "peaceful hermitage" is too
obvious to have escaped Marvell's attention. An immense sympathy
for his friend is evident in "On . . . *Paradise Lost*." Marvell pays Milton the homage of taking his claim to prophetic stature literally, and

accepting it publicly. But this does not preclude his awareness that, within the prophet who transmits the vision of the Muse, an unreconstructed republican asserts his unyielding sense of righteousness. Surely, Marvell realized that calling Milton a prophet, he seconds his friend's declaration that, appearances notwithstanding, his power is undiminished and his position more exalted than ever.

Declaring himself a prophet, Milton declared himself possessed of an insurmountable status and a unique authority beyond the reach of any human question or criticism. It hardly matters, from this point of view, whether he is an instrument of the Muse or one of God's solitary heroes; his self-proclaimed identity gives him a voice of unquestionable authority. A voice that cannot be challenged or even engaged, it is doubly hedged against discourse or disputation by reason either of its discrete, particular message or of the disputant's lack of faith. The prophetic voice, audacious and unconquerable, must have the last word because it *is* a voice, pure and simple, which, as such, cannot hear or respond to other voices. At the same time that it emphatically declares itself unavailable to ordinary human intercourse, the prophetic voice professes to be the voice of all insight, knowledge, and wisdom. It is no wonder that Milton's infuriated enemies charged him with impiety. In "On Mr. Milton's *Paradise Lost*," Marvell appropriated Milton's own language about himself to stabilize its meaning, transforming words that detractors saw as boastful, deluded, or sacrilegious into objective reports and awed declarations of praise.

Notes

1. Gary A. Stringer, "Milton's 'Thorn in the Flesh': Pauline Didacticism in *Sonnet XIX*." *Milton Studies* 10 (1977), ed. James D. Simmonds (Pittsburgh, Pa.: University of Pittsburgh Press, 1977), 147–48.

2. Christopher Hill, "Milton and Marvell." In *Approaches to Marvell. The York Tercentenary Lectures*, ed. C. A. Patrides (London: Routledge, 1978), 5.

3. Quoted in Joseph A. Wittreich, "Perplexing the explanation: Marvell's 'On Mr. Milton's *Paradise Lost*.'" In *Approaches to Marvell*, 284. See 283–85.

4. Steven N. Zwicker, "Lines of Authority: Politics and Literary Culture in the Restoration." In *Politics of Discourse. The Literature and History of Seventeenth-Century England*, eds. Kevin Sharpe and Steven N. Zwicker (Berkeley: University of California Press, 1987), 246.

5. Carol Gilbertson, " 'Many *Miltons* in This One Man': Marvell's Mower Poems and *Paradise Lost*." *Milton Studies* 22 (1986):152; Judith Scherer Herz, "Milton and Marvell: The Poet as Fit Reader," *MLQ* 39 (1978): 248.

6. Herz, "Fit Reader," 256. "Il Penseroso" was written some years before "Lycidas" and its perspective differs from that of the later poem, which Joseph A. Wittreich reads as "a prophecy about transforming all the Lord's people into prophets." See " 'A Poet Amongst Poets': Milton and the Tradition of Prophecy." In *Milton and*

the Line of Vision, ed. Joseph A. Wittreich (Madison: University of Wisconsin Press, 1975), 113.

7. Quotations of Marvell's poems are from *The Poems and Letters of Andrew Marvell*, ed. H. M. Margoliouth, 3d ed. rev. by Pierre Legouis with E. E. Duncan-Jones, vol. 1 (London: Oxford University Press, 1971).

8. On Milton's misreading of "The Squire's Tale," see Donald R. Howard, "Flying Through Space: Chaucer and Milton." In *Line of Vision*, 9–11.

9. Stella Revard identifies Melancholy as the Muse, Urania, who "has the power to call up the souls of dead poets." " 'L'Allegro' and 'Il Penseroso': Classical Tradition and Renaissance Mythography," *PMLA* 101 (1986): 344.

10. Robert Wilcher, *Andrew Marvell* (Cambridge: Cambridge University Press, 1985), 157. Although several other works have been suggested as models for, or influences on, Marvell's "Upon Appleton House," in this essay I restrict myself to Milton's "Il Penseroso." See Wilcher, 147; Margoliouth, 280–81; and Elizabeth Story Donno, ed. *Andrew Marvell. The Complete Poems* (1972; Middlesex: Penguin, 1983), 248.

11. Thomas Hobbes, *Leviathan*, ed. Michael Oakeshott (New York: Macmillan, 1962), 272–73.

12. Kenneth Gross, " 'Pardon Me, Mighty Poet': Versions of the Bard in Marvell's 'On Mr. Milton's *Paradise Lost.*'" *Milton Studies* 16 (1982): 77.

13. Wittreich, "Perplexing the explanation," 285.

14. William Kerrigan, *The Prophetic Milton* (Charlottesville: University Press of Virginia, 1974), 106; 105–6.

15. Ibid., 138.

16. John R. Mulder, "The Lyric Dimension of *Paradise Lost.*" *Milton Studies* 23 (1987): 151.

17. Kerrigan, *Prophetic Milton*, 178.

18. Gross, "Versions of the Bard," 87.

19. George de F. Lord, "Milton's Dialogue with Omniscience in *Paradise Lost.*" In *The Author in His Work: Essays on a Problem in Criticism*, eds. Louis L. Martz and Aubrey Williams (New Haven: Yale University Press, 1978), 39.

20. Margoliouth, *Marvell*, 337n.

21. Quoted in Donno, *Complete Poems*, 302n.

22. Wittreich, "Perplexing the explanation," 290.

Milton, Bunyan, and the Clothing of Truth and Righteousness

DENNIS DANIELSON

Clothes in that country are not a disguise: the spiritual body
lives along each thread and turns them into living organs. A
robe or a crown is there as much one of the wearer's features
as a lip or an eye.

> For we by rightful doom remediless
> Were lost in death, till he that dwelt above
> High-thron'd in secret bliss, for us frail dust
> Emptied his glory, ev'n to nakedness.

I dreamed, and behold *I saw a Man cloathed with Raggs,
standing in a certain place, with his face from his own House, a
Book in his hand, and a great burden upon his Back.*[1]

In the first of these epigraphs, from *The Great Divorce*, a work deeply
informed by the imaginative writings of Milton and Bunyan,
C. S. Lewis adumbrates a model of regained, heavenly innocence in
which clothing, instead of having to be discarded, *reveals* rather than
covers up, becomes natural, integral, rather than artificial. In the second epigraph, from "Upon the Circumcision" (17–20), Milton points
to the revealing, the uncovering, of the innocent Christ and his mission through his being stripped, almost simultaneously, of heavenly
glory and of that integral piece of human-fleshly covering whose
removal circumcision accomplishes. And in the third, from the
beginning of *The Pilgrim's Progress*, John Bunyan introduces his character Christian along with two of the book's most significant images
of the unregenerate human condition: the filthy rags of our righteousness (from Is. 64:6) and of course the burden of iniquity (from Ps.
38:4), which Christian *experiences* as integral because he cannot take
it off.[2]

In the present essay on Milton and Bunyan I highlight this theme of nakedness and clothing not only because it helps to reveal their common, radical vision of spiritual integrity, but also because it provides us with a metaphor for the practice and mission of their literary imaginations. Or to put the matter another way, it gives us a model for understanding Milton's and Bunyan's use of metaphor itself, broadly conceived. For to the Puritan mind that Milton and Bunyan shared, literature must not simply involve the replacement or displacement of truth. If art entailed the mere making of images, then the theaters must be closed and the idols must be torn down. But the careers of Milton and Bunyan stand as a decisive affirmation of the value of art, not because they abandoned their insistence on the sanctity and radical integrity of truth's body, but precisely because they allowed the implications of that insistence to encompass art itself. To clothe the naked truth is not to cover it up. Art, fiction, "metaphor"—as Lewis says of clothing in his imagined heavenly country of "the Solid People"—is "not a disguise." And "must I needs want solidness," Bunyan asks,

> because
> By metaphors I speak; was not Gods Laws,
> His Gospel-laws in older time held forth
> By Types, Shadows and Metaphors?
>
> *(PP,* 4)

—a biblical appeal also made in *Paradise Regained,* where the "True Image of the Father" declares Hebrew monotheistic culture to be the true source of "Arts / And Eloquence," whereas in classical Greece, literature disintegrates into a covering up of sin: "swelling Epithets thick laid / As varnish on a Harlot's cheek" (*PR,* 4.596, 240–42, 343–44).

Puritanism and Christianity

Before tracing this common thread in more textual detail, however, I would like briefly to recapitulate a few crucial definitions. Most current writing on Bunyan, and to some extent on Milton, seems to proceed on the assumption, as Vincent Newey has put it (citing Philip Rieff), that ours is "an all but deconverted world."[3] S. J. Newman refers to "the faith on which [*The Pilgrim's Progress*] floated" as receding and leaving the work "stranded like a quaint Noah's ark" (Newey, 225). If the Christian faith is becoming less well known, then it is all the more important for critics to be as precise as they can in defining it and its components.

Apart from their status as seventeenth-century authors, then, what Milton and Bunyan most conspicuously have in common is their Puritanism. Puritanism is a part of Protestantism, which in turn is part of Christianity, the religion based on the teachings of Jesus Christ and his apostles. According to Christianity, human beings—originally created in God's image but then fallen into sin, and hence also subject to death and separated from their Creator—have received a divine offer of forgiveness and eternal life through the miraculous birth, life, death, and resurrection of Jesus Christ, the Son of God. Protestantism, beginning in the early sixteenth century, was a reaction within Christianity against the Roman Catholic church, which the reformers came to see as an institution acting as a sort of wholesaler or multinational corporation that mediated business dealings between God on the one hand and ordinary human beings on the other, between (so to speak) the Producer of forgiveness and the consumer. Martin Luther claimed in effect that the Roman Catholic church as *Zwischenhändler*, by making up rules to further its own interests, was damaging the interests of both its "customers" while growing rich, materially rich, in the process. Therefore, Luther, based on his reading of the Bible alone (*sola scriptura*), declared that salvation—forgiveness, reconciliation, eternal life—is a free gift of God (*sola gratia*) given directly to the individual, Christ himself being the only intermediary; and that the individual human being receives the gift, again without earthly intermediary, merely by faith (*sola fides*). In spite of its various forms and divisions, and in spite of the many nondoctrinal factors in its development, Protestantism (or the "Evangelical" or "Reformed" religion) for the most part kept this gospel (*evangelium*) of Christ-as-savior-and-sole-mediator as its essential emphasis.[4]

In England, the national church, which had been officially reformed (had become Protestant) under Henry VIII and *doctrinally* reformed under Edward VI, still exhibited many features of *discipline*—church government, the administration of the sacraments, and so on—that even later in the sixteenth century had still not been brought into line with the church's reforms of doctrine. At least so some argued, and these were branded by their opponents as "Puritans," because they wanted to purify, to reform further, the practices of the church in keeping with the essential themes of Protestant theology. Until about 1625 at the earliest, "Puritan" should thus not be understood primarily as a doctrinal designation, nor simplistically treated as a contrary of "Anglican," which is also often used anachronistically. For as George Carleton put it in 1626: in the reigns of Edward and in the beginning of the reign of Elizabeth,

> albeit the *Puritans* disquieted our Church about their conceived *Discipline*,
> yet they never moved any quarrell against the Doctrine of our Church . . .
> Both the *Bishops* and . . . the *Puritanes* . . . embraced a mutuall consent in
> Doctrine, onely the difference was in matter of inconformity: Then hith-
> erto there was no *Puritane Doctrine* known.[5]

It should thus also be clear that Puritanism was not initially nor
essentially a separatist movement, though the failure of the Church of
England to reform itself—and of course the decisive movement away
from reform in the 1620s and 1630s—drove an increasing number of
Puritans to leave the national church altogether.

A further, overlapping point worth making here is that the seventeenth-century doctrinal debate between "Arminians" and "Calvinists" about matters of election and predestination has virtually no role
to play in a definition of Puritanism. It is true that in England the
term *Arminian* became associated with the anti-Puritan forces of
Archbishop Laud, and likewise with his successors after the Restoration in 1660.[6] By that time most Puritans had in fact separated, and
Arminianism had acquired a clearly political meaning, one distinct
from its still authentic doctrinal denotations. In any case, some Puritans, such as John Goodwin and John Milton, were doctrinally Arminian, while many other Puritans, such as John Bunyan, were Calvinist.
And what characterizes these Puritans is not "single-issue" theology,
but rather their adherence to the Protestant, "evangelical" theology of
Christ (and the need for an individual response to it),[7] *combined with* a
determination to pursue the implications of that gospel into the full
life of the church and often indeed into society and culture as a whole.

Whether this radical project was attempted within the national
church or beyond it is not of the essence, but rather was contingent on
history and circumstance. In this context, the distinction that Richard
L. Greaves makes between Puritanism and Sectarianism—Bunyan
was "a sectary and not a Puritan"[8]—is simply unhelpful. Puritanism's
mission to quicken and purify the church—the body of believers, the
communion of saints—cannot be defined simply according to its field
of operation. Milton's Puritanism clearly found its first exercise
within the Church of England, "to whose service," he says, "by the
intentions of my parents and friends I was destin'd of a child, and in
mine own resolutions"—until he was "Church-outed by the Prelats,"
whose conditions for the "sacred office" of ministry would have
required Milton to "forswear" and perjure himself. Milton accordingly devoted himself to the cultivation of his poetic abilities, which

> are of power beside the office of a pulpit, to imbreed and cherish in a great
> people the seeds of vertu and publick civility, to allay the perturbations of

the mind, and set the affections in right tune, to celebrate in glorious and lofty Hymns the throne and equipage of Gods Almightinesse, and what he works, and what he suffers to be wrought with high providence in his Church, to sing the victorious agonies of Martyrs and Saints, the deeds and triumphs of just and pious Nations doing valiantly through faith against the enemies of Christ, to deplore the general relapses of Kingdoms and States from justice and Gods true worship. (*CG, CPW,* 1:822–23, 816–17)

The grandeur of Milton's Puritan vision revealed in these words written in 1642 causes one to wonder how his prophetic voice might have been exercised had he been able to ascend the pulpit rather than Parnassus. Had he been born twenty years earlier, he might have done so. Twenty years later, his Puritanism might, like Bunyan's, have taken him down the path of Nonconformity, or "sectarianism." But in the 1640s and 1650s, Puritanism's battle for the English Church was not yet quite lost; and by the time it was lost, Milton's ministerial calling had taken him irrevocably into the realm of poetry rather than preaching. Nevertheless, and in spite of their huge differences in education and milieu, we can see Milton and Bunyan as sharing their combative Puritanism together with a profound allegiance to the unmediated Christian gospel and a determination to use their imaginative and literary powers in its service, as "ministers."

The Exercise of Faith and of Its Champions

Milton and Bunyan not only engaged in spiritual combat but also believed in its value. Each in his own voice affirms the Christian need for such "exercise," Milton most famously in *Areopagitica*, in his defense of freedoms conducive to "the triall of vertue, and the exercise of truth" (*CPW,* 2:528), but Bunyan too in his declaration, at the beginning of one of his first published controversial works, that

it is very expedient that there should be heresies among us, that thereby those which are indeed of the truth might be made manifest; and also that the doctrine of GOD, and his son JESUS CHRIST, might the more cast forth its lustre and glory. For the Truth is of the nature, that the more it is opposed, the more glory it appears in; . . . which doth give me and all that stand for it . . . much boldness and incouragment.[9]

In his preaching career, occasionally Bunyan recognized that some "scorching portion of the Word" he was preparing to expound condemned himself, and he was tempted to "mince it as to make way for

[his] own escape." But his practice, he tells us, was "rather, as Samson," to bow

> myself with all my might, to condemn sin and transgression wherever I found it, yea though therein also I did bring guilt upon my own conscience; *Let me die*, thought I, *with the Philistines* (Judg. 16:29, 30) rather than deal corruptly with the blessed Word of God . . . It is far better that thou do judge thyself . . . than that thou, to save thyself, imprison the truth in unrighteousness.[10]

Bunyan's identification of himself with the blinded, imprisoned judge (whom Hebrews 11 includes in its catalogue of heroes of faith) naturally brings to mind Milton's Samson in *Samson Agonistes*, who in turn can be viewed side by side with Bunyan's own character Faithful in *The Pilgrim's Progress*. Like Bunyan, both characters are tempted to renounce their vocation and to save themselves by abandoning allegiance to the truth.

We can view Samson and Faithful, in whom Milton and Bunyan may have sublimated their own personal concerns with martyrdom, as a kind of thematic diptych, with Milton's words as a caption: "the victorious agonies of martyrs and saints." Both Samson and Faithful exemplify the pattern of temptation, "progress" in faith, and death that bears witness in the face of forces hostile to faith. Most colorfully, both are lured by temptations of the flesh, Samson by Dalila, and Faithful by Wanton, who (as Faithful puts it) "had like to have done me a mischief." He adds,

> You cannot think . . . what a flattering tongue she had: she lay at me hard to turn aside with her, promising me all manner of content.
> *Chr. Nay, she did not promise you the content of a good conscience.*
> *Faith.* You know what I mean, all carnal and fleshly content.
>   . . .
> *Chr. Why, I tro you did not consent to her desires?*
> *Faith.* No, not to defile my self; for I remembered an old writing that I had seen, which saith, *Her steps take hold of Hell.* So I shut mine eyes, because I would not be bewitched with her looks: then she railed on me, and I went my way. (*PP,* 56–57)

Milton's Samson is similarly tempted—by Dalila and her "Life yet hath many solaces, enjoy'd / Where other senses want not their delights" (*SA,* 915–16). Although he need not shut his eyes, Samson too refuses the temptress's touch (952) and remembers, not an old writing, but instead his own experience of the hell her "delights" have already brought him. And when he resists, Dalila rails on him.

Another temptation comes to Faithful in the person of the "Old Man," and to Samson in the person of his father, Manoa. Although by no means identical, both temptations represent the lure of this-world-liness, of a comfortable immanence that excludes any rising up above the concerns of this life. While motivated not by hostility but by fatherly benevolence, Manoa's appeal to Samson is aptly summarized by the words of Faithful's Old Man: *"Wilt thou be content to dwell with me . . .?"* In Bunyan's allegory, this *"Adam the first"* dwelt *"in the Town of Deceit"* and would prevent Faithful from climbing "the Hill called *Difficulty"* (*PP,* 57). In Milton's drama, Manoa's temptation consists in an appeal to "self-preservation" together with the persistent assumption that God's "high disposal" functions on a plane of existence that does not intersect with that of "timely care" and human "means" (*SA,* 505, 602–3). Both temptations seek to prevent the faithful heroes from transcending the lower plane through a faith enlivened by the personal address of Providence.

Samson's last individual tempter, the giant Harapha, can be seen, like Faithful's last tempter Shame, as objecting "against Religion it self" (*PP,* 59). Harapha's vaunting appeal to traditional muscular heroism ("glorious arms . . ."; *SA,* 1130) and his scornful atheism ("Presume not on thy God, whate'er he be"; 1156) engage Samson in the same contest of foundations as that with which Shame challenges Faithful. If one judges by worldly criteria of "manliness," then Faithful ought to give up his pilgrimage, and Samson ought to cringe under the giant's insults. But if instead one is unashamed of one's faith in God—if it is not "a pitiful, low, sneaking business for a man to mind Religion" (*PP,* 59)—then Faithful is wise to remember that "at the day of doom" we shall "be doomed to death or life . . . according to the Wisdom and Law of the Highest" (*PP,* 60), just as Samson is wise to acknowledge God and to

> despair not of his final pardon
> Whose ear is ever open; and his eye
> Gracious to re-admit the suppliant.
>   (*SA,* 1171–73)

In this way, for Samson and for Faithful, it is a practical and characterological as well as a theoretical principle that "the more [the truth] is opposed, the more glory it appears in." And such opposition drives both Samson and Faithful back upon their foundations in the "evangelical" promises of God.

Milton and Bunyan apparently see the same principle applying to the conclusions of Samson's and Faithful's lives. Faithful is in fact executed by the enemies of the truth in Vanity Fair; Samson's death, amid his enemies, brought about by his last feat of strength, is certainly more problematical. But both deaths are presented as the deaths of characters faithful to the truth and faithful to the meaning of their lives and of their names. Evangelist warns Christian and Faithful that one of them will die in Vanity Fair, and he encourages them to base their faithfulness on the faithfulness of their God: "quit your selves like men; and commit the keeping of your souls to your God, as unto a faithful Creator" (*PP,* 72). Samson, having arrived at the insight that God may "dispense with" him as he sees fit, and having felt "rousing motions" within himself (*SA,* 1377, 1382), goes forth to die destroying the Philistines. "*Samson* hath quit himself / Like *Samson,*" declares his father after his death (1709–10). In spite of the this-worldliness and denial that characterize the rest of Manoa's speech, I think the reader is inclined to agree that Samson, like Faithful, has quit himself in a manner befitting his calling and his name: Samson (the name means "like the sun"), "though blind of sight . . . With inward eyes illuminated" (1687–89).

Finally, in the conclusions of Samson's and Faithful's lives, both characters are also linked to the revelation of truth and, through association with the Phoenix, to its Christian propagation. A proverb included by John Clarke in his catalogue of proverbs in 1639 states: "A faithfull friend is like a *Phoenix.*"[11] Bunyan would seem to apply some similar principle to Faithful's truthfulness amid trial, and to his resulting execution, whose immediate effect is the "new birth" of Hopeful: "Thus one died to make Testimony to the Truth, and another rises out of his Ashes to be a Companion with *Christian*" (*PP,* 80). "Hope," as Milton comments in *Christian Doctrine,* "has its origin in faith"; and "it is generally by martyrdom that the gospel is propagated" (*CPW,* 6:476, 702).

The image of the Phoenix in addition links Faithful and Samson to Christ himself, whose resurrection, together with its propagative effect, the Phoenix traditionally symbolizes. As John Ford wrote in 1613, in his meditation on the death of Christ:

> [Christ] like the *Phoenix* burning in the Sun,
> That from his ashes may spring up a younger,
> Doth beate himselfe to death, and will not shun
> The fire, that weake men may in him grow stronger:
>   A perfect *Phoenix,* that most gladly dyes,
>   That many in his only death may rise.[12]

The Phoenix image thus is a marker of the Christ-likeness of Faithful and of Samson (God's "faithful Champion"; 1751), another indication of the "evangelical" foundation of Bunyan's and of Milton's visions. To be sure, there does not appear to be any "gospel response" within *Samson Agonistes* itself—unless it is Samson's own. Yet some readers continue (after the pattern of Hebrews 11) to see Samson as a hero of faith, whose story and whose death do point beyond law to grace.[13]

Faith and Family Responsibilities

There are further "literary diptychs" to which a simultaneous study of Milton and Bunyan may likewise draw our attention. One, which I shall merely mention, is that of Adam and Eve in *Paradise Lost* overcoming despair and the temptation of suicide by remembering the so-called *protevangelium*, the promise of the "Seed" who will "bruise / The Serpent's head" (*PL*, 10.1031–32); and of Christian, escaping from the Giant Despair by remembering that he carries "a *Key* in [his] bosom, called *Promise*" (*PP*, 96).[14]

Yet another such diptych, one in which the focus is a contrast rather than a similarity, involves Bunyan's depiction of Christian's "praiseworthy" desertion of his wife and family and Milton's presentation of Adam's "culpable" solidarity with Eve in *Paradise Lost*, in his acceding to join her in sin and death. Even though, within the moral cosmos of *The Pilgrim's Progress*, Christian does the right thing, some critics have complained that a story that premises a hero abandoning his family to Destruction to pursue his own salvation is by nature morally inconsistent. As T. R. Glover puts these critics' question, "can a work stand as a picture of the Christian life, in which the family and the city are discarded?"[15]

Similarly, critics such as A. J. A. Waldock have charged that *Paradise Lost*, because it demands a condemnation of Adam precisely at the point where he exhibits "love" by joining Eve in her sin, cracks at its moral center.[16] I have argued elsewhere why I think that the apparent dilemma in *Paradise Lost* dissolves when we recognize alternative scenarios adumbrated in the background of the "picture" that Milton paints, in particular the self-sacrificial possibility hinted at in Adam's typological status as a "first Christ" analogous to Christ's status as "second Adam," who sinlessly sacrificed himself to atone for the sinful.[17]

The picture Bunyan paints of Christian, however, is both starker and simpler. At the time of his departure from his family and the City of Destruction, Christian's choice is merely whom to listen to: either Evangelist, or the others, including his wife and children. It is a hard scene because it is based on a "hard saying" of Jesus: "If any man come to me and hate not his father, and mother, and wife, and chil-

dren, and brethren, and sisters, yea, and his own life also, he cannot be
my disciple" (Luke 14:26; cited by Bunyan, *PP*, 10). It is thus a genuinely Christian problem, not only a literary one for Bunyan. And it
has, I think, a genuinely Christian answer. First, in one sense Christian is leaving behind "his own life," his life as Graceless. The principle here is that "whosoever shall lose his life for my sake and the
gospel's, the same shall find it" (Mark 8:35). But still more pertinent is
another saying of Jesus: "There is no man that hath left house, or parents, or brethren, or wife, or children, for the kingdom of God's sake,
who shall not receive manifold more in this present time, and in the
world to come life everlasting" (Luke 18:29–30). Moreover, the interpretation of this verse that *The Pilgrim's Progress* as a whole supports
is not at all an exclusively personal or selfish one so far as Christian is
concerned. First, by remaining in the City of Destruction Christian
would clearly do nothing to further the welfare of his wife and children—whatever the merely sentimental or romantic appeal of that sort
of solidarity may be. But the second and more telling point is that it is
precisely Christian's obedience to the call of Evangelist that establishes the pattern for Christiana and the children to follow (*PP*, 145).

While the opening scene by itself may seem to pose a dilemma,
therefore, *The Pilgrim's Progress* as a whole reveals this appearance to
be just a function of the myopia that typifies the city that Christian
leaves behind. As N. H. Keeble points out in his fine discussion of
this issue, "Milton and Bunyan share the Puritan [I would simply say
Christian] perception that absolute devotion to any human being leads
not to blissful freedom but to servitude."[18] The diptych of Adam and
of Christian in this context thus displays a sobering antithesis: one
man myopically, sentimentally, choosing sin as a prologue to servitude, death, and woe for himself and all his offspring (see *PL*,
10.729–41); the other following the call of the *evangelium* as a prologue to the salvation of those he was faithful enough initially to leave
behind.

The Gospel and the Regaining of Nakedness

The *evangelium* to which Christian responds is associated by Milton,
in *The Reason of Church Government*, with prelapsarian nakedness. In
his attack on prelatical ceremony, including vestments, Milton issues
the following challenge:

> Tell me ye Priests wherfore . . . these roabs and surplices over the
> Gospel? is our religion guilty of the first trespasse, and hath need of

cloathing to cover her nakednesse? what does this else but cast an ignominy upon the perfection of Christs ministery by seeking to adorn it with that which was the poor remedy of our shame? . . . he that will cloath the Gospel now, intimates plainly, that the Gospel is naked, uncomely . . . Do not, ye Church-maskers, while Christ is cloathing upon our barenes with his righteous garment to make us acceptable in his fathers sight, doe not, as ye do, cover and hide his righteous verity with the polluted cloathing of your ceremonies. (*CPW,* 1:828)

Clearly there is a gospel or innocent nakedness, in Milton's view, that is antithetical to the nakedness of shame, just as there is a clothing of righteousness that is antithetical to the prelates' polluting robes.

Our first glimpse of innocent nakedness in *Paradise Lost,* however—of Adam and Eve, "clad / In naked Majesty" (4.289–90)—is one that participates in this postlapsarian ambiguity, and is a glimpse we share with Satan. Even the language Milton uses to describe Eve's hair—"Dishevell'd, . . . in wanton ringlets" (*PL,* 4.306)—"surprises" us, to use Stanley Fish's famous formulation, with thoughts of sin even amid our perception of innocence.[19] When Milton says Eve wore her hair "as a veil down to the slender waist," he not only draws our eye downward, but also allows us to picture Eve's hair "as a veil"—as "clothing" that covers that which lies between the head and the waist. In other words, we are permitted (Fish might say "tempted") to treat the innocent, integral "clothing" of Eve's hair *as* postlapsarian covering of something shameful—which Milton then tells us is an inappropriate response, characteristic of now, not of *then:* for "Then was not guilty shame . . . Of Nature's works" (*PL,* 4.304, 314 –15).

Later in book 4 of *Paradise Lost* Milton exposes the same polemical contrast of innocence and sin, of nakedness and nonintegral, nonauthentic clothing, in his swift transition from divine prayer to connubial embrace:

> into thir inmost bower
> Handed they went; and eas'd the putting off
> These troublesome disguises which wee wear,
> Straight side by side were laid.
>
> (4.738–41)

Milton pans away from the happy couple to the strains of his famous hymn to "wedded Love" (750 ff.)—and then he finishes the scene by zooming in again on the embracing couple, on whose "naked limbs the flow'ry roof / Show'r'd Roses" (772–73). Perhaps one remembers here the earlier mention of that now potentially painful flower—"and without Thorn the Rose" (4.256). But again the contrast of then and now obtrudes; and again, as he does with Eve's hair earlier in the

same book, Milton provides an organic covering that, without participating in the guilty nature of postlapsarian clothing, decorously
shields innocent nakedness from our polluting gaze.[20]

In the next book Raphael, on his way to visit the naked couple, is
described in a way that may remind us of Lewis's comments about the
clothing of the "Solid People" in *The Great Divorce*—for "clothed"
and "unclothed" almost fail here as distinct categories. Like Eve,
Raphael is "Veil'd" (5.250) by something integral and organic:

>   six wings he wore, to shade
> His lineaments Divine; the pair that clad
> Each shoulder broad, came mantling o'er his breast
> With regal Ornament; the middle pair
> Girt like a Starry Zone his waist, and round
> Skirted his loins and thighs with downy Gold
> And colors dipt in Heav'n; the third his feet
> Shadow'd from either heel with feather'd mail
> Sky-tinctur'd grain

>   (5.277–85)

This magnificence of "clothing"—Raphael is really not *wearing* anything—finds its counterpart in the mere unfallen simplicity of the
angel's welcoming host, whom Milton cannot resist contrasting favorably to postlapsarian princes with their "rich Retinue . . . and Grooms
besmear'd with Gold" (5.355–56), a contrast for which Raphael's genuinely "regal Ornament" too has prepared us.

But Milton most richly weaves together the various themes relating
to nakedness in his depiction of Raphael's meeting with Eve:

>   but *Eve*
> Undeckt, save with herself more lovely fair
> Than Wood-Nymph, or the fairest Goddess feign'd
> Of three that in Mount *Ida* naked strove,
> Stood to entertain her guest from Heav'n; no veil
> Shee needed, Virtue-proof, no thought infirm
> Alter'd her cheek. On whom the Angel *Hail*
> Bestow'd, the holy salutation us'd
> Long after to blest *Mary*, second *Eve*.
>   Hail Mother of Mankind, whose fruitful Womb
> Shall fill the World more numerous with thy Sons
> Than with these various fruits the Trees of God
> Have heap'd this Table.

>   (5.379–91)

Here we have the familiar contrast of then and now: in the face of a
"god-like Guest" (5.351) *she* needs "no veil," and *she* doesn't blush.

Moreover, Eve is explicitly compared with two other specific females, Milton's mention of the first implying a contrast: Eve's innocent beauty outstrips the naked charms even of Venus, the fairest goddess of mythology. The second comparison implies closeness rather than distance: Raphael greets Eve with the same salutation (Luke 1:28) with which the virgin Mary is greeted by the angel Gabriel at the Annunciation—"*Hail.*"

This brief scene of salutation stands in a long tradition of pairing Eve and Mary typologically.[21] It establishes, of course, an affinity, one that in context reflects great honor on Eve. The salutation can create in the reader, however, ambivalence of at least two kinds. First, and familiar, is that associated with the Fishian guilty-reader syndrome. Here we behold the angel greeting a superlatively beautiful naked woman in a way that twins her with the most religiously venerated woman in the history of the world. Nor are (at least) a heterosexual male's possible efforts at an appropriately spiritual reading of the scene assisted by the fact that the angel at once mentions the woman's sexual organs.

But second, and I think more profoundly, the evocation of Mary brings to the foreground of our consciousness not the state of innocence but the framework of the gospel story, in particular the Incarnation, along with the need for redemption that that story presupposes. If Milton, in his depiction of innocent nakedness, surprises us with sin, then he also accordingly includes in that surprise an adumbration—from our point of view, a reminder—of sin's remedy. For the Eve/Mary typology is an outgrowth of the Adam/Christ typology, which posits a symmetry between type and antitype: the AVE (hail) spoken to Mary begins the reversal of the misdeed of EVA; and "as in Adam all die, even so in Christ shall all be made alive" (1 Cor. 15:22). The clothing of salvation that the Gospel offers is thus quietly advertised to those whose response to (among other things) nakedness in *Paradise Lost* may show that they need saving. There is nothing here so bold or explicit as the later words of Charles Wesley ("Veiled in flesh the Godhead see, Hail th' incarnate Deity"), but the prelapsarian "presence" of Mary in the poetry side by side with the naked Eve and with an angelic congratulation of her fruitful womb weaves into the poem's fabric an incarnational premonition, a thread attaching directly to the one who, as Eve's and Mary's seed, empties "his glory, ev'n to nakedness."

Bunyan, in his *Exposition on the First Ten Chapters of Genesis*, exploits a different typological reading of Eve, yet one that similarly, if less subtly, imports a consciousness of the Gospel into his consideration of Eden before the Fall. Bunyan's commentary is highly imaginative, often even fanciful; but when he associates Eve with the church, he is participating in a tradition that goes back at least as far as St. Augustine, who summed up the parallel with the aphorism: "Eva de latere dormientis, Ecclesia de latere patientis"—"Eve from the side of the sleeping one, the Church from the side of the suffering one."[22] "Adam's wife," as Bunyan says, "was a type of the church of Christ; for that she was taken out of his side, it signifies we are flesh of Christ's flesh, and bone of Christ's bone."[23]

Bunyan's commentary on nakedness, however, reveals many parallels with Milton's treatment, though in general (in keeping with the commentary genre) he uses physical or narrative details to make theological points rather than, like Milton in *Paradise Lost*, and like himself in *The Pilgrim's Progress*, poetically melding concrete experience with theology. Both agree that before the Fall Adam and Eve even in their nakedness were in one sense "clothed." Milton's "clad / In naked Majesty" has its counterpart in Bunyan's less organic but no less enthusiastic "O! they stood not naked before God! they stood not without righteousness, or uprightness before him" (*Works*, 2:431–32). Similarly, the recognition of nakedness after the Fall—"And they knew that they were naked" (Gen. 3:7)—both Bunyan and Milton interpret as involving more than consciousness of bare skin. As Bunyan puts it:

> Not only naked of outward clothing, but even destitute of righteousness; they had lost their innocency, their uprightness, and sinless veil, and had made themselves polluted creatures. (2:431)

After the fall, Milton's Adam says:

> we know
> Both Good and Evil, Good lost, and Evil got,
> Bad Fruit of Knowledge, if this be to know,
> Which leaves us naked thus, of Honor void,
> Of Innocence, of Faith, of Purity,
> Our wonted Ornaments now soil'd and stain'd.
> (9.1071–76)

Second, in keeping with this interpretation of guilty nakedness, Milton and Bunyan both see Adam and Eve's clothing of themselves in fig leaves (Gen. 3:7) as a picture of the hopelessness of human attempts to cover one's own guilt. "Vain Covering," comments Milton, "if to hide / Thir guilt and dreaded shame; O how unlike / To that first naked Glory" (*PL*, 9.1113–15). But on this particular topic Bunyan lingers longer than does Milton, exclaiming:

as if because fig-leaves would hide their nakedness from their [own] sight, that therefore they would hide it from the sight of God. . . . Fig-leaves! . . . But was that a sufficient shelter against either thorn or thistle? Or was it possible but that after a while these fig-leaves should have become rotten, and turned to dung? So will it be with all man's own righteousness.[24]

This interpretation is based on a vivid, concrete, almost amusingly literal apprehension of the implications of fig leaves and their inadequacy as protection against such hazards as tall thistles (see Gen. 3:18). It shares in the imaginative energy that enlivens *The Pilgrim's Progress* just as decisively as it expresses its underlying soteriology.

Milton's and Bunyan's interpretations of the next verse, Genesis 3:8, is worth noting on our way to Adam and Eve's next change of clothes. "And they heard the voice of the Lord God walking in the garden in the cool of the day: and Adam and his wife hid themselves." Bunyan's identification of "the voice" as the Word, as Christ, and his insistence on the simultaneity of divine grace and wrath, are an effective gloss on Milton's similarly Christocentric reading:

by voice here, we are to understand the Lord Christ himself; wherefore this voice is said to walk . . . This voice John calls the word . . . 'And . . . in the cool of the day.' The gospel of it is, in the season of grace; for by the cool of the day, he here means, in the patience, gentleness, goodness and mercy of the gospel; and it is opposed to the heat, fire, and severity of the law. (*Works*, 2:432)

The presence of the Gospel from the beginning (Milton and Bunyan both treat Adam and Eve as the first Christian converts)[25] is emphasized also in *Paradise Lost*, where it is the Son himself who appears in

> The Ev'ning cool, when he from wrath more cool
> Came the mild Judge and Intercessor *both*
> To sentence Man: the voice of God they heard
> Now walking in the Garden.
> (10.95–98; italics added)

This same *both* is repeated in Milton's transition from divine condemnation to divine clothing: "So judg'd he Man, both Judge and Savior sent, . . . then pitying how they stood / Before him naked. . . ."

> As Father of his Family he clad
> Thir nakedness . . .
>   .   .   .
> Nor hee thir outward only with the Skins
> Of Beasts, but inward nakedness, much more

> Opprobrious, with his Robe of righteousness
> Arraying cover'd from his Father's sight.

> (10.209–23)

Again to use Bunyan as a gloss upon Milton: "By this action the Lord God did preach to Adam, and to his wife, the meaning of that promise that you read in ver. 15 [the *protevangelium*]. Namely, That by the means of Jesus Christ, God himself would provide a sufficient clothing for those that accept of his grace by the gospel" (*Works,* 2:240). In *Paradise Lost,* moreover, the Son returns immediately after this clothing episode to his Father's presence, where he makes his report, "mixing intercession sweet" (10.228). The "Prevenient Grace" (11.3) that later descends to soften Adam's and Eve's hearts is apparently already in operation during the Son's judgment and in his clothing of fallen nakedness.

If the animal skins in Genesis 3:21 thus represent for Milton and Bunyan Christ's "robe of righteousness" (Is. 61:10; *PL,* 10.222; *Misc. W,* 10:172), the question remains wherein that righteousness consists. The answer that both Milton and Bunyan give has everything to do with Christ's work and effectively nothing to do with our works. The technical account of justification, or redemption, is most often expressed in the *satisfaction* Christ makes for us. Milton sees this satisfaction as being twofold:

CHRIST AS [*théanthropos*—"God-Man"] FULLY SATISFIED DIVINE JUSTICE BY FULFILLING THE LAW AND PAYING THE JUST PRICE ON BEHALF OF ALL MEN. (*CD, CPW,* 6:663)

These last two words ("ALL MEN") reveal Milton's Arminianism; however, the rest of the definition accords with Bunyan's:

this obediential Righteousness of Christ, consisteth of two parts: 1. In a doing of that which the Law commanded us to. 2. In a paying that price for the transgression, which Justice hath said shall be required at the hand of man; and that is the cursed death.[26] (*Misc. W,* 10:173).

Christ's "merit" and Christ's "death" are what make up this "propitiation" (*PL,* 11.34–36; cf. 3.210–12). It is Christ's active obedience—that in which Adam failed—*and* his "passive" obedience in death (*PL,* 12.395–410) that accomplish justification. The love of Christ, as Milton says in "Upon the Circumcision,"

> that great Cov'nant which we still transgress
> Entirely satisfi'd,

And the full wrath beside
Of vengeful Justice bore for our excess.

(21–24)

If there is a contrast between Milton and Bunyan in their literary treatment of this twofold satisfaction of Christ, it is to be seen in Milton's apparent taste for the beginnings of human history and of human stories, over against Bunyan's leisurely meditation on the end. To be sure, *Paradise Lost* does adumbrate the cross, and Christian pilgrimage, and the *eschaton* (e.g. 3.227–343; 12.415–65, 486–550); but these occupy little more than a few hundred lines of poetry. And *Paradise Regained* focuses as it were on *the first part* of the first part of Christ's satisfaction, which is why the angels' song ends as it does: "on thy glorious work / Now enter, and begin to save mankind" (4.634–35).

The Pilgrim's Progress finds many more opportunities for meditation on the blood of Christ, in particular the "satisfaction" achieved by his death, and on the river of death itself that all must cross. In part 1, Hopeful summarizes Christ's two-fold redemption: "I must look for righteousness in his person, and for satisfaction for my sins by his blood" (*PP,* 117). In part 2, after Christiana is dressed in new garments, "*fine Linnen, white and clean,*" she and her company "came to the place where *Christians* Burthen fell off his Back, and tumbled into a Sepulchre." And Great-heart tells her that her pardon too has been obtained by Christ "in this double way. He has performed Righteousness to cover you, and spilt blood to wash you in" (*PP,* 171–73).

When it comes to "the last things," Bunyan, in keeping with the book of Revelation, continues to develop the language of clothing. Revelation describes the rider on the white horse, who is "called Faithful and True . . . clothed with a vesture dipped in blood; and his name is called The Word of God"; he is followed by the army of those "clothed in fine linen, white and clean" (Rev. 19:11–14; cf. *CPW,* 6:486). And once Christian and Hopeful, in part 1, have crossed the River of Death, they find that they have "left their Mortal Garments behind them in the River" (*PP,* 129). Here Bunyan brilliantly renders his own, apocalyptic vision of paradise regained. The mortal body, like the burden of sin (*PP,* 31), which had likewise once seemed an integral part of Christian's being, now slips lightly from his shoulders like an unfastened bathrobe. But just as Adam and Eve's fig leaves were replaced with the typological animal skins of righteousness, so Christian and Hopeful, on their way now "to the Paradise of God," are promised "white Robes": "There also you shall be cloathed with Glory and Majesty, and put into an equipage fit to ride out with the King of Glory" (*PP,* 130).

Fitting Clothes, Telling Truths

Earlier I suggested that clothing also provides us with a metaphor that characterizes the practice and mission of Milton's and Bunyan's literary imaginations. The antithesis that this metaphor assumes is that between wholeness and brokenness—between, on the one hand, clothes-and-nakedness as a fused integrity, as implying one another, like the prelapsarian bodies of Adam and Eve, "clad / In naked Majesty"; and on the other hand nakedness as revealing want of clothing and want of righteousness, clothes as falsifying, disguising, mere tatters, rags, fig leaves, like "varnish on a Harlots cheek." Now in writing their *Hauptwerke*, Milton and Bunyan both have to strive, especially given the profoundly biblical nature of their subjects, to dress the Word decorously—in one sense to leave it naked; in another, but complementary sense, to clothe it both modestly and attractively. For them to render the Word other than naked, or to clothe it in "tinsel Trappings," would be to commit the sin of which Milton accuses the prelates, who put "roabs and surplices over the Gospel" (*CPW*, 1:828). Yet unless Milton and Bunyan clothe it somehow attractively in a way that does not disguise its true form, they fail in their vocation as ministers.[27]

Milton does not describe his undertaking in precisely these terms, though as the invocations in *Paradise Lost* make clear, his epic, in keeping with its "great Argument," must also be something more than an epic. Its inspiration—we might also say its pattern and its fabric—must derive from the Word, from the inspirer of the Bible itself (*PL*, 1.6–13). And as early as "On the Morning of Christ's Nativity," one has the clear sense of Milton the poet seeking to harmonize with the "holy Song" of the spheres, which can "Enwrap our fancy." In this Ode likewise Milton apocalyptically envisages Truth, Justice, and Mercy as being "clothed"—in the sign of the Noahic covenant— "Th'enamel'd *Arras* of the Rainbow wearing" (*Nat*, 131–35, 141–44).

Bunyan, having arrived at his "mode" for *The Pilgrim's Progress* almost by accident, has fewer resources than Milton with which to justify his allegory *sui generis*. But he does not lack biblical example nor, apparently, poetic wit and poetic conviction of his own. The attractiveness of his "mode" he defends with reference to the "fishers of men" metaphor from the Gospels (Matt. 4:19; Mark 1:7). Some fish "must be grop'd for, and be tickled too, / Or they will not be catcht, what e're you do" (*PP*, 3). Furthermore, he declares the possibility that truth may emerge in its integrity from what we might call fiction, from "feigning words": "Some men by feigning words as dark as mine, / Make truth to spangle, and its rayes to shine" (*PP*, 3). And he implies the humility of his project by identifying it with the simplicity of Truth itself: the impartial reader will

> take my meaning in these lines
> Far better then [the carper's] lies in Silver Shrines.
> Come, Truth, although in *Swadling-clouts*, I find
> Informs the Judgement, rectifies the Mind,
> Pleases the Understanding, makes the Will
> Submit; the Memory too it doth fill
> With what doth our Imagination please.
>   (*PP*, 5; italics added)

By thus identifying his "mode" with the "Swadling-clouts" that clothed the Word-become-flesh—with the very sign by which the shepherds should recognize the Christ-child (Luke 2:12)—Bunyan brilliantly establishes both the humility and the Christocentricity of his undertaking. Moreover, by identifying the incarnate Christ with the Truth, he indicates the "evangelical" hermeneutic whereby his allegory might best be read. He effectively implies, as Luther says in his *Preface to the New Testament*, that one should "not be searching for commandments and laws, when one should be looking for the Gospel and promise of God."[28]

This fundamentally Protestant, "evangelical" hermeneutic also explains, I think, much of the enduring vitality of both *Paradise Lost* and *The Pilgrim's Progress*. First, it teaches one, when reading biblical or biblically-based texts, to seek primarily not for propositions but for a person, the incarnation of divine promise. It emphasizes the Word less as words that express doctrine, and more as a *Verb* that unifies and brings it to life, creates syntax, makes the story hang together. How much the Reformation used "Word" as a noun standing both for Scripture and for Jesus Christ also indicates how deeply the medium and the Messiah were thought of (to exaggerate only slightly) as co-essential.[29] And for this reason, the message must not be deprived of its personhood. "Mind you don't make Christ into a Moses," warns Luther, "nor the Gospel into a book of law or doctrine."[30]

Furthermore, because the Bible is like that—personal and narrative—it encourages the production of other literature that focuses on persons, story, process. Thus Bunyan catalogs the Bible's use of "Dark figures, Allegories," "parables," "Types, Shadows and Metaphors" to justify his own literary mode, to declare the appropriateness of thus continuing to clothe the Truth:

> The Prophets used much by Metaphors
> To set forth Truth; Yea, who so considers

Christ, his Apostles too, shall plainly see,
That Truths to this day in such Mantles be.

(*PP,* 4)

Considering that the Christian faith centers on the "metaphor" of the *logos*, which was with God in the beginning, became flesh, and dwelt among us (John 1:1–14), it is not too surprising that among the most memorable Christian works expounding or "clothing" that faith are those which, like the Gospels themselves, are narrative, "incarnational," metaphorical.

On the other hand, only if we have a rather artificial, freeze-dried notion of what "theology" is, or if we treat its controversial details as if they constituted its essence, will we be compelled, as Gordon Campbell repeatedly does, to drive a wedge between poetry and theology. The superiority of *Paradise Lost* over *Christian Doctrine*, or of *The Pilgrim's Progress* over the flat doctrinal prose of *Some Gospel-Truths Opened*, demonstrates not the inferiority of "theological writing" but the inferiority of theology that excludes images, persons, events, and perhaps ambiguity. If Bunyan's theology is reduced to his uncritical reliance on nonbiblical material as if it were biblical, and to Campbell's tendentious rendering of Bunyan's "cruel God" and his "victims," then of course we will conclude that "Bunyan's imagination transcends his theological convictions."[31] If theology is weak or poor, let it be strengthened and enriched, not abandoned. Let it be clothed with imagination. But theology need not thereby be stripped of its name or its mission.

There are accordingly ways of complimenting Milton's and Bunyan's poetic powers without concluding, as Campbell does of *The Pilgrim's Progress*, that their imaginative works "create their own truths."[32] For Milton or Bunyan, indeed, such praise would vitiate and contradict their achievements, like clothes that *un*made the man or the woman, that displaced or disguised rather than enhanced or revealed their wearer. My aim is not to declare Milton's or Bunyan's works above criticism, or to hide them behind any merely dogmatic assertion of theological or poetic truth. Rather it is to suggest that those works be read as culminating their authors' radical Puritan, Protestant, "Evangelical," Christian mission to retell parts of the story that they believed all our brief chapters are bound up together with. And I think it is a measure of the achievement of Milton and Bunyan, as well as a measure of their profound kinship amid all differences, that in their greatest works *logos* and *mythos* (to use terms introduced by Milo Kaufmann)[33] are as nearly integrated as they are. Or to return to our primary metaphor, while *Paradise Lost* and *The Pilgrim's Progress* are indeed "mythic," they continue to unsettle us and to declare their own coherence by virtue of their proximity, like the "clouts" that swaddle the Truth in Bunyan's "Apology," to a *logos* we can recognize as wearing human flesh.[34]

Notes

1. C. S. Lewis, *The Great Divorce: A Dream* (London: Geoffrey Bles, 1946), 97–98; cf. 29. John Bunyan, *The Pilgrim's Progress*, ed. N. H. Keeble (Oxford: Oxford University Press, 1984), 1. Hereafter cited in the text as *PP* and page number.

2. William Blake captures beautifully this sense of the "integral" burden—he makes it appear almost like an attached tumor—in his *Christian Reading in His book*, in the Frick Collection, New York.

3. *"The Pilgrim's Progress": Critical and Historical Views*, ed. Vincent Newey (Liverpool: Liverpool University Press, 1980), 21.

4. For an effective summary of the early Reformation and especially of Luther's role in it, see James Kittelson, *Luther The Reformer: The Story of the Man and His Career* (Minneapolis, Minn.: Augsburg, 1986), chaps. 4–14.

5. George Carleton, *An Examination* (London, 1626), 5–6.

6. See Nicholas Tyacke, "Puritanism, Arminianism and Counter-Revolution," in *The Origins of the English Civil War*, ed. Conrad Russell (London: Macmillan, 1973), 119–43. Most Arminians did not reject "predestination" or "prevenient" grace, *pace* Gordon Campbell, "Fishing in Other Men's Waters: Bunyan and the Theologians," *John Bunyan: Conventicle and Parnassus: Tercentenary Essays*, ed. N. H. Keeble (Oxford: Clarendon Press, 1988), 147. Rather, they and orthodox Calvinists had differing interpretations of predestination and grace (both terms being biblical and hence authoritative).

7. See Milton, *CPW*, 6:118: "God . . . demands of us that any man who wishes to be saved should work out his beliefs for himself." See also Dayton Haskin's discussion of this issue in relation to both Milton and Bunyan, in "The Burden of Interpretation in *The Pilgrim's Progress*," *Studies in Philology* 79 (1982): 256–78.

8. Richard L. Greaves, *John Bunyan*, Courtenay Studies in Reformation Theology, 2 (Appleford: Sutton Courtenay Press, 1969), 23. Greaves is followed by Gordon Campbell, "The Theology of *The Pilgrim's Progress*," in Newey, 251.

9. *A Vindication of the Book called Some Gospel-Truths Opened* in *The Miscellaneous Works of John Bunyan*, gen. ed. Roger Sharrock (Oxford: Clarendon Press, 1988), 1: 34. This edition is hereafter cited as *Misc. W* with volume and page number.

10. *Grace Abounding to the Chief of Sinners*, ed. W. R. Owens (London: Penguin, 1987), 73.

11. John Clarke, *Paroemiologia Anglo-Latina . . . Or Proverbs English and Latine, methodically disposed according to the Common-place heads*, in *Erasmus his Adages* (London, 1639), 26. [STC #5360] See also James Whaler, "Animal Simile in *Paradise Lost*," *PMLA* 47 (1932): 544–45.

12. John Ford, *Christes Bloodie Sweat*, ed. D. Danielson, lines 277–82; in *The Non-Dramatic Works of John Ford*, ed. L. E. Stock et al. (Binghamton, N.Y.: MRTS, 1991). See also *The Book of Beasts: Being a Translation from a Latin Bestiary of the Twelfth Century*, ed. T. H. White (London: Jonathan Cape, 1954), 125–26.

13. See, for example, Joan S. Bennett, *Reviving Liberty: Radical Christian Humanism in Milton's Great Poems* (Cambridge: Harvard University Press, 1989), chap. 5: "For Milton, the Old Testament God is the New Testament God" (153).

14. See Georgia Christopher, "Milton and the Reforming Spirit," *The Cambridge Companion to Milton*, ed. Dennis Danielson (Cambridge: Cambridge University Press, 1989), 201.

15. T. R. Glover, "On the Permanence of *The Pilgrim's Progress*," *"The Pilgrim's Progress": A Casebook*, ed. Roger Sharrock (London: Macmillan, 1976), 121. For other complaints, see Robert Bridges in *Casebook*, 108; and Christopher Hill, *A Turbulent, Seditious, and Factious People: John Bunyan and his Church 1628–1688* (Oxford: Oxford University Press, 1988), 226–30.

16. A. J. A. Waldock, *"Paradise Lost" and Its Critics* (Cambridge: Cambridge University Press, 1947), 54–56.

17. Dennis Danielson, "Through the Telescope of Typology: What Adam Should Have Done," *Milton Quarterly* 23 (1989): 121–27.

18. N. H. Keeble, "Christiana's Key: The Unity of *The Pilgrim's Progress*," in Newey, 13.

19. Stanley Fish, *Surprised by Sin: The Reader in "Paradise Lost"* (1967; rpt. Berkeley: University of California Press, 1971), 92 ff.

20. The situation is reversed in "On the Morning of Christ's Nativity" (37–44), in which an "organic" covering—snow—covers an unholy object from a holy gaze. Nature "woos the gentle Air / To hide her guilty front with innocent Snow, . . . Confounded, that her Maker's eyes / Should look so near upon her foul deformities."

21. See my "Through the Telescope of Typology," cited above, and Ernst Guldan, *Eva und Maria: Eine Antithese also Bildmotif* (Graz and Cologne: Hermann Böhlaus, 1966), passim.

22. *Patrologia Latina*, ed. J. –P. Migne (Paris, 1844–80), 37:1785. See also Mary Ruth Brown, "*Paradise Lost* and John 15: Eve, the Branch and the Church," *Milton Quarterly* 20 (1986):127–31.

23. *The Works of John Bunyan*, ed. George Offor (Glasgow, 1860–62), 2: 427. Subsequent citations of the *Commentary* will likewise be from *Works* with volume and page number.

24. *Works*, 2: 432. Compare Bunyan, *The Pharisee and the Publican*, in *Miscs. W,* 10:161: "the true Gospel-teacher still . . . condemneth all [pharisaical] righteousness as to be *menstruous rags* . . . and nothing but loss and *dung*."

25. See Bunyan's catechism, *Instruction For the Ignorant*, in *Misc. W*, 8:12.

26. See also Greaves, *John Bunyan*, 39.

27. For a discussion of the "language of accommodation" in Milton and Bunyan, see Roland Mushat Frye, *God, Man, and Satan* (Princeton: Princeton University Press, 1960), chap. 1.

28. Luther, *Werke: Kritische Gesamtausgabe*; *Die Deutsche Bibel*, 6 (Weimar: Hermann Böhlaus, 1929): 2: "auff das er nicht gepott unnd gesetze suche, da er Evangeli unnd verheyssung Gottis suchen sollt."

29. See Georgia Christopher's discussion of how "one encounters the Real Presence in biblical promise," and of Luther's and Calvin's belief that Christ is "in" the biblical narratives; in *Milton and the Science of the Saints* (Princeton: Princeton University Press, 1982), 12.

30. Luther, *Die Deutsche Bibel* 6: 8: "Darumb sihe nu drauff, das du nit aus Christo eyn Mosen machist, noch aus dem Evangelio eyn gesetz oder lere buch."

31. Campbell, in Keeble, 138, 150, 148.

32. Campbell, in Newey, 261.

33. Milo Kaufmann, *The Pilgrim's Progress and Traditions in Puritan Meditation* (New Haven: Yale University Press, 1966), 9–15.

34. The clothing metaphor (which most likely has its roots in the etymology of the

word *text*: Lat. *textus*, "fabric," from the past participle of *texere*, "to weave") recurs often in sixteenth- and seventeenth-century discussions of the role of poetry. To cite but a few further examples: Sidney notes that "the senate of poets hath chosen verse as their fittest raiment"; and, attaching the covering even more tightly to the "body," he declares that "in the body of [Plato's] work, though the inside and strength were philosophy, the skin, as it were, and beauty depended most on poetry" (*A Defence of Poetry*, ed. Jan Van Dorsten [Oxford: Oxford University Press, 1973], 27, 19). In another variation, Donne in his Christmas sermon of 1621 exhorts one "*to search the Scriptures*, not as though thou wouldest make a *concordance*, but an *application*; as thou wouldest search a *wardrobe*, not to make an *Inventory* of it, but to finde in it something fit for thy wearing" (Potter and Simpson, 3:367). Clothing as a metaphor for literature appears at the heart of Herbert's "Jordan [2]": "Nothing could seem too rich to clothe the sun" (line 11). And Milton, in his *Prolusions*, refers to authors who transmitted their learning, "arraying them [all the sciences which are known today] in the charming cloak of fable"; and to Pythagoras, who "followed the example of the poets . . . who never display before the eyes of the vulgar any holy or secret mystery unless it be in some way cloaked or veiled" (*CPW*, 1:224, 235–36).

Milton, Dryden, and the
Politics of Literary Controversy

STEVEN ZWICKER

Questions of influence—of imitation and adaptation, of pedagogy
and admiration—exercise a steady interest for students of literary
relations; they seem especially appropriate when posed to relations
among writers who were contemporaries, perhaps acquaintances or
friends, intimates or collaborators: Eliot and Pound, Ford and Conrad, Coleridge and Wordsworth, Swift and Pope, Milton and Dryden.
But recent work on the relations between authors and among texts has
so complicated our notions of influence that the word itself seems
slightly worn. Indeed, the question of influence has come to imply
models of acquisition and contest that subsume and all but exclude
imitation and admiration. Without denying the older language, I want
here to consider "contest" as the shadow under which negotiations
between Milton and Dryden took place, to suggest that while adaptation and admiration describe aspects of Dryden's encounter with Milton—surely admiration inflects the lines that Dryden wrote for the
frontispiece portrait of the 1688 *Paradise Lost*[1]—it was contestation,
perhaps envy and denial, that rather more powerfully determined Milton's response to Dryden.

Notions of influence, of literary dominance and strong writing,
perhaps even literary histories of a slightly Whiggish cast, have so
long determined our reading of relations between Milton and Dryden
that it takes a special effort to allow the possibility of literary anxiety
moving in more than one direction during the 1660s.[2] We are ready
enough to concede the political anxiety that Cromwell's Latin Secretary felt after 25 May 1660, and we have become increasingly atten-
tive to the ways in which political anxiety and resistance are written
into Milton's great epic.[3] But having acknowledged the political qui-
etism, Milton's necessary revision of the politics of election after
1660, we often assume that Milton swept the literary field, that the

massive self-confidence of the opening lines of *Paradise Lost*, the poem's manifest ambition and majesty, determined the poet's dominance over the whole of midcentury literary endeavor. What we know of the reception and printing history of *Paradise Lost* resists such accounts of literary relations at midcentury; and yet knowing how the story would eventually be told, it is difficult to keep that knowledge at bay. Biographical sketches only confirm the familiar contours of the story. In such accounts, the protagonist is an aging republican beached on the shores of an alien culture, writing poetry that casts into doubt the very premise of Stuart court culture, and the antagonist is the ambitious new man aiming at success and sinecure from that court, but nervously acknowledging and sidestepping the master's great achievement. What better secures the model than Dryden's, shall we say ridiculous, adaptation of *Paradise Lost* as a rhymed heroic drama?

This story is a staple of our literary histories; it has been told often, and always to the same effect. In its sharpest renditions not only are we led to discover the diminution of epic into opera, but Milton's spiritual grandeur and generic ambitions are made everywhere to reflect on the laureate's servitude, his partisan allegories and satires, his fulsome prefaces, timeserving odes and panegyrics. In such accounts we are led to observe an anxious Dryden trying to maneuver bits of Milton into strategic corners of his own verse, and *Paradise Lost* is made to hover luminously or perhaps ominously over Dryden's whole career, the monument that blocked Dryden's own epic ambitions. In the renditions of Dryden's visit to Milton, we are asked to look on as the blind sage politely but contemptuously allows the eager neophyte—now in fact aged forty-one and both laureate and historiographer royal—to tag his verses.[4] Nor is the story an invention of our time; at its origin we might be surprised to find Dryden himself: "This Man Cuts us All Out," or so Jonathan Richardson reported of Dryden's response to *Paradise Lost*.[5]

If this were the only construction to be made of their relations, it would hardly be worth another recitation; perhaps a detail or two might be adjusted, another citing of *Paradise Lost* might be added to our store of borrowings and allusions.[6] But without reconceiving the outlines of the story, without adjusting the model to allow contestation and ambivalence running in both directions, it is familiar enough to forbid retelling. What I propose is to reconceive the story by narrating it, at first, from what I shall suggest might have been Milton's point of view. Like the familiar version of their relations, this is a story of influence and anxiety; it begins, however, with Milton's nerves. And the anxiety of influence, since it has been told of Dryden,

I want to attribute to Milton, to suggest why Dryden might have made
Milton nervous, where in Milton's work the anxiety might be confronted, and how it might have shaped his masterpiece *Paradise
Regained*. For I want to suggest that *Paradise Regained* is a response
to something other and more formidable than Thomas Ellwood's
"Thou hast said much here of Paradise Lost, but what hast thou to say
of Paradise Found?";[7] that Milton orchestrates not only a variety of
sacred themes, rewriting the Book of Job and the Gospels, but that he
also wished to engage, indeed to put into question, to controvert the
formidable literary challenge posed by the new drama and the astonishing career of its foremost apologist, theorist, and practitioner, John
Dryden. Milton shaped his brief epic, in part, as an answer to, and a
repudiation of, the heroic drama: its rhyming couplets, its bombast
and cant, its aristocratic code of virtue and honor, its spectacle and
rhetoric, its scenes and stage machinery, its exotic lands and erotic
intrigues, its warring heroes and virgin queens, its exaltation of passion and elevation of empire. Milton conceived *Paradise Regained* as
a drama in the form of an epic in order to display "deeds above heroic," while demonstrating what literary mode might best express heroic
virtue, and how heroic colloquy ought truly to sound. I want, that is,
to readjust the story of literary relations in the late 1660s to allow the
contestatory force of *Paradise Regained*, its challenge to the form,
style, and ethos of the heroic drama, to its theoretical defense of the
form, and to Dryden's astonishing career as the central protagonist of
a new literary culture, its laureate, a commercial and critical success
beyond anything that Milton had experienced or could now hope to
achieve.

Of Milton's anxieties over the new drama and its defence, there can
I think be no doubt.[8] It would be wrong to suggest that Milton had lost
control over the tone of his headnote to *Paradise Lost*, but surely his
remarks on rhyme have an odd and urgent ring. If Milton were defensive in 1668 as he prepared the remarks on blank verse and rhyme, it
was with some reason.[9] Who among the English, Italian, or French
epic poets had written a blank verse epic poem? All had chosen
rhyme. But consider this language, "rhyme being. . . the Invention of
a barbarous Age, to set off wretched matter and lame metre" (Hughes
210), and note the proud political gesture at the close where Milton
argues *Paradise Lost* as an epic of "ancient liberty" and explicates that
powerful term by glossing rhyme as "troublesome and modern
bondage." The extraordinary combativeness of the headnote signals
not only a generic and formal sensitivity, but suggests as well that
Milton had hold of a very large cultural project in his repudiation of
rhyme. In the delineation of that project, rhyme was a key term, but it

was only one term. For what the diffuse epic of 1667 and the brief epic of 1671 attempt is a full definition and demonstration of heroic action and the literary forms best suited to its enactment and display. In the prefatory note on verse, *Paradise Lost* is explicitly pitched into contest with classical and continental models, and yet more pointedly, it is positioned against a very powerful and articulate literary world identified by the discourse on rhyme.[10] But it is more than tone that surprises in the headnote; it is also the presence of the drama. In mapping the critical terrain for *Paradise Lost* we might well have expected Spenser, the Fletchers, Davenant, or Cowley, but Milton's concentration on rhyme, that key term in the defense of the new drama, reveals a particular and peculiar alignment, not with English epic poetry but with English blank verse tragedy. The odd skewing came about not because *Paradise Lost* is a blank verse *tragedy*, but because the poem is positioned in relation to its own literary culture, that of the mid– and late–1660s. The primary contexts that Milton summoned for *Paradise Lost* are Scripture and classical poetry; but the inventions of a barbarous age also comprise a setting for *Paradise Lost*, one rather fractiously admitted by the headnote on verse.

The companion piece to the note on verse added to the 1668 issue of *Paradise Lost* is the prefatory "Of that sort of Dramatic Poem which is called Tragedy," printed with the first issue of *Paradise Regained and Samson Agonistes* (1671). The note prefaces *Samson Agonistes*, but it signals for the whole volume Milton's continuing engagement with the heroic drama: "This is mention'd to vindicate Tragedy from the small esteem, or rather infamy, which in the account of many it undergoes at this day with other common Interludes; happ'ning through the Poet's error of intermixing Comic stuff with Tragic sadness and gravity; or introducing trivial and vulgar persons, which by all judicious hath been counted absurd; and brought in without discretion, corruptly to gratify the people. And though ancient Tragedy use no Prologue, yet using sometimes, in case of self defense, or explanation, that which *Martial* calls an Epistle; in behalf of this Tragedy coming forth after the ancient manner, much different from what among us passes for best, thus much beforehand may be Epistl'd. . . ." (Hughes 550) What is then epistled is the modeling of verse and stanza on classical and Italian examples and some fairly routine remarks on the unities. *Paradise Regained* lacks a preface, but both the 1668 preface to *Paradise Lost* and the note for *Samson Agonistes* function on behalf of *Paradise Regained*, announcing the presence of the heroic drama as a continuous literary context for Milton's late work.

The development of a new dramatic genre and, more generally, the reinvigoration of the stage dominated the production of literature and literary theory in the 1660s. The polemical verse of the mid–1660s, a form most brilliantly practiced by Marvell in *The Last Instructions to a Painter*, predicts the genius of satire for the whole of Restoration culture, but for writers in the 1660s, the dominant form was the heroic drama. It was practiced, imitated, praised, defended, defined, and finally canonized in Buckingham's *Rehearsal*. And though the form was loosely identified with a group of aristocrats and courtiers—Sir Robert Howard, Sir William Davenant, and Roger Boyle, Earl of Orrery—its hero was John Dryden. It was Dryden who theorized the form in a series of works beginning with *An Essay of Dramatic Poesy* (1668) and culminating in *Of Heroic Plays* (1672), and it was Dryden whose work was most completely identified with the new drama through theatrical production and publication: *The Indian Queen* (1664/1665); *The Indian Emperor* (1665/1667); *Tyrannick Love; or, The Royal Martyr* (1669/1670); *The Conquest of Granada* (1670–71/1672); and *Aureng-Zebe* (1675–76).

It may be difficult from our distance quite to appreciate the impact of the heroic drama on courtly and popular culture in the first decade of the Restoration, but it is not difficult to imagine Milton's sensitivity to the new form. His interest in dramatic forms and themes was long-standing;[11] *Comus* and *Samson* witness the early and late public engagement and experimentation with theatrical forms, but the Trinity College manuscript in which Milton records schemes for the theater is also crucial. Thought to date from the early 1640s, the manuscript discovers Milton thinking on Old Testament tragedies, on New Testament theater, and on several British and Scottish topics. Milton identifies various scriptural and national themes, but the notes also display a vivid theatrical imagination: the severities of Greek choric tragedy but as well a theater rather more luxurious in its deployment of scenes and machines—angels girt with flame; the burning and destruction of cities and temples; slaughter, battle, and mayhem; witchcraft and ghosts. The Trinity manuscript also reveals Milton's interest in theatrical music and song, hymns, masques, dances, and allegories. His heroes are drawn after the examples of God's servants, prophets, and witnesses; but Milton also imagines a rather more spectacular theater, centered in murder, lust, and mayhem, and figuring the defeat of tyrants, the martyrdom of Christians.

Some of the dramas are set in ancient Israel, but there are also pastoral settings, monasteries and nunneries, battlefields, and castles where Milton's casts are imagined in combat and intrigue as well as in revelry and adulterous union. His casts include warrior kings, princes, and heroes; noble ladies and ravished virgins; whores and concubines; and whole armies of Saxons, Angles, Northumbrians, and Danes. Milton drew from several sources: Bede, Geoffrey of Monmouth, Holinshed, and Speed as well as myth and sacred history. But the shorthand multiplicity of these notes looks less like a considered plan for a historical drama than sketches for an epic theater. The settings do not quite rival the exotic realms of the Restoration epic theater, but distance and antiquity are clear effects in Milton's sketches; so too is the epic dimension of Milton's theater: love and honor are prominent among his themes, and heroic action is the aim of theatrical representation. Here is Milton musing on epic theater set in Alfred's reign: "A Heroicall Poem may be founded somwhere in Alfreds reigne. especially at his issuing out of Edelingsey on the Danes. whose actions are wel like those of Ulysses" (*CPW*, 8:571). Tragedy on the Greek model is among Milton's preoccupations, but just as clearly epic drama is another, a theater that would compact diffuse action, heighten the themes of virtue and honor, alternate and redeem love with combat. Such had been Milton's notions for an epic theater in the early 1640s; and such a theater was preeminent among the aims of the heroic drama as it was shaped by Dryden in theory and practice over the first decade of the Restoration. How else could Milton have responded but with intense curiosity and competitiveness when a form suddenly appeared in the mid–1660s that claimed to do exactly what had preoccupied him in the 1640s and toward which he had made his own notes and plans? It is the very engagement signaled in the prefaces to *Paradise Lost* and *Samson Agonistes*, and in the construction of that heroic drama cast as brief epic, exploring and redefining the themes of love and empire, the nature of glory, the uses of wealth and wisdom, observing the unities, spare in style and severe in manner, which Milton published in 1671 under the name of *Paradise Regained*.

By the rather slow standards of literary evolution, the heroic drama looks like an instantaneous creation; but it was not produced full blown from Dryden's imagination. According to Dryden's own history of the genre, Davenant provided the initial model in *The Siege of Rhodes*, heroic drama disguised as opera to escape censorship in 1656 and then refashioned in 1662 as "a just drama" in rhyming couplets.[12] Dryden's theorizing of the genre begins with the defense of rhyme for the stage in the preface to *The Rival Ladies* (1664): rhyme offers the advantages of rapidity, grace, point, sweetness and beauty; it "bounds and circumscribes the fancy"; without rhyme the imagination grows luxuriant (*Essays*, 1:8, 96). The arguments are developed in *The Essay of Dramatic Poesy* (1665/1668), but even in the preface to *The Rival Ladies* the strength of the defense is surprising. What it lacks in 1664 is the assertion of a new dramatic idiom; and that comes with the

Essay, the last quarter of which is devoted to a debate over the rival literary claims of rhyme and blank verse. Dryden's management of the argument in favor of rhyme is well known, as is the rivalry here begun with Sir Robert Howard which, through the 1660s, takes rhyme as its overt subject. For our immediate purposes, however, it is the connection that Dryden makes between rhyme and the *new* literary mode that presents the most sensitive issue, for that explicit declaration of modernity brings us to what must have been the pressure point for Milton.

In contending with that age of giants—Jonson, Fletcher, and Shakespeare—Dryden stakes his claim with the moderns: "either not to write at all, or to attempt some other way. There is no bays to be expected in their walks: *tentanda via est, qua me quoque possum tollere humo*" (*Essays,* 1:99). The tag from Virgil might well remind the reader that Dryden's is an informed radicalism, but the flag of novelty, argued out of a rather melodramatic literary desperation, flies high over this literary camp: "We acknowledge them our fathers in wit; but they have ruined their estates themselves, before they came to their children's hands. There is scarce an humour, a character, or any kind of plot, which they have not blown upon. All comes sullied or wasted to us; and were they to entertain this age, they could not make so plenteous treatment out of such decayed fortunes . . . . This way of writing in verse they have only left free to us"; the way, that is, of rhymed heroic drama, the "serious plays written since the King's return . . . *The Siege of Rhodes, Mustapha, The Indian Queen,* and *Indian Emperor*" (*Essays,* 1:99–100). Heroic rhyme, Dryden argues, is "the noblest kind of modern verse"; and here Dryden puts into direct contest rhyme and blank verse, a mode "too low for a poem, nay more, for a paper of verses; but if too low for an ordinary sonnet, how much more for Tragedy, which is by Aristotle, in the dispute betwixt the epic poesy and the dramatic, for many reasons he there alleges, ranked above it?" (*Essays,* 1:101)

It would have been difficult to invent a literary program more galling to Milton in the mid–1660s than the one sketched here with its aggressive modernism, elevation of drama above epic, fluent alignment with Latin literary culture, celebration of court taste, and attack on blank verse. I suspect that Milton was galled as well by the casual elegance of the prose, a style he may not have affected but one that was clearly not native to his talent. But more than the elegant and knowing manner of the *Essay,* it is the program of rhymed heroic drama here first enunciated, that must at once have angered Milton and caused a sense of despair, as if the last boat had just sailed, a craft not only missed by Milton but one he had already determined was not even in the race. Of course, Milton had had some experience as the prophet of lost causes; he composed and published *The Ready and Easie Way* within weeks of Charles Stuart's restoration. Dryden's enunciation of the new drama together with its triumph on the London stage created another circumstance in which Milton must have felt that he was pitching his tent in a whirlwind.[13] How else are we to understand the banked fury and contempt of the prefatory note to *Paradise Lost*? But Milton's encounter with the heroic drama was hardly over when he had added the angry note on verse to his epic. The encounter had a deeper and more lasting form in the poems of 1671: in the repudiatory challenges of the note prefatory to *Samson*, in the choric forms and gestures of the drama, and I think most intriguingly and most subtly in the brief epic. It is almost as if Milton anticipated in *Paradise Regained* the formula Dryden would achieve in the *Essay of Heroic Plays*: "an heroic play ought to be an imitation, in little, of an heroic poem" (*Essays*, 1:150). That imitation in little—compact, "no time was then / For long indulgence to their fears and grief" (*PR*, 1.109–10), observant of the unities, redefining love and valor—is *Paradise Regained*.

Milton's brief epic has not had an easy or an appreciative critical history. Its identity as sequel to *Paradise Lost* contributes, of course, to the difficulty—as literary project it seems in no way sequential to the diffuse epic—but the brief epic presents barriers to appreciation in ways quite independent of its relation to *Paradise Lost*. It is not brevity, exactly, that presents the problems; it is rather the poem's severity that has been at the heart of resistance. Despite critical appreciation of its variety of figurative speech, the levels and patterning of Milton's rhetoric, the poem's metrical subtlety, *Paradise Regained* remains so insistently and programmatically fixed in the plain style, that defenses of the poem's art seem almost plaintive, votive exercises in special pleading. To rescue the stylistic program of *Paradise Regained* by appreciating the rhetorical flair and figurative richness of its bleached pages seems wholly to miss the contestative energy of this poem, a program that begins to come clear when we observe the style conjoined to that other striking feature of the epic, its dramatic form. The poem is more than three-quarters dramatic colloquy, and nothing in the literary models that have been adduced for the brief epic—from Sannazaro and Marino to Aylett or Fletcher—prepares us for the poem as drama.[14] *Paradise Regained* does not simply fall into dramatic colloquy or occasionally deploy the unities: the poem is designed for their display, it engages in the most central concerns of drama as they had been debated from Aristotle's *Poetics* through Sidney's *Defence of Poesy*, and as they were once again under scrutiny in the lively critical forum that fostered the creation of the heroic drama.

Paradise Lost makes brilliant use of soliloquy and colloquy, but we do not for a moment doubt its epic gestures, its conjuring of Homer and Virgil, its broad scope and epic themes. This is hardly the case with *Paradise Regained* whose technical features so clearly suggest the drama that some critics argue the poem's origins as a drama originally written near the time of the Trinity manuscript.[15] Yet, despite the density of colloquy, the thrust of point and counterpoint in the temptations, the poem as drama is framed by a narrative voice that balances one set of generic imperatives against another. Part of the effect is the familiar Miltonic mixture of genres, though the generic interplay in *Paradise Regained* is narrower and sharper than in *Paradise Lost*.[16] Here the center of generic mixture is drama and epic with occasional adversion to pastoral. Yet the density of dramatic effect is overwhelming. None of Milton's contemporaries asked permission to dramatize *Paradise Regained*, but it would have been less daunting than the task Dryden assumed in *The State of Innocence*. Not only had Milton created soliloquy and dialogue: he also very nearly provided copy text for production. A small cast and unities of time, action, and—by means of Satan's optic skill—place suggest the technical and aesthetic requirements of the stage more exactly than they accommodate the models of brief epic.

The poem begins with generic signals: the allusions to *Paradise Lost*, to Virgil and Spenser, give certain definition at the outset of the journey; and yet the modesty of the invocation and Milton's immediate qualifying of the epic cast of poem and hero—"obscure, / Unmarkt, unknown" and "deeds / Above heroic, though in secret done" (*PR*, 1.24–25, 14–15)—not only remind us of Milton's earlier contest with epic heroism but also anticipate the unfolding temptations that argue, with great clarity, that while epic may be the formal genre, the poem intends to subject the genre to severe scrutiny, to formal challenge, and to moral redefinition. So much we have come to expect from Milton, but the redefinition of epic is so radical here that the formal composition of the poem seems almost wholly to deny epic expectations. Combat and empire are the familiar idioms of epic poetry, even when they are subsumed by and spiritualized in the vast design of *Paradise Lost*, but this brief epic will insist on static denial, on inwardness, submission, and patience, on perseverance, "Humiliation and strong Suffrance" (*PR*, 1.160), on poverty and solitude as epic conditions and attributes. Here simplicity defeats cunning; plain style subverts guile and double sense; weakness overcomes a martial foe. The encounter is heroic: from Satan's perspective the contest is epic battle. But Christ's idiom is meditative, his weapons are instruction and high thoughts. With each temptation and each denial we are further distanced from the familiar landscape, both literal and literary, of the epic mode. Against pomp, state, and regal mystery, the stylized architecture of heroic poetry and heroic drama, against "Palaces adorn'd, / Porches and Theaters, Baths, Aqueducts, / Statues and Trophies, and Triumphal Arcs," "Turrets and Terraces, and glittering Spires" (*PR*, 4.35–37; 54), Milton contrasts Christ's "Cottage low," "Sheepcote" (*PR*, 2.28, 287), and private house (*PR*, 4.639). The heroic landscape of this poem is "barren waste," a "pathless Desert, dusk with horrid shades" (*PR*, 1.354, 296), and the battle of epic attributes is waged between the hero who "reigns within himself" (*PR*, 2.466) and a tyrant who would "Subject himself to Anarchy within, / Or lawless passions" (*PR*, 2.471–2). To identify kingship with sexual luxury, to discover the passions lurking in "Courts and Regal Chambers" (*PR*, 2.183), is more than to glance at the fabled sexual indulgence of Charles II's court—a subject brilliantly, indelibly etched in the satires of the mid–1660s—but the broad references to abstinence and constancy, to the regulation of the will and the passions, also have a literary target, for Milton's hero counterpoints both the historical figure and the literary representation of outlandish passions.

The aesthetic challenge is posed by such allusions and applications, by Milton's shaping of the satanic colloquies, and directly by that last and most controversial of the temptations, the arts and eloquence of classical antiquity. The final temptation frames Milton's poignant address to literary culture; it also enfolds a review of literary types that suggests the generic dilemma Milton faced and solved with *Paradise Regained*.

The formal structure of the last temptation is announced at its opening: "Look once more . . . behold . . . *Athens*, the eye of *Greece*" (*PR*, 4.236–40). The vision that follows is divided between the aesthetic and the rhetorical modes; the rationale for the temptation to rhetorical skill is obvious enough, and Satan provides the necessary links between rhetoric and politics:

> And with the *Gentiles* much thou must converse,
> Ruling them by persuasion as thou mean'st,
> Without thir learning how wilt thou with them,
> Or they with thee hold conversation meet?
> How wilt thou reason with them, how refute
> Their Idolisms, Traditions, Paradoxes?
> Error by his own arms is best evinc't.
> Look once more, ere we leave this specular Mount,
> Westward, much nearer by Southwest, behold

> Where on the *Aegean* shore a City stands
> Built nobly, pure the air, and light the soil,
> *Athens*, the eye of *Greece*, Mother of Arts
> And Eloquence.
>
> <div align="right">(<i>PR</i>, 4.229–41)</div>

Though the temptation to the powers of oratory does not belong to the Gospel, the idea that rhetoric, and more particularly political rhetoric, should constitute half the final temptation is an obvious expression of Milton's long engagement with the role of rhetoric in the constitution of the just state. The temptation to rhetorical power is, moreover, anticipated by the opening lines of book 4 where Satan waxes nostalgic over the powers of "persuasive Rhetoric / That sleek't his tongue, and won so much on *Eve*" (*PR*, 4.4–5); the defeat of Satan reprises the Fall in detail. Nor is the culminating position of rhetoric in these temptations hard to decide in formal and aesthetic terms, for rhetorical skill and philosophical authority are the most abstracted of temptations. The line of ascent from the feast in the wilderness to Demosthenes and Pericles, Socrates and Plato is clear enough.

What is not quite so clear, though it exercises a crucial and climactic role in Satan's temptations, as in Milton's poem, is the role of the literary genres in such an argument:

>   within the walls then view
> The schools of ancient Sages: his who bred
> Great *Alexander* to subdue the world,
> *Lyceum* there, and painted *Stoa* next;
> There thou shalt hear and learn the secret power
> Of harmony in tones and numbers hit
> By voice or hand, and various-measur'd verse,
> *Aeolian* charms and *Dorian Lyric* Odes,
> And his who gave them breath, but higher sung,
> Blind *Melesigenes* thence *Homer* call'd,
> Whose Poem *Phoebus* challeng'd for his own.
> Thence what the lofty grave Tragedians taught
> In *Chorus* or *Iambic*, teachers best
> Of moral prudence, with delight receiv'd
> In brief sententious precepts, while they treat
> Of fate, and chance, and change in human life,
> High actions, and high passions best describing.
>
> <div align="right">(<i>PR</i>, 4.250–66)</div>

The temptation of classical eloquence is linked to the schooling of Alexander the Great, Milton's acknowledgement of the relations between arts and empire. The passage that follows from Milton's invocation of that "secret power / Of harmony in tones and numbers" seems like free-standing praise of attic literary modes. Nor is such panegyric surprising from the greatest literary classicist of the English Renaissance. What is of course surprising is that the panegyric is issued not by the narrator but by the tempter, that it is Satan who sings these praises of classical literary culture. The temptation to eloquence is not of course part of the Gospel account; moreover, it is difficult to see how exactly to accommodate literary eloquence, attic or modern, to Satan's other schemes. That this particular temptation must therefore be accommodated to Milton's biography is obvious, but the ways in which it is autobiographical are not; rather than dismiss the models of classical antiquity, Milton had long admired and practiced them. And while the rejection of gentile wisdom is not difficult to grasp when we have allowed the consoling intervention of theology, the rejection of classical antiquity as a cultural model is not so neatly adjudicated by theology. Finally, the arrangement of genres—love poetry, pastoral, ode, epic, and tragedy—is slightly unusual in the setting of this poem, for epic here is superseded by tragedy. And the allusion to tragedy, by comparison with Milton's treatment of the other genres, is surprisingly full. Moreover, in Christ's counterpointing of Greek by Hebrew literary genres—hymns and psalms, Hebrew songs and harps, for "various-measur'd verse" and *"Dorian Lyric Odes"*—he offers nothing from Scripture with which to answer the claims of drama. Earlier we hear of "Celestial measures," of "Odes and Vigils tun'd" (*PR*, 1.169, 182)—perhaps these are the divine counterpart to *"Sion's* songs" (*PR*, 4.347). Christ's dismissive reference to "swelling Epithets, thick-laid / As varnish on a Harlot's cheek" (*PR*, 4.343–4) surely glosses Greek epic; but what is summoned to answer the lofty tragedians? If Milton is replaying, in Christ's answer to the arts and eloquence of Greece, his own confrontation with and triumph over classical genres, from pastoral elegy through Homeric epic, it was not until publication of *Paradise Regained and Samson Agonistes* that he could have felt the colloquy with classical antiquity complete. *Samson Agonistes* is part of the answer—so much is obvious—and its choric method and exacting echoes of Greek tragedy juxtapose the Hebraic spirit against and perfect the Attic model.

Paradise Regained is the second part of Milton's response to the challenge posed by tragedy; but here the model of Greek drama is extended, not to say distorted, by the latest innovation of the Restoration stage, the heroic drama. Rewriting classical tragedy had been made a task especially urgent through the triumph of the heroic drama: its swooning excesses, its rhetoric, and its rhymes, and not least by the drama's exaltation of a court whose acts and ethos were celebrated in the guise of exotic emperors and queens, and whose military adventurism had been puffed by a newly dignified laureate who dominated the Restoration theater, using its forms to shadow under such names as Achilles and Almanzor the debauched principals of that court and to replay, in the most exaggerated of manner, its corruption, its moral squalor, its manners, arms, and arts. Satan's offer of classical literary eloquence reprises Milton's recovery of and triumph over the forms of classical literary antiquity; but in the case of tragedy, a form that he had not attempted until the composition of *Samson Agonistes*, Milton faced a particularly vexing challenge, for he needed to outgo not only the classical model, but also to triumph over and correct the contemporary enactment of that mode. The radical answer that he now proposed was a poem challenging the heart of the drama not by accepting the outward form, but by mimicking and inverting its devices, at once acknowledging the gauntlet laid down by ancient and modern drama and rejecting utterly its premises and central modes of expression.

That Milton did not shy of competition is clear from the obvious and forthright challenges the poet issued in those highly exposed invocations to *Paradise Lost*; it is evident as well in the allusions to and adumbrations of Homer and Virgil, Ovid and Horace, his Italian predecessors, and his near-contemporaries Spenser, Shakespeare, Jonson, and the Fletchers. But when we come closer to the home Milton had to make after 1660 in a literary London that could not have been much to his taste, it is not difficult to imagine the ambiguities folded within his sense of literary competition, or to think that Milton may have been reluctant to acknowledge the promise, the fluency, the literary sophistication of his younger contemporaries, or the considerable challenge offered by the most fluent and the most sophisticated of those contemporaries, John Dryden. So much is to cross familiar territory. The argument that I have tried to make concerning Milton's contestation of the heroic drama allows not only the poet's competition but also suggests, I hope, some of its aesthetic consequences. Milton created an exacting, a severe, and a beautifully controlled poem, in response not only to his own sense of canon and career but as well to that most extravagant of contemporary literary forms. Nor does it matter how many of those among Milton's audience would have understood that *Paradise Regained* was shaped by Milton's argument, in the most and least exalted senses of that word, with texts calling themselves *The Siege of Rhodes*, *Mustapha*, *The Conquest of Granada*, or *The Indian Emperor* and *The Indian Queen*. Nor was Milton concerned to address himself to one such production in particular; he surely could not have thought them individually worth the dignity of *Paradise Regained*. But to save the idiom, to refurbish the epic drama, such an ideal was worthy of his address. And to that ideal he gave himself in a book containing *Paradise Regained* and *Samson Agonistes*.

But to attribute those competitive impulses to Milton alone, to adjust the story of literary relations between the two greatest poets of the later seventeenth century by suggesting that only Milton combined the higher kinds of literary ambition with less sublime forms of competition and contestation, is perhaps to apply a corrective that renders the relations of Milton and Dryden difficult to recognize. And I want to close by allowing the circumstances and aspects of *The State of Innocence* that comprehend both the higher and lower forms of the question about literary relations with which we began.

Perhaps Dryden had made Milton's acquaintance during the 1650s; we know that both, together with Andrew Marvell (who turns up later, triangulating the relations between Milton and Dryden), walked in the funeral cortege for Cromwell;[17] and we know by anecdote of Dryden's response to the copy of *Paradise Lost* that Dorset had sent him in 1669. But Dryden's first extended meditation on Milton's poetry came with his adaptation of *Paradise Lost*. Again by anecdote, we know of Dryden's visit to Milton.[18] The results were mixed. It is impossible to know what Dryden thought he was doing in choosing to render the epic as opera, but we can sense some defensiveness about the results. At first, the text of *The State of Innocence* was not published; perhaps it was intended for performance at the Duke of York's marriage to Mary of Modena.[19] When it was published, Dryden fixed to his text an "Author's Apology for Heroic Poetry and Poetic Licence" and a *Dedication* to the new Duchess of York, a dedication that outgoes the panegyric idiom of all his dedicatory prose. As we have come to expect from the materials with which Dryden surrounds his poems and plays, these texts make a surprising and fascinating context for and commentary on the works themselves.

First, the more conventional of the pieces, the "Apology"; as in the earlier defenses of the heroic drama, Dryden celebrates the nobility and profusion of the form. He aligns the heroic drama with Greek tragedy and defends what have, by this date, become standard targets: its boldness of language, its excessive figures, its interrogations, exclamations, and hyperbata, its "disordered connection of discourse."[20] Yet more intriguing is Dryden's defense of *Paradise Lost* against these charges, his denial that Milton's poem is guilty of those lapses of taste, "strained . . . all fustian, and mere nonsense" (*Works,* 5:116). If Dryden had seen Milton's prefatory notes to *Paradise*

Regained and to *Samson Agonistes*, he may be indulging, by defending *Paradise Lost*, a taste for revenge here: not directly answering Milton's accusations, but rather aligning Milton with and indeed praising him for the very excesses he had deplored.

But Dryden also suggests some uneasiness over the text of *The State of Innocence*; he claims that he has been forced to publish the work because so many pirated and false copies have been put in circulation, "I was also induced to it [publication] in my own defence; many hundred copies of it being dispersed abroad without my knowledge, or consent: so that every one gathering new faults, it became at length a libel against me; and I saw, with some disdain, more nonsense than either I, or as bad a poet, could have crammed into it, at a month's warning; in which time it was wholly written, and not since revised. After this, I cannot, without injury to the deceased author of "Paradise Lost," but acknowledge, that this poem has received its entire foundation, part of the design, and many of the ornaments, from him. What I have borrowed will be so easily discerned from my mean productions, that I shall not need to point the reader to the places: And truly I should be sorry, for my own sake, that any one should take the pains to compare them together; the original being undoubtedly one of the greatest, most noble, and most sublime poems which either this age or nation has produced" (*Works,* 5:111–12).

We need not doubt Dryden's admiration any more than we should have difficulty glossing the lovely self-deprecation; just as certainly, some of the anxiety that Dryden expresses about false copies of his text represents a genuine nervousness about fitting Milton's epic into the confines of his opera. But my suspicion is that we have still not unfolded all the work here, that Dryden's anxiety was driven not only by the sublimity of Milton's poem but also by his hostility to *Paradise Lost*, perhaps even by his fear that the hostility was all too obvious in the adaptation he had made. *The State of Innocence* may not have been adequate to the task as we would wish he had understood it, but it may have been quite adequate to the job that Dryden wanted to do on *Paradise Lost*. Moreover, it is difficult to believe that if we find Dryden's text trivializing, domesticating, perhaps ridiculous or comic, the poet himself could have been wholly insensitive to those possibilities. Perhaps Dryden's remark that the circulating copies had become "a libel" on him betrays a sensitivity to textual corruption, but it may also reveal the poet's admission that he had been only too well understood, perhaps that he was content to have managed this comic diminution.

And what are we to make of Dryden's dedication? Having chosen to render the greatest work of this most sublime poet in operatic form, having taken this theologically dense argument of Protestant radicalism, this poetic statement of republican utopianism, and having eradicated both its politics and theology, Dryden then proceeded to lay his opera at the feet of a fifteen-year-old Roman Catholic, princess of the Este House, niece of Louis XIV, bride of the Duke of York—in 1674 the most famous and the most feared Roman Catholic in England.[21] If this were not enough, the Dedication is a continuous rapture over the beauty and virtue of this Catholic princess, a panegyric that indulges not simply the conventional excesses of courtly praise but conjures the language of Roman Catholic baroque;[22] Dryden exalts the mystery and glory of her beauty and virtue in an idiom that he adopts pointedly from the writings of St. Theresa.[23] Mary's beauty is a sacred revelation, a "mystery left behind" to express God's perfection: "I confess myself too weak for the inspiration: the priest was always unequal to the oracle: the god within him was too mighty for his breast: he laboured with the sacred revelation, and there was more of the mystery left behind than the divinity itself could enable him to express. I can but discover a part of your excellence to the world; . . . Like those who have surveyed the moon by glasses, I can only tell of a new and shining world above us, but not relate the riches and glories of the place" (*Works,* 5:103). The temptation when faced with such language is always to quote Jonson's quip on the *Anniversaries*: "If it had been written of the Virgin Mary it had been something."[24] If this were not quite enough, Dryden next turns to the Duke, "a prince who only could deserve you; whose conduct, whose constancy to his friends, whose bounty to his servants, whose justice to merit, whose inviolable truth, and whose magnanimity in all his actions, seem to have been rewarded by Heaven by the gift of you" (*Works,* 5:104).[25] And if this were not quite enough, Dryden toys with the familiar idioms of popish politics: "You render mankind insensible to other beauties, and have destroyed the empire of love in a court which was the seat of his dominion. You have subverted (may I dare to accuse you of it?) even our fundamental laws; and reign absolute over the hearts of a stubborn and freeborn people, tenacious almost to madness of their liberty" (*Works,* 5:105–6).

This may remind us of Milton's application of the language of bondage and liberty to heroic verse in the prefatory note to *Paradise Lost*. But we need not hear that echo to find Dryden's Dedication an astonishing way in which to pay court to the new princess. Dryden's language is at once daring and wry; but even if the wonderful exaggeration of the passage is understood as part of the complimentary manner, the choice of political idioms is not. And there are two kinds of work the passage performs, one related to Dryden's patronage relationship with this particular branch of the Stuart court, the other bearing on the more intimate matter of Dryden's relation to Milton. Perhaps in working through the idioms of patronage and praise Dryden was indulging in a bit of scandalous flirtation; he all but dares his audience to apply the praise of Mary's beauty to the danger of a Roman Catholic succession, a succession quite clear by 1674 both in the obvious barrenness of Charles II's marriage and in the now public Roman Catholicism of the Duke of York and his bride.[26] The idioms of popery and absolutism would be violently stirred a few years later during Exclusion, but even in 1674 the language is daring, the tone—hovering between amusement and contempt for public fears—difficult exactly to fix. This, then, is a piece of service. But there is another kind of service that Dryden indulges in relation to the poet whose work he had adapted. To dedicate Milton's work to James and Mary, to exalt the virtue and honor of this particular Catholic prince and his new bride, is to subject *Paradise Lost* to an astonishing application and to subjugate Milton's Protestant poetry and poetics in a most humiliating way. For Dryden to prepare an adaptation of Milton's epic for the marriage festivities of the Duke of York and then to preface the printed text with such a dedication is not simply to neglect the ideology of his great original or to indulge in a recondite form of ridicule, it is utterly to deny its spiritual and ideological authority.

Of course Dryden's relations with Milton went beyond the literary events of 1673–74, and he returns to Milton's poetry at different times and in quite different moods. The comments on *Paradise Lost* in the *Preface* to *Sylvae* (1685) still display a sharp defensiveness; Dryden acknowledges Milton's importance but resists the pressure of the sublime: "*Paradise Lost* is admirable; but am I therefore bound to maintain, that there are no flats amongst his elevations, when 'tis evident he creeps along sometimes for above an hundred lines together?" (*Essays*, 1:268) But a less defensive response begins to unfold after Dryden's conversion; Milton's presence can often be felt in *The Hind and the Panther*; the "Lines on Milton" date from the year of the Revolution; and echoes of *Paradise Lost* color a number of lines in the Virgil translations.[27] And in the *Discourse of Satire* (1693) Dryden balances resistance with affection, "As for Mr. Milton, whom we all admire with so much justice, his subject is not that of an Heroic Poem, properly so called. His design is the losing of our happiness. . . . But I will not take Mr. Rymer's work out of his hands. He has promised the world a critique on that author; wherein, though he will not allow his poem for heroic, I hope he will grant us, that his thoughts are elevated, his words sounding, and that no man has so happily copied the manner of Homer, or so copiously translated his Grecisms, and the

Latin elegancies of Virgil. 'Tis true, he runs into a flat of thought, sometimes for a hundred lines together, but it is when he is got into a track of Scripture. . . . Neither will I justify Milton for his blank verse, though I may excuse him, by the example of Hannibal Caro, and other Italians, who have used it; for whatever causes he alleges for the abolishing of rhyme, (which I have not now the leisure to examine,) his own particular reason is plainly this, that rhyme was not his talent; he had neither the ease of doing it, nor the graces of it" (*Essays,* 2:29). Perhaps it is surprising that after so many years Dryden still wants the last word on rhyme. But this poet had a long memory:[28] he held in mind a vast body of literature, but we must allow that memory served Dryden in other ways; it took Dryden a long time to make peace with Milton.

Yet what is most interesting about the curve of Dryden's relation to Milton is the increasing ease with which he turned to his poetry after the conversion to Catholicism, and then after the Revolution. Dryden was able to reread Milton with greater sympathy once he had come to embrace, and then been forced to accept, a minority position in his own culture. Part of the openness must be sympathy for the marginal; so much is obvious. But there is also a sense that the strong ambitions and bitter partisanship of Dryden's laureate years have given way to broader literary sympathies, to a sense of kinship within an extended family of poets:[29] Homer and Virgil, Horace and Ovid, of course, but as well Chaucer and Spenser, Jonson, Waller, and now Milton: "Milton was the poetical son of Spenser, and Mr. Waller of Fairfax; for we have our lineal descents and clans as well as other families. Spenser more than once insinuates, that the soul of Chaucer was transfused into his body; and that he was begotten by him two hundred years after his decease. Milton has acknowledged to me, that Spenser was his original; and many besides myself have heard our famous Waller own, that he derived the harmony of his number from Godfrey of Bulloign, which was turned into English by Mr. Fairfax."[30] Are we wrong to hear in this language a new intimacy with Milton, the affection of one poet for another, a glimpse of that Parnassus where poets speak across the years, Dante to Virgil, Spenser to Chaucer, Dryden to Milton? There is something quite touching about the sentence that begins, "Milton has acknowledged to me, that Spenser was his original"; Dryden allows us to overhear a moment of shoptalk when affinities can be affirmed without competition. It took Dryden a long time to arrive at this sentence, but it would be nice to think that the last sentence Dryden wrote about Milton tells us something important about both competition and admiration, about the journey and the arrival.

Notes

1. Hugh Macdonald, *John Dryden, A Bibliography of Early Editions* (Oxford: Clarendon Press, 1939), 48, notes that the epigram was first published anonymously and that Dryden's name was attached when the epigram was reprinted in *Miscellany Poems*, 1716; for the text see *The Poems of John Dryden*, ed. James Kinsley (Oxford: Clarendon Press, 1958), 2: 540.

2. Richard Garnett and Edmund Gosse's *English Literature, An Illustrated Record in Four Volumes* (London: Heinemann, 1903) on Dryden and the challenges of Restoration literature is fairly typical of the Whiggish mode: "But a writer like Dryden, responsible for the movement of literature in the years immediately succeeding the Restoration, had a grave task before him. He was face to face with a bankruptcy; he had to float a new concern on the spot where the old had sunken. That uniformity of manner, that lack of salient and picturesque individuality, which annoy the hasty reader, were really unavoidable. Dryden and Tillotson, Locke and Otway, with their solicitude for lucidity of language, rigidity of form, and closeness of reasoning, were laying the foundations upon which literature might once more be built" (3:174).

3. Christopher Hill's *Milton and the English Revolution* (London: Viking, 1978) was crucial to this revaluation, but see as well, among several more recent works, Hill's own *The Experience of Defeat* (New York: Viking, 1984); Andrew Milner, *John Milton and the English Revolution: A Study in the Sociology of Literature* (Totowa, N.J.: Barnes and Noble, 1981); Mary Ann Radzinowicz, "The Politics of *Paradise Lost*," *Politics of Discourse*, eds. K. Sharpe and S. Zwicker (Berkeley: University of California Press, 1987), 204–29.

4. The story originates with Aubrey; see *The Early Lives of Milton*, ed. Helen Darbishire (London: Constable, 1932), 7; and commentary by Morris Freedman, "Dryden's 'Memorable Visit' to Milton," *Huntington Library Quarterly* 18 (1955): 99–109.

5. J. Richardson, *Explanatory Notes and Remarks on Milton's Paradise Lost* (London, 1734), cxix–cxx.

6. See, for example, David Hopkins, "Dryden's 'Baucis and Philemon' and *Paradise Lost*," *Notes and Queries*, N.S., 29 (1982): 503–4, or Edward Sichi, " 'A Crowd of Little Poets': Dryden's Use of Milton's Serpent in His *Aeneid*, II," *ANQ* 2 (1989): 94–97.

7. David Masson, *The Life of John Milton* (London, 1859–94), 6:496.

8. Morris Freedman in "Dryden's 'Memorable Visit'" first proposed this argument; see as well Jackson Cope, "*Paradise Regained*: Inner Ritual," *Milton Studies* 1 (1969): 53–54; Cope alone among Milton critics proposes the idea that *Paradise Regained* might be read as a response to the heroic drama.

9. See William Riley Parker, *John Milton, A Biography* (Oxford: Clarendon Press, 1968), 2:1108, n. 29.

10. On the debate and its literary context, see Arthur Kirsch, *Dryden's Heroic Drama* (Princeton: Princeton University Press, 1965), 22–33; Eric Rothstein, *Restoration Tragedy* (Madison: University of Wisconsin Press, 1967), 29–40; and Robert Hume, *The Development of English Drama in the Late Seventeenth Century* (Oxford: Clarendon Press, 1976), 172–3; and, more recently, see the discussion of rhyme and republicanism in the 1688 headnote to *Paradise Lost* in David Norbrook's review of *The Faber Book of Political Verse*, ed. Tom Paulin, *London Review of Books*, July 3, 1983 (vol. 8, no. 10, p. 7), and the subsequent exchange of letters between Norbrook and Craig Raine on this theme (vol. 8, nos. 12, 13, 15, 16, 20, and 22, and vol. 9, no. 1)

11. See John G. Demaray, *Milton's Theatrical Epic* (Cambridge: Harvard University Press, 1980), chap. 2, "Inconstant Theatrical Designs."

12. *Essays of John Dryden*, ed. W. P. Ker (Oxford: Clarendon Press, 1900), 1:150. Hereafter cited in the text as *Essays* with volume and page numbers.

13. I owe this figure to Barbara Lewalski's foreword to "The Political and Religious Tracts of 1659–60," *The Prose of John Milton*, ed. J. Max Patrick et al. (New York: Anchor Books, 1967), 439: "Trying to cope with the English political crisis of 1659–60 was for the Puritans like trying to tame a whirlwind."

14. Barbara Lewalski reviews the models in *Milton's Brief Epic* (Providence: Brown University Press, 1966), "Part I: The Genre."

15. See John T. Shawcross, *Paradise Regain'd* (Pittsburgh, Penn.; Duquesne University Press, 1988), 17–28.

16. On generic mixture in Milton's poetry, see Barbara Kiefer Lewalski, *Paradise Lost and the Rhetoric of Literary Forms* (Princeton: Princeton University Press, 1985).

17. Macdonald, *John Dryden, A Bibliography*, 6, n. 4.

18. See above, n. 4.

19. Macdonald, *John Dryden, A Bibliography*, 115 and 115, n. 5; cf. Demaray, *Milton's Theatrical Epic*, 16.

20. *The Works of John Dryden*, ed. Sir Walter Scott, revised by George Saintsbury (Edinburgh, 1882–93), 5:119. Hereafter cited in the text as *Works* with volume and page numbers.

21. See Ronald Hutton, *Charles the Second* (Oxford: Oxford University Press, 1989), 309: "During the previous two years, James had courted another Catholic princess, of Austria, without arousing any disapproval in England. Nor had the faith of Catherine of Braganza provoked any, ten years before. But again, James's conversion changed everything and the new match was regarded as another stage in England's betrayal to Rome."

22. Cf. James Winn, *John Dryden and His World* (New Haven: Yale University Press, 1987), 294–96.

23. See the commentary by Montague Summers in his edition, *Dryden: The Dramatic Works* (London: Nonesuch Press, 1931–1932), 3:580.

24. Ben Jonson, *The Complete Poems*, ed. George Parfitt (Harmondsworth: Penguin, 1975), 462.

25. On Dryden and his patronage relationship with the Duke of York, see George McFadden, *Dryden, the Public Writer, 1660–1685* (Princeton: Princeton University Press, 1978), 88–94.

26. Winn suggests that the dedication was an effort by the poet to identify his position in the crises brewing between the King and Parliament in February of 1677, *John Dryden and His World*, 296; for Winn the language is "humorously exaggerated," but "humor" does not seem quite the effect of the dedication.

27. See the commentary and annotation in vol. 3, edited by Earl Miner, and vol. 6, edited by William Frost, in the California edition, *The Works of John Dryden*, eds. E. N. Hooker and H. T. Swedenberg, Jr., et al. (Berkeley: University of California Press, 1956—).

28. See Dryden writing of Virgil and himself in *The Dedication of the Aeneis* (1697), *The Poems of John Dryden*, 3:1016, "But one poet may judge of another by himself. The vengeance we defer is not forgotten."

29. On this theme, see David Bywaters, *Dryden in Revolutionary England* (Berkeley: University of California Press, 1991), chap. 4, "The Poet, Not the Man: Poetry and Prose, 1692–1700."

30. *The Poems of John Dryden*, 4:1445.

Notes on Contributors

DIANA TREVIÑO BENET is Director of Great Books at the Gallatin Division of New York University. In addition to essays on Milton and other seventeenth-century figures, she is the author of *Secretary of Praise: The Poetic Vocation of George Herbert* and *Something to Love: The Novels of Barbara Pym*. With Michael Lieb, she has recently co-edited *Literary Milton: Text, Pretext, Context* (1994).

CHARLES CANTALUPO is Associate Professor of English at Penn State University where he has taught since 1980 after completing his Ph.D. at Rutgers University. He has been poetry editor of *Studia Mystica* and has produced and staged his own poetry in Morocco, Puerto Rico, and the United States as well as publishing it in a variety of periodicals. He has recently edited and introduced a collection of essays, interviews, and poetry called *The World of Ngugi wa Thiong'o* (1993). He is also the author of *A Literary Leviathan: Thomas Hobbes's Masterpiece of Language* (1992).

JOHN CREASER, formerly English Fellow and Vice-Principal of Mansfield College, Oxford, has been Hildred Carlile Professor of English literature at Royal Holloway, University of London, since 1985. He is Executive Secretary of the Malone Society and Co-Director of the Index of English Literary Manuscripts. His publications on Jonson and Milton include an edition of *Volpone* (1978). He is writing a critical study of Milton's earlier work.

DENNIS DANIELSON is Associate Professor of English at the University of British Columbia and a former Alexander von Humboldt Fellow at the University of Bonn. In addition to numerous periodical publications, he is author of *Milton's Good God: A Study in Literary Theodicy* (1982) and the editor of *The Cambridge Companion to Milton* (1989; rpt. 1992) and of *Christes Bloodie Sweat* for *The Nondramatic Works of John Ford* (1991).

MARY JANE DOHERTY received her B.A. from Regis College in Massachusetts (1967) where she later served as Assistant Dean of Students (1975–77). Since completing her Ph.D. at the University of Wisconsin (Madison) in 1977, she has taught at the University of Missouri (Columbia), Vanderbilt University, and the University of Wisconsin. Her articles, notes, reviews, and poems have appeared in numerous Renaissance journals, and she is the author of *The Mistress-Knowledge: Sir Philip Sidney's Defence of Poesie and Literary Architectonics in the English Renaissance* (1991).

DAVID A. KENT teaches at Centennial College, Toronto. Following studies at the University of Winnipeg and Queen's University, he did his Ph.D. at York University in

Toronto. In addition to editing a collection of essays and writing a monograph on Canadian poet Margaret Avison, he has edited *The Achievement of Christina Rossetti* (1987) and *Christian Poetry in Canada* (1989), and co-edited *Romantic Parodies. 1797–1831* (1992).

PAUL A. PARRISH is a Professor of English and former Associate Dean in the College of Liberal Arts at Texas A & M University, where he teaches courses on Renaissance and seventeenth-century literature. He is the author of *Richard Crashaw* (1980) and has written articles on Donne, Crashaw, Cowley, Gascoigne, and Milton. He is the Commentary Editor for the first published volume of *The Variorum Edition of the Poetry of John Donne* and is the 1994–95 president of Phi Beta Delta, the Honor Society for International Scholars.

STELLA P. REVARD is Professor of English at Southern Illinois University, Edwardsville. She is the author of *The War in Heaven* (1980) and of numerous articles on Milton and other subjects. She is currently at work on a book on Milton and Neo-Latin poetry.

THOMAS P. ROCHE, JR. is Murray Professor of English Literature at Princeton University and author of studies of Spenser, Petrarch, Ariosto, Tasso, and Shakespeare. He is editor of the Penguin *Faerie Queene* and is completing a book on the iconography of the Muses from Hesiod to Milton.

MAREN-SOFIE RØSTVIG was born in Norway in 1920. Candidate of Philology (Oslo University, 1947) and Ph.D. (UCLA, 1950), she taught English literature at Oslo for her entire career. After retiring in 1988, she continued there as senior research fellow in 1988–90. Her most recent publication is *Configurations. A Topomorphical Approach to Renaissance Poetry* (1994). Among her other publications, she has contributed a chapter on Marvell and the Caroline poets to the *Sphere History of Literature*, volume 2 (1970 and 1986).

P. G. STANWOOD is Professor of English at the University of British Columbia. He received the Ph.D. from the University of Michigan-Ann Arbor. He has edited John Cosin's *A Collection of Private Devotions;* Henry More's *Democritus Platonissans;* William Law's *A Serious Call to a Devout and Holy Life* and *The Spirit of Love; John Donne and the Theology of Language* (with Heather Ross Asals); Richard Hooker's *Of the Laws of Ecclesiastical Polity* (Books VI, VII, VIII); Jeremy Taylor's *Holy Living* and *Holy Dying* (2 vols.). *The Sempiternal Season: Studies in Seventeenth-Century Devotional Writing* (1993) is a collection of his own essays.

MARGO SWISS has taught at York University, Toronto, since receiving her Ph.D. there in 1981. From 1988 to 1990 she held a Social Sciences and Humanities Research Council Fellowship (Canada) to begin work on the theology of tears in relation to seventeenth-century English poetry. She has published on Milton in *Milton Quarterly* and on Donne in *English Studies in Canada*. Her own poetry has appeared in various Canadian periodicals and has been anthologized twice.

STEVEN N. ZWICKER is Professor of English at Washington University, St. Louis. He has written on Marvell, Milton, and Restoration politics and literature, including *Dryden's Political Poetry: The Typology of King and Nation* (1972); *Politics and Language in Dryden's Poetry: The Arts of Disguise* (1984); *Lines of Authority: Politics and English Literary Culture, 1649–1689* (1993), and has co-edited *Politics of Discourse: The Literature and History of Seventeenth-Century England* (1987).

Bibliography

Almasy, Rudolph. "Richard Hooker's Book VI: A Reconstruction." *Huntington Library Quarterly* 42 (1979): 115–39.

Alter, Robert. *The Pleasures of Reading in an Ideological Age.* New York: Simon Schuster, 1989.

Ambrose, Saint. *De Poenitentia.* In *Pat L.* 16:387–440.

Arnold, Marc H. "The Platan Tree in *Paradise Lost.*" *Papers on Language and Literature* 11 (1975): 411–14.

Arthos, John. *Milton and the Italian Cities.* London: John Murray, 1962.

Attwater, Aubrey. *Pembroke College, Cambridge: A Short History.* Cambridge: Cambridge University Press, 1936.

Aubrey, John. "Thomas Hobbes." In *Brief Lives.* Edited by Oliver Lawson Dick. Ann Arbor: University of Michigan Press, 1972.

Augustine, Saint. *On the Trinity.* Translated by Arthur West Haddam. Edinburgh: T. & T. Clark, 1873.

———. *Oeuvres de Saint Augustin.* Vols. 7 and 8. Paris: Desclée, de Brouwer et Cie., 1951.

———. *Confessions.* Translated by Vernon J. Bourke. Vol. 21. New York: Fathers of the Church Publications, 1958.

———. *On Christian Doctrine.* Translated by D. W. Robertson. Indianapolis, Ind.: The Liberal Arts Press, 1968.

Avis, Paul. *Anglicanism and the Christian Church: Theological Resources in Historical Perspectives.* Minneapolis, Minn.: Fortress Press, 1989.

Barkan, Leonard. *The Gods Made Flesh: Metamorphosis & the Pursuit of Paganism.* New Haven: Yale University Press, 1986.

Barker, Arthur. "Milton's Schoolmasters." *Modern Language Review* 32 (1937): 517–36.

———. "The Pattern of Milton's *Nativity Ode.*" *University of Toronto Quarterly* 10 (1940–41): 167–81.

———. *Milton and the Puritan Dilemma 1641–1660.* Toronto: University of Toronto Press, 1942.

Bars, Henry. "A La Source des Larmes." *Vie Spirituelle* 39 (1934): 140–50.

Barton, Anne. *Ben Jonson, Dramatist.* Cambridge: Cambridge University Press, 1984.

Basil, Saint. *Regulae Brevius Tractate*. In *Pat. G.* 31:414–526.

Bauman, Michael. *Milton's Arianism*. Regensburger Arbeiten zur Anglistik und Amerikanistick 26. Frankfurt: Peter Lang, 1987.

Beaty, Nancy Lee. *The Craft of Dying: A Study in the Literary Tradition of the Ars Moriendi in England*. New Haven: Yale University Press, 1970.

Becon, Thomas. *Workes*. London, 1564.

Bell, Barbara Currier. " 'Lycidas' and the Stages of Grief." *Literature and Psychology* 25 (1975): 166–74.

Bennett, Joan S. *Reviving Liberty: Radical Christian Humanism in Milton's Great Poems*. Cambridge: Harvard University Press, 1989.

Bernard of Clairvaux, Saint. *Saint Bernard, His Meditations: or Sighes, Sobbes, and Teares, upon our Saviours Passion*. Translated by W. P. London, 1631.

———. *Sermones in Cantica* 26. In *Pat. L.* 183:1353–1359.

Bertonasco, Marc. *Crashaw and the Baroque*. University: University of Alabama Press, 1971.

Bonaventura. *Collationes in Hexaemeron*. Darmstadt: Wissenchaftliche Buchesellschaft, 1964.

Bongo, Pietro. *Numerorum mysteria*. Bergamo, 1591.

The Book of Beasts: Being a Translation from a Latin Bestiary of the Twelfth Century. Edited by T. H. White. London: Jonathan Cape, 1954.

The Book of Common Prayer 1559. The Elizabethan Prayer Book. Edited by John E. Booty. Charlottesville: University Press of Virgina, 1976.

Bourdette, Jr., Robert E. "Mourning Lycidas: 'The Poem of the Mind in the Act of Finding What Will Suffice.'" *Essays in Literature* 11 (Spring 1984): 11–20.

A Breviate of the Prelates intollerable usurpations. London, 1637.

Broadbent, J. B. "The *Navitity Ode*." In *The Living Milton: Essays by Various Hands*. Edited by Frank Kermode. London: Routledge and Kegan Paul, 1960.

Brown, Cedric C. *John Milton's Aristocratic Entertainments*. Cambridge: Cambridge University Press, 1985.

Brown, Marianne. "Spenserian Technique: *The Shepheardes Calender*". *REAL. The Yearbook of Research in English and American Literature* 2 (1984): 55–118.

Brown, Mary Ruth. "*Paradise Lost* and John 15: Eve, the Branch and the Church." *Milton Quarterly* 20 (1986): 127–31.

Bunyan, John. *The Works of John Bunyan*. Vol. 2. Edited by George Offor. Glasgow, 1860–62.

———. *The Pilgrim's Progress*. Edited by N. H. Keeble. Oxford: Oxford University Press, 1984.

———. *Grace Abounding to the Chief of Sinners*. Edited by W. R. Owens. London: Penguin, 1987.

———. *The Miscellaneous Works of John Bunyan*. General editor Roger Sharrock. Oxford: Clarendon Press, 1980– .

Bush, Douglas. *English Literature in the Earlier Seventeenth Century, 1600–1660*. Oxford History of English Literature, 5. Revised edition. Oxford: Clarendon Press, 1966.

Butler, Martin. "Politics and the Masque: *The Triumph of Peace*." *The Seventeenth Century* 2 (1987): 117–41.

———. "Ben Jonson and the Limits of Courtly Panegyric." In *Culture and Politics in Early Stuart England*. Edited by Kevin Sharpe and Peter Lake. Houndmills, Hants.: Macmillan Press, 1994.

Buxton, John. "Two Dead Birds: A Note on 'The Phoenix and the Turtle.'" In *English Renaissance Studies Presented to Dame Helen Gardner in Honour of Her Seventieth Birthday*. Edited by John Carey. Oxford: Clarendon Press, 1980.

Bywaters, David. *Dryden in Revolutionary England*. Berkeley: University of California Press, 1991.

Campbell, Gordon. "Fishing in Other Men's Waters: Bunyan and the Theologians." In *John Bunyan: Conventicle and Parnassus: Tercentenary Essays*. Edited by N. H. Keeble. Oxford: Clarendon Press, 1988.

Cannon, Nathaniel. *The Cryer*. London, 1613.

———. *Lacrimae: Lamentations over the Dead*. London, 1616.

Cantalupo, Charles. "How to be a Literary Reader of Hobbes's Most Famous Chapter." In *The Literature of Controversy*. Edited by Thomas N. Corns. London: Frank Cass & Company, 1986.

Capella, Martianus. *The Marriage of Philology and Mercury*. Translated by William Harris Stahl and Richard Johnson. New York: Columbia University Press, 1977.

Carleton, George. *An Examination Of those things wherein the Author of the late Appeale holdeth the Doctrines. . . .* London, 1626.

Cassiodorus. *Expositio Psalmorum*. Corpus Christianorum Series Latina. Vols. 97 and 98. Turnholt Press, 1958.

———. *An Introduction to Divine and Human Readings*. Translated by Leslie Webber Jones. New York: Octagon Books, 1966.

Chernaik, Warren L. *The Poetry of Limitation: A Study of Edmund Waller*. New Haven: Yale University Press, 1968.

Christopher, Georgia. *Milton and the Science of Saints*. Princeton: Princeton University Press, 1982.

———. "Milton and the Reforming Spirit." In *The Cambridge Companion to Milton*. Edited by Dennis Danielson. Cambridge: Cambridge University Press, 1989.

Christs Teares over Jerusalem: Or a Caveat for England . . . London, 1624.

Clark, Donald Lemen. *John Milton at St. Paul's School: A Study of Ancient Rhetoric in English Renaissance Education*. 1948. Reprint. New York: Archon Books, 1964.

Clarke, John. *Paroemiologia Anglo-Latina . . . Or Proverbs English and Latine, methodically disposed according to the Common-place heads, in Erasmus his Adages*. London, 1639.

Claudian, Claudianus Claudius. *Epigram de Phoenice*. Edited and translated by M. Platnauer. 2 vols. London: William Heinemann, 1956.

Clayton, Jay and Eric Rothstein, eds. *Influence and Intertextuality in Literary History*. Madison: University of Wisconsin Press, 1991.

Collinson, Patrick. *The Elizabethan Puritan Movement*. Oxford: Clarendon Press, 1967.

———. *The Religion of Protestants*. Oxford: Clarendon Press, 1982.

Complaynt of the Lover of Cryst Saynt Mary Magdaleyn. London, 1520.

Cooper, Charles Henry. *Annals of Cambridge*. Vol. 3. Cambridge, Eng.: Warwick and Co., 1845.

Cope, Jackson. *"Paradise Regained:* Inner Ritual." *Milton Studies* 1 (1969): 51–65.

Corns, Thomas N. *The Development of Milton's Prose Style.* Oxford: Clarendon Press, 1982.

———. "'Some rousing motions': The plurality of Miltonic ideology." In *Literature and the Civil War.* Edited by Thomas Healy and Jonathan Sawday. Cambridge: Cambridge University Press, 1990.

Crashaw, Richard. *The Complete Poetry of Richard Crashaw.* Edited by George Walton Williams. 1970. Reprint. New York: Norton, 1974.

Creaser, John. "'The present aid of this occasion': The setting of *Comus.*" In *The Court Masque.* Edited by David Lindley. Manchester: Manchester University Press, 1984.

———. "Enigmatic Ben Jonson." In *English Comedy.* Edited by Michael Cordner, Peter Holland, and John Kerrigan. Cambridge: Cambridge University Press, 1994.

Cullen, Patrick. *Infernal Triad: The Flesh, the World and the Devil in Spenser and Milton.* Princeton: Princeton University Press, 1974.

Curtis, Mark. *Oxford and Cambridge in Transition, 1558–1642: An Essay on Changing Relations Between the English Universities and English Society.* Oxford: Clarendon Press, 1959.

Daniells, Roy. *Milton, Mannerism and Baroque.* Toronto: University of Toronto Press, 1963.

Daniélou, Jean. *From Shadows to Reality.* London: Burus & Oates, 1960.

Danielson, Dennis. *Milton's Good God: A Study in Literary Theodicy.* Cambridge: Cambridge University Press, 1982.

———. "Through the Telescope of Typology: What Adam Should Have Done." *Milton Quarterly* 23 (1989): 121–27.

Darbishire, Helen, ed. *The Early Lives of Milton.* London: Constable, 1932.

Davies, H. Neville. "Milton and the Art of Cranking." *Milton Quarterly* 23 (1989): 1–7.

Davies, Stevie. *The Feminine Reclaimed: The Idea of Woman in Spenser, Shakespeare and Milton.* Lexington: University of Kentucky Press, 1986.

Davis, Robert Leigh. "That Two-Handed Engine and the Consolation of *Lycidas.*" *Thoreau Literary Quarterly* 20 (May 1986): 44–48.

de Guibert, Joseph. *The Jesuits, Their Spiritual Doctrine and Practice: A Historical Study.* Chicago: Loyola University Press, 1964.

de Man, Paul. "The Epistemology of Metaphor." In *On Metaphor.* Edited by Sheldon Sacks. Chicago: University of Chicago Press, 1979.

Demaray, John G. *Milton's Theatrical Epic.* Cambridge: Harvard University Press, 1980.

Derrida, Jacques. *Margins of Philosophy.* Translated by Alan Bass. Chicago: University of Chicago Press, 1982.

Dickson, Donald R. *The Fountain of Living Waters: The Typology of the Waters of Life in Herbert, Vaughan, and Traherne.* Columbia: University of Missouri Press, 1987.

Diekhoff, John. *Milton on Himself.* New York: Humanities Press, 1965.

Doherty, M. J. *The Mistress-Knowledge: Sir Philip Sidney's Defence of Poesie and Literary Architectonics in the English Renaissance.* Nashville, Tenn.: Vanderbilt University Press, 1991.

Donne, John. *The Sermons of John Donne.* Edited by George R. Potter and Evelyn N. Simpson. 10 vols. Berkeley: University of California Press, 1962.

———. *John Donne and the Theology of Language.* Edited by P. G. Stanwood and Heather Ross Asals. Columbia: University of Missouri Press, 1986.

Draper, John W. *The Funeral Elegy and the Rise of English Romanticism.* New York: New York University Press, 1929.

Dryden, John. *The Works of John Dryden.* Edited by Sir Walter Scott, revised by George Saintsbury. 18 vols. Edinburgh, 1882–93.

———. *Essays of John Dryden.* Edited by W. P. Ker. Oxford: Clarendon Press, 1900.

———. *The Works of John Dryden.* Edited by E. N. Hooker and H. T. Swedenberg, Jr., et al. Berkeley: University of California Press, 1956 – .

———. *The Poems of John Dryden.* Edited by James Kinsley. 4 vols. Oxford: Clarendon Press, 1958.

———. *Fables Ancient and Modern* (1700). In *Essays.* Edited by W. P. Ker. 2 vols. 1900. Reprint. New York: Russell and Russell, 1961.

———. *Dryden: The Dramatic Works.* Edited by Montague Summers. 6 vols. London: Nonesuch Press, 1931–32.

———. *Selected Criticism.* Edited by James Kinsley and George Parfitt. Oxford: Clarendon Press, 1970.

Edwards, Philip. *Threshold of a Nation.* London: Cambridge University Press, 1979.

Eccleshall, Robert. "Richard Hooker and the Peculiarities of the English: The Reception of the *Ecclesiastical Polity* in the Seventeenth and Eighteenth Centuries." *History of Political Thought* 2 (1981): 63–117.

Eliot, T. S. "Tradition and the Individual Talent." In *Selected Essays.* New York: Harcourt, Brace & World, 1932.

Emerson, Everett H. *English Puritanism from John Hooper to John Milton.* Durham, N.C.: Duke University Press, 1968.

Empson, William. *Milton's God.* Revised edition. London: Chatto and Windus, 1981.

Evans, Robert C. *Ben Jonson and the Poetics of Patronage.* Lewisburg, Penn.: Bucknell University Press, 1989.

Fallon, Stephen. "Milton's Sin and Death: The Ontology of Allegory in *Paradise Lost.*" *English Language Review* 17 (1987): 329–50.

———. *Milton Among the Philosophers: Poetry and Materialism in Seventeenth-Century England.* Ithaca: Cornell University Press, 1991.

Featley, Daniel. *Ancilla pietatis.* London, 1625.

———. *House of Mourning.* London, 1640.

Featley, John. *A Fountaine of Teares.* London, 1646.

———. *Teares in Time of Pestilence.* Amsterdam, 1665.

Ferry, Anne. *Milton's Epic Voice: The Narrator in Paradise Lost.* Cambridge: Harvard University Press, 1986.

Ficino, Marsilio. *Théologie Platonicienne de l'Immortalité des Ames.* Translated by Raymond Marcel. Paris: Société d'Edition "Les Belles Lettres," 1964.

———. *Commentary on the Symposium.* Translated by Sears Reynolds Jayne. 1944. Reprint. Dallas, Texas: Spring Publications Inc., 1985.

Filmer, Robert. *Observations Concerning the Originall of Government.* London, 1652.

———. *Patriarcha*. London, 1680.

Finnis, J. M. *Natural Law and Natural Rights*. Oxford: Clarendon Press, 1980.

Fiore, Peter A. *Milton and Augustine: Patterns of Augustinian Thought in Paradise Lost*. University Park: Pennsylvania State University Press, 1981.

Fish, Stanley. *Surprised by Sin: The Reader in "Paradise Lost."* 1967. Reprint. Berkeley: University of California Press, 1971.

———. "Authors-Readers: Jonson's Community of the Same." *Representations* 7 (1984): 26–58.

Fletcher, Giles and Phineas. *Poetical Works*. Edited by Frederick S. Boas. Cambridge: Cambridge University Press, 1908.

Fletcher, Harris F. *The Intellectual Development of John Milton*. 2 vols. Urbana: University of Illinois Press, 1961.

Foakes, R. A. *Shakespeare: From the Dark Comedies to the Last Plays—From Satire to Celebration*. London: Routledge & Kegan, 1971.

Fogel, E. G. "Milton and Sir Philip Sidney's *Arcadia*." *Notes and Queries* 196 (1951): 115–17.

Ford, John. *Christes Bloodie Sweat*. Edited by D. Danielson. In *The Non-Dramatic Works of John Ford*. Edited by L. E. Stock et al. Binghamton, New York: MRTS, 1991.

Fowler, Alastair. "The Silva Tradition in Jonson's *The Forrest*." In *Poetic Traditions of the English Renaissance*. Edited by George de Forest Lord. New Haven: Yale University Press, 1982.

Fraistat, Neil, ed. *Poems in Their Place: The Intertextuality and Order of Poetic Collections*. Chapel Hill: University of North Carolina Press, 1986.

Freedman, Morris. "Dryden's 'Memorable Visit' to Milton." *Huntington Library Quarterly* 18 (1955): 99–109.

French, J. Milton, ed. *The Life Records of John Milton*. Vol. 1. New Brunswick, N.J.: Rutgers University Press, 1949.

Fretheim, Terence E. *The Suffering of God: An Old Testament Perspective*. Philadelphia: Fortress Press, 1984.

Frey, William. *Crying: The Mystery of Tears*. Minneapolis, Minn.: Winston Press, 1985.

Frye, Northrop. *Anatomy of Criticism*. Princeton: Princeton University Press, 1957.

———. "Criticism, Visible and Invisible." In *The Stubborn Structure: Essays on Criticism and Society*. London: Methuen, 1970.

———. *Words with Power: Being a Second Study of the Bible and Literature*. New York: Harcourt Brace Jovanovich, 1990.

Frye, Roland Mushat. "The Teachings of Classical Puritanism on Love in Marriage." *Studies in the Renaissance* 2 (1955): 148–59.

———. *God, Man, and Satan*. Princeton: Princeton University Press, 1960.

Gabler, Hans Walter. "Poetry in Numbers: A Development of Significative Form in Milton's Early Poetry." *Archiv* 220 (1983): 54–61.

Galinsky, G. Karl. *The Herakles Theme. The Adaptations of the Hero in Literature from Homer to the Twentieth Century*. Oxford: Basil Blackwell, 1972.

Gardeil, Fr. Ambroise. "La Béatitude des larmes." *Vie Spirituelle* 57 (1938): 129–36.

Gardiner, Judith Kegan. *Craftsmanship in Context: The Development of Ben Jonson's Poetry*. The Hague, the Netherlands: Mouton, 1975.

Garnett, Richard and Edmund Gosse. *English Literature, An Illustrated Record in Four Volumes*. London: Heinemann, 1903.

The Geneva Bible, A Facsimile of the 1560 Edition. Introduction by Lloyd E. Berry. Madison: University of Wisconsin Press, 1969.

The Geneva Bible: The Annotated New Testament. 1602 Edition. Edited by Gerald T. Sheppard. New York: The Pilgrim Press, 1989.

Gibbs, Lee W. "The Source of the Most Famous Quotation from Richard Hooker's *Laws of Ecclesiastical Polity*." *Sixteenth Century Journal* 21 (1990): 77–86.

Gilbertson, Carol. "'Many *Miltons* in This One Man': Marvell's Mower Poems and *Paradise Lost*." *Milton Studies* 22 (1986): 151–72.

Gillet, Lev. "The Gift of Tears." *Sobornost* (December 1937): 5–10.

Glover, T. R. "On the Permanence of *The Pilgrim's Progress*." In *"The Pilgrim's Progress": A Casebook*. Edited by Roger Sharrock. London: Macmillan, 1976.

Greaves, Richard L. *John Bunyan*. Courtenay Studies in Reformation Theology, 2. Appleford: Sutton Courtenay Press, 1969.

Greene, Thomas M. *The Light in Troy: Imitation and Discovery in Renaissance Poetry*. New Haven: Yale University Press, 1982.

———. *The Vulnerable Text: Essays on Renaissance Literature*. New York: Columbia University Press, 1986.

Greville, Fulke. *Life of the Renowned Sir Philip Sidney* (1652). Edited by Warren W. Wooden. Delmar, New York: Scholar's Facsimiles and Reprints, 1984.

Gross, Kenneth. "'Pardon Me, Mighty Poet': Versions of the Bard in Marvell's 'On Mr. Milton's *Paradise Lost*.'" *Milton Studies* 16 (1982): 77–96.

Guibbory, Achsah. "John Donne and Memory as 'The Art of *Salvation*.'" *Huntington Library Quarterly* 43 (1979–80): 260–74.

Guillory, John. *Poetic Authority: Spenser, Milton, and Literary History*. New York: Columbia University Press, 1983.

Guldan, Ernest. *Eva und Maria: Eine Antithese also Bildmotif*. Graz and Cologne: Hermann Bühlaus, 1966.

Haigh, Christopher, ed. *The English Reformation Revisited*. Cambridge: Cambridge University Press, 1987.

Hale, John K. "Milton's Self-Presentation in *Poems . . . 1645*." *Milton Quarterly* 25.2 (May 1991): 37–48.

Halkett, John. *Milton and the Idea of Matrimony: A Study of the Divorce Tracts and "Paradise Lost"*. New Haven: Yale University Press, 1970.

Haller, William. "'Hail Wedded Love.'" *English Literary History* 13 (1946): 79–97.

Hanford, James Holly. "The Youth of Milton." In *Studies in Shakespeare, Milton and Donne by Members of the English Department of the University of Michigan, University of Michigan Publications: Language and Literature* 1 (1925): 89–163.

——— and James G. Taafe. *A Milton Handbook*. 5th edition. Englewood Cliffs, N.J.: Prentice Hall, Inc., 1970.

Hannay, Margaret W. *Philip's Phoenix: Mary Sidney, Countess of Pembroke*. Oxford: Clarendon Press, 1989.

Hardacre, Paul. "A Letter from Edmund Waller to Thomas Hobbes." *Huntingdon Library Quarterly* 11.2 (1948): 431–33.

Harland, Paul. "Imagination and Affections in John Donne's Preaching." *John Donne Journal* 6 (1987): 33–50.

Harrington, James. *The Political Writings of James Harrington.* Edited by Charles Blizter. New York: Columbia University Press, 1955.

Hartwell, Kathleen Ellen. *Lactantius and Milton.* Cambridge: Harvard University Press, 1929.

Hartwig, Joan. "Tears as a Way of Seeing." In *On the Celebrated and Neglected Poems of Andrew Marvell.* Edited by Claude J. Summers and Ted-Larry Pebworth. Columbia: University of Missouri Press, 1992.

Haskin, Dayton. "The Burden of Interpretation in *The Pilgrim's Progress.*" *Studies in Philology* 79 (1982): 256–78.

Hausherr, Irénée. *Penthos: The Doctrine of Compunction in the Christian East.* Translated by Anselm Hufstader. Kalamazoo, Mich.: Cistercian Publications, 1982.

Hayes, T. Wilson. *Winstanley the Digger.* Cambridge: Harvard University Press, 1979.

Hawkins, Sherman. "Mutabilitie and the Cycle of the Months." In *Form and Convention in the Poetry of Edmund Spenser.* Edited by William Nelson. New York: Columbia University Press, 1961.

Hefferman, Carol Falvo. *The Phoenix at the Fountain: Images of Woman and Eternity in Lactantius's Carmen de Ave Phoenice and the Old English Phoenix.* Newark, Delaware: University of Delaware Press, 1988.

Helgerson, Richard. *Self-Crowned Laureates: Spenser, Jonson, Milton, and the Literary System.* Berkeley: University of California Press, 1983.

Heninger, Jr., S. K. *Sidney and Spenser: The Poet as Maker.* University Park, Pennsylvania: Pennsylvania State University Press, 1989.

Herschel, Abraham J. *The Prophets.* 2 vols. New York: Harper & Row, 1962.

Herz, Judith Scherer. "Milton and Marvell: The Poet as Fit Reader." *Modern Language Quarterly* 39 (1978): 239–63.

———. "Epigrams and Sonnets: Milton in the Manner of Jonson." *Milton Studies* 20 (1984): 29–41.

Hertz, Neil. "Wordsworth and the Tears of Adam." In *The End of the Line: Essays on Psychoanalysis and the Sublime.* New York: Columbia University Press, 1985.

Heyworth, P. L. "The Composition of Milton's *At a Solemn Musick.*" *Bulletin of the New York Public Library* 70 (1966): 450–58.

Hieatt, A. Kent. *Chaucer, Spenser, Milton: Mythopoeic Continuities and Transformations.* Montreal: McGill-Queen's University Press, 1975.

Hill, Christopher. *Milton and the English Revolution.* New York: Viking Press, 1978.

———. *The Experience of Defeat.* New York: Viking, 1984.

———. *A Turbulent, Seditious, and Factious People: John Bunyan and his Church 1628–1688.* Oxford: Oxford University Press, 1988.

Hinnant, Charles. *Thomas Hobbes.* Boston: G. K. Hall & Co., 1977.

Hobbes, Thomas. *Leviathan* (1651). Edited by C. B. Macpherson. Harmondsworth: Penguin Books, 1968.

———. *Behemoth.* London, 1679.

———. *The English Works.* Edited by Sir William Molesworth. 11 vols. London: J. Bohn, 1839–45.

———. *Leviathan.* Edited by Michael Oakeshott. Oxford: Basil Blackwell Press, 1947.

Hooker, Richard. *Of the Laws of Ecclesiastical Polity: Preface, Books I to IV.* Edited by Georges Edelen. The Folger Library Edition of the Works of Richard Hooker. Cambridge: Belknap Press of Harvard University Press, 1977.

———. *Laws: Books VI, VII, VIII.* Edited by P. G. Stanwood. The Folger Library Edition of the Works of Richard Hooker. Cambridge: Belknap Press of Harvard University Press, 1981.

———. *Of the Laws of Ecclesiastical Polity.* Edited by Arthur Stephen McGrade. Cambridge Texts in the History of Political Thought. Cambridge: Cambridge University Press, 1989.

———. *Tractates and Sermons.* Edited by Laetitia Yeandle and Egil Grislis. The Folger Library Edition of the Works of Richard Hooker. Cambridge: Belknap Press of Harvard University Press, 1990.

Hopkins, David. "Dryden's 'Baucis and Philemon' and *Paradise Lost.*" *Notes and Queries,* N.S., 29 (1982): 503–4.

Howison, Patricia M. "Donne's Sermons and the Rhetoric of Prophecy." *English Studies in Canada* 15 (June 1989): 134–48.

Hume, Robert. *The Development of English Drama in the Late Seventeenth Century.* Oxford: Clarendon Press, 1976.

Hunter, W. B., C. A. Patrides, and J. H. Adamson. *Bright Essence: Studies in Milton's Theology.* Salt Lake City: University of Utah Press, 1971.

Hunter, Jr., William B., gen. ed. *A Milton Encyclopedia.* 9 vols. Lewisburg, Penn.: Bucknell University Press, 1978–83.

———. "The Provenance of the *Christian Doctrine.*" *Studies in English Literature* 32 (1992): 129–66.

Hunnis, William. *Seven Sobs of a Sorrowfull Soule.* London, 1583.

Hutton, Ronald. *Charles the Second.* Oxford: Oxford University Press, 1989.

Hvidberg, Flemming Friis. *Weeping and Laughter in the Old Testament.* Amsterdam: E. J. Brill, 1962.

Ignatius, Saint. *The Spiritual Exercises of Saint Ignatius.* Translated by Thomas Corbishley. Wheathampstead, Hertfordshire: Anthony Clarke, 1963.

Innovations in Religion & Abuses in Government in University of Cambridge. British Museum Ms. Harley 7019, fol. 73.

Jardine, Lisa. *Still Harping on Daughters: Women and Drama in the Age of Shakespeare.* Sussex: Harvester Press, 1983.

Janzen, Waldemarr. *Mourning Cry and Woe Oracle.* Berlin, New York: Walter de Gruyter, 1972.

Jerome, Saint. "Letter 58" of *The Principal Works of Saint Jerome.* Translated by W. H. Fremantle. In *A Select Library of Nicene and Post-Nicene Fathers*, Second Series. Vol. VI. Edited by Philip Schaff and Henry Wace. 1892. Reprint. Grand Rapids, Mich.: Wm. B. Eerdmans Publishing Company, 1979.

———. *De Poenitentia.* In *Pat. L.* 22: 890–900.

———. *In Ieremiam Prophetam.* In *Pat L.* 24: 833–1092.

Johnson, Barbara A. "Fiction and Grief: The Pastoral Idiom of Milton's *Lycidas.*" *Milton Quarterly* 18.3 (1984): 69–76.

Johnson, Samuel. *Lives of the English Poets* (1779). 2 vols. London: Oxford University Press, 1952.

———. "Milton." In *Lives of the English Poets*. London: J. M. Dent, 1925.

Jonson, Ben. *Ben Jonson*. Edited by C. H. Herford, Percy and Evelyn Simpson. 11 vols. Oxford: Clarendon Press, 1925–52.

———. *Ben Jonson: Sejanus*. Edited by Jonas A. Barish. New Haven: Yale University Press, 1965.

———. *Ben Jonson: The Complete Poems*. Edited by George Parfitt. Harmondsworth: Penguin, 1975.

———. *Volpone or, The Fox*. Edited by R. B. Parker. The Revels Plays. Manchester: Manchester University Press, 1983.

Jordan, Constance. *Renaissance Feminism: Literary Texts and Political Models*. Ithaca: Cornell University Press, 1990.

Kaplan, Fred. *Sacred Tears: Sentimentality in Victorian Literature*. Princeton: Princeton University Press, 1987.

Kaufmann, Milo. *The Pilgrim's Progress and Traditions in Puritan Meditation*. New Haven: Yale University Press, 1966.

Kay, Dennis, ed. *Sir Philip Sidney, An Anthology of Modern Criticism*. Oxford: Clarendon Press, 1987.

Kelley, Maurice. *This Great Argument: A Study of Milton's 'De Doctrina Christiana' as a Gloss Upon 'Paradise Lost.'* 1941. Reprint. Gloucester, Mass.: Peter Smith, 1962.

Kempis, Thomas à. *Imitation of Christ*. Translated by Thomas Rogers. London, 1580.

Kerrigan, William. *The Prophetic Milton*. Charlottesville: University Press of Virginia, 1974.

———. *The Sacred Complex: On the Psychogenesis of Paradise Lost*. Cambridge: Harvard University Press, 1983.

King, John N. "Milton's Bower of Bliss: A Rewriting of Spenser's Art of Married Love." *Renaissance and Reformation* 10 (1986): 289–99.

Kinney, Arthur F., et. al., ed. *Sidney in Retrospect: Selections from ELR*. Amherst: University of Massachusetts Press, 1988.

Kirby, W. J. Torrance. *Richard Hooker's Doctrine of the Royal Supremacy*. Leiden: E. J. Brill, 1990.

Kirsch, Arthur. *Dryden's Heroic Drama*. Princeton: Princeton University Press, 1965.

Kittelson, James. *Luther The Reformer: The Story of the Man and His Career*. Minneapolis, Minn.: Augsburg, 1986.

Knight, Samuel. *The Life of Dr. John Colet*. London, 1724.

Knott, Jr., John R. *The Sword of the Spirit: Puritan Responses to the Bible*. Chicago: University of Chicago Press, 1980.

Krouse, Michael. *Samson and the Christian Tradition*. Princeton: Princeton University Press, 1949.

Lake, Peter. *Puritan and Anglican? Presbyterianism and English Conformist Thought from Whitgift to Hooker*. London: Allen & Unwin, 1988.

Lambert, Ellen Zetzel. *Placing Sorrow: A Study of the Pastoral Elegy Convention from Theocritus to Milton*. Chapel Hill: University of North Carolina Press, 1976.

"Larmes." *Dictionnaire d'Archeologie Chrétienne et de Liturgie* 8, part 1 (1928): 1393–1402. Paris: Letouzey et Ané.

———. *Dictionnaire de Spiritualité Ascétique et Mystique Doctrine et Histoire* 9 (1976): 287–303. Paris: Beauchesne et ses fils.

Larsen, Kenneth J. "Some Light on Richard Crashaw's Final Years in Rome." *Modern Language Review* 66 (1971): 492–96.

Latham, James E. *The Religious Symbolism of Salt. Théologie Historique* #64. Paris: Beauchesne, 1982.

Lawry, Jon S. *The Shadow of Heaven: Matter and Stance in Milton's Poetry.* Ithaca: Cornell University Press, 1968.

Le Comte, Edward. *Milton and Sex.* New York: Columbia University Press, 1978.

Le Vay, John. "Crashaw's 'Saint Mary Magdalene, or The Weeper.'" *Explicator* 50.3 (Spring 1992): 142–44.

Leighton, William. *Teares or lamentations of a sorrowfull soule.* London, 1613.

Leites, Edmund. *The Puritan Conscience and Modern Sexuality.* New Haven: Yale University Press, 1986.

Leonard, John. *Naming in Paradise: Milton and the Language of Adam and Eve.* Oxford: Oxford University Press, 1990.

Lewalski, Barbara Kiefer. *Milton's Brief Epic.* Providence: Brown University Press, 1966.

———. "The Political and Religious Tracts of 1659–60." In *The Prose of John Milton.* Edited by J. Max Patrick et. al. New York: Anchor Books, 1967.

———. *Paradise Lost and the Rhetoric of Literary Forms.* Princeton: Princeton University Press, 1985.

———. "Writing Women and Reading the Renaissance." *Renaissance Quarterly* 44 (Winter 1991): 792–821.

———. *Writing Women in Jacobean England.* Cambridge: Harvard University Press, 1993.

Lewis, C. S. *The Great Divorce: A Dream.* London: Geoffrey Bles, 1946.

Lieb, Michael. *Poetics of the Holy, A Reading of Paradise Lost.* Chapel Hill: University of North Carolina Press, 1981.

———. "Milton's 'Unexpressive Nuptial Song': A Reading of *Lycidas.*" *Renaissance Papers* (1982): 15–26.

———. *The Sinews of Ulysses: Form and Convention in Milton's Works.* Pittsburgh, Pa.: Duquesne University Press, 1989.

Lindenbaum, Peter. "Lovemaking in Milton's *Paradise Lost.*" *Milton Studies* 6 (1974): 277–306.

Lipking, Lawrence. "Life, Death, and Other Theories." In *Historical Studies and Literary Criticism.* Edited by Jerome J. McGann. Madison: University of Wisconsin Press, 1985.

Little, Bryan. *The Colleges of Cambridge.* New York: Arco Publishing Co., 1973.

Loeffelholz, Mary. "Two Masques of Ceres and Proserpine: *Comus* and *The Tempest.*" *Shakespeare Quarterly* 10 (1959): 177–83.

Lord, George de F. "Milton's Dialogue with Omniscience in *Paradise Lost.*" In *The Author in His Work: Essays on a Problem in Criticism.* Edited by Louis L. Martz and Aubrey Williams. New Haven: Yale University Press, 1978.

————, ed. *Anthology of Poems on Affairs of State 1660-1714*. New Haven: Yale University Press, 1975.

Lowenstein, David, and James Grantham Turner, *Politics, poetics, and hermeneutics in Milton's prose*. Cambridge: Cambridge University Press, 1990.

Luther, Martin. *Werke: Kritische Gesamtausgabe: Die Deutsche Bibel 6*. Weimar: Hermann Bühlaus, 1929.

MacCallum, Hugh. *Milton and the Sons of God: The Divine Image in Milton's Poetry*. Toronto: University of Toronto Press, 1986.

Macdonald, Hugh. *John Dryden, A Bibliography of Early Editions*. Oxford: Clarendon Press, 1939.

Macrobius. *Commentary on the Dream of Scipio*. Translated by William Harris Stahl. Records of Civilization, Sources and Studies. Vol. 48. New York: Columbia University Press, 1952.

Mansbridge, Albert. *The Older Universities of England: Oxford and Cambridge*. Boston: Houghton Mifflin, 1923.

Marcus, Leah S. *The Politics of Mirth*. Chicago: University of Chicago Press, 1986.

Maries Exercise. London, 1597.

Marie Magdalens Love. London, 1595.

Martz, Louis L. *The Poetry of Meditation: A Study in English Religious Literature of the Seventeenth Century*. 1954. Reprint. New Haven: Yale University Press, 1962.

————. "The Action of the Self: Devotional Poetry in the Seventeenth Century." In *Metaphysical Poetry*. Edited by Malcolm Bradbury and David Palmer. Bloomington: Indiana University Press, 1971.

————. *Poet of Exile: A Study of Milton's Poetry*. New Haven: Yale University Press, 1980.

————. "Donne and Herbert: Vehement Grief and Silent Tears." *John Donne Journal* 7.1 (1988): 21–34.

Marvell, Andrew. *The Poems and Letters of Andrew Marvell*. Edited by H. M. Margoliouth. 3d edition revised by Pierre Legouis with E. E. Duncan-Jones. Vol. 1. London: Oxford University Press, 1971.

————. *Andrew Marvell. The Complete Poems*. Edited by Elizabeth Story Donno. 1972. Reprint. Middlesex: Penguin, 1983.

Mary Magdalens Lamentations for the Loss of her Master Jesus. London, 1601.

Masson, David. *The Life of John Milton*. 7 vols. London, 1859–94.

Maus, Katharine Eisaman. *Ben Jonson and the Roman Frame of Mind*. Princeton: Princeton University Press, 1984.

McColley, Diane Kelsey. *Milton's Eve*. Urbana: University of Illinois Press, 1983.

McCown, Gary M. "Milton and the Epic Epithalamion." *Milton Studies* 5 (1973): 44–55.

McDonnell, Sir Michael. *A History of St. Paul's School*. London, 1909.

McFadden, George. *Dryden, the Public Writer, 1660–1685*. Princeton: Princeton University Press, 1978.

McGann, Jerome J. *The Textual Condition*. Princeton: Princeton University Press, 1991.

Milner, Andrew. *John Milton and the English Revolution: A Study in the Sociology of Literature*. Totowa, N.J.: Barnes and Noble, 1981.

Milton, John. *Complete Prose Works of John Milton.* Edited by Don Wolfe et al. 8 vols. New Haven: Yale University Press, 1953–83.

———. *The Prose of John Milton.* Edited by J. Max Patrick et al. New York: Anchor, 1967.

———. *The Poems of Milton.* Edited by John Carey and Alastair Fowler. London: Longmans, 1968.

———. *Poetical Works.* Edited by Douglas Bush. London: Oxford University Press, 1969.

———. *Poems* (1645). Menson, Eng.: Scolar Press, 1970.

———. *A Variorum Commentary on the Poems of John Milton.* Edited by A. S. P. Woodhouse and Douglas Bush. Vol. 2, part 1. New York: Columbia University Press, 1972.

———. *John Milton: Complete Poems And Major Prose* . Edited by Merritt Y. Hughes. New York: Odyssey Press—Bobbs-Merrill, 1973.

Miller, Leo. "Milton Dines at the Jesuit College: Reconstructing the Evening of October 30, 1638." *Milton Quarterly* 13 (1979): 142–46.

Mintz, Samuel. *The Hunting of Leviathan: Seventeenth-Century Reactions to the Materialism and Moral Philosophy of Hobbes.* Cambridge: Cambridge University Press, 1962.

———. "The Motion of Thought: Intellectual and Philosophical Backgrounds." In *The Age of Milton: Background to Seventeenth-Century Literature.* Edited by C. A. Patrides and Raymond B. Waddington. Manchester: Manchester University Press, 1980.

Mohl, Ruth. *John Milton and His Commonplace Book.* New York: Frederick Ungar Publishing, 1969.

More, St. Thomas. *De Tristitia Christi.* Translated and edited by Clarence H. Miller. New Haven: Yale University Press, 1976.

Moryson, Fynes. *An Itinerary. . . .* (1617). Reprint. Glasgow: James MacLehose and Sons, 1907.

Moseley, C. W. R. D. *Milton: The English Poems of 1645.* Harmondsworth, England: Penguin Books, 1992.

Mulder, John R. "The Lyric Dimension of *Paradise Lost.*" *Milton Studies* 23 (1987): 145–63.

Mullinger, James Bass. *A History of the University of Cambridge.* London: Longmans, Green, and Co., 1888.

———. *The University of Cambridge.* Vol. 3. Cambridge: Cambridge University Press, 1911.

Munz, Peter. *The Place of Hooker in the History of Thought.* 1952. Reprint. London: Routledge & Kegan Paul, 1970.

Murphy, Avon Jack. "The Critical Elegy of Earlier Seventeenth-Century England." *Genre* 5.1 (1972): 75–105.

Myhr, Ivar Lou. *The Evolution and Practice of Milton's Epic Theory.* Folcroft: The Folcroft Press, 1969.

Myrick, Kenneth. *Sir Philip Sidney As a Literary Craftsman.* Cambridge: Harvard University Press, 1935.

Nardo, Anna K. *Milton's Sonnets & The Ideal Community.* Lincoln: University of Nebraska Press, 1979.

Nashe, Thomas. *Christs Teares over Jerusalem.* London, 1593.

Newey, Vincent, ed. *"The Pilgrim's Progress": Critical and Historical Views.* Liverpool: Liverpool University Press, 1980.

Newton, Richard C. *"'Ben./Johnson':* The Poet in the Poems." In *Two Renaissance Mythmakers.* Edited by Alvin Kernan. Baltimore: The Johns Hopkins University Press, 1977.

Nicolson, Marjorie. "Milton and Hobbes." *Studies in Philology* 23 (July 1926): 405–33.

Norbrook, David. *Poetry and Politics in the English Renaissance.* London: Routledge and Kegan Paul, 1984.

———. Review of *The Faber Book of Political Verse,* ed. Tom Paulin. *London Review of Books* 8.10 (July 3, 1986): 7.

Novarr, David. *The Making of Walton's Lives.* Ithaca: Cornell University Press, 1958.

Nyssa, Saint Gregory of. *De Vita S. Patris Ephraem Syri.* In *Pat. G.* 46: 819–50.

Orgel, Stephen. *The Jonsonian Masque.* New York: Columbia University Press, 1965.

Origen, Saint. *In Ieremiam Homilia* 19. In *Pat. G.* 13: 262–76.

Ovid. *Metamorphoses* 15. Translated by Frank Justus Miller. 2 vols. London: William Heinemann, 1916.

Ozment, Steven. *The Age of Reform, 1250–1550: An Intellectual and Religious History of Late Medieval and Reformation Europe.* New Haven: Yale University Press, 1980.

Panofsky, Erwin. *Hercules am Scheidewege.* Leipzig, 1930.

Parker, William Riley. *Milton, A Biography.* 2 vols. Oxford: Clarendon Press, 1968.

Parrish, Paul. *Richard Crashaw.* Twayne's English Authors Series. No. 299. Boston: G. K. Hall, 1980.

Patrides, C. A, ed. *Milton's Lycidas: The Tradition and the Poem.* New York: Holt, Rinehart & Winston, 1961.

———. *Milton and the Christian Tradition.* Oxford: Clarendon Press, 1966.

———. ed. *Approaches to Marvell. The York Tercentenary Lectures.* London: Routledge, 1978.

Patrologiae, cursus completus. Series graeca, 161 vols. Edited by J. P. Migne. Paris, 1857–1912; *Series latina,* 220 vols. Paris, 1844–80.

Patterson, Annabel. *Censorship and Interpretation: The Conditions of Writing and Reading in Early Modern England.* Madison: University of Wisconsin Press, 1984.

———. "Couples, Canons, and the Uncouth: Spenser-and-Milton in Educational Theory." *Critical Inquiry* 16 (Summer 1990): 773–93.

Pecheux, M. Christopher. "'At a Solemn Musick': Structure and Meaning." *Studies in Philology* 75 (1978): 331–46.

Peile, John. *Christ's College.* London: F. E. Robinson & Co., 1900.

Peterson, D. L. *Time, Tide, and Tempest: A Study of Shakespeare's Romances.* San Marino, Calif.: Huntington Library, 1973.

Peterson, Richard S. *Imitation and Praise in the Poems of Ben Jonson.* New Haven: Yale University Press, 1981.

Petrarch, Francesco. *Petrarch's Lyric Poems: The Rime sparse and Other Lyrics.* Ed. Robert M. Durling. Cambridge: Harvard University Press, 1976.

Philip, John. *The Phoenix Nest* (1593). Edited by Hyder Edward Rollins. Cambridge: Harvard University Press, 1931.

Pigman, III, G. W. "Suppressed Grief in Jonson's Funeral Poetry." *English Literary Renaissance* 13 (1983): 203–20.

———. *Grief and English Renaissance Elegy.* Cambridge: Cambridge University Press, 1985.

Plato. *Platonis Opera Quae Extant Opera.* 3 vols. Geneva: Henri Estienne, 1578.

Pope, Alexander. *Poetry and Prose of Alexander Pope.* Edited by Aubrey Williams. Boston: Houghton Mifflin Company, 1969.

Porter, H. C. *Reformation and Reaction in Tudor Cambridge.* Cambridge: Cambridge University Press, 1958.

Potter, George Reuben. "Milton's Early Poems, the School of Donne, and the Elizabethan Sonneteers." *Philological Quarterly* 6 (1927): 396–400.

Praz, Mario. *The Flaming Heart: Essays on Crashaw, Machiavelli, and Other Studies in the Relations between Italian and English Literature from Chaucer to T. S. Eliot.* 1958. Reprint. Gloucester, Mass.: Peter Smith, 1966.

Prince, F. T. *The Italian Element in Milton's Verse.* Oxford: Clarendon Press, 1954.

Prudentius. *Peristephanon Liberii.* Translated by H. J. Thompson. 2 vols. London: William Heinemann, 1953.

Puttenham, George. *The Arte of English Poesie* (1589). Facsimile Edition. Introduction by Baxter Hathaway. Kent, Ohio: Kent State University Press, 1970.

Pye, Christopher. "The Sovereign, the Theatre, and the Kingdome of Darknesse: Hobbes and the Spectacle of Power." In *Representing the English Renaissance.* Edited by Stephen Greenblatt. Berkeley: University of California Press, 1988.

Quarles, John. *Englands Complaint.* In *Fons Lachrymarum.* London, 1648.

Quilligan, Maureen. *Milton's Spenser: The Politics of Reading.* Ithaca: Cornell University Press, 1983.

Quint, David. "David's census: Milton's politics and *Paradise Regained.*" In *Re-Membering Milton.* Edited by Mary Nyquist and Margaret W. Ferguson. New York: Methuen, 1987.

Radzinowicz, Mary Ann. *Towards Samson Agonistes: The Growth of Milton's Mind.* Princeton: Princeton University Press, 1978.

———. *Milton's Epics and the Book of Psalms.* Princeton: Princeton University Press, 1989.

Randall, Dale B. J. *Jonson's Gypsies Unmasked.* Durham, N.C.: Durham University Press, 1975.

Revard, Stella. "'L'Allegro' and 'Il Penserso': Classical Tradition and Renaissance Mythography." *PMLA* 101 (1986): 338–50.

Richardson, J. *Explanatory Notes and Remarks on Milton's Paradise Lost.* London, 1734.

Richetti, John. *Philosophical Writing: Locke, Berkeley, Hume.* Cambridge: Harvard University Press, 1983.

Ricks, Christopher. "What is at stake in the 'battle of the books.'" *The New Criterion* 8 (September 1989): 40–44.

Riggs, David. *Ben Jonson: A Life.* Cambridge: Harvard University Press, 1989.

Rivers, Isabel. *The Poetry of Conservatism, 1600–1745.* Cambridge: Rivers Press, 1973.

Roberts, John R., ed. *New Perspectives on the Life and Art of Richard Crashaw*. Columbia: University Press of Missouri, 1990.

Robinson, Thomas. *The Life and Death of Mary Magadelene*. London, 1620.

Roche, Jr., Thomas P. "*Astrophil and Stella*: A Radical Reading." *Spenser Studies* 3 (1982): 139–91.

———. "Autobiographical Elements in Sidney's *Astrophil and Stella*." *Spenser Studies* 5 (1984): 209–29.

———. *Petrarch and the English Sonnet Sequences*. New York: AMS Press, Inc., 1989.

Rollins, Hyder Edward, ed. *The Phoenix Nest* (1593). Cambridge: Harvard University Press, 1931.

Roscelli, William John. "The Metaphysical Milton (1625–31)." *Texas Studies in Language and Literature* 8 (1966): 463–84.

Rose, Mark. *Heroic Love: Studies in Sidney and Spenser*. Cambridge: Harvard University Press, 1968.

Ross, Maggie. *The Fountain & the Furnace: The Way of Tears and Fire*. New York: Paulist Press, 1987.

Roston, Murray. *Milton and the Baroque*. Pittsburgh: University of Pittsburgh Press, 1980.

Røstvig, M.-S. "*The Shepheardes Calender*—A Structural Analysis." *Renaissance and Modern Studies* 13 (1969): 49–75.

———. "Ars Aeterna: Renaissance Poetics and Theories of Divine Creation." *Mosaic* 3 (1970): 40–61.

———. "Images of Perfection." In *Seventeenth-Century Imagery*. Edited by Earl Miner. Los Angeles: University of California Press, 1971.

———., ed. *Fair Forms*. Cambridge: D. S. Brewer Ltd., 1975.

———. "Golden Phrases: The Poetics of Giles Fletcher." *Studies in Philology* 88.2 (1991): 169–200.

———. *Configurations: A Topomorphical Approach to Renaissance Poetry*. Oslo, Copenhagen, and Stockholm: Scandinavian University Press and London: Oxford University Press, 1994.

Rothstein, Eric. *Restoration Tragedy*. Madison: University of Wisconsin Press, 1967.

Rowse, A. L. *Milton the Puritan: Portrait of a Mind*. London: Macmillan, 1977.

Sacks, Peter. *The English Elegy: Studies in the Genre from Spenser to Yeats*. Baltimore: Johns Hopkins University Press, 1985.

Saint Mary Magdalens Conversion. London, 1603.

Samuel, Irene. *Plato and Milton*. Ithaca: Cornell University Press, 1947.

Santirocco, Matthew S. *Unity and Design in Horace's Odes*. Chapel Hill: University of North Carolina Press, 1986.

Seaton, Edith. "Comus and Shakespeare." *Essays by Members of the English Association* 31 (1945): 68–80.

Sells, A. Lytton. *The Paradise of Travellers*. Bloomington: Indiana University Press, 1964.

Shakespeare, William. *The Riverside Shakespeare*. Edited by G. Blakemore Evans. Boston: Houghton Mifflin Co., 1974.

Sharpe, Kevin. *The Personal Rule of Charles I.* New Haven: Yale University Press, 1992.

Shawcross, John T. ed. *Milton, the Critical Heritage.* London: Routledge and Kegan Paul, 1970.

———. *With Mortal Voice: The Creation of Paradise Lost.* Lexington: University of Kentucky Press, 1982.

———. *Paradise Regain'd: Worthy T'Have Not Remain'd So Long Unsung.* Pittsburgh: Duquesne University Press, 1988.

———. *John Milton and Influence: Presence in Literature, History and Culture.* Pittsburgh: Duquesne University Press, 1991.

Shelley, Percy Bysshe. *Shelley's Prose.* Edited by David Lee Clark. Reprint. London: Fourth Estate, 1988.

Sichi, Edward. " 'A Crowd of Little Poets': Dryden's use of Milton's Serpent in His *Aeneid,* II." *ANQ: A Quarterly Journal of Short Articles, Notes, and Reviews* 2 (1989): 94–97.

Sidney, Sir Philip. *The Complete Works of Sir Philip Sidney.* Edited by Albert Feuillerat. 4 vols. Cambridge: Cambridge University Press, 1912.

———. *The Poems of Sir Philip Sidney.* Edited by William A. Ringler. Oxford: Clarendon Press, 1962.

———. *A Defence of Poetry.* Edited by Jan van Dorsten. Oxford: Oxford University Press, 1973.

———. *The Defence of Poesie.* In *Miscellaneous Prose of Sir Philip Sidney.* Edited by Katherine Duncan-Jones and Jan van Dorsten. Oxford: Clarendon Press, 1973.

———. *The Countess of Pembroke's Arcadia.* Edited by Maurice Evans. Harmondsworth, Middlesex: Penguin Books, 1977.

———. *The Countess of Pembrokes Arcadia.* Edited by Victor Skretkowicz. Oxford: Oxford University Press, 1987.

Simonds, Peggy Munoz. "The Marriage Topos in *Cymbeline*: Shakespeare's Variations on a Classical Theme." *English Literary Renaissance* 19 (1989): 94–117.

Sissa, Guila. *Greek Virginity.* Translated by Arthur Goldhammer. Cambridge: Harvard University Press, 1990.

Sisson, C. J. *The Judicious Marriage of Mr. Hooker and the Birth of The Laws of Ecclesiastical Polity.* Cambridge: Cambridge University Press, 1940.

Sloane, Thomas O. *Donne, Milton and the End of Humanist Rhetoric.* Berkeley: University of California Press, 1985.

Smith, Hallett. *Shakespeare's Romances: A Study of Some Ways of the Imagination.* San Marino, Calif.: Huntington Library, 1972.

Spenser, Edmund. *The Poetical Works of Edmund Spenser.* 3 vols. Edited by J. C. Smith and E. de Selincourt. Oxford: Clarendon Press, 1909.

———. *The Faerie Queene.* Edited by Thomas P. Roche, Jr. Harmondsworth, Middlesex: Penguin, 1989.

———. *The Yale Edition of the Shorter Poems of Edmund Spenser.* Edited by William A. Oram et. al. New Haven: Yale University Press, 1989.

Steadman, John M. "Milton and St. Basil: The Genesis of Sin and Death." *Modern Language Notes* 73 (1958): 83–4.

———. "Grosseteste on the Genealogy of Sin and Death." *Notes and Queries* 204 (1959): 367–68.

———. "Leviathan and Renaissance Etymology." *Journal of the History of Ideas* 28 (1967): 575–6.

———. *Redefining a Period Style: "Renaissance," "Mannerist" and "Baroque" in Literature.* Pittsburgh: Duquesne University Press, 1990.

Steiner, George. *Real Presences.* Chicago: University of Chicago Press, 1989.

Stevens, Paul. *Imagination and the Presence of Shakespeare in Paradise Lost.* Madison: University of Wisconsin Press, 1985.

———. "Subversion and Wonder in Milton's Epitaph 'On Shakespeare.'" *English Literary Renaissance* 19 (Autumn 1989): 375–88.

Stillman, Carol A. "Politics, Precedence, and the Order of the Dedicatory Sonnets in *The Faerie Queene." Spenser Studies* 5 (1984): 132–48.

Stock, Richard. *The Churches Lamentation for the losse of the godly.* London, 1614.

Stockholder, Kay. *Dream Works: Lovers and Families in Shakespeare's Plays.* Toronto: University of Toronto Press, 1987.

Stringer, Gary A. "Milton's 'Thorn in the Flesh': Pauline Didacticism in *Sonnet XIX." Milton Studies* 10 (1977): 141–54.

Summers, Claude J. and Ted-Larry Pebworth, eds. *Classic and Cavalier: Essays on Jonson and the Sons of Ben.* Pittsburgh: University of Pittsburgh Press, 1982.

———. *"The muses common-weale": Poetry and Politics in the Seventeenth Century.* Columbia: University Press of Missouri, 1988.

Summers, Claude J. "Tears for Herrick's Church." *George Herbert Journal* 14. 1–2 (Fall 1990—Spring 1991): 51–71.

Summers, Joseph H. "The Two Great Sexes." In *The Muse's Method.* Cambridge: Harvard University Press, 1962.

Sundby, Ove Kr. "Musiske Perspektiver i Platons Dialog *Lovene." Studia Musicologia Norvegica.* Vol. 5: 67–104.

Sweetman, John. *S. Mary Magdalens Pilgrimage to Paradise.* London, 1617.

Sylvia Mary, Sr. "St. Symeon the New Theologian and the Way of Tears." *Studia Patristica* 10, part 1 (1970): 431–35.

Symonds, J. A. *Sir Philip Sidney.* London: Macmillan, 1886.

Sypher, Wylie. *Four Stages of Renaissance Style: Transformations in Art and Literature, 1400–1700.* Garden City, N.Y.: Doubleday, 1955.

Tacitus, Cornelius. *The Annals.* Translated by John Jackson. London: William Heinemann, 1937.

Tasso, Torquato. *Opere.* Edited by Ettore Mazzali. Vol. 2. Naples: Casa Editrice Fulvio Rossi, 1969, 1970.

———. *Opere.* Edited by Bartolo Tommaso Sozzi. 3d edition. Turin: Union Tipografico-Editrice, 1974.

———. *Creation of the World.* Translated by Joseph Tusiani and annotated by Gaetano Cipolla. MRTS 12. Binghamton, New York: Center for Medieval & Early Renaissance Studies, 1982.

Taylor, Mark C. *Tears.* Albany: State University of New York Press, 1990.

The Teares of our Saviour in the Garden. London, 1601.

Terrein, Samuel. *The Elusive Presence: The Heart of Biblical Theology.* San Francisco: Harper & Row, 1978.

Thompson, Charlotte. "Love in an Orderly Universe: A Unification of Spenser's *Amoretti*, 'Anacreontics,' and *Epithalamion*." VIATOR 16 (1985): 277–335.

Thompson, W. D. J. Cargill. "The Philosopher of the 'Politic Society': Richard Hooker as a Political Thinker." In *Studies in Richard Hooker: Essays Preliminary to an Edition of His Works*. Edited by W. Speed Hill. Cleveland, Ohio: Press of Case Western Reserve University, 1972.

Tillyard, E. W. *Milton*. London: Chatto & Windus, 1930.

Toliver, Harold. *Transported Styles in Shakespeare and Milton*. University Park: Pennsylvania State University Press, 1989.

Trevor-Roper, H. R. *Catholics, Anglicans, and Puritans*. London: Secker & Warburg, 1987.

Tricomi, A. H. "Milton and the Jonsonian Plain Style." *Milton Studies* 13 (1979): 129–44.

Trimpi, Wesley. *Ben Jonson's Poems: A Study in the Plain Style*. Stanford, Calif.: Stanford University Press, 1962.

Tromly, Frederic B. "Milton Responds to Donne: 'On Time' and 'Death Be Not Proud.'" *Modern Philology* 80 (May 1983): 390–93.

Turner, James Grantham. *One Flesh: Paradisal Marriage and Sexual Relations in the Age of Milton*. Oxford: Clarendon Press, 1987.

Tyacke, Nicholas. "Puritanism, Arminianism and Counter-Revolution." In *The Origins of the English Civil War*. Edited by Conrad Russell. London: Macmillan, 1973.

Ulreich, Jr., John C. "'And by Occasion Foretells': The Prophetic Voice in *Lycidas*." *Milton Studies* 18 (1983): 3–23.

van Dorsten, Jan, Dominic Baker-Smith, and Arthur F. Kinney, eds. *Sir Philip Sidney: 1586 and the Creation of a Legend*. Leiden: E. J. Brill, 1986.

Vann, Gerald. *The Pain of Christ and the Sorrow of God*. London: Aquin Press, 1947.

Von Hildebrand, Dietrich. "Bienheureux Ceux Qui Pleurent." *Dieu Vivant* 18 (1951): 79–90.

Vincent-Buffault, Anne. *Histoire Des Larmes XVIIIe–XIXe siècles*. Paris: Rivages, 1986.

Waldock, A. J. A. *"Paradise Lost" and Its Critics*. Cambridge: Cambridge University Press, 1947.

Walker, Caroline Bynum. *Jesus as Mother: Studies in the Spirituality of the High Middle Ages*. Berkeley: University of California Press, 1982.

Walker, Julia, ed. *Milton and the Idea of Woman*. Urbana: University of Illinois Press, 1988.

Walker, Thomas A. *Peterhouse*. Cambridge, Eng.: W. Heffer & Sons, 1935.

Wallerstein, Ruth. *Studies in Seventeenth-Century Poetic*. Madison: University of Wisconsin Press, 1950.

Warden, Blair. "Commentary." *Times Literary Supplement*. 21 July 1978: 20.

Warnke, Frank. *European Metaphysical Poetry*. New Haven: Yale University Press, 1961.

———. *Versions of Baroque*. New Haven: Yale University Press, 1972.

Warren, Austin. "Crashaw's Residence at Peterhouse." *Times Literary Supplement*. 3 November 1932: 815.

————. *Richard Crashaw: A Study in Baroque Sensibility.* University: Louisiana State University Press, 1939.

Wedgwood, C. V. *The King's Peace 1637–1641: The Great Rebellion.* London: Collins, 1955.

West, Michael. "The *Consolatio* in Milton's Funeral Elegies." *Huntington Library Quarterly* 34 (1970–71): 233–49.

Whaler, James. "Animal Simile in *Paradise Lost.*" *PMLA* 47 (1932): 534–53.

Whately, William. *Charitable Teares.* London, 1623.

Wickert, Max A. "Structure and Ceremony in Spenser's *Epithalamion.*" *English Literary History* 35.2 (1968): 135–57.

Wilcher, Andrew. *Andrew Marvell.* Cambridge: Cambridge University Press, 1985.

Wilde, Oscar. "Two Biographies of Sir Philip Sidney." *Pall Mall Gazette* 44 (1886): 5.

Williams, Kathleen. "Milton, Greatest Spenserian." In *Milton and the Line of Vision.* Edited by Joseph Anthony Wittreich, Jr. Madison: University of Wisconsin Press, 1975.

Williams, R. Darby. "Two Baroque Poems on Grace: Herbert's 'Paradise' and Milton's 'On Time.'" *Criticism* 12 (1970): 180–94.

Wilson, A. N. *The Life of John Milton.* Oxford: Oxford University Press, 1983.

Wilson, Thomas. *The Arte of Rhetorique* (1560). Edited by G. H. Mair. Oxford: Oxford University Press, 1909.

Wiltenburg, Robert. "Damnation in a Roman Dress: Cataline, *Cataline,* and *Paradise Lost.*" *Milton Studies* 25 (1989): 89–108.

Winn, James. *John Dryden and His World.* New Haven: Yale University Press, 1987.

Winstanley, Gerrard. *The True Levellers Standard Advanced: Or, The State of Community Opened, and Presented to the Sons of Men.* London, 1649.

Winters, Yvor. "The 16th Century Lyric in England: A Critical and Historical Reinterpretation." *Poetry* 53 (1939): 258–72; and 54 (1939): 35–51.

Wittreich, Jr., Joseph A., ed. *The Romantics on Milton: Formal Essays and Critical Asides.* Cleveland: Case Western Reserve University Press, 1970.

————, ed. *Milton and the Line of Vision.* Madison: University of Wisconsin Press, 1975.

————. *Visionary Poetics: Milton's Tradition and His Legacy.* San Marino, Calif.: Huntington Library, 1979.

————. *Interpreting "Samson Agonistes."* Princeton: Princeton University Press, 1986.

————. *Feminist Milton.* Ithaca: Cornell University Press, 1987.

Wolfe, D. M. "Milton and Hobbes, a Contrast in Social Temper." *Studies in Philology* 41 (September 1944): 410–26.

Wolin, Sheldin. "Paradigms and Political Theories." In *Politics and Experience.* Edited by Preston King and B. C. Parekh. Cambridge: Cambridge University Press, 1968.

Woodhouse, A. S. P. *The Heavenly Muse: A Preface to Milton.* Edited by Hugh MacCallum. Toronto: University of Toronto Press, 1972.

Zarlino, Gioseffo. *Institutioni Harmoniche.* Venice, 1558.

————. *Supplimenti Musicali.* Venice, 1588.

————. *Opere*. Venice, 1589.

Zwicker, Steven W. "Lines of Authority: Politics and Literary Culture in the Restoration." In *Politics of Discourse. The Literature and History of Seventeenth-Century England*. Edited by Kevin Sharpe and Steven N. Zwicker. Berkeley: University of California Press, 1987.

Index